A Seventeenth-Century Chinese Classic

Ling Mengchu

Amazing Tales

First Series

Translated by Wen Jingen

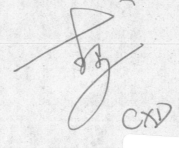

Panda Books

First Edition 2005

ISBN 7-119-03351-4

©Foreign Languages Press, Beijing, China, 2005

Published by Foreign Languages Press

24 Baiwanzhuang Road, Beijing 100037, China

Website: http://www.flp.com.cn

E-mail Address: info@flp.com.cn

sales@flp.com.cn

Distributed by China International Book Trading Corporation

35 Chegongzhuang Xilu, Beijing 100044, China

P.O. Box 399, Beijing, China

Printed in the People's Republic of China

CONTENTS

轉運漢遇巧
洞庭紅

Mr Fortune Comes Across Red Fruit from Dongting

A Persian Merchant Discerns the Shell of a Drum Dragon

姚滴珠避羞惹羞

Escaping Disgrace Yao Dizhu Encounters Disgrace

鄭月娥將錯就錯

Making an Error Zheng Yue'e Utilizes the Error

劉東山誇技
順城門

Liu Dongshan Brags of His Prowess at a City Gate

十八兄奇踪村酒肆

Eighteenth Brother Shows off Marvels in a Village Tavern

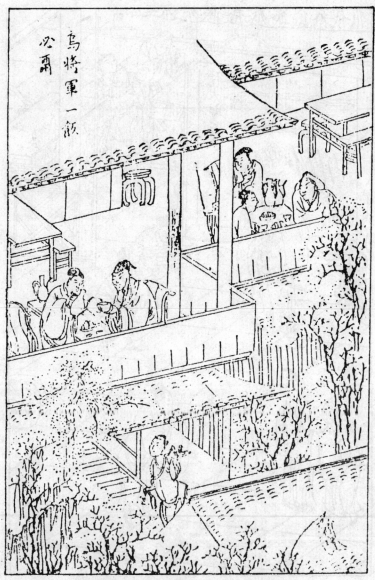

General Woolly Pays the Debt of a Dinner

陳大郎三人重會

Chen Dalang Reunites with His Lost Kinfolk

韓秀才乘亂
聘嬌妻

Scholar Han Acquires a Pretty Wife Amidst the Chaos

吳太守憐才
主姻簿

Prefect Wu Confirms a Marriage Contract in Favor of Talent

悪船家計賺
假屍銀

An Evil Boat Owner Takes Money for an Unidentified Corpse

狼僕人誤投
真命狀

A Base Servant Files an Accusation about an Alleged Murder

趙六兒詆犢
袁成生

Zhao the Sixth Dies at the Hand of His Pampered Son

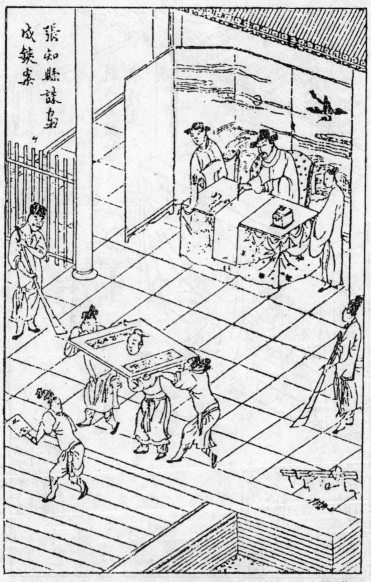

張知縣誅惡成鐵案

Magistrate Zhang Punishes the Evil with an Irrevocable Death Verdict

酒謀財千郊
肆惡

To Steal Money, Yu Dajiao Murders a Drunk Man

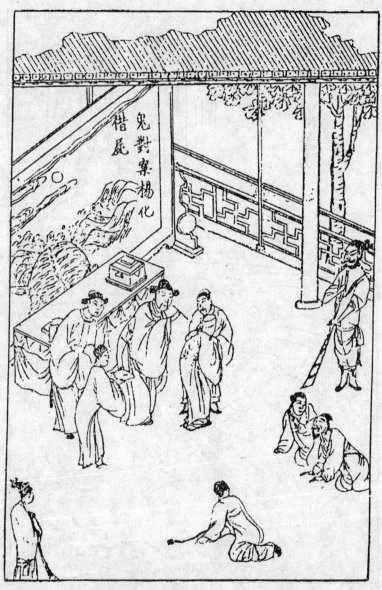

鬼對寨楊化惜屍

To Confront his Enemy, Yang Hua Haunts a Living Lady

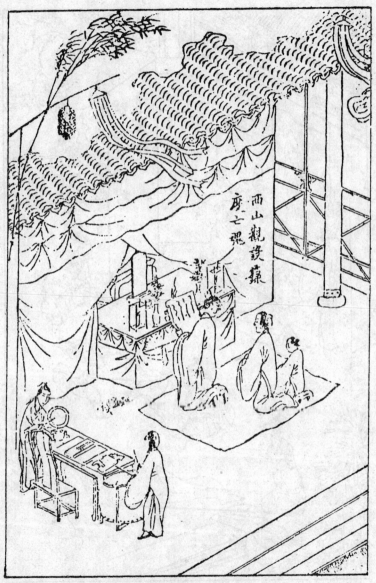

西山觀設醮
度亡魂

A Soul is Redeemed in West Mountain Monastery

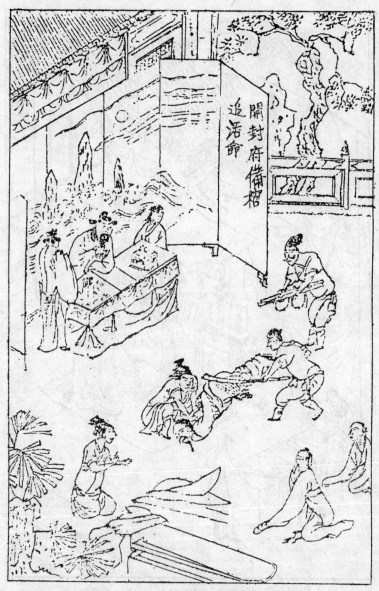

A Breathing Body is Encoffined in Kaifeng Prefecture Court

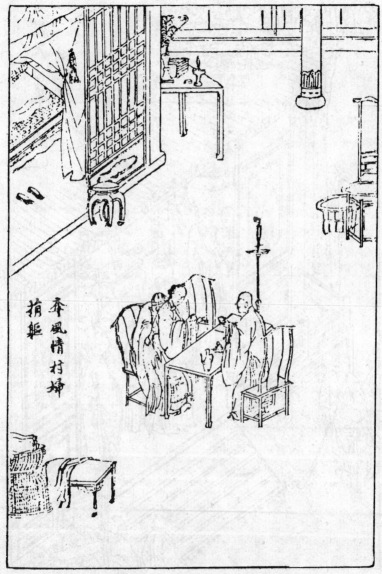

奉風情村婦捐軀

Fighting for Affection a Village Woman Gives Her Life

假天語幕僚斷獄

Conversing with Heaven an Assistant Governor Settles a Case

通閨閨堅心
燈火

Faithful Lamplight Conducts to a Boudoir

開囹圄捷報旗鈴

Glad Tidings Break into a Cell

喬氏換胡
子宣淫

By Exchanging Wives, Mr Hu Indulges in Debauchery

To Expound Retribution a Prelate Sinks into Meditation

后土之神

張員外
義撫頃
姈子

Charitable Squire Zhang Fosters an Orphan

Witty Prefect Bao Extracts a Contract

Introduction

*A*mazing Tales, the books you have in hand, are tales that have been read, retold and enjoyed by the Chinese people for nearly four centuries.

The author, Ling Mengchu (凌濛初 1580-1644), was a native of Wucheng (present-day Wuxing) of Zhejiang Province. In his time the only way for an intellectual to prosper was to pass the imperial examinations for official candidates. The examinees were required to write stereotyped essays on a few Confucian classics. Ling Mengchu, like many brilliant minds of that time, made slow progress in passing those examinations. (The great scientist, Li Shizhen. author of the encyclopaedic *Compendium of Materia Medica*, failed the imperial examinations also!) Seeing no hope as he reached his late forties, Ling Mengchu turned to fiction writing. His first book, *Amazing Tales* (拍案惊奇), which contained forty tales, was printed in 1628 and made a hit. So the publisher urged him to write a sequel. Five years later he completed forty more tales and gave them the title *Amazing Tales*, *Second Series* (二刻拍案惊奇). Since this was the second series, the previously published book acquired the name "First Series" (初刻拍案惊奇), the name by which it is generally known today. In his fifties, Ling Mengchu was finally made a county magistrate and he was later promoted to prefect. In 1644 he died during a vain attempt to resist a peasant insurrection army. Apart from these two "series", he wrote twenty or so other works, but none of them were as successful as his tales.

These tales were not invented by Ling Mengchu. He took plots from different sources. Speaking of his sources, we had better review part of the tradition of Chinese literature. Chinese prose fiction has two main streams. One is literary sketches and stories written by men of letters in "classical" language, that is, a style patterned on writings produced before the first century and in the language used for all formal and official literature over thousands of years in China. (This was a situation similar to that of Europe where through the middle ages important documents were all written in Latin rather than in colloquial local languages.) Chinese literature abounds in witty, cursory anecdotes, tales in scholars' jottings, parables in philosophical mode and other works. Such stories have matured since the seventh century. The other stream of fiction is stories in a vernacular language developed from ballad-singing and oral story-telling. Understandably, as the "classical" language was not spoken in everyday life, vernacular literature captured the largest audience. By the tenth century stories in the vernacular began to emerge in large numbers. In the fourteenth century great novels such as the *Three Kingdoms* (三国演义) and *Outlaws of the Marsh* (水浒) appeared. In Ling Mengchu's time, short stories in the vernacular had become quite popular among townsfolk. Works belonging to the two categories, however, often borrowed material from one another. Writers of vernacular stories often took their plots from literary sketches which provided outlines for the stories, or from pithy stories written in classical language. Despite this, great writers like Ling Mengchu developed the borrowed plots with such originality and imagination, and infused them with such strong feelings, that one can hardly say the tales were not their creation (much as we don't doubt Shakespeare's creativity although he invented little). This can be exemplified by a comparison between Ling Mengchu's story "Zhao the Sixth Dies in the Hand of His Pampered Son..." in the first series (Tale 8 in our selection) and the two sketches from which he derived the content for this tale.

In the Zhejiang area there was a son who hit his seventy-year old father and knocked out his teeth. The father presented the teeth to the authorities as evidence against his son. The son in panic sought advice from a pettifogger, offering him a hundred liang of silver. The pettifogger shook his head, saying, "It's too difficult." But as the son offered a higher reward and pleaded for his help, the pettifogger promised to think the matter over for three days. The next day he said, "I've got it! Come to a place where nobody can listed to us and I'll tell you of my plan." When the son put his ear close to the pettifogger's mouth, the man gave it a sudden bite and tore half of it away causing the ear to bleed profusely. The son was shocked. The pettifogger said, "Don't cry! This is my plan to help you out. Keep the torn off portion of your ear and show it to the authorities when they question you." When the case was investigated in court, the son explained that his father's teeth had fallen out when he bit his ear. The magistrate realized that the ear could not have been bitten off by the son himself and believed that the old man's loose teeth might have fallen out in the nipping. Thus the son was pardoned. (Zhi Nang Bu 智囊补, Vol. 2)

When Finance Minister Zhang Jin was on the Criminal Board, there was a man who lived separately from his father. The man was wealthy. One night the father cut a hole in the wall and entered his house to take some of the man's property. The son thought the person who had entered his home must be a robber and so he hit at him and killed him. After he lit a candle and looked at the body, he discovered it was his father. The clerks of the court discussed the matter and decided that the son should not be absolved of the crime, but as he had done it in an attempt to stop a thief, he should not be put to death. They hesitated for *a time. Zhang Jin wielded his brush and commented, "To kill a thief is forgivable, but an unfilial son should be executed. The son has more than enough wealth but his father was driven to theft in poverty. His unfilialty is clear enough." So the man was killed. (Zhi Nang Bu, Vol. 7)*

Influential and successful as Ling Mengchu's tales were, little textual study was conducted on them until early in the last century. For a long time they were read from *Jin Gu Qi Guan* (今古奇观 *Wonders of Old and Today*), a selection of stories by Ling and another author. As literature researchers collected and collated the various versions of the tales, they found no edition was complete. Perhaps this was because not long after the publication of Ling Mengchu's tales, a dynasty fell and another was founded. In the change of state power there was a war, as there always was in dynastic changes in China, and presumably because of this all or some printing wood blocks of the tales were destroyed. So far no authentic and complete first edition has been discovered. The Shang You Tang (尚友堂) edition, found in the collection of a Japanese library, is believed to be the edition closest to the original first printing. Over the last few decades many scholars have made painstaking efforts and have scored great achievements in the textual study of these tales. Wang Gulu (王古鲁) spent almost his whole life in studying them. His researches resulted in a good edition of the tales that was published in 1957. After him Zhang Peiheng (章培恒), Chen Erdong (陈迩冬) and Guo Juanjie (郭隽杰) took pains to further Wang's study. Tan Zhengbi (谭正璧) has perused many works of ancient fictions and identified almost all the sources of Ling's tales. Our translation benefits much from this scholarship.

Each "series" of Ling Mengchu's books is divided into 40 "volumes" (the tales have been renumbered in our selection). This translation has selected nearly half of the tales in the first series. We cannot yet say that the "best" tales have been selected — the tales are so uniformly pleasing that one may find the unselected ones no less interesting. Each volume contains one or more prelusive tales and one main tale. The prelusive ones often expound a moral preaching from the same or opposing point of view in relation to the main tale. The prelusive tales have largely been left out in the translation but in a few cases they have been kept. For example, Tale 3, Tale 5, Tale 7, Tale 8 and Tale 13. From these the readers may have a glimpse of the tales' original structure. The author also inserted many rhymes in his tales. As he confessed, most of them were composed by himself and a small number were taken from works of former times. He called those verses "seasonings". Most of the rhymes are didactic doggerels and may not be to today's readers' taste. We have cut some of the rhymes. We have also kept a few with a view to suggesting the original style. The author claimed that he did not use obscene descriptions in his love stories. But this is not true. There *is* explicit depiction of sex. We cut some such portrayals, and in some places we have used less direct wording. Apart from these, we have tried our best to avoid straying far from the original text. As for terms and expressions peculiar to Chinese, we explain them in several ways: 1. at the end of the book we add a glossary of the names of measurement and of ancient academic titles (in the text they appear in italic type); 2. we put footnotes to clarify some sentences; 3. we put our explanations in square brackets ([]); and 4. we put in parentheses those words omitted by the author without which the meaning is unclear.

If this translation is readable and our readers' literary taste is not strongly offended, the credit should go partly to our editor Foster Stockwell. Thanks must also be extended to Liu Liangming (刘良明) of the Wuhan University and our colleague Wu Lijuan (武丽娟) who helped us in finding the meanings of some difficult words.

As for the tales themselves their titles in antithetical couplets serve as a good guide for readers and we don't think it necessary to repeat their contents here. In these tales the author praised what he thought praiseworthy and condemned what he thought condemnable. On the whole a good part of his moral standards is shared by the Chinese people. People of different times and different national backgrounds may have different values. Our English speaking readers may read the tales and pass their own judgement.

The Translator

Tale 1

Mr Fortune Comes Across Red Fruit from Dongting; A Persian Merchant Discerns the Shell of a Drum Dragon

It is related that during the reign of Chenghua [AD 1465-1487] of our [Ming] dynasty, outside of Changmen Gate of Changzhou County in Suzhou Prefecture there lived a man surnamed Wen, whose given name was Shi and whose style name was Ruoxu. A clever man by nature, he was capable of doing almost everything and was quick at learning. As a dabbler in many a trade, he knew a little about playing the *qin*, chess and pipes, and he could do calligraphy, paint, sing and dance. When he was a child, a physiognomist predicted that he would become a millionaire. Quite confident of his talent, he never bothered to learn a trade to support himself. By and by the wealth handed down from his ancestors gave out. Then he understood there was a limit to his family fortune. Seeing that other people doubled and redoubled their profit out of their investment in business, he thought of engaging in trade. But every time he tried to do so, he misplaced his capital.

One day he learned that fans sold well in Beijing. Thereupon he found a partner and began to purchase fans. The top-quality fans were delicate and graced with golden decorations. He presented gifts to some famous artists and asked them inscribe poems or to paint something on these fans. A few casual strokes by these celebrities such as Shen Zhou, Wen Zhengming and Zhu Yunming could raise the price of a single fan up to one *liang* of silver. On the second-rate fans he had some quacks produce imitations of the works of renowned artists. This would allow him to pass them off as genuine works. Wen Ruoxu himself was also good at copying famous works. Even the low-quality fans, which were not decorated or painted, would sell for several dozen coins. That meant he would be assured of a hundred-percent profit. He chose an auspicious date, packed the fans in boxes and transported them to Beijing.

Unexpectedly it was raining one day after another from the beginning of summer and there was no sign of a heat wave at all in Beijing. Therefore his fans sold very slowly. When autumn set in the weather cooled down considerably, and fans went out of season. Fortunately it was sunny every day and there was still a demand among noble offspring's who liked to put on airs by swinging Suzhou-made fans with their hands protruding from broad sleeves. However, when Wen Ruoxu opened the boxes, he was dismayed by what he saw. It happens that during the seventh and eighth months of the year the air in Beijing is moist and fabrics get damp and mildewy easily. That year the rain made it worse. This caused the glue contained in the ink to be moistened and to percolate through the surface, and the fans were stuck to each other as a result. As he pulled the fans apart, the paintings on them either had patches of color chipped off or were badly smeared, so that they became worthless. Only the blank fans remained intact, but they were worth little. The returns from the sales were barely enough to cover the expenses for his journey home, while the capital he had put out went with the wind. Such was the case for several years. Not only did he lose money, but his partner suffered losses as well. Because of this he got the nickname "Mr Misfortune".

In a few years, Mr Misfortune wasted away all his possessions and he couldn't even get a wife. He eked out a living by inscribing calligraphic scrolls or painting for clients, but he could make little from this even though he was constantly on the go. Fortunately, with a gift of gab he was liked for his humorous talk and jokes. Wherever his friends met to amuse themselves, he was a regular guest. This provided him with a chance to scrounge meals, but not to make a fortune. Furthermore, he had been used to ostentatious way of living, and was not fit to be a literary hack. Some people took pity on him and recommended him to various houses as a family tutor, but decent families disliked him because of his superficial learning. He was unfit for a respected job and yet he was too proud to accept a humble position. For this, both the hacks and the family tutors, on seeing him, would make faces and laugh at him, the "Mr Misfortune".

One day some of his neighbors who went overseas to traffic in goods were about to set off. There were forty or so of them, headed by Big Brother Zhang, Second Brother Li, Zhao the Senior and Qian the Junior. When Wen Ruoxu learned of this, he mused, "I am in such a pitiable state that I lack means to support myself. If I go overseas with them and enjoy the sights of a strange land, my life will be worthy. And I don't think they will turn me down if I join them. This will save me the worries about everyday food. Isn't that great?"

As he was thus musing, Big Brother Zhang came up. His real name was Zhang Chengyun. He engaged exclusively in overseas business. Having a keen eye for rare treasures, he was straight-forward, generous and always ready to offer help. For this his country fellows called him Goods-Appreciator Zhang. Wen Ruoxu told him of his intention. "Good, good," said Zhang. "We can't stand the monotony on the ship at sea. If you go with us, your humorous talks will make our voyage less unbearable. I believe our brothers will be happy to have you as their traveling companion. But I'd remind you of one thing. We all have goods to sell, but you don't. What a pity you are going on a sea voyage yet will come back empty-handed! Let me go and talk with my friends and have them offer you some money so that you, too, can buy goods to sell." "It's very kind of you," said Wen Ruoxu, "but I'm afraid nobody is as generous as you." "Let me try," replied Zhang as he went away.

Just then a blind fortune-teller, rattling a pair of clappers in hand, passed by. Fumbling in his pocket, Wen Ruoxu took out a coin. He handed it to the blind man and asked him to tell him his fortune. "You'll make an enormous fortune, sir," said the blind man. "A big sum, not an ordinary one." Hearing this, Wen Ruoxu thought, "I'm going to waste some days by joining the merchants. I'm not going to do business. What's the use of pooling financial aid for me? Even if I get the financial aid, it won't be a large sum. Does that point toward wealth? The fortune teller is talking rubbish!"

Then Zhang came up in anger, "Indeed, talk of money and friends will turn away! How ridiculous it is! When I told them you'll join us, they were overjoyed. But when I asked them to offer you some help, nobody responded. A couple of my good friends and I gathered one *liang* of silver for you. It's too little for you to purchase any goods, but you can buy some fruit with it. We'll look after your meals on the ship." Wen Ruoxu thanked him profusely and took the silver. "Be quick to get ready," Big Brother Zhang urged him. "The ship is about to set off." "I'll be there in a moment," replied Wen Ruoxu. "I haven't much to collect."

Looking at the silver in his hand, Wen Ruoxu smiled again and again. What can I buy with this, he wondered. As he walked forward, he saw fruit in baskets for sale along the street. They were:

as red as flames and as large as hanging bells. When their skin was green, they tasted slightly sour; before the frost bit, you could not eat many of them.

This fruit came from Dongting Mountain near Taihu Lake. The soil on the mountain was as fertile as that in Fujian and Guangdong provinces where tangerines known far and wide were grown. The tangerines from Dongting Mountain were similar in color and flavor but a little sourer when not ripe. But when they were ripe, they tasted just as sweet. And they sold at only one tenth of the price of the tangerines from Fujian. People called this kind of tangerine "Red Fruit from Dongting". Wen Ruoxu thought to himself, "With my one *liang* of silver I can buy more than one hundred *jin* of these fruit. It will quench my thirst on the voyage and besides, I can spare some for my companions to express my gratitude for their help." He bought the fruit, packed them in a bamboo basket and hired a man sitting by the side of the road to haul his fruit and luggage onto the ship.

At the sight of this, everyone clapped their hands, "Look, here's Mr Wen's valuable goods!" Blushing with embarrassment, Wen Ruoxu got on the ship silently. He dared say nothing about his purchase of the tangerines.

As the ship was sailing out of the sea port, they saw

Snow-white foam jump on silvery wave-crests,
Silvery sparks dart among the snow-white swelling tides;
The torrent scares the sun and moon;
The swirling water overturns the galaxies.

This ship drifted with the wind for nobody knows how long, and after three to five days it pulled into a place. Looking from the deck of the ship they could see that the place was thronged with people and the city walls were high. Realizing that they had arrived at a metropolis, they steered their ship into a haven where the water was smooth, fixed a post, cast the anchor and tied the ship to the post. After this, they climbed ashore and found they were in Jiling, a country they had visited before. The prices of Chinese goods tripled here and, likewise, goods from Jiling sold in China at high prices. Thus a voyage to and from Jiling could net a nine-fold profit, and that was why people went there to do business at all risks.

The people on the ship had all carried on transactions there in the past and each had his own agents, interpreters and lodging place. They got off the ship and went to deliver their goods. Wen Ruoxu was left alone to watch over the boat. He did not know the way and had nowhere to go. In boredom, he thought to himself, "I've not opened my basket to look at my tangerines since I got aboard. They might have become rotten by now. Let me take a look at my tangerines while my fellows are gone." He asked a seaman to bring out his basket from under the deck board. When he opened it, he found the tangerines on the top were good. Anxious to know how the rest were, he laid all of them out on the deck.

Maybe this was a time his star was rising or that luck turned in his favor. Looked at from afar the fiery-red tangerines on the deck were like a sea of torches or stars in the night sky. The people on shore came close to ask, "What are those?" Wen Ruoxu didn't answer. He picked out a tangerine from among the few that had moldy spots on them, broke it and bit into it. The crowd on the bank grew larger. Someone laughed in surprise, "It is edible!" One of them asked, "How much for one?" Wen Ruoxu didn't understand their language, but one of the seamen did. The seamen improvised a price. Raising one finger, he said, "One coin per fruit."

The asker untied his robe, exposing his red brocaded money belt, and fished a silver coin out of it. "I'll buy one to have a taste," he said. Wen Ruoxu took the coin, weighed it in his hand and guessed it weighed about one *liang*. He wondered how many the man meant to buy with this silver, and because he didn't have scales to weigh the fruit he decided to give the man one tangerine as a sample. Picking a large and impressively red one, he handed it to the man. "Good," the buyer said as he tossed the tangerine in his hand and broke it in two, sending the sweet smell into the air. The aroma drew applause from many bystanders. The buyer did not know how to eat the tangerine so he simply imitated Wen Ruoxu and peeled it but did not break it into segments. Cramming the whole fruit in his mouth, he swallowed it without spitting out the seeds. "Ha, ha!" he laughed, "Great!" Then he took out ten silver coins from his belt and said, "I'll buy ten as a contribution." Overjoyed, Wen Ruoxu gave him ten. Following the man's example, the lookers-on began to buy the fruit, one, two or three at a time. All paid with silver coins, and left in total satisfaction.

The currency of that country was made of silver and the coins bore different designs. The coins with designs of a dragon and phoenix were the most valuable, those with human figures were worth less and those with trees, still less, while those with weeds were the least valuable. Despite the difference in face value, the coins were all made of silver and weighed exactly the same. The people who had just bought tangerines all paid coins bearing the signs of weeds. They believed that they had got a good bargain for a pittance of money. That's why they were greatly pleased. They, like we Chinese, were inclined to go after petty benefits.

Soon two thirds of the tangerines were sold. One man regretted having brought no money with him, and he hurried away to get some money. When he returned, not many oranges were left, Wen Ruoxu feigned reluctance to part with them. "I'll keep these for myself," he said. "I won't sell them." The would-be buyer willingly offered double the price and bought two tangerines with four coins, grumbling, "What a pity! It's too late." Seeing him pay a higher price, other people grumbled, "We wanted to buy a couple more. Why did you pay him so much?" one of them asked. But the buyer replied, "Didn't you just hear him say he'd not sell any more?"

While these people were talking the matter over, the first buyer of ten tangerines returned to the scene on a galloping white piebald horse.

As he approached the ship, he demounted and elbowed his way through the crowd, shouting at the ship, "Stop! Stop! Don't sell retail! I'll buy all of the fruit. My master wants to pay a tribute to the Khan." Hearing this, the other people stepped back and looked on at a distance. Quick-witted as Wen Ruoxu was, he was aware that this was a good customer. He immediately dumped what remained in the basket onto the deck and found there were only fifty-two tangerines left. As he counted he feigned reluctance again. "I've just said I'll keep these for myself. I don't want to sell them. If you'd like to offer a better price, I'll let you have some. I sold one for two coins a moment ago."

The buyer unloaded a big sack from the horse's back and took out a coin with the pattern of trees on it, asking, "Will you accept one such coin for one fruit?" "No " replied Wen Ruoxu, "I'd rather have the kind of coin you paid before." The man smiled and took out a dragon-and-phoenix coin, asking again, "How about one like this for one fruit?" "No," Wen Ruoxu insisted, "I'd rather have two coins like the one you paid me before for the tangerine." The man laughed, "A coin like this is worth a hundred coins of that type. I haven't got so many coins of this type for you. I was teasing you. What a fool you are, preferring coins of that type to this one! If you give all your fruit to me, I don't mind paying one more coin of that type." Wen Ruoxu counted out all the fifty-two tangerines and got one hundred and fifty six silver coins with weed signs on them in return. The buyer took the fruit together with the basket. Throwing down a handful of coins, he tied the basket onto the horse's back and trotted away, his face glowing. Seeing no tangerines left, the lookers-on broke up in a hubbub.

As the people dispersed, Wen Ruoxu went into the cabin and weighed a coin on a pair of scales. The weight of a single coin was found to be about eight *qian* and seven *fen*. He scaled several more coins and found them to be of the same weight as the first one. He counted the coins and found he had earned a thousand of them. He gave the seaman two coins as a prize and wrapped up the rest. "The blind man's word was really accurate!" he chuckled. In good spirits he waited for his companions to return so he could chat with them.

You are wrong, story teller — my gentle readers may say — if the silver in that country is worth so little and the business is done that way, why don't the merchants who often deal in silk overseas sell their goods for silver coins and make a hundred-fold profit? The answer is, my readers, you don't understand the reason. The people of that country always barter goods for silk. The Chinese merchants, too, accept goods as payments and this turns out to be profitable. If one insists on being paid in money, they will pay you with dragon-and-phoenix coins, which means a high price to them but no more than the weight of the silver to us. You'll get no advantage. They buy something to eat with coins that they take to be of low value, while we accept them as one *liang* of silver, and thus we gain.

You are wrong again, story-teller — my readers may say — if so, why didn't the businessmen make money by exchanging food for the foreigners' low-valued coins? Why should they buy goods with a good deal of capital? The matter is not that simple, my readers. It's by good luck that this man made an unexpected fortune. If he were to try to do this a second time, he might find that three to five days' delay on the sea would cause his tangerines to rot like pulp. Remember Wen Ruoxu's fans when his luck was out. Even goods as durable as fans could bring no profit, let alone fruit! You can't predict one's fortune or misfortune.

Enough of this digression. Let's return to the merchants. As they brought their agents to the ship, Wen Ruoxu told them the story of his tangerines. They were all surprised. "Good luck for you. We came together, but you were the first to make a fortune with a little capital!" Clapping his hands, Big Brother Zhang said, "People say he's unlucky. Now his luck must have turned!" And then he said to Wen Ruoxu, "Your silver coins are worth little if you use them to purchase goods here. You can use them to buy some Chinese goods from your companions that would be worth hundreds of *liang* of silver and barter them for some rare native products. Then you'll make a big profit when you get back home. Wouldn't that be better than keeping the money with you?" "I am always unlucky," replied Wen Ruoxu, "and every time I go out to make a profit I lose my capital. Now thanks to your help I have made a profit without any investment. It's a windfall. How can I fancy more profit? If I lose as I did in the past, will I ever find another opportunity as lucrative as the 'Red Fruit from Dongting'?" Many of his companions proposed, "We are in need of silver yet we have abundant goods. Why don't we supply each other's needs to the benefit of both sides?" "Once bitten by a snake," answered Wen Ruoxu, "one shies at a coiled rope for as long as ten years. Speaking of goods, I am dispirited. I think I'd better return home with this much silver." Clapping their hands, his companions sighed, "You are letting a handsome profit slip through your fingers. What a pity!"

Wen Ruoxu and his companions left the boat, and went to shops to barter. This went on for about half a month, during which time Wen Ruoxu saw many interesting things. He was contented with what he had earned and showed no interest in their wares.

As they finished their business, they got on board the ship, offered sacrifices to the gods for blessing, held a feast and set off. After a few days on the sea, the weather changed all of a sudden. They saw

Dark clouds veiled the sun
Black waves mounted to the sky;
Dancing dragons and serpents soared high,
Frightened fish and turtles hid deep.

Seeing the hurricane coming, the people on the ship hoisted the half-mast sail. The ship, now at the mercy of the wind, drifted along. An island came faintly in sight, so they lowered the sail and oared the ship toward the island. As they reached it, they found it to be a desert island, where

> *Towering trees scraped the sky,*
> *Grass covered the ground;*
> *On this desolate place were found*
> *Only footprints of hares and foxes.*
> *In the barren earth*
> *Neither dragons nor tigers could have nests;*
> *No one knows to which domain it belonged,*
> *Or if anybody had ever set his foot on it.*

Thereupon they lowered the anchor over the stern, fixed a post on the bank and tied the ship to it. The seamen told their passengers in the cabin, "Sit inside at ease and wait until the wind falls."

With his sum of money, Wen Ruoxu wished he could fly home, but he had to wait until the wind died down. He was irritable. "I'll climb onto the island and have a look at it," he said. "Is there anything worth seeing on such a desert island?" his companions asked. "I have nothing to do anyway," Wen Ruoxu replied. "There's no harm in looking at it."

Having gotten dizzy from the jolting ship in the storm, his companions yawned. Nobody wanted to go with him. Wen Ruoxu collected his spirits and jumped ashore by himself. His visit to the island, however, brought unexpected consequences, alas! — As a result:

> *The spirit was brought back into an abandoned crust*
> *And an enormous wealth befell a poor scholar.*

If the story-teller were born in the same year as the hero of this story and could foresee what happened later, he would have accompanied

Wen Ruoxu to the island — even if he couldn't move his legs, he would walk with a stick!

I am telling you about Wen Ruoxu, who, seeing that nobody wanted to go with him, made up his mind to climb onto the island by clutching at vines and canes. The island was not high and it took him little effort to reach its peak. There was wild grass everywhere and no path to be found. He looked around only to see an expanse of nothingness. He felt as if he was a leaf hovering in the air. Sadness welled up inside him and tears came to his eyes. "I am a clever man," he thought to himself, "but I am always unlucky. My family fortune has waned and I am all alone. I've just journeyed overseas. Although I've got a thousand silver coins in my pocket, who knows if they are destined to be mine or someone else's? Now I am on an isolated island, far from the continent. Even my life is shared by the sea god." As he was musing, he raised his head and saw a big object sticking up above the grass far ahead. When he went to investigate, he found it to be a turtle shell. He was surprised: "Imagine there can be so large a turtle shell in the world! If I tell my fellows in the ship about it, they will not believe me. I haven't brought anything back from my overseas voyage. If I take this shell home, I will have an unusual object to show. Otherwise my statement will be taken to be a fabricated story, and they will say a Suzhou native like me is good at lying. Besides, if I break the cover and bottom apart and fix four legs to each part, I'll have two beds! What an original idea!" He untied his puttees, joined them together, put them through the shell and tied a knot. Then he hauled the turtle shell towards the ship.

Seeing him coming, the people on the ship laughed: "From where did you tow this, Mr Wen?" "I want you all to know that I, too, have acquired goods from abroad," he replied. Then, as they raised their heads to see the turtle shell, which looked like a big legless bed, they were surprised, "What a big crust!" some of them remarked. "Why have you brought it here?" "It's a rare object," said Wen Ruoxu, "so I wanted to bring it." "Instead of valuable goods," every one mocked, "you just take something like this?" Someone said, "It is useful in that if you are in doubt about an important matter, you can divine an answer by burning it. But such a large shell is useless as a medical prescription!" "If a physician were to make turtle-shell plaster with it," another man put in, "this shell, cracked and boiled down, would equal a hundred ordinary shells." "Useful or not," explained Wen Ruoxu, "it is an unusual object and it cost me nothing. Why can't I take it home?" He called to a seaman and together they carried the shell into his cabin. When it had been lying in the open space on the island, it had looked as big as it was supposed to be; now, in the cabin, it appeared much larger. If it had not been a sea ship, it wouldn't have had enough room for such a mammoth object.

His companions laughed a lot, saying, " If someone asks us when we get home, we'll say Mr Wen has dealt in large turtles in foreign countries." "Don't laugh at me," Wen Ruoxu said. "I think it may be of use one way or another — It's definitely not a castaway." No matter how he was laughed at, he was pleased about his new possession. He fetched water, washed the whole turtle shell clean and wiped it dry. Then he put his purse and luggage into the shell and bound it with a rope. The whole object served as a huge suitcase. "Look," he said, laughing, "isn't this its usage?" "A great idea!" others said. "Mr Wen is a clever man indeed." Everybody laughed too. Thus the night passed.

The wind ceased the next day, and the ship set off again. In a few days they arrived at a place that turned out to be Fujian Province. As they moored the ship, they were thronged by a group of petty brokers who used to wait on merchants from abroad. One broker tried to persuade them to go to Zhang's shop, while another claimed the Li's shop was the best. There was a lot of dragging and pulling. Wen Ruoxu's companions followed a broker they knew well and only then did the rest of them give up.

The merchants stopped at a big shop run by a Persian and sat down in it. Hearing that overseas traffickers had come, the master of the shop immediately handed out some silver to his servants, ordering them to lay out a feast of a dozen tables. Then he walked into his shop. He was a Persian and, strangely had the surname of Ma written in the Chinese character for "manao" (agate), and his given name was Baoha.* He specialized in dealing with traffickers with rare goods from abroad. He owned a great deal of capital, so much so that nobody knew exactly how many thousands of *liang* of silver he had. Everyone from the ship knew him well, except Wen Ruoxu. As Wen Ruoxu raised his head to look at him, he found the Persian man, who had been in China for a long time, wore clothes in a way not much different from the Chinese and he acted like a Chinese. But his eyebrows had been shaved, his beard was cut short, and he looked odd with high nose-bridge and deep eye sockets. The Persian greeted his guests and seated them. After a cup or two of tea, he stood up and ushered them into a hall where the tables had been set beautifully. As the convention went, when an ocean-going ship arrived, the shop master would treat the merchants to a dinner before bargaining with them. Now, with an enamel plate decorated with chrysanthemum patters in hand, the Persian gestured a salute, saying, "Show me your lists of items please, so I can arrange your seats."

Do you know why the Persian said this? The answer lies in the fact that the Persian set much store by interests. He would offer the most honored seat to the merchant whose list of items contained rarities worth over ten thousand *liang* of silver. The other guests were seated in the order of the value of their goods; age and rank were out of consideration. This had been an established tradition. The merchants from the ship naturally knew the quantity and worth of each other's

---

*Many Chinese Muslins bear a family name Ma, which is derived from Mohammed "Baoha" may be the Chinese transliteration of Abu Hassan or Abu Hamid.

goods. So they each took a proper seat and held up a cup. Only Wen Ruoxu stood there alone. The Persian master said, "I've never seen this distinguished guest before. I suppose he must be a new hand at overseas trade and returns with little purchase." "He's our good friend and he has been abroad with us just for fun," replied the companions. "He has silver, but he didn't do any purchasing. So we have to let him sit in a humble seat." Blushing, Wen Ruoxu took the humble seat. The master sat on a flank. During the wining the merchants vied with each other to parade their goods. One claimed he had this many sapphires while another pretended to have that many emeralds. Wen Ruoxu was silent. He felt a little regret. "I should have taken their advice the other day and purchased some goods. Now, despite the silver I have in pocket, I cannot utter one word." On second thought he sighed, "Considering that I had no capital at all, I am fortunate enough. I should be content with my lot." As he brooded over this situation, he was in no mood to drink. His tipsy companions played the finger-guessing game as they drank, making a terrible mess of the tables. The master was a worldly-wise man. He discovered Wen Ruoxu was in low spirits, but instead of trying to find out what was the matter, he perfunctorily proposed toasts to Wen Ruoxu. "We've drunk our fill," said the merchants. "It's late. We'd better return to our ship before it gets too dark. We'll deliver our goods tomorrow." And they said good-bye to the master, who then put away the plates and dishes and retired for the night.

The Persian got up early next morning and went to the shore to see the merchants on the ship. As he stepped onto the deck, he caught a glimpse of the huge object in Wen Ruoxu's cabin. He was surprised. "Whose treasure is that?" he asked. "Nobody mentioned it d ring the feast yesterday. I guess it's not for sale?" Everyone laughed, pointing to Wen Ruoxu. "It's our friend Mr Wen's treasure," they said. "And it's unsalable," added one. The Persian cast a glance at Wen Ruoxu. He scowled at Wen's fellow travelers, and said, "I've been a good friend to you for years. Why did you play such a joke on me so that I've offended this new guest? It's outrageous that you've made me humiliate him by giving him the humble seat!" Grasping Wen Ruoxu by the arm, he said to the merchants, "There's no hurry in delivering your goods. Let me go back to my shop and apologize to him." The merchants could not make head or tail of the matter. Some who knew Wen Ruoxu well and some who were just curious — there were a dozen of them altogether — followed the two of them to the shop to see what would happen. As they watched, the Persian pulled Wen Ruoxu with one hand and set a chair in place with another. Disregarding the other merchants, he said, gesturing at the chair, "Excuse me for my offense. Please sit down." Wen Ruoxu was baffled, thinking, "It's incredible that what I have is such a valuable thing! Can I be so lucky?"

The Persian master entered the inner room and came out soon after. He ushered the merchants to the hall where the feast had been held the day before. The tables had been reset, the one in the lead more sumptuous than what it looked like the previous time. The Persian held up a cup and made an obeisance to Wen Ruoxu. He said to the other guests, "This guest should sit in the honor seat. All your shipload of goods is no match for his. Excuse me for having been disrespectful!" The merchants thought it ridiculous and strange. A little skeptical, they sat down at the tables. After they each drank three cups of wine, the master asked, "Please, my esteemed guest, is the rarity of yours that I've just seen for sale?" A quick-witted man, Wen Ruoxu replied, "Why not if a good price is offered?" Hearing this affirmative answer, the master was exhilarated. With a broad smile he stood up, saying, "If so, set a price and I dare not cut it."

Wen Ruoxu did not know how much the turtle shell was worth. If he demanded too little, he would expose his ignorance in trade; if he demanded too much, he would be mocked. Thinking over and over again, and becoming flushed, he could not set a price. Big Brother

Zhang looked at him and put his hand on the back of the chair. He raised the middle, ring and little fingers — three together — and pointed his forefinger upward, saying, "Ask him for this number!" Shaking his head, Wen Ruoxu raised one finger, "I dare not even demand this much." Their gestures, however, were not lost on the Persian. "How much do you want?" he asked. Big Brother Zhang lied to him, "Mr Wen's gesture might suggest ten thousand." Breaking into laughter, the Persian said, "I see you don't want to sell. You are joking with me by giving this price. How can such a treasure be sold at such a low price!"

Hearing this, every one was dumb-struck. They stood up and pulled Wen Ruoxu aside, saying "It's good luck for you. It must be worth a far higher price. But we don't know the exact price. Mr Wen, you'd better make a big bid and let him counter it." Wen Ruoxu, however, was shy and he faltered. "Don't' be timid," they said, encouraging him. "Don't hesitate to tell me how much you are asking," the Persian urged him. Wen Ruoxu then asked for fifty thousand *liang* of silver. The Persian shook his head: "No kidding! It's unreasonable." Pulling Big Brother Zhang aside the Persian asked him in private, "You have engaged in trade overseas many times and you are called Goods-Appreciator Zhang. How come you do not know the price of this object? I suppose he doesn't want to sell it and so he makes fool of my humble shop in this way." "To tell the truth," said Big Brother Zhang, "he is a good friend of mine. He went overseas with us just for the fun of it. That's why he didn't purchase anything. The object you mentioned was accidentally discovered on an island when we took shelter from the wind. Because it was not purchased, we don't know its price. If you pay fifty thousand, it's enough to let him live the rest of his life in luxury. He should be content." "If that's the case," said the Persian, "I will ask you to be the guarantor on my behalf. I'll thank you with a huge reward. No one must go back on his word!" Thereupon the Persian bade a waiter to fetch ink, a brush and paper.

He folded a sheet of paper used for writing statements in court — and handed the brush to Big Brother Zhang. "May I trouble you to write a contract so that I can make the deal?" he asked. Pointing to a companion, Big Brother Zhang said, "This is Chu Zhongying. He writes a good hand." He passed the brush and paper to him. Mr Chu ground the ink slab until the ink was dark enough, spread out the paper and committed the brush to it. Then he wrote:

The agreement singed by Zhang Chengyun and his party testifies:

As Wen Shi, a merchant of Suzhou origin, has brought back one huge turtle shell from abroad to the shop of Ma Baoha, the Persian merchant, Ma Baoha is willing to offer a price of fifty thousand liang of silver for the shell. Upon signing this agreement the selling party will deliver the goods and the purchasing party will deliver the silver. Neither party must break the promise. If either party violates the agreement, that party will be fined the sum declared in this agreement plus one tenth thereof.

The contract was copied, dated and signed by Zhang Chengyun and his dozen companions. Chu Zhongying, as the writer, signed his name at the end of the list. Then they folded each copy at the margin of the date line, put the two edges together and wrote a line of characters across the junction that read, "An Agreement between Wen Shi, the seller, and Ma Baoha, the purchaser." The people listed in the contract signed their names on the line, beginning with the last one on the list. When it was Zhang Chengyun's turn, he said, "The deal will be smoothly made if we are offered a handsome fee for the signatures." "Certainly, certainly," smiled the Persian.

After that the Persian went into his inner room and carried out a box of silver, saying, "Let me pay the fee to the signers first. I have something to say after that." The merchants craned their necks as the Persian opened the box, and they saw twenty packs of silver in it, each containing fifty *liang* and the entire amount was one thousand *liang*. The Persian presented the silver to Zhang Chengyun with both hands saying, "My honorable guest, please distribute this to your companions." When the merchants were feasted and the contract was drawn up, they were clamoring for the fun of it — none of them were sure the transaction could ever be made. Only when the glittering silver were brought out did they realize that the business was for real.

As if in a dream or being tipsy, Wen Ruoxu was dumbstruck and stared blankly ahead of him. Nudging him, Big Brother Zhang said, "It's up to Mr Wen to decide how to divide the silver among us." Only then did Wen Ruoxu find his tongue. He said, "Let's take our time after the business is settled."

The Persian, with a smile, said to Wen Ruoxu, "My esteemed guest, I'd like to discuss one thing with you. The silver is in the garret. The weight has been checked and is exact to the full value. It should be enough for one or two of you to enter the garret, count the packs and weigh one pack. It's not necessary to weigh every pack. But I'd remind you of a problem. So much silver cannot be carried away in a short time. Besides, Mr Wen is a single man. How can he carry it onto the ship? It's rather inconvenient for him to carry it on an overseas voyage." Thinking for a moment Wen Ruoxu said, "I see your point. What should I do?"

"In my opinion," said the Persian, "Mr Wen cannot go home right away. I have a silk shop with a capital of three thousand *liang* of silver. The adjoining large and small houses, halls and storied houses have a total of more than a hundred rooms. It's a large piece of property, worth two thousand *liang* of silver. It is half a *li* away from here. I would like to give you the shop with the goods in it and the title deed by way of paying five thousand *liang* of silver. You may stay there and engage in business. You may transport your silver to the shop in several batches without being noticed. When you want to visit your home in future, you may trust your estate to a confidential servant. In this way you can come and go unburdened. Otherwise, it's not difficult for me to pay the whole sum but it's difficult for you to store it. That's my proposal."

Hearing the eloquent remarks, Wen Ruoxu and Big Brother Zhang stamped their feet in admiration. "You are indeed a master mind of business," they said. "Every word is convincing!" "I haven't a wife yet," said Wen Ruoxu, "and my family fortune is gone. Even if I were to take the silver home, I could find no place to dispose of it. I'll take his advice and make a home here. Why not? My lucky hit was predestined by Heaven. What I should do is but to let fate take its own course. Even though the goods and houses are less than the fifty thousand *liang* of silver, it doesn't matter, since I am getting them without much pain." Turning to the Persian he said, "What you've put forward is a flawless plan. I'll adopt it."

The Persian then led Wen Ruoxu into the garret and beckoned to Big Brother Zhang and Chu Zhongying, "You two come with us. The rest may sit here and wait for a moment." When the four of them entered the garret, Wen Ruoxu's companions outside stretched their necks and exchanged remarks. One of them said, "What a wonderful adventure! What luck! If we had known the outcome, we would have gone onto the island when the ship moored there. You can never tell if we, too, might have come across something strange." "The greatest fortune came by itself," another said, "and was not obtained through labor."

As they were marveling at the good fortune, Wen Ruoxu came out with Big Brother Zhang and Chu Zhongying. "What's up?" the companions asked them. "There's a lofty garret inside, a storehouse of silver. The silver is stored in barrels. When I went in I saw ten large barrels, each with four thousand *liang* of silver in it and five small barrels each with one thousand. This amounts to forty-five thousand *liang*. They were sealed with paper strips bearing Mr Wen's signature. As soon as the turtle shell is delivered, those barrels belong to Mr Wen."

The Persian walked out. "Here is the title deed for the houses and an account of the silk. They add up to the sum of five thousand *liang*. Now let me get the turtle shell from the ship." The merchants all went to the ship.

On the way Wen Ruoxu warned his companions, "There are more of our fellows in the ship. Please don't tell them the whole story! I'll repay you for your kindness." His companions, too, feared that the others in the ship might want to have a share of their fee. So they all maintained a tacit understanding.

Going onto the ship, Wen Ruoxu took his pack from within the shell, and running his fingers over the shell, he thought to himself, "I am indeed lucky!" The Persian had two young waiters from his shop carry the turtle shell, telling them, "Be careful to carry it to the shop, and don't leave it in the open."

As the shell had been carried away, the people in the ship said, "Such unsalable goods are now sold. What price did you ask?" With his pack in hand, Wen Ruoxu did not answer but instead made for the bank. His companions who had been to the shop with him followed him. They scrutinized the shell from one end to the other, peeped into it and felt its inner side. Looking at each other they were perplexed, "What is the good of this?"

The Persian took them into his shop and then said, "Now let's go with Mr Wen to see his shop and houses." As they followed the Persian there, they found it to be a gigantic mansion on a busy street. In front of the gate was the shop with a lane nearby. They entered the lane, took a turn at a corner and saw huge gate consisting of two stone-plate planks, beyond which was a spacious courtyard. In the yard was a grandiose hall with a panel reading "Treasure Presenting House". On either side of the hall was a side room, along three walls of which were shelves full of various kinds of silk. At the back there were many chambers and storied houses. Wen Ruoxu mused, "Such an edifice is no less luxurious than that of a prince. And besides, the silk business will bring me boundless profits. I'll settle down here. Why should I think of my native place anymore?" So he told the Persian: "It's good to live here, but I am single. I will need some waiters and servants." "No problem," the Persian assured him, "I'll take care of that matter."

Pleased, Wen Ruoxu and his companions returned to the Persian's shop. Having ordered some tea, the Persian said, "Mr Wen, you may stay overnight in the shop and need not go back to your ship. The servant in the shop will wait upon you and I'll engage more for you by and by." Wen Ruoxu's companions said, "Now that the business is done and we need not talk about it anymore, we would like to know more about the turtle shell. Why does it cost so much? We hope you'll tell us." "Just so," echoed Wen Ruoxu.

The Persian smiled, and said, "My honorable guests, how come you don't know about this since you have traveled overseas so many times? Haven't you heard that a dragon has nine offspring? One of its offspring is a drum dragon. Its skin is used to cover drums. Such a drum sends its sound over a hundred *li* distance. For this it is called the dragon drum. At the age of ten thousand years, the drum dragon casts off its shell and becomes a dragon. This shell has twenty-four ribs, a number matching the twenty-four solar terms in the sky. Within the joint of every rib is a big pearl. The drum dragon cannot slough it off and become a dragon until its ribs are fully grown. A drum dragon caught alive is useless except that its skin can be used to cover a drum, because it has nothing in the joints of its ribs. Only when all its ribs are full grown and every joint has a pearl in it can it slough off the shell and fly into the air as a dragon. Then its shell falls by itself, the skeleton fully nurtured by nature is perfect and the joints of its ribs are fully developed. It's quite different from the shell taken from a killed drum dragon that hasn't lived its full life span. That's why it is so large.

Although we know this, we don't know when it will cast its shell off and where to wait for the moment! The shell is worth nothing, but the pearls, which all emit light at night, are priceless treasures. Today I have come across it without pains."

Wen Ruoxu's companions, however, were still skeptical about this. Thereupon the Persian went inside and came out smiling. He took out a wrapping of western-made cloth from within his sleeve, saying, "Please look at this, gentleman." When he unwrapped the cloth, they saw a dazzling bright pearl one *cun* in diameter. He asked for a black lacquer tray, and put it with the pearl in darkness. The pearl kept rolling, radiating glistening rays as far as one *chi* away. Everyone stared at it in awe, and with their tongues sticking out. Turning himself around, the Persian thanked them one by one: "It is very kind of you to help me. This pearl alone, when taken to my country, will be worth the sum I've paid for the shell. The other pearls are your presents to me." Everyone was shocked to hear this, but they could not go back on their own word. Discerning a slight change on their facial expressions, the Persian put the pearl away, hurried in and emerged with a couple of footmen carrying a trunk of silk. Delivering two bolts of silk to each of them except Wen Ruoxu, he said, "I've caused you a lot of trouble. Please take this material to make a couple of robes. It's a token of respect from my humble shop." And he took out a dozen strings of fine beads from within his sleeve and gave each a string. "This paltry present," he added, "may be used to buy a cup of tea on your way home." To Wen Ruoxu he gave four strings of thicker beads and eight bolts of silk, saying, "This may be used to make some clothes." Wen Ruoxu and his companions gladly thanked him.

Now the Persian and the companions escorted Wen Ruoxu to the silk shop. He commanded the waiters and assistants to meet Wen Ruoxu: "From today on he is your master."

Then the Persian took leave, saying, "I am going back to my shop and I'll return in a few moments." Soon tens of footmen carried up loads of ten barrels and five boxes of silver that had Wen Ruoxu's own seals on them. Wen Ruoxu hid the silver in a secluded bedroom. He came out and said, "Thank you for helping me gain this unexpected fortune. My gratitude is beyond expression." From his packs he took out the silver coins that he had acquired from selling the "Red Fruit from Dongting" and gave ten coins as a present to each of his companions except Big Brother Zhang and the couple of close friends who had aided him when he was setting off. To each of the latter he gave twenty, adding, "This may be a token of my gratitude." By then Wen Ruoxu no longer needed these coins, while his friends rejoiced and were grateful. Handing dozens of coins to Big Brother Zhang, Wen Ruoxu said, "Would you mind dividing these coins among our colleagues who have stayed in the ship? Let each of them have one coin that may serve as the tip for tea. I will stay here. When I have put everything in order I'll visit home at leisure. I can't go home with you now. So let's say good-bye here."

"But we haven't got our share of a thousand *liang* of silver as a commission yet," said Big Brother Zhang to Wen. "How shall we handle that? Nobody will complain only if you can take the trouble of dividing it up for us." "Oh, I almost forgot that!" Wen Ruoxu said. He talked the matter over with his companions and decided to hand out one hundred *liang* among those who had remained in the ship. The remaining nine hundred *liang* was divided into equal shares according to the number of the companions ashore, but two more shares were set aside, so that while each man got his share, Big Brother Zhang, the head of them all, and Chu Zhongying, the writer of the contract, received two shares.

All were greatly pleased and nobody complained. One of them said, "But that Uygur* has got an easy bargain! Mr Wen should have asked

---

*Uygur is an ethnic group dwelling in Northwest China. In ancient times the term Uygur was used as a general name for Chinese and foreign muslins.

an extraordinary price." "One mustn't be too covetous," said Wen
Ruoxu, "I used to be in misfortune and would lose my capital every
time I engaged in a trade. By chance I gained an easy fortune. This
shows that every man's lot is predestined and it's no use making an
effort for any purpose. But for the Persian master who recognized the
shell, we'd have taken it as a castaway. It is his instruction that has
made us understand what the shell is. How can we be so ungrateful as
to demand more from him?" "You're right, Mr Wen!" they replied.
"It's because you are honest and kind, that you've become wealthy."
With repeated thanks these people collected their things, and returned
to the ship to deliver their goods.

After this Wen Ruoxu became a rich merchant in Fujian Province.
He took wives and concubines and settled down there. He did not visit
his old friends and acquaintances in Suzhou until several years later.
His line of descendants has continued until today and they are all
prosperous.

Tale 2

Escaping Disgrace Yao Dizhu Encounters Disgrace; Making an Error Zheng Yue'e Utilizes the Error

It is related that during the reign of Wanli [AD 1573-1619] of our [Ming] dynasty in Suntian Village, Xiuning County, Huizhou Prefecture, there lived a man named Yao, who had a daughter by the name of Dizhu. When the daughter was sixteen, she was as beautiful as a flower and was regarded as the most attractive woman in her native place. The parents were healthy and the family was well off. The daughter was doted on and indulged in many ways. She was brought by a match-maker to the house of Pan Jia in Tunxi Village and became his wife. — It seems that the least believable thing in the world is a match-maker's word. A match-maker can describe the number one millionaire as a man without a pin-point of land or describe a scholar in starvation as a millionaire. Your wealth is at the tip of his tongue and your appearance depends on his caprice.

The Pans of Tunxi Village, once an influential family, were reduced to poverty. The male members had to engage in business and the women took up all sorts of heavy housework such as fetching water and pestling rice. None in the family could lead an idle life anymore.

Pan Jia was a good youth and had a somewhat impressive bearing, but he had given up the study of Confucian classics and taken up a trade. His parents, however, were atrocious, and they would reprimand their daughter-in-law at the slightest provocation in all sorts of abusive language. Because Dizhu's parents had believed the match-maker's assurance that the Pans were a good family, they had married off their dearly loved daughter to the Pans. The young couple loved each other tenderly, but as Dizhu experienced the hard life she had to lead, she was upset and often shed tears in secret. Knowing the reason of her sadness, Pan Jia comforted her with soft words. Soon two months had elapsed since the wedding. The father reproached the son, "You two indulge in love and stay together all the time. Can you make a living this way? Why don't you leave home and do some business?" When the helpless young man told Dizhu about this, the couple couldn't stop crying. They talked all the night through.

The next day the father forced his son to leave the house. Left alone, Dizhu was depressed. Besides, she had been pampered by her parents, and as a new wife in a new house she did not know the way in which the Pan's house was managed. So she always made mistakes. Because of this she was in low spirits all the time. Seeing her like this, the parents-in-law garrulously scolded her, "For whom is the bitch lovesick? There must be a paramour!" When she was living with her parents, she had never heard such harsh words. But she dared not talk back, so she had to stifle her anger and sobbed by herself.

One morning Dizhu got up a little later than usual. When the parents-in-law called for breakfast, she failed to serve it promptly. The father-in-law berated her, "What a lazy and greedy slut! She sleeps until the sun is high! Only a prostitute can lead such a carefree life. If you prefer such a comfortable life, you may go to brothel and flirt with dandies. You certainly cannot maintain a family this way!" "I am a daughter from a decent family," said Dizhu, "how can you insult me like this, even if I've done something wrong!" And she broke into a fit of tears. Since she had nobody to pour out her woes to, she could not get to sleep the whole night. The more she thought about the matter, the more angry she became: "It's really too outrageous for the old idiot to talk to me that way. How can I stand this? Let me return home and tell my father and mother. They will bring him to account for his words! Besides, I can stay at my parents' home for a time, and thus save myself much of the frustration here." As she made up her mind, she got up early the next morning and departed without dressing herself up. She covered her head with a silk scarf and ran towards the ferry. — Well, if the story-teller had lived at the same time as she did and knew that she would come into trouble, he would have held her back by seizing her by the waist or pushing her at the breast so as to save her from the trouble in which she would later be involved!

When she departed, it was still early. Though some people might have already risen, scarcely a soul could be seen in the wild. The ferry was tranquil. There happened to be a villain by the name of Wang Xi who specialized in evil doing. He bore the sobriquet "Maggot in the Snow", meaning he was not afraid of cold or hunger. It seemed that Yao Dizhu was doomed to meet with rotten luck: she faced the villain poling a raft towards the ferry. Seeing the young lady, who was as beautiful as a flower, standing alone on the bank, hair disheveled and with tear stains on her cheeks, he realized something was wrong with her. "Are you going across the river, Madam?" he asked. "Just so," replied Dizhu. "Get in please," he said. And with a "Take care!" he reached out his hand and helped her onto the raft.

As he poled the raft to a secluded place, he asked, "May I ask, Madam, from which family do you come? Where are you going by yourself?" "I am going to my parents in Suntian Village." Dizhu answered. "Just take me across the river; I know my way home. Why should you bother about me?" "I see your hair is not combed, your face is not washed, there are tears in your eyes, and you are alone. I guess there must be a reason for this. Tell me what it is and I'll take you across," said Wang Xi. Now in the middle of the river, Dizhu was eager to get home. She had to tell him, with tears in her eyes, how she had been wronged while her husband was away. On hearing this, Wang Xi had an idea. He turned around, saying, "If so, I cannot ferry you across. You don't mean well by running away. If I take you to the opposite bank, you might escape or commit suicide or someone might kidnap you. If it is discovered that I have ferried you across, I'll be answerable for the legal consequences." "Stop your nonsense!" said Dizhu. "I am going to my parents. How can you say I am escaping? If I wanted to die, why didn't I drown myself in the water? Why should I commit suicide after you have ferried me across the river? I know my way to my home and it's impossible for anybody to kidnap me." "But I don't believe you. If you are going to your parents' home, you may first stop at my house — it is near. Let me go and ask your parents to come to take you home. Thus both sides will be assured of your security." "All right," said Dizhu. She was a woman of little worldly experience. In a helpless situation such as this she could not disobey him. Believing he was acting out of good intentions, she followed him. They arrived at the other bank and, after traveling down a winding path, reached the place he said was his home. Walking through several gates they arrived at a yard with a number of quiet houses. She saw the rooms were attired

With bright windows and clean tables,
Brocade curtains and designed drapes;
Flowers in pots stood without,
Cane chairs lay within.
On the walls hung scrolls by great artists;
On the tables were purple ceramic tea-pots from master
     craftsmen.
Though the rooms, small, were no match for a noble residence;
The serene paths pointed to an edifice other than an average one.

The place turned out to be Wang Xi's snare, to which he induced women from respectable families. When he entrapped such women, he would say they were his relatives and solicit lavish and light-hearted men to carry on with them. The couples might spare a short moment of sensual pleasure together, or, if an attachment developed, the place would serve as their villa. This earned Wang Xi a great deal of silver. As for the women who were of hazy background, Wang Xi would sell them to traders in women who would offer him a high price, and the traders in turn would sell the women to brothels. This business had been carried on for long time. At a glance of Yao Dizhu, an evil plot entered his mind, and so he lured her to his den.

Dizhu was a daughter of a respectable family and was fond of leisure. Because of the ill-tempered parents-in-law, the everyday chores had tormented her enough, not to speak of the heavy work of cooking and fetching water. The quiet place somewhat pleased her, making her ignorant of the situation she was in. When Wang Xi saw Dizhu was pleased instead of being scared, he felt his urges kindled. He stepped forward, knelt down and begged Dizhu to make love with him. Dizhu glowered at him, "How dare you!" she said. "I am a daughter of a good family. You said you would keep me here waiting while you passed a message to my family. But you've lured me here and you are trying to defile me in broad daylight! If you pressure me, I'll commit suicide." She picked up an iron bar from the table, which was used to light the lamp, and was about to stab at her own throat. Flurried, Wang Xi said, "Please take it easy. I dare not be so audacious." Wang Xi said this because his kidnapping business was conducted for money rather than sex. He feared that if Yao Dizhu did what she had said she would do, he would lose a big sum. His flaming urges were thus dampened.

He entered an inner room and, after a long while, called out an old woman. "Mom Wang," he said to the old woman, "please sit here and keep company with this lady. I'll go to her home and report to her parents." Dizhu asked him to wait a moment so she could tell him the whereabouts of her home and the names of her parents, adding, "Be sure to ask them to come soon. I'll thank you with a bounty gift."

After Wang Xi left, Mom Wang brought a basin of water and toilet articles for Dizhu to wash and dress. While Dizhu was dressing herself, the old woman stood by, dropping the question, "Whose wife are you, may I ask? Why are you here?" Dizhu told her story in detail. Hearing this, the old woman stamped her feet, feigning indignation, "Oh, the short-lived wretches are blind! A beautiful daughter-in-law like you is far beyond what they deserve! Why should they insult you with such abusive words? They are too heartless. How can you get along with them?" These words struck at the pent-up grief in Dizhu's mind, and tears welled up in her eyes. "Where are you going?" the old woman asked her. "I'm going to my parents' house to tell them what had happened to me, and to stay with them for some time until my husband returns." "When will your husband return home?" the old woman asked. "Only two months after the wedding he was reprimanded and forced to leave," Dizhu replied in tears. "Who knows when he will come home? Heaven only knows!"

"It's unbearable that a flower-like girl such as you is left alone and abused!" exclaimed the old woman, " Madam, let me give you a little advice. You may stay with your parents for some time, but you will have to return to your parents-in-law some day. Can you take shelter from them at your parents' home all your life? Years of frustration are ahead of you. How can you get rid of this?" "Since such is my fate," said Dizhu, "I have no choice but to accept it." "But, if you take my humble advice," said the old woman, "I can assure you of a life of joy and leisure." "What advice is that?" asked Dizhu. "My humble self has contact with many offspring of wealthy and ranking families," said the old woman. "Among them are many handsome and refined young men. You needn't ask any of them for their consent. Simply choose one to your liking and I will go and persuade him to take you. He'll treat you as a invaluable treasure. You'll enjoy an easy life free from worries about food or clothing. You'll not toil with your delicate hands in labor, but you'll have servants and maids to wait upon you. Such a life is worthy of your charming looks. It's far better than your present life of solitude, crude labor and humiliations." Dizhu could not sustain such a hard life, and she was a young woman who had no definite view. Hearing the old woman's words, she thought of the many unhappy experiences at her husband's home. She wavered. "It won't do," she said. "What if somebody learns about this?" "No stranger dares to tread on my territory," the old woman assured her. "Neither a god nor a ghost knows this secret place. Stay here a couple of days and you'll not be able to part, even for paradise." "But I have just asked the raft man to inform my parents," said Dizhu. "He is my adopted son," said the old woman. "It is very thoughtless of him to deliver that meaningless message."

At this point a man broke in. Seizing the old woman he shouted, "You are abetting the lady to shack up with a lover in the light of day! I'll report you to the authorities." Dizhu was taken aback by this sudden development, but as she cast her eye on the man, she found him to be none other than Wang Xi, the raft man. "Have you handed the message to my parents?" she asked him. "Shit! I eavesdropped outside for a long time. What Mom Wang said is a well-deliberated plan for your future. Think it over," he said. Dizhu heaved a sigh, "Since I am in misfortune and snared, I have no other choice. But you must not make a clumsy arrangement for me!" "I've just said," the old woman assured her, "you may pick one to your liking by yourself and you two will be matched by mutual consent. How then can you be mismated?" Unable to keep her own counsel, Dizhu believed the old woman. Seeing the tidy and clean rooms with refined bedding and drapes, she settled down relaxed. The old woman and Wang Xi waited upon her hand and foot, serving everything promptly at her order. This made Dizhu happy and caused her to forget her cares and fears.

Eventually Wang Xi departed and met with a magnet of Shangshan in the native county, whose name was Wu Dalang. A millionaire and a lady's man, Wu had many friends among loafers, and Wang Xi was one of them. He asked Wang Xi, "Do you know of any place for fun these days?" "I have good news for you, sir," replied Wang Xi. "One of my nieces was recently widowed. She's captivating and she's not found a new spouse yet. Is this not a piece of goods for your stock? But the price may be high." "May I have a look?" Wu Dalang asked. "Why not?" said Wang Xi, "But she is from a respectable family and she is shy. Let me return first and, after I talk with her in the sitting room, you may burst in upon her and have a good look." Wu Dalang saw his point and agreed.

After Wang Xi returned to his house he saw Dizhu sitting in her room meditating. "Why not sit in the sitting room, Madam?" he asked. "It's boring here." Hearing his voice, Mom Wang entered the room, and said, "Just so, Madam! Please come out and have a conversation with me." Dizhu agreed and went to the sitting room, whereupon Wang Xi secretly bolted the door to her room. "Mom," Dizhu said, "I'd better go home." "Don't be impatient, please." Mom Wang replied, "We keep you here because we treasure your lovely looks and can't bear to see you live in hardship. Wait a few days and you'll surely meet a good mate." As they were talking, a man broke in. Do you, my readers, know how he looked like? He

> wore a roof-shaped bamboo hat over his head,
> and a vermilion amber pendant on either side;
> He was in a narrow-collared and broad-sleeved blue robe
> and had a pair of low-soled and flat-faced red silk shoes.

When he entered the sitting room, he asked, "Is Wang in?" Flurried, Dizhu stood up, facing him, and then rushed to the door of her own room, only to find it bolted. She was embarrassed but could not find anywhere to hide. The old woman smiled, "It's you, Mr Wu. Why didn't you announce yourself before you came?" and she turned to Dizhu, "Be at ease. He's one of our regular customers." To Wu Dalang she said, "Come meet this lady."

Wu Dalang greeted her with a deep bow, hands clasped in front of his chest. Dizhu had to return the salute. As she stole a glance at the visitor, she found him to be a lovely and handsome young man. She immediately took a liking to him. Wu Dalang, on other hand, sized up Dizhu with his eyes and found her, dressed in plain clothes and without make-up, to be a virtuous lady, a far cry from the kind of easy-virtued women he often saw. An expert womanizer, Wu Dalang naturally sensed Dizhu's affection for him. He was half paralyzed. "Sit down please, Madam," he said. Dizhu, after all, was from a good family and shy at such a meeting. She begged Mom Wang, "Let's enter the inner room." "There's no hurry," Mom Wang said as she departed with Dizhu.

In a moment she returned and asked Wu Dalang, "Is she to your mind, sir?" "Please help me win her, Mom," he entreated. "I'll never forget your kindness." "You have enough silver and to spare, sir," Mom Wang replied. "Simply pay a thousand or so *liang* of silver and marry her." "She's not from a parlor house, so why is the price so high?" Wu Dalang asked. "You've seen how attractive she is," Mom Wang replied. "Isn't she worth a thousand *liang* of silver if she becomes your concubine?" "The silver does not matter," said Wu Dalang, "but my atrocious wife is a bully. I don't fear her, but I am afraid this woman will suffer because of her. That's why I cannot take her home." "That's no problem!" said the old woman. "You may rent a house here and live with her in it. Isn't it a good idea that you should have two wives in separate houses? The other day the Jiangs said they'd rent out a garden. Let me ask them if they'd like to rent it to you. What's your opinion of that idea?" "This is a good one," Wu Dalang said, "but if I live in another house, I'll need to hire attendants and servants and set up a new kitchen. Such things, though, pose no great difficulty. But sooner or later the truth will leak out. Then my first wife will come to share the new house and the situation will stink!" "If so, I have a solution," said the old woman. "You pay the bride-price and marry her and hold the wedding ceremony here. You may pay me several *liang* of silver every month as a fee and I'll wait upon her. You may come from time to time on the excuse that you have some business outside your home. Thus the secret will not leak out. How about that?" "Great!" laughed Wu Dalang. Thereupon they set a price of eight hundred *liang* of silver. They further agreed that clothes and jewelry would be bought and brought over, and these together would amount to one thousand *liang* of silver. The monthly expense for Dizhu and the pay for the old woman amounted to ten *liang* of silver, which would be paid each month. Wu Dalang accepted these conditions and hurried away to get his silver.

Then the old woman entered the room of Dizhu and asked her, "What do you think of the looks of the gentleman who's just been here?" Though Dizhu had been shy at first, after she entered her own room she realized that she had been reluctant to part with Wu Dalang. She kept peeping at him from the darkness of the other room and thus savored his looks to her heart's content. As Wu Dalang and the old woman talked, they could see beyond the door. Sometimes they had seen part of her face appear. If no other people had been present and they were not utter strangers, Dizhu and Wu Dalang would have flirted with each other right there. Now, hearing Mom Wang ask her about the man, she countered with a question of her own, "Which family is he from?" "He is a member of the family of Wus," responded Mom Wang, "a reputed family in Shangshan of Huizhou Prefecture, and he himself is the top magnate, called 'Millionaire Wu'. He fell in love with you as soon as he saw you. He wanted to take you home, but there's something inconvenient about doing this. So he wants to marry you and let you remain here. What do you think of that?" Having become fond of her clean and tidy bedroom and infatuated with Wu Dalang because of his appearance, Dizhu was quite happy to hear that she would live there, as if at her home. "Now that I am here, I will trust everything to you, Mom. But you must be careful not to divulge anything." "How can I let out anything?" Mom Wang said. "It's you who must be careful! After you and he have been together for a long time, be sure you do not tell him of your origin, or he'll look down upon you. Simply regard me as a senior relative and have a secret, pleasant life."

Wu Dalang came in a sedan chair, followed by two handsome footmen, each holding a container in his hand. He entered the house of Wang Xi and handed over the silver. "When shall I hold the wedding?" he asked. "Do as you please, sir," said the old woman. "You may choose an auspicious date or you may not. And it will be all right if you take her this very night." "I haven't prepared my family yet," said Wu Dalang, "so I cannot be so rash as to pass the night here. Tomorrow I'll leave home on the excuse of offering a sacrifice to the gods and collecting debts in Hangzhou. Then I'll come and stay with her. Is it really necessary to choose a date?" — Because Wu Dalang was indulging in sex, he was too impatient to wait for an auspicious date. Marriage is, in fact, an important event and therefore choosing a good date is necessary. Wu Dalang's rash act may have offended an evil ghost, which led to the breaking up of the union in no more than two years, as the later development of the story will reveal.

As for Wu Dalang, he left after delivering the silver. Having exchanged opinions with Wang Xi, the old woman came to Dizhu: "Congratulations, Madam, on your wedding!" And she took out four hundred *liang* of silver and smiled, "The bride-price is eight hundred *liang* of silver. Half of it goes to you and the rest will be divided between me and Wang Xi as our fee." Saying this, she put the glittering silver on the table. Dizhu was happy, too.

You're wrong, story-teller! — My readers may say. Seeing silver, the villain and the procuress would be like flies seeing blood. How could they be so kind as to offer a share to the girl? The answer is, gentle readers, in the first place, the old woman wanted to parade her wealth so as to set Dizhu's mind at rest; in the second, the silver was, after all, in her house, and could not run away. By and by the old woman would cheat the girl out of it. If she had not given some to Dizhu, when she and Wu Dalang were together, she might tell him the truth. Then Wu Dalang would insist that they give some to Dizhu and she would be taken at a disadvantage. Indeed, the old procuress was crafty and foresightful!

The next day Wu Dalang, dressed more beautifully than ever, came to Wang Xi's home for the wedding. Fearing outsiders might learn of the event, he didn't bring any attendants, nor did he hire musicians. He only told Wang Xi to set a couple of tables and ask Dizhu to have dinner with him before entering the bedroom. At first Dizhu was bashful and refused to emerge; later, as she could not resist the persuasion, she sat down at the table for a moment, but she soon returned to the bedroom again on an excuse. She blew out the lamp and went to bed by herself, leaving the door unbolted. "She is a young girl and shy by nature," said the old woman, "let's join in the fun." Holding a lamp in her hand, she led Wu Dalang into the bedroom, lit a lamp there, and then went out and shut the door. Wu Dalang was a careful man. He bolted the door and moved the lamp to the bedside. As he opened the curtain, he saw Dizhu asleep, her face covered. He dared not stir her, but silently took off his clothes, blew out the lamp and crept under her quilt. Dizhu heaved a sigh and huddled up. Cooing and crooning, Wu Dalang gently turned her around and mounted her in one swoop. Dizhu accepted him with quivering. There was a lot of pricking and piercing, rocking and rolling, until Dizhu felt herself comfortably numb all over. Although Dizhu had been married for two months, her husband Pan Jia was a new hand at it and she had never tasted such a sensation of pleasure. Wu Dalang, on the other hand, was a champion in the arena of love who had never failed to exhibit his prowess in bed. The joy they felt in their sensual union was beyond expression. Dizhu even felt regret that she met him so late. They expressed their appreciation and gratitude for each other and thus spent a blissful night.

The next morning Mom Wang and Wang Xi came to extend their congratulations. Wu Dalang rewarded them both. After that he stayed and spent a happy time together with Dizhu. He would visit his home once in every other month. But soon afterward he would come back.

Shouldn't the Pans have done something about their daughter-in-law being missing, story-teller — my readers may ask — and not just let her enjoy herself there? The answer is, gentle readers, the story has two threads. But I cannot evolve them simultaneously. Now let me tell you about the Pans. The other morning the mother-in-law did not find her daughter-in-law in the kitchen. She guessed that she must have overslept again. So she came to her room and shouted for Dizhu angrily. As she heard no answer, she entered the room, opened the curtains and looked at the bed, but saw no sign of Dizhu. "Where has the slut gone?" the mother-in-law cursed. When she told the father-in-law, he said, "She's making trouble again. Maybe she's gone to her parents' home." He hurried to the ferry crossing, and inquired about her. Someone told him, "I saw a woman being ferried across the river in the early morning." Another person who knew Dizhu said the woman on the raft was the daughter-in-law of the Pans. "I gave the wench a talking-to yesterday," he said, "and she is going to tell her parents. She's really fretful. Let her stay with her parents. I'll not go and take her back. See what she can do!" He angrily returned home and told his wife what he had heard.

About ten days after that, the Yaos, who missed their daughter, sent boxes of pastry to her by way of two servants, one a boy and the other a girl. As they asked about the daughter, the father-in-law replied,

"She has been at your place for ten days or so, why did you come and ask me about her?" The servants were surprised. "What are you saying?" they asked. "It has been just two months since she came to your house. We haven't come to take her, how could she return home by herself? Because her parents worry about her, they've sent us here. Why should you say this?" "The other day I gave her a talking-to," said the father-in-law, "in a fit of anger she left for her parents' home. Some people saw her at the ferry crossing. Where can she be if not at her parents' house?" "But she is not there," the servants said. "Are you sure you are not making a mistake?" "She must have made a false account to her parents of what happened here," the father-in-law replied with irritation, "and you want to annul the matrimonial union and marry her to another. So you have worked out this scheme to come to ask me about her whereabouts. Am I right?" "She's disappeared from your place," said the servants, "and you are landing blame on us. There must be some reason for this!" Hearing the words "some reason," the father-in-law flew into rage, "You bastards! I'll report this to the authorities and see if you can cancel the marriage!" The servants saw that the situation had turned ugly. They returned home without delivering the pastry in the boxes.

When they told the Yaos what had happened, both the father and mother were astounded. "If so," they cried, "our daughter may have been pressured to death by the two short-lived wretches. Let's prepare a complaint and demand that he pay for our daughter's life." And they went to a pettifogger and consulted him. The father of Pan Jia, however, stated categorically that the Yaos had hidden their daughter somewhere. He sent for his son. Both the Pans and the Yaos lodged written complaints and both their statements were put on file for investigation.

When Li, the magistrate of Xiuning County, summoned the plaintiffs and the accused to court and interrogated them, they all tried to shift the responsibility on the other party. Magistrate Li was furious.

He ordered that Mr Pan be tortured by clamping his legs. "Some people saw Dizhu go across the river," explained Pan. "If she drowned herself in the river, there should be signs of her body. It is obvious that they have hidden their daughter somewhere." "You are right," said the magistrate. "She has been missing for more than ten days. If she's dead, why hasn't her body been seen anywhere? So she must have been hidden by her parents." So thinking, he removed the torture clamp from Mr Pan and began to clamp Mr Yao. "My daughter has been at his house for two months," said Mr Yao, "and she never returned home. If she had really returned, why in the last ten days or so hasn't Pan sent a man to my house and ask what's up? A human body is six *chi* long and is not easily hidden anywhere in the world. If I have hidden her and plan to marry her to another man, there must be someone in the world who knows this. Can I hide the truth? I hope my lord will conduct a thorough investigation." The magistrate thought it over and said, "You are right, too. How can you hide her? And what's the use of hiding her? She must have a lover and the two of them must have eloped." "Your servant's daughter-in-law," said Pan, "though pampered and lazy, has been disciplined. I've never seen any sign that she was having an affair." "Then she might have been kidnapped," said the magistrate, "or she's hidden herself at a relative's house." Then he said to Mr Yao, "Your daughter is not well-bred. And you, as her father, know her ways. You cannot just throw off your responsibility. I order you to find out her whereabouts. On every fifth day you and the police will come and check your findings." Thereupon Mr Pan and his son were bailed out. Yao was escorted out of the yamen, arms tied.

With his daughter missing, Mr Yao was broken-hearted. Now he was wronged by the magistrate. Helpless, he could only lament to heaven and earth. He had to post "Lady Lost" notices everywhere, offering a reward for those who would provide any clue. But no one responded. On the other hand, Pan Jia, who had lost his wife, was burning with anger. All he could do was to come to the magistrate on every fifth and tenth day and inquire about the results of the searching. For this Mr Yao was whipped many times. This made a sensation in the towns and villages of Xiuning County. Mr Yao's relatives felt indignation on his behalf, but none of them could find a solution.

Let us turn now to another man by the name of Zhou Shaoxi, a close relative of Mr Yao's wife. He happened to traffic in goods in Quzhou in Zhejiang Province. As he wandered along a street of ill fame, he saw a prostitute casting amorous smiles at passers-by. The woman looked familiar. As he ransacked his memory, he found her to be a perfect picture of Yao Dizhu. "The legal suit has been going on fruitlessly for two years at home, but she's here," he thought to himself. He wanted to go forward and ask her, but on the second thought he decided not to. "No, it will not do. She may not wish to tell the truth. If I lay bare her origin, she might escape this very night. Then I'd have nowhere to look for her. I'd better report this to her family and let them come to look for her." Though Quzhou and Huizhou prefectures belonged to Zhejiang and South Zhili [present-day Jiangsu and Anhui] provinces respectively, the two prefectures bordered on each other.

In a few days Zhou Shaoxi arrived in Huizhou and reported to Mr Yao in detail what he had seen in Quzhou. "I see," said Mr Yao. "She must have been kidnapped and sold to a brothel by a villain." Thereupon he bade his son, Yao Yi, go to Quzhou in secret with one hundred *liang* of silver as ransom. Then he thought, "We might not succeed if we try to ransom her in private." So he reported this to the magistrate of Xiuning County and, having offered a bribe, he acquired from the magistrate an arrest warrant. In case of failure, he could produce the warrant and bring the matter to the authorities. Yao Yi took the order. Mr Yao begged Zhou Shaoxi to accompany his son to Quzhou.

At Quzhou, Zhou Shaoxi stayed with his old host and found a hotel for Yao Yi, depositing his luggage there. When Zhou Shaoxi took him to the brothel, the prostitute happened to be standing by the door. Yao Yi found her to be his sister. But as he called her diminutive name several times, she simply smiled and didn't answer. "She is my sister," he said to Zhou Shaoxi, "but she didn't answer when I called her several times. It is as if she doesn't know me anymore! Can she refuse to recognize her own brother because she is happy here?" "You don't know the reason," said Zhou Shaoxi. "All runners of brothels are cruel. Since your sister's background is unknown, to prevent her from divulging anything, the procuress must have warned her in advance. She dares not recognize you because she fears that someone may discover it." "How can I make her know my intention, then?" asked Yao Yi. "It's easy," replied Zhou Shaoxi. "You can pretend to be a whorehouse frequenter, set a table, offer one *liang* of silver to the brothel plus a pack of coins for the sedan chair bearers, and have her carried to your hotel. Then you can talk to her in detail. If she is your sister, you may recognize each other in secret and then arrange for the future. If not, sleep with her for a night and let her go." "Wonderful!" Yao Yi exclaimed.

Having stayed in Quzhou for a long time, Zhou Shaoxi knew the local ways and people. He found a footman and gave him some silver. After a while, a sedan chair was carried up to Yao Yi's hotel. "If she is his sister," Zhou Shaoxi thought to himself, "It will be inconvenient for them if I stay there." So he left on a pretext. Yao Yi, too, believed the girl was his sister and it was inconvenient to have Zhou Shaoxi with him. So he didn't ask him to stay. There Yao Yi saw a slim and slender girl gracefully step down from the sedan chair.

Believing that the girl was his sister, he fixed his eyes on her; the girl, thinking he was a customer, beamed with delight. One wondered why she did not come out calling him "brother", while the another may be perplexed that the man did not rush to the sedan chair to greet his "sister".

Looking at the woman, Yao Yi found her to be exactly like his sister. Radiant with smiles, she dropped an affected curtsy whereupon Yao Yi told her to take a seat. Daring not claim her as his kin at once, he asked, "What's your name, sister, may I ask? And where are you from?" "My family name is Zheng and my humble name, Yue'e. I am a native." Discerning a Quzhou accent in her voice that was quite different from that in Dizhu's voice, Yao Yi became suspicious. "Where are you from, sir?" the girl asked him. "Your servant is surnamed Yao and is a native of Suntian Village of Xiuning County, Huizhou Prefecture. His father is so and so and his mother, so and so." He gave a full account of his father and grandfather and his ancestor's home places, as if someone was probing into his origins and his ancestors' ranking and deeds. He did so because he thought the girl would certainly recognize who he was if she was his sister. Zheng Yue'e, however, found his account wordy. "I haven't asked you about your origin," smiled she, "why should you have told me about your ancestors?" Blushing, Yao Yi realized this was not Dizhu.

As the table was laid, they drank a couple of cups together. Seeing Yao Yi looking at her face for a while and then mumbling something to himself, Zheng Yue'e was suspicious. "I have never met with you," she said, "except the day before yesterday when you walked up and down before my door. When you saw me, you pointed at me. My sisters and I found it funny and laughed in secret. Now I am fortunate to be invited to your place, and yet you are still staring at me. It seems to me that there is something troubling your mind. Can you tell me what it is?" Yao Yi hummed and hawed. An extremely clever girl who had received many clients, Zheng Yue'e immediately understood that there was something odd in this encounter. She questioned him closely. "It is a long story," said Yao Yi. "Let's talk about it in bed." So they put the things away and went into the bed, and there, naturally, they enjoyed sensual pleasures.

Then Zheng Yue'e resumed her questioning. Yao Yi had to tell her in detail what had happened at home. "Because you and she look so much alike," he said, "I've invited you here on an excuse so as to find out your identity. Beyond my expectation, you are not my sister." "Do I really look like her?" asked Zheng Yue'e. "Both your countenance and your manners are exactly like hers," replied Yao Yi, "but there's a slight difference in your facial expression. Except for close relatives who are together with her every day and examine you closely, none could recognize the difference. But for your accent, even I myself have almost mistaken you to be her." "If so, let me be your sister!" said Yue'e. "You are joking." said Yao Yi. "I am not joking," said Yue'e, "but I'm asking your opinion. You lost your sister and the lawsuit will never drop until your sister comes to the authorities. I am the daughter of a respectable family here and was married to a *xiucai*, Jiang, as his concubine. His wife is narrow-minded and intolerant. Later even the *xiucai* himself forgot what is right at the sight of wealth. He sold me to the brothel of Mom Zheng. The brothel owner and his wife would scourge me on any excuse. Since I could not endure their torment, I am looking for a way to escape. Now you can categorically state that I am your sister and I will claim you as my brother. If we make the same statement to the authorities, they will certainly pronounce that I should be returned to yo   amily. In this way I'll be free from hell and avenge myself on the evil doers. Then I'll go with you to your home and be your sister and the lawsuit will be concluded. Isn't that a perfect plan?"

"It is a good idea all right," said Yao Yi, "but your voice is not like my sister's. Besides, if you come to my home and pretend to be my sister, you should know all my relatives in different places, or you'll not be believed. I'm afraid we'll get into trouble." "What really matters is the likeliness of the faces," said Yue'e, "the accent is changeable. Your sister has been missing for two years. If she is in Quzhou, who knows whether or not she speaks the same dialect as I!

As for your relatives, you may teach me who they are. And you have to report this to the authorities and wait for the judgment. There is enough time for me to learn things about your home. I can also learn to speak your dialect. The housework is not a problem — you can teach me and I will learn day by day. What do you need to worry about?"

Eager to put an end to the lawsuit, Yao Yi thought over the words of Zheng Yue'e and found her plan practicable. "I have the warrant with me," he said. "If I ask the authorities to made an arbitration, it will not be difficulty for me to have you. But you should insist that you are my sister from beginning to end and mind that your tongue never slips." "I am making good on the opportunity to flee from here, how can I go back on my word?" Zheng Yue'e replied. "But I am anxious about one thing: what kind of a man is your brother-in-law? Can I get along with him?" "He is a traveling businessman," said Yao Yi, "and he is an honest young man. It will be good for you to live with him." "Anyhow, it is better to be his wife than to be a prostitute," said Zheng Yue'e. "Furthermore I will be a wife and no longer a concubine as I am now. Thus my youth will not be wasted." Thereupon she and Yao Yi took an oath: "We two are of one heart and neither shall betray the other. Whoever divulges this oath will be stricken to death by the gods." Saying this, they felt a surge of pleasure. So they made love again and slept in each other's arms till day-break.

Yao Yi got up, and without combing his hair, went to Zhou Shaoxi. He didn't tell him the truth. "She is my sister," he said. "What should I do?" "The owner of a parlor house cannot be reasonable," said Zhou Shaoxi. "She might refuse if you try to ransom your sister in private. Let me invite a dozen of Huizhou natives who are here at present Then we can produce a petition to the prefect. In front of the public, the prefect must be fair. Besides, you have the arrest warrant from our county. The prefect will certainly pronounce that she should be returned to you. But first, you will have to send several *liang* of silver to the brothel owner to ask her permission to keep your sister for a few days at your place. In this way we can set them at rest and take the opportunity to get prepared." Yao Yi accepted his advice. When they were ready, Zhou Shaoxi gathered a group of Huizhou natives and they, together with Yao Yi, went to see the prefect. There they gave an account of the lost lady and Yao Yi submitted the warrant from Xiuning County for the prefect to examine. The prefect immediately issued a summons to bring the brothel owner to court. Zheng Yue'e appeared too. She called him "brother" and he called her "sister". Except for Zhou Shaoxi, few Huizhou natives knew Yao Dizhu. They all said "Yes, she is!" with one voice.

Quite ignorant of what had happened, the brothel owner could not understand what was happening. She shouted in protest. "Slap her mouth!" the prefect ordered. As the prefect questioned her as to where she had kidnapped the girl, she dared not hide the fact. "She was a concubine of *Xiucai* Jiang," she confessed. "She's not kidnapped, but was bought for eighty *liang* of silver." The prefect ordered the guards to bring *Xiucai* Jiang to court. Feeling guilty, the *xiucai* hid himself to avoid the prefect. The prefect pronounced that Yao Yi should pay the brothel owner forty *liang* of silver as the ransom price and take the girl home. He also condemned the brothel owner for her crime of buying a prostitute from a respectable family. *Xiucai* Jiang was disqualified from any further promotion in scholarly honors. Thus Zheng Yue'e worked off her anger.

Yao Yi happily took Zheng Yue'e to his hotel, where they stayed a few days until the files from the yamen were prepared, the ransom price was transferred to the receiver and they got their things ready. Then they left for Huizhou Prefecture. During these days he was able to sleep with Zheng Yue'e. To the public he said she was his sister, but in private they lived as man and wife. By chattering endlessly with her in bed, he gave her a complete lecture about what to say and how to behave herself when they arrived home.

Soon they approached Suntian Village. Some people saw them.

"Thank heaven!" they clapped their hands, "the lawsuit has come to an end." Someone rushed to herald their coming. The parents came to the gate to greet them. Zheng Yue'e pretended to know them all, and with full composure she stepped into the courtyard, calling out "father" and "mother". These, of course, were among the persons in the family who had been identified by Yao Yi. Once a prostitute, she was quick to accommodate to the situation and she let nothing go amiss. "My child," cried Mr Yao, "where have you been in the last two years? Dad has suffered a great deal because of you!" Zheng Yue'e put on a show of broken-hearted sobs, too. "Have you been well in recent years, father and mother?" she asked. Hearing her voice, Mr Yao said, "Two years away from home and your voice has been changed so!" As the mother grasped her hand and stroked it, she said, "You wear beautiful, long nails. You didn't when you left home." Everyone wept for a time. Only Yao Yi and Zheng Yue'e knew what was what. Mr Yao had suffered jitters during the two years of endless lawsuit. When he saw his "daughter", he felt unloaded of a heavy burden. He was too relieved to have a close examination of the girl who looked exactly like his daughter. As for her experience, knowing that she was ransomed from a brothel, he didn't think it proper to ask her for more details. As soon as the day broke, he bade his son, Yao Yi, and the "sister" to see the county magistrate.

As the county magistrate convened court, he let the new arrivals give an account of their story. The magistrate, who was bored with the complicated two-year-long case, immediately realized what "Dizhu" had been. "Who kidnapped you?" he asked. "A man whose name I don't know," answered the "Dizhu". "Without any explanation he sold me to a *xiucai* from Quzhou by the name of Jiang. Afterward, the *xiucai* sold me to the brothel. But I don't know where the man who kidnapped me went." The magistrate recognized that "Dizhu" had been kidnapped and sold in Quzhou, which was situated in another province, and that it was not easy to conduct an investigation there. He was eager to put an end to the case that he decided not to probe more deeply. He summoned Pan Jia and his parents to court and let them claim the girl. When Mr Pan and his wife came in and saw "Dizhu", they said, "My dear child, where have you been these last few years?" Pan Jia said, "Fancy I can see you at last!" As they recognized each other, they went home. At the gate to the county court, the two old couples reciprocated apologies for the troubles they had caused to each other. They both believed that their lawsuit had been settled once and for all.

The next day Magistrate Li opened court and, when he was about to mark the files about the case as "settled" and put them in the archives, Pan Jia came, saying, "The lady I took home yesterday is not my wife." The magistrate was enraged. "You shrewd slave!" he growled. "Haven't you implicated your father-in-law enough? Why don't you give up?" He ordered the runners to drag Pan Jia out of the court and give him ten blows. Pan Jia shouted his grievance. "The document from Quzhou Prefecture clearly states what she is," the magistrate rebuked him, "and your brother-in-law brought her home. Your father-in-law and mother-in-law recognized her as their daughter and your parents recognized her as their daughter-in-law. How can you have a different idea?" "I have entered a lawsuit," said Pan Jia, "to get my own wife back, not someone else's wife. Now that she is obviously not my wife, how can I take her? And how can my lord force me to take her? If you demand me to take a false wife as the genuine one, I'd rather have no wife at all." "How do you know she is not your wife?" asked the magistrate. "She looks exactly like my wife," said Pan Jia, "but when she and I were together, I found differences." "Don't be silly!" said the magistrate, "maybe her manners have changed because she was a prostitute for a time?" "Not at all, my lord," said Pan Jia, "not only is her private talk totally discrepant, but there are slight differences in her skin and body parts — this I know clearly, but I am too embarrassed to tell you about them. If she was my wife, I would be eager to see her since we were separated only two months after our wedding. Why should I cause trouble out of nothing? My lordship is insightful and will make a fair judgment." Hearing his sensible reasoning, the magistrate was astounded, but he did not want to acknowledge his mistake. "Please be patient," he enjoined Pan Jia in a secretive voice. "You may feign ignorance. Don't reveal her identity to anybody, even to your parents and relatives. I will have a solution."

Thereupon Magistrate Li had notices posted everywhere saying "Yao Dizhu was found on this and that date and brought to the county court. The families Pan and Yao willingly dropped the lawsuit and none of them will file any further complaint on this matter." In the meantime he secretly set up a high prize and dispatched a dozen runners to observe the readers of the notices. If anything strange occurred, they were to take note and report back to him.

Now let us put them aside. As for Yao Dizhu, she and Wu Dalang had lived together for two years. By and by Wu Dalang's family got wind of this and seldom allowed him to go out, so he came to see her less and less often. Yao Dizhu once told Wu Dalang that she needed a maid servant to assist her. Wu Dalang, in turn, asked Wang Xi for help. Wang Xi, who used to kidnap girls, was too reluctant to hire a girl. He wanted to seize one at an opportune place and time. Those days he often saw a maid servant of Wang Ruluan's house in Shexian County doing the family washing by the river. He thought she might be an easy prey.

One day as Wang Xi was walking in the street, he heard of the county government's notice that Yao Dizhu had been found. He rushed to Mom Wang saying, "Somebody has filled the vacancy! This girl will now be our property for sure." As the old woman was suspicious of his words and wanted to see with her own eyes, she and Wang Xi went together to the place where he had seen the notice. Having read it, Wang Xi pointed his hand here and there and read it aloud to Mom Wang. This was observed by the runner from the government who was on the lookout there. He followed them. As they reached a quiet place, he heard Wang Xi and the old woman say, "Great! Now we can set our minds at rest and enjoy a peaceful sleep at night!" Jumping at them in one swoop, the runner shouted, "Your nefarious plot has come to light. Where are you running!" Scared out of his wits, Wang Xi said, "Please don't scare me. Will you please go and sit a while in a restaurant?" He and the old woman invited the runner to a restaurant and sat down to drink. Wang Xi fled on the excuse of urging the waiters to serve dishes. As Mom Wang and the runner sat for awhile without being served, they went downstairs only to find that Wang Xi had run away. The runner tied Mom Wang up. "I'll take you to the magistrate," he said. Kneeling down, the old woman pleaded, "Please spare me! Come with me to my house and I'll thank you with a sum of silver." The runner had found her and Wang Xi's behaviors strange, but he didn't know the real cause. However, as he bluffed her, she revealed her guilty conscience.

The runner anticipated some clue from the old woman, so he kept a tight watch over her and followed her closely to Wang Xi's lodging and knocked at the door. He then saw a woman come to answer the door. At the sight of her, the runner was surprised: "Isn't this the lady that was escorted from Quzhou the other day?" Then he realized that this must be the real Yao Dizhu. But he didn't lay the matter bare. Having taken a cup of tea and receiving the money from Mom Wang, he left. Believing the crisis over, Mom Wang set her fears at rest.

The next day the runner went to the county magistrate and reported his findings. The magistrate assigned to him a dozen enforcements and ordered them to arrest the old woman and Yao Dizhu immediately. The runners, like a host of beasts of prey, dashed to the Wang Xi's residence and broke in, howling. There they found the desperate Mom Wang had hanged herself from a beam. The runners took Dizhu to the court. Seeing her, the magistrate said, "This is the lady they wanted the other day." And issuing another summons, he called in Pan Jia and his "wife". The assumed Dizhu and the real Dizhu looked so much alike that the magistrate could not tell who was who. He had to ask Pan Jia to tell them apart. Pan Jia, of course, knew which one was his wife. He and the real Dizhu whispered something to each other. Then the magistrate questioned the real Dizhu. She related how she had been cheated by Wang Xi. "Has anybody seduced you?" asked the magistrate. Cherishing the kindness of Wu Dalang, Dizhu didn't want to betray him. So she said she didn't know the man's name. As the magistrate questioned the assumed Dizhu, she confessed, "My name is Zheng Yue'e. Because I wanted to avenge myself and Yao Yi wanted to drop the lawsuit and he told me that I looked like his sister, we together worked out this plot." At that the magistrate ordered the arrest of Wang Xi, but he had run away. The magistrate wrote a report about the case and submitted it together with the arrested to the prefectural government.

When Wang Xi ran away from the restaurant, he ran into Cheng Jin, one of his cronies. They together went to the domain of Shexian County and chanced to see the maid servant of Wang Ruluan's house washing clothes at the riverside. Grabbing her with one hand Wang Xi shouted, "You are my maid servant. You ran away from my house and are here!" With this he seized her laundry, tied her with it and tried to drag her onto the bamboo raft. The maid screamed. Wang Xi covered her mouth with his sleeve, but the maid uttered muffled cries. Cheng Jin strangled her throat. Because he exerted too much effort and her mouth was gagged, she gave up the ghost in a short while. Many local people swarmed up and took them to the county court.

The magistrate of Shexian County, who's name was Fang, sentenced Cheng Jin to be strangled and Wang Xi to perform military servitude at a remote garrison. When they were brought to the prefecture court, the real and assumed Dizhus were escorted there too. As they appeared in the court, the real Dizhu shouted, "Isn't this Wang Xi?" The prefect, by the name of Liang, was a just man. Seeing that the files from the two counties were both about Wang Xi, he was indignant. "Wang Xi is the chief criminal," he said. "Why is his sentence so lenient as to be only servitude in a garrison?" Thereupon he ordered his runners to flog Wang Xi severely sixty times, which ended his life. The real Dizhu was returned to her husband; the assumed Dizhu was to be sold by the government; and because Yao Yi used the government's warrant to conduct a fraud, he was sentenced to forced servitude in a garrison. Only Wu Dalang, who had connections among the functionaries of the government and, on hearing of the case, bribed his way out of the case and escaped punishment.

Pan Jia took the real Dizhu home, and thus the family was reunited. Yao Yi was to be banished under guard to a remote place for penal servitude along with his wife. But he was not married yet. Hearing this, Zheng Yue'e cried, "It is because I wanted to free myself from humiliation and avenge myself on my enemy that he and I worked out the plot. I never expected this would ruin Yao Yi. I will go with him to live or die. I've made a laughing-stock of myself, so let things remain that way." Mr Yao was reluctant to let his son leave home alone. When he heard about Zheng Yue'e's remarks, he used a false name and bought her out. Zheng Yue'e assumed a new name and went with Mr Yao's son in exile as his wife. Later on, Yao Yi returned home on a chance of general amnesty. Then he and Zheng Yue'e became real man and wife. This manifested the good-heartedness of Zheng Yue'e. That the sisters-in-law, Yao Dizhu and Zheng Yue'e, looked so much alike remains an interesting anecdote in Huizhou.

Tale 3

Liu Dongshan Brags of His Prowess at a City Gate; Eighteenth Brother Shows off Marvels in a Village Tavern

During the Tang Dynasty there was a candidate for the imperial examinations whose name and native place I cannot remember. He was extremely strong and possessed extraordinary martial arts skill. A warm-hearted man, he was always ready to champion those who were bullied. Whenever he saw an injustice, he would come to the weaker side's rescue. When he went to the capital city for the examinations, he didn't take any servant or bodyguard with him. Proud of his ability, he set off by himself on a good horse, with arrows and a bow on his back and a broadsword hanging down from his hips. Along the way he hunted pheasants and hares, game that he ate with wine when he stopped overnight at an inn.

One day the horse galloped so fast along a road in Shandong (Province), that he overpassed a hotel. Toward evening he reached a village. Then he realized that he could travel no further. Thereupon he saw light coming through an open gate of a household. He got down from his horse and, leading it, moved closer. He found empty ground inside the gate, upon which were three or four boulders from Taihu Lake. Facing the gate were three rooms, on either side of which was a side room. An old woman was sitting there spinning hemp thread. When she heard steps in the yard, she stood up to ask who was there. "Auntie," the young man said loudly, "I have lost my way and want to stay for the night. May I?" "No, sir," replied the old woman. "I don't have the say here." Discerning a trace of sadness in her voice, the man became suspicious. "Where are the male members of your family?" he asked. "Why do you sit here alone?" "I have been a widow for years," she said. "I have only one son. He left home to do some business." "Do you have a daughter-in-law?" the man asked. "Yes," the old woman answered, knitting her brows, "I have one. She is stronger than a man and so she can support this family. But she has tremendous strength and is fierce and short-tempered. If you make a slight error in speech, you'll incur her wrath; a prick of her finger and you'll fall down. I am always in jitters around her and carefully adjust myself to her expression. But she is always unpleasant and I am always insulted by her. So I cannot make the decision to let you stay for the night." With these words tears streamed down her cheeks.

Hearing this, the young man glared, his eyebrows rising upward. "Should there be such outrageous behavior in the world!" he shouted. "Where is the bitch? I'll get rid of her on your behalf." He tied his horse to a rock and drew out his sword. "Please don't court trouble, sir," said the old woman. "My daughter-in-law isn't a woman to be trifled with. She does not do needlework, but after lunch every day she goes by herself into the mountains to hunt a few hares or a deer. These she salts for sale, and by this earns a few strings of coins for the family. She often returns home at the second watch of the night. The daily living expenses come from her hunting. Because of this I dare not disobey her." The young man put his sword back into the sheath. "I am a man who never cringes in defying bullies and I champion people in distress. I will see how strong a woman such as she can be. Since your daily life depends on her, I will spare her life. But I will give her a sound beating to teach her to mend her ways." "She's coming," said the old woman, "but I think you'd better not stir up trouble." The young man, however, waited in anger.

A huge, dark figure entered through the gate. Throwing a sack-like object on the ground, the figure shouted, "Old Mom, light a lamp and pick things up." "What treasure do you have?" the old woman asked in a trembling voice. As she lit a lamp and looked at it, she was startled to see that it was a dead tiger. No sooner did the young man's horse see the tiger in the lamplight, than it shied and jumped up and down in fear. Seeing the horse, the figure asked, "From where has the horse come?" The young man standing in the dark caught a glance of a tall, dark-skinned woman. On seeing her shape and the tiger on her back, he thought to himself that this was indeed an able woman, and he was a little awed. He immediately led his horse away and tied it. Stepping forward, he answered, "I am going to sit for the examinations and have been delayed on my way. I overpassed a hotel, but I am blessed to have come to your honorable place. Seeing your gate not shut yet, I came in. May I make bold to ask permission to put up here for the night?" "Old Mom is really too mannerless," the woman laughed. "Why does she let a distinguished guest stand in the open at such a late hour?" And pointing to the tiger, the woman said, "I met this spotted beast in the mountains today. After quite a long and strenuous struggle, I subdued it. Because of this I've come home late. Please don't blame me." Seeing her speak so frankly and straightforwardly and accept him in perfect etiquette, the young man thought that she was reachable by reasoning. He said "Certainly not" repeatedly.

The woman entered the room and brought out a chair. "I should have ushered you into the room, but both my mother-in-law and I are women and it's not right for us to mix with men. So I will have to ask you to sit on the porch." Putting a table before him and lighting a lamp, she went to the yard and brought the tiger into the kitchen. In awhile she served a pot of warm wine, a large plate of piping hot tiger-meat, a plate of meat from a deer's breast and five or six dishes of salted meat of hare or pheasant. "Please don't despise my crude food, my distinguished guest," she said. Seeing her to be hospitable, the young man accepted the dishes and began to help himself to wine. Soon he finished the meal. Cupping his hands the young man thanked her, saying, "Thank you for your generous repast." "I dare not accept your extravagant praise," said the woman, who began to collect the plates and dishes.

Seizing this moment, the young man said, "I can see you are a heroic lady and act with refined manners, but it seems to me that you could be more respectful towards your elders." Hearing this, the woman pushed the plates aside and stopped cleaning the table. "What lie did the old devil tell you?" she asked, glaring. "No, nothing at all," the young man explained, "but I do discern a trace of arrogance in the way you addressed her, not in the way a daughter-in-law should act toward her mother-in-law. As I saw you received a guest with perfect manners and find your ability above that of ordinary people, I know that you are not an unreasonable person. So out of good intentions I have asked you about this." Thereupon the woman seized the young man by the sleeve and, with lamp in hand, moved towards the huge rocks. "Let me tell you all about it." The young man could not struggle to get free. Still, he planned to give her a beating when she turned unreasonable. The woman, leaning against the rocks and patting them, said that the other day there was such and such a thing, she did this and that and her mother-in-law this and that. "Was it her fault or mine?" she asked, and with this she made a sign in the rock with her forefinger. "That's the first," she said. The sign she made was more than one *cun* deep. Thus, when she finished telling about three happenings, three notches had been made in the rock by her finger. Each notch was more than one *cun* deep, as if chiseled. The young man sweated in fear.

Blushing, he said repeatedly, "You were right all the time." His ambition to give her a lesson was by now extinguished, just as if ice cold water had been poured over his head. He held his breath in fear.

The woman brought out a bed, let the young man sleep on it, and fed his horse. Then she entered the room of the old woman, bolted the door, put out the lamp and went to bed herself. The young man could not fall asleep the whole night through. He admired her strength and thought to himself, "It is amazing that there should be such a strong woman in the world! Fortunately I did not fight with her, otherwise my life would have been lost!" At dawn he saddled his horse, thanked the hostess and quietly left without saying any more.

After that the young man pulled in his horns. He never concerned himself with other's affairs, fearing that if he met an opponent like this woman he would eat humble pie.

Now let me tell you of another man who suffered from fright and made a fool of himself because of his bragging about his valor. Just as a rhyme says:

Before the tiger, the beasts' king,
All animals lie prostrate and still.
But as the lion utters a roar,
The tiger's might is reduced to nil.

It is said that during the reign of Jiajing [522-566] of our [Ming] dynasty in Jiaohe County, Northern Zhili Province* there lived a man surnamed Liu, named Qian and styled Dongshan. He was the head of a police team in a police station of Beijing. Well versed in riding and shooting arrows, he never missed a target. He was thus nicknamed

---

*Northern Zhili Province (北直隶省) in the Ming Dynasty covered present-day Beijing, Tianjin, and a large part of Hebei, Henan and Shandong provinces.

"running shooter". He could catch any tough gangster as if he were catching a turtle from an urn. This earned him some family fortune. When he was on the wrong side of thirty, he got tired of the job. So he resigned and started a new trade in his native county.

One late winter day, Liu Dongshan made a hundred *liang* of silver by reselling a dozen donkeys and horses in Beijing. When the business was done, he hired a mule at the Shuncheng Gate, which he intended to ride on his way home. In the inn run by the owner of the mule he came across his neighbor, Zhang Erlang, who had come to the capital from their native county. They took meal together in the same inn. "Where are you going, Dongshan?" asked Zhang Erlang. Liu Dongshan told him what he had done and added, "I've hired a mule. I will put up for the night here and tomorrow I will be on my way home." "It is very dangerous to make such a journey now," said Zhang Erlang. "Bandits are frequenting the regions around Liangxiang and Zhengzhou and they rob travelers even in daylight. You are traveling by yourself without a companion and with a great deal of money on you. You may be victimized. Be careful." Hearing this, Liu Dongshan's face lit up, his eyebrows dancing and his lips pursing. He clenched his fists, gestured as if he was drawing a bow and pealed out in laughter. "I have been chasing criminals over the last twenty years," he said, "and my arrow has never missed its target. And I haven't met a rival. I don't think I'll lose my capital in this last transaction." Hearing his loud talk, all the guests in the inn turned to see him. Some of them asked his name. When they learned who he was, they said, "We have heard about you for a long time." Being aware of his slip of tongue, Zhang Erlang left the inn.

Liu Dongshan got up at the daybreak the next morning, washed and got dressed. He wrapped his silver in a belt purse and tied it around his waist. He slung a bow over his shoulder, wore a sword and hid twenty

---

*Shuncheng Gate is the present-day Xuanwu Gate in Beijing.

arrows in his boots. He mounted a tall and robust mule and, cracking a whip, set off. When he arrived at Liangxiang thirty or forty *li* away from Beijing, he saw a man galloping up on horseback behind him. The man stopped when he approached the mule of Liu Dongshan. Liu Dongshan cast a glance at the man and saw he was a handsome young man of about twenty, who was beautifully dressed —

With a yellow blouse and felt hat on head,
He wore a short sword and held a long bow.
He had twenty new arrows in his arrow bag;
His horse wore red tassels on its forehead.
With a gold-and-jade adorned belt
The young man had a fair-skinned face.
As he drew on the bridle, the horse neighed —
His horse was tall and robust.

As Liu Dongshan was looking at the youth, the youth shouted from a distance. "Let's journey together." And with a cupped-hand salute he said, "I'm presumptuous enough to want to keep you company. May I venture to ask your name?" "My humble family name is Liu, given name Qian and style name Dongshan," replied Liu Dongshan, "I'm usually called by the style name of Dongshan." "I have heard your exalted name for a long time," the youth replied. "I am really very lucky to meet up with you. Where are you going, may I ask?" "I am going to my native county, Jiaohe," answered Liu Dongshan. "Great!" exclaimed the young man. "My hometown is Linzi. I am from a family of long-standing fame. I learned to read and write when I was a child, but I have a disposition to ride and shoot. By and by I have forgotten what I learned from books. Three years ago I acquired some capital to invest in a business in Beijing and I have earned quite a lot of profit. Now I am going home to get married and I just happened to tread on the same road as you. Let us keep company so that we can build up our courage. We'll say good-bye when we arrive at Hejian Prefecture. I think I am really very fortunate." Seeing the young man had heavy luggage with him, spoke discretely, bore handsome features and a nimble figure, Liu Dongshan guessed that the youth was not an evil man. Besides, Liu Dongshan thought that with a companion on road he would feel less lonely. So he said, gladly, "It's right for us to be companions."

That night they put up at an inn and ate and slept together like brothers.

The next day they rode side by side out of the town of Zhuozhou. The young man on horseback said, "I've heard for long time that you are skilled at capturing criminals. How many have you caught? And have you ever met with a tough opponent?" The question triggered Liu Dongshan's desire to brag about his prowess. He thought his companion was too young to know the truth, so he boasted, "With my two hands and one bow, I have laid hold of so many greenwood men that I can not remember the precise number, but I have never met my match. These villains are not worth mentioning. Now in my middle age I've lost interest in that job, so I gave it up. If we run into bandits on our way, I'll show you my skills by catching one or two." The young man gave a light sneer. "My I have a look at your bow?" As Liu Dongshan on the mule handed over the bow, the young man held it in the left hand and pulled the string with the right hand, drawing the bow full with ease. He repeatedly drew it as if drawing soft silk lace.

Liu Dongshan blanched in awe. He then borrowed the young man's bow, which was about twenty *jin* in weight. Liu Dongshan strained all his muscles till his face turned red, but he could not even draw it to a half moon shape, let alone to its full. In embarrassment, Liu Dongshan said, "What a tough bow! My brother, your might is miraculous, far beyond what I expected." "My strength is far from miraculous," said the young man, "but your bow is too soft." While Liu Dongshan was profuse in his praise, the young man expressed extreme modesty.

That night they stayed in another hotel together.

The next day they set out together. As the sun began to decline in the west, they passed by Xiongxian County. The young man patted his horse and the horse flew ahead like the wind. As Liu Dongshan looked on, the young man rode out of sight. Being well experienced in dealing with bandits, Liu was naturally horrified by this queer behavior. "It's my fate that will make a sight of me," he thought to himself, "If he is evil-minded and yet he has such supernatural strength, how can I beat him? Then I am doomed to die." Nervously he shuffled along. After he proceeded twenty *li* or so, he saw the young man a hundred steps ahead, with his bow drawn full and an arrow aimed at Liu. The man addressed Liu Dongshan, "I have heard for a long time that you are unmatched. Please listen to my arrow's sound first." No sooner had he finished these words, than a "whiz" was heard, as if a bird flew by Liu Dongshan's ears, but Liu emerged unscathed. Then the young man loaded another arrow, and aimed it at Liu Dongshan's face. He laughed, saying, "Liu Dongshan is clever enough to present me with the money from reselling mules and horses, or I'll take it by myself." Liu Dongshan understood he could not beat the young man. He was quite flustered. He had to jump down from his mule, untie the purse from his waist and hold the money in both hands as he moved forward on his knees to the young man's horse, where he kowtowed. "Here's the silver for you," he said. "I only beg you to spare my life." The young man on horseback reached out his hand for the silver. "Why should I take your life?" he shouted. "Get lost! Be quick! Your dad has his business here and cannot go with you." The young man turned around and galloped in the northern direction, leaving billowing yellow dust behind him. Soon he was out of sight.

Liu Dongshan was stupefied. After a long while he stood up, beating his chest and stamping his feet. He said to himself, "The loss of the silver is not as great as the humiliation I have suffered. I've been known as a hero all my life, but my fame is ruined today. Indeed, the devil-summoner is mystified by devils! What a disaster! It's most annoying." Crestfallen he limped home to Jiaohe empty-handed. When he told the story to his wife, they both fell into low spirits. They had a discussion about their means of livelihood and collected some capital and opened a tavern in the east suburbs. After that Liu Dongshan never used his bow. He was afraid that if the truth was leaked out, his fame would be ruined. So he had to swallow his humiliation silently.

One freezing winter day three years later, when Liu Dongshan and his wife were selling wine in their tavern, a group of mounted guests arrived. There were eleven of them, each on a tall and robust horse, beautifully saddled. The men, who wore short and close-fitting garments and had bows, arrows and swords, demounted, removed the saddles and bridles from their horses and entered the tavern one by one. Liu Dongshan ushered them in and led their horses to the trough. There a waiter fed the horses with fodder and grain.

Among the guests one eight-*chi*-tall teenage boy of about fifteen did not dismount. He said to the other people, "I, your Eighteenth Brother, will stay in the hotel on the opposite side." "We'll go over and wait upon you after a short rest here," the others said in chorus. When the teenage boy had gone through the door, his companions began drinking. The host served chicken, pork, beef and mutton to go along with wine. Soon they had wolfed down sixty to seventy *jin* of meat and six or seven jugs of wine. They told the host to take dishes to the teenage boy in the house across the street. When they finished everything on the tables, they felt they were still not full. So they opened their leather sacks and took out deer-hoofs, pheasants, roasted hares and other food they had brought with them. "It's our turn to treat," they said, smiling, "let's invite our host to join us."

With great formality Liu Dongshan sat down at the table. He looked at the guests one by one. As his eyes darted left and fell on the man sitting at the northern side of the table, he could not see his face clearly because it was partly covered by the rim of a felt hat. But when that man suddenly raised his head, Liu Dongshan had a clear look and was scared out of his wits. He groaned inwardly. Do you know who the man was? He was none other than the young man who had taken Liu's money on the road in Xiongxian County. "I am doomed today," Liu Dongshan thought to himself. "The small sum I have accumulated will not meet their demands. If I could not resist that one man the last time, how can I beat so many today? — They must be equally well versed in martial arts." His heart thumped in his chest like a jumping deerlet. He stared at his cup but dared not utter one word. In the meantime the guests all stood up and proposed a toast to him.

After a round of wine, the young man at the northern side of the table took off his felt hat and said, "How have you been these days, Dongshan? I've been missing you very much since we kept each other company on the journey the other year." Ashen faced, Liu Dongshan could not help but drop on his knees. "Please excuse me for my offense," he said. The young man jumped away from the table, knelt down also, and lifted him up. "Please don't be like this," he said, taking Liu Dongshan by the hand, "I am really embarrassed by your saying that. When my brothers and I heard you bragging about your unmatched skill at the tavern near Shuncheng Gate, we were not convinced. So my brothers let me do such a flippant thing on the road as a practical joke on you. I broke my promise that I would not say good-bye to you until we arrived at Hejian. Since then our travel on the way to Renqiu on horseback has lingered in my memory, even in my dreams. Thank you for your kindness! I'll repay you tenfold." With this, he took out a thousand *liang* of silver from his purse and put it on the table, "This is just a token of my respect for you. Please take it." Liu Dongshan was mesmerized, as if drunk or dreaming. Fearing that it might be a joke, he dared not take it. Seeing him in hesitation, the young man clapped his hands. "How can a man tell a lie! Dongshan," he said. "You are a hero, too. Why are you so timid? Could my brothers and I take your silver in earnest? Be quick to take it." Hearing him speak forthrightly, Liu Dongshan realized that he was in earnest. As if awakening from a dream or drunkenness, he accepted the silver without further hesitation. He entered the inner room, told his wife what had happened and asked her to come out and collect the silver.

After Liu Dongshan and his wife put away the silver, they concluded, "These are real heroes and they are so generous towards us. We must not give them a cold treatment. Let's butcher more animals, and serve more wine to them, or better, let's ask them to stay for a few days." Liu Dongshan came out, expressed his gratitude and told the young man his intention. The young man relayed this to his fellows. "Why not," they said, "if this is your old friend. But we will have to ask the Eighteenth Brother for consent." They all went over to the teenage boy in the opposite house, and Liu Dongshan followed them. He saw that these men were all respectful towards the teenager, who accepted them with great dignity. As they told the boy that the host wanted to keep them for a time, the teenage boy said, "Good! But you mustn't oversleep after you have drunk and eaten your fill, or you'll be unworthy of your host's kindness. If anything unexpected happens, my swords will taste blood." "Yes, we all see," the guests said in chorus. Liu Dongshan thus became more perplexed.

Thereupon they all returned to the tavern and drank to their hearts' content. Then they brought wine to the inn opposite the tavern, but they dared not drank while the boy drank by himself. The meat and wine he used equaled the amount five men had consumed in the tavern. When he was tipsy, he took out a pure-silver strainer from his bag, lit a charcoal fire and began cooking pastries to eat. He ate more than one hundred pastries at one sitting. After putting away his things, he strode out the door and went to nobody-knew-where. He didn't return to the inn for the night until dusk and he did not pay a single visit to Liu Dongshan's house, where his companions ate and played. When they went over to pay a visit to the teenage boy, the boy was reticent and arrogant. Liu Dongshan was puzzled. He pulled the young man who had been his companion aside and asked, "Who is this Eighteenth Brother?" The young man did not answer him, but passed the question to his fellows, all of whom broke out in laughter. They did not tell who the boy was, but loudly recited two lines:

When willows and poplars are green, peach blossom blows
You don't know which in the spring breeze glows!

And these lines were followed by another peal of laughter.

Three days later they bid farewell. They got dressed and mounted. The teenage boy took the lead while the others followed behind. Liu Dongshan never found out who they were. Now with the thousand *liang* of silver that had come unexpectedly, he was comfortably well off. Fearing that he might meet trouble, he moved into the town and opened another business.

Later, when he talked to others about this, a worldly experienced man said, "The two lines suggest a plum.* That must be the family name of the teenage boy, the Eighteenth Brother. He is their leader. From his words to his fellows, he was vigilant against possible assassination. He lived in the house opposite yours so that he and his fellows could keep watch for each other. Besides, he did not eat and lodge with the others. This showed his special rank. He must have had done something special when he went out alone at night, but we may never find out what it was."

Liu Dongshan had been a hero, but after he met with these people, he never dared to mention his skill in arms. He put away the bow and arrows and made a living by honest business. At the end of a peaceful life he died a natural death. That proves that one must not be carried away by one's ability. The conceited ones will eventually meet tougher opponents.

---

*In poems the plum is often mentioned along with willow, poplar and peach.

Tale 4

Nun Zhao Ensnares a Beauty with Narcotic Wine; Scholar Jia Takes His Revenge with an Ingenious Plot

It is related that at Wuzhou [present-day Jinhua, Zhejiang Province] there lived a young *xiucai* by the name of Jia. He was well learned and had surpassing ability and wisdom. His wife, Lady Wu, was extremely beautiful and virtuous. Attached to each other like fish and water, the couple never bickered. The *xiucai* tutored the children of an influential family. He usually stayed away for his work and visited home only once every half year, leaving his wife with a maid servant by the name of Chun Hua. The wife excelled in needle work. Once she created a brocade portrait of Avalokitesvara. The graceful portrait was lifelike. Quite proud of it, she bade the *xiucai* to have it mounted in a picture-mounter's shop where every one who saw the portrait admired it. When it was brought home, she hung it in a clean room. Every morning and evening the lady would light incense before it. Because she worshipped Avalokitesvara so piously, a nun by the name of Zhao from a nunnery in the street often visited her. When the *xiucai* was away, the wife frequently had the nun stay at her home for a couple of days. The nun also invited her to the nunnery, but since she was a woman who kept to what is proper, she did not leave her house without a reason. She went to the nunnery no more than twice a year.

One spring day the nun went to see Wu when her husband was away. After they chatted for awhile, the lady stood up and saw the nun off. "What a lovely day!" the nun said. "Why not go for an outing?" — Well, it was her bad luck to meet something unexpected! As she walked with the nun to the gate and stuck her head out to look, she saw a vagrant swaggering directly towards her. The lady drew herself back in a hurry and hid behind the gate. The nun stood there. The man apparently knew the nun. "Abbess Zhao," he said, "I have been looking for you everywhere but I didn't know you were here. I need to have a word with you." "I'll go with you after I say good-bye to this lady," said the nun. She entered the gate and bid good-bye to Lady Wu. The lady shut the gate and went inside.

The vagrant who greeted the nun was Bu Liang, a lecherous good-for-nothing in the town of Wuzhou. Whenever he caught sight of a good looking woman, he would scheme to find a way to seduce her, and he never gave up until he achieved his end. He was so promiscuous he ravished beautiful and ugly victims alike. That's why many nuns consorted with him. Sometimes the nuns procured women for him; sometimes, when opportunity presented itself, they themselves went at it with him. Nun Zhao had a disciple whose religious name was Ben Kong. She was in her early twenties and attractive, and she was more of a whore in a nunnery than a nun. By sleeping with clients she made money. This business, of course, was carried out in secret. Bu Liang was one of Zhao's clients.

As Nun Zhao departed from Wu and caught up with Bu Liang, she asked him, "What's up, Mr Bu?" "Is the house you've just left *Xiucai* Jia's?" he asked. "Yes." the Nun answered. "I have heard for some time that his wife is beautiful," he said. "I suppose she was the lady who walked out with you and then hid herself behind the gate. Am I right?" "You are really smart!" said the Nun. "Can there be another woman as beautiful as she? Not only in his house, but in the whole street there is no woman as graceful as she." He responded, "Her beauty suits her reputation well! But when will I have a chance to have a good look at her?" "That's easy," the nun replied. "The nineteenth of the second month is the birthday of Avalokitesvara. By then there will be a street gathering in honor of the god and thousands of people will come out. You can rent a room in the house opposite her's and stay there. She is alone at home. Let me invite her to view the pageant at her gate and she will certainly stand there for a long time. Then you can look at her from behind your window to your heart's content." "Marvelous!" Bu Liang exclaimed.

By the day of the gathering Bu Liang had checked into house across the street, as he had been instructed, from where he could clearly see the inside of Jia's gate. He saw Nun Zhao enter it and come out with Wu, who was, of course, unaware of his presence. Besides, since she was at her own gate, she was vigilant against peepers within the crowd, but was not on guard against someone peeping from the top floor of the opposite house. Bu Liang had a clear and full view of her, and he did not descend until the lady went back through her gate. Thereupon he ran into Nun Zhao, who had come out from Jia's house. "Have you had a satisfactory look?" Nun Zhao asked, smiling. "Yes," he replied. "But it is useless to think of her. The more I look at her, the more infatuated I become. How can I approach her?" "You are like a toad that lusts after a swan's flesh!" the nun rebuked him. "She is a *xiucai*'s wife. She never comes out without a special reason and, besides, you are not her relative or clan member and she does not know you. How can you get in touch with her? You have to be satisfied with the opportunity to peep at her." Saying this, she entered the nunnery.

Bu Liang entered the nunnery at her heels and knelt down before her. "Since you often visit her house," he said, "I can only turn to you for a plan. Please find a way for me to seduce her." "It's very difficult!" the nun said, shaking her head. Bu Liang entreated, "If only I can have a taste of her, I will die without regrets!" "But she is not like other women," said the nun, "one can't easily get an opportunity to talk with her. If you want to rouse her desires and have her engage in a secret meeting with you, you will never achieve your end, not even after a thousand and one years of effort! If you just want to have a taste of her, it may be possible to take her with or without her consent. But you must be patient." "Do you mean I should rape her?" asked Bu Liang. "No," said the nun, "but under special circumstances she will not be able to resist."

At this, he asked, "What strategy would you employ? I will commission you as the general in my campaign." The nun replied, "As the old saying goes, on a slow-oared boat you can catch drunken fish. The only way is to make her drunk so that you can do what you please with her. What do you think of this?" "It's good all right," said Bu Liang, "but how can we make her drunk?" "She never drinks," said he nun. "Since she insists on abstaining from wine, you cannot force her to drink. If you propose so repeatedly, she may get suspicious or angry. In the end you cannot force her to drink. Even if you could force one cup or two down her throat, she will become tipsy quickly and then sober up easily. That will not make her." "What shall we do then?" asked Bu Liang. "I have worked out a plan," said the nun. "Don't ask about it now." But as Bu Liang insisted that the nun tell him the plan, the nun whispered to him that she would do this and that to achieve the end. "What do you think of the idea?" she asked. "Great!" Bu Liang laughed, stamping his feet, "the most brilliant scheme that has ever been devised since primeval times!" "But you have to remember one thing," said the nun. "If I entrap her with this trick, she may blame it on me after she sobers up, and she may fall out with me. What should I do then?" "I only fear that I cannot take her," said Bu Liang. "As long as I can take her, will she be that serious about the matter? With honeyed words I will soothe her so that she might willingly become

my long-time lover. If she blames you, I'll repay you generously.
Maybe when she and I get closely attached, I will speak to her on your
behalf!" "You nasty guy!" the nun teased him. They both laughed
before saying good-bye.

After that, Bu Liang went to the nunnery every day for information.
The nun, on her part, was preparing a trap for Lady Wu.

A few days later the nun prepared a couple of boxes of snacks and
went to Jia's house and see the lady. As the lady invited her to stay for
dinner, the nun took the chance to exchange a little small talk. Then
the nun embarked on her main reason for being there. She said, "You
and your husband are both at the prime of your youth and you have
been married for a long time. It is time that you had a baby." "That's
right," replied Lady Wu. "Why not be pious and pray to the gods?"
asked the nun. "I light incense before the portrait of Avalokitesvara
that I embroidered myself every morning and evening," said the lady,
"and I have prayed in silence to the god for a son, but so far nothing
has happened." "You are too young to know the way to pray for a son,
Madam," explained the nun, "If you pray for a son, you have to pray to
the Pandaravasini*. There is a volume of sutras entitled "Dharani of
Pandaravasini" (白衣经). The god is not the Avalokitesvara we are
familiar with, nor is the sutra *Everyone's Way to Redemption.* (普门品
观音经). *The Dharani* has shown many miracles, which are mostly
noted in a volume kept in my humble nunnery. It's a pity I haven't
brought it with me, otherwise you could have a look at it. I'll not
mention other places, just those in and out of the town of Wuzhou who
print and distribute the sutras and the people who have chanted it. All
of them have had their own babies. The god responds to every plea."

"If the volume is so efficacious," said the lady, "may I trouble you
to bring it to my house and chant it here?" "You don't know how to

---

*Pandaravasini, another name for Avalokitesvara, who is believed to wear a white
dress and sit on a white lotus. That the nun said Pandaravasini was not Avalokitesvara
reveals her ignorance of Buddhism.

chant it, Madam," replied the nun. "It's not easy to start reciting a sutra. I would have to invite you to my nunnery and have you tell the statue of the Pandaravasini how many volumes you'll chant. My humble self will send a message to the god and then I will chant the first chapters on your behalf. After that I can go to your house and teach you the way to chant them. When you are familiar with the citation, you may go on by yourself." "That is alright," said the lady. "I'll abstain from meat and offensive-smelling food for a couple of days before I go to your nunnery and start chanting." "That you will have meatless food for a few days manifests your piety towards the gods." said the nun. "When you have begun reciting the sutra, you'll have to eat a meatless breakfast. After reciting the paragraph for a day, you may eat meat." "If that's the case," replied Lady Wu, "it will be easy." Thereupon Lady Wu and Nun Zhao fixed a date. The lady gave the nun five *qian* of silver to cover the expenses on the sutras and sacrificial offering to the god. The nun went away and immediately informed Bu Liang about all this.

The lady, as she had promised, abstained from meat for two days. On the third day she got up before daybreak, and having dressed herself, with her maid servant Chun Hua she made for the nunnery. There were few people outside. — Gentle readers take warning: no nunnery or monastery is a place for children from good families to go. If the story teller lived at the same time as the lady and heard what they had talked about, he would block the way at the door to stop her, so that not only could the lady maintain a good name, but Nun Zhao would stay alive. But, alas, because of Lady Wu's going to the nunnery,

A beauty from a reputed family ended in disgrace;
And a sinful nun smeared the ground with her blood.

That was a later development. Now let's resume our story. Nun Zhao gladly received Lady Wu, ushered her into the room and seated her. Having offered her a cup of tea, the nun led her to the statue of Pandaravasini and paid respects to the god. While the lady prayed in silence, the nun murmured to the god on behalf of the lady: "Your pious disciple, Lady Wu from the family of Jia, will willingly chant the *Dharani of Pandaravasini*, hoping that you will grant her a noble male offspring as soon as possible and good auspices in everything!" After that the nun began to chant incantations beating a wooden fish — at first magic words to clear away foul speeches from the mouth, and then spells to inform the earth on the spot. After chanting these incantations, she made obeisance to the Buddhas addressing their titles for a long time and then she chanted the inscriptions twenty times in one breath.

The nun was indeed crafty! Knowing that Lady Wu must not have had breakfast because she came early and had offered sacrifices to gods the day before, the nun pretended to have forgotten about it. She neither served any food nor did she ask her if she had had breakfast at home. She purposefully starved Lady Wu for the morning in order to get the better of her. The lady, however, was very delicate. Having gotten up early without eating anything and having prayed to the Buddhas for a long time, she was tired out and hungry, but she was too shy to ask for something to eat. So she called her servant, Chun Hua, and whispered in her ear, "Go and see if there is hot water in the kitchen. If there is, fetch me a bowl of water." Seeing this, the nun feigned ignorance. "I have been concentrating on our important matter," she said, "and I've forgotten to ask about your breakfast!" "I came here early," replied Lady Wu, "and to tell you the truth, I did not have breakfast at home." "I am really forgetful and muddle-headed!" exclaimed the nun. "I haven't prepared breakfast and it's too late to prepare it now. What shall I do? Let's have an early lunch." "To be honest, I am hungry. Anything will do," said the lady.

The nun apologized profusely on purpose before she went to her room and then to the kitchen, where she bade her disciple, Ben Kong, serve a plate of food and a pot of tea. With her insides grumbling the lady thought the fresh fruit on the plate would not allay her hunger, but the piping hot cakes on a big plate would. Taking a cake, she found it soft and sweet. Because she was very hungry, she ate several cakes before she realized how many she had eaten. When the young nun poured tea for her, the lady sipped it and then she ate more cakes. Then she had more tea. Before she had two or three sips, her face was flushed and everything in her eyes started turning. She yawned and collapsed in the chair. The nun pretended to be surprised, "What is wrong with her?" she asked. "Maybe she's dizzy because she got up too early this morning. Support her to the bed and let her sleep a while." She and her disciple carried the chair with the lady in it to the bed, put her in bed and laid her head on the pillow.

Do you know why the cakes were so potent? It was because they had been specially prepared by Nun Zhao, who knew the lady did not drink. She ground glutinous rice into fine flour and mixed it with wine, baking the flour until it was dry, and then grinding the flour again and mixing in more wine. After repeating this process two or three times, she put in one or two kinds of powdered drugs that were disproportionately mixed. Having tampered with the flour like this she made the cakes. Taken along with hot water, the cakes released the effects of all the wine and drugs contained in them so that they were like ferments of wine. Nobody could remain sober with them, let alone Lady Wu who might become drunk at the tasting of a bit of the distiller's grain. Besides, she ate many of them with an empty stomach. When she swallowed hot tea, the drugs and wine all acted up. How could she withstand it? Indeed, just as the saying goes, none can beat a woman cheat!

Thus Nun Zhao put the lady down. Seeing her mistress asleep on the bed, the servant Chun Hua was glad to seize the free moment to go out for fun with the young nun, leaving the lady alone. The nun immediately called out Bu Liang from his hiding place, "The cunt is lying in bed," she told him. "Now you may do what you please with her. How will you thank me?"

Bu Liang bolted the door, drew the curtain aside and looked in. He found the drunk lady with pink cheeks as attractive as a fully-blown crabapple flower. Flaming with the sudden urge of desire, he kissed her lips. The lady was senseless. He lightly pulled off her trousers, exposing her private parts, mounted her, and gloatingly said, "How lucky I am!" Too feeble to move her limbs, the lady faintly felt a man above her, but she believed it was her husband. Thus she let him relish her for quite awhile. After this, the lady was still deep in sleep. Laying a hand on her body, Bu Liang lay beside her, his cheek against hers.

After a good while the potency of the medicine ebbed away. and Lady Wu came to. Seeing a strange man lying beside her, she was surprised and broke out into a cold sweat, shouting, "Calamity!" She sat up at once, her drunkenness evaporating into thin air. "Who are you? How dare you defile a decent lady!" she rebuked him. Bu Liang was flustered too. Kneeling down, he begged her for mercy, "Please be kind, Madam, and excuse me for my impudence." Seeing her trousers were off, she realized she had been victimized. Saying nothing, she put on her trousers back on and calling her maid, Chun Hua, she jumped down from the bed and dashed off. Fearing that somebody might see him, Bu Liang dared not follow her. He remained in the room. As the lady opened the door and fled from the room, she called again, "Chun Hua!" The maid servant, however, due to having risen so early that morning, was dozing off in the room of the young nun. Hearing her mistress's voice, she went up yawning. "You base slave!" yelled Lady Wu, "why didn't you stay with me when I slept?" As she had nowhere to vent her anger, she got furious and hit at the servant. Nun Zhao came forward to dissuade her. Seeing the nun, the lady was even more furious. Slapping Chun Hua twice, she shouted, "Collect our things and go home! Be quick!" "Will you not chant the sutras?" asked Chun

Hua. "Shut up, you slave!" Lady Wu retorted her. "You have no say in my business." The lady, face flushed a deep red in anger, paying no attention to the nun, said nothing but left the nunnery straight away for home with Chun Hua.

As she opened her gate, entered her room and shut the door, she sat down in a sulky mood. After awhile, she calmed down. "I remember eating cakes in hunger," she said to the servant, "but how did I fall asleep in bed?" "When you ate cakes, Madam, and had sips of tea," replied Chun Hua, "you fell down in the chair. It was Nun Zhao and her disciple who helped you into bed." "Where were you then?" she asked. "When you were asleep," said the servant, "I, too, was hungry. I ate the cakes you had left and had a cup of tea in the young nun's room. Then I was a little tired and dozed off. When I heard you calling, I came up." "Did you see anyone get into the room where I slept?" "No one, except the nuns." Lady Wu was wordless. She faintly recalled what she had felt in her dream. "So that's it, I see," sighed Lady Wu, "I never realized that bitch nun was so evil. She helped a wretched scoundrel to defile my spotless body. How can I now be regarded as a good woman?" She felt annoyed, her eyes brimming with tears. She thought of committing suicide, but she could not leave the world without seeing her husband once more. Turning to the portrait of Avalokitesvara that she had embroidered, she wept, praying, "Your disciple was wronged. She pleads with you to display your magic power and help her to reap revenge." Having prayed to the god, she sobbed for awhile thinking of her husband. Then she fell asleep dispirited. Chun Hua could not make head or tail of the events.

Let's now put the doleful lady aside and turn to Nun Zhao. When she saw the lady leave the nunnery in anger without saying good-bye, she realized that Bu Liang had achieved his end. She entered the room and saw him lying in the bed with one finger in his mouth, lost in a reverie. Lust aroused, she mounted him, "Why not thank your match-maker?" she asked. "My gratitude is beyond expression," said Bu

Liang. "I will keep you company tonight. Besides, I want to know your arrangement for the future." "You said you just wanted to have a taste," replied the nun, "but you are talking about an arrangement for the future!" "It's natural for a man to covet more pleasure after he has tasted a bit of it," said Bu Liang. "How can I be content only with this? I ravished her without her consent. It will be most interesting when she comes gladly and willingly and enjoy my company." "You are really insatiable!" said the nun. "You forced her. She looked angry and left without saying good-bye. I don't know how she feels now. How can you expect to meet her again? If she continues to contact me, then you may find an opportunity to talk about it with her." "You are right," said Bu Liang. "It all depends on your marvelous schemes." That night, to express his thanks to the old nun, he stayed in the nunnery and did all he could to please her in bed. So much for the two of them.

As for *Xiucai* Jia, that night he had a dream at his school. In the dream he saw a lady dressed in white enter his room. As he moved forward to ask her what she was doing, she went into the inner room, and as he followed her with big strides, he saw her ascend into the portrait of Avalokitesvara on the wall. Then, as he raised his head, he saw these lines:

What comes in the mouth, will go from the mouth again;
To revenge yourself, you should turn to my discipie.

Having read the lines aloud, he turned around and saw his wife kneeling on the ground. He held her up and thereupon he awoke from the dream. "What an enigmatic dream!" he said to himself as he brooded over it. "Is my wife ill and thus the Avalokitesvara sent a message via a dream?" The next day he took leave of the children's parents and went home. All the way back he racked his brain over the lines he had read in the dream. As he could not make out their meaning, he was full of misgivings.

When he arrived at his home and knocked on the door, Chun Hua came to answer it. "Where is the lady?" he asked. "The lady is lying in bed, sleeping," she answered. "Why is she staying in bed at such an hour?" the *xiucai* asked. "She was depressed," replied the servant, "and she cried a lot calling your name." The *xiucai* hurried in. Seeing him, the lady rolled out of bed and jumped up. The *xiucai* saw her hair was disheveled and her eye-sockets red. Walking a few steps, she cried and threw herself down on the ground prostrate. Startled, the *xiucai* asked, "Why all this?" And he held her up. "Stand by me, my master!" she cried. "Who has wronged you?" asked the *xiucai*. The lady bade the servant prepare a meal in the kitchen and tearfully told him, "Since I was married to you, we have never had a quarrel and we have never fallen out. But now I am guilty and I am only waiting for death. I was waiting for your return, and only if I pour out my distress to you and you back me, will I die content." "What has happened?" the *xiucai* asked her, "and why do you use these ominous words?" Thereupon the lady told him how she had been lured to the nunnery by Nun Zhao on the pretext of sutra chanting, how she had lost consciousness after eating cakes, and how the nun had arranged for her to be raped by seizing the opportunity of her drunkenness. Finishing the account, she threw herself to the ground again, weeping.

Hearing this, the *xiucai* fumed. All his hairs bristled and he shouted, "Should there be such an outrage!" Then he asked her, "Do you know who the man was?" "How can I know?" she replied. Drawing a broadsword out from beside the bed, he smote the table, and said, "I cannot be a man if I do not kill all such villains! But since we don't know who the man is, if we are not careful, he may escape. We must work out tactics." "I have told you everything," the lady said, "and nothing is unsettled in my mind. I would like to die using the broadsword in your hand right here and now." "Don't be short-sighted!" the *xiucai* replied. "This is not your flaw in morals, but is your misfortune! Your conscience is clean. If you commit suicide, there will be much inconvenience." "I won't care if there is any inconvenience!" the lady insisted. "If you die," explained the *xiucai*, "people from your maternal family and the neighbors will ask the reason. If I tell them, you'll bear ill fame after your death. Besides, my future will be ruined.* But if I don't tell them the truth, they will not leave the matter at that, and I myself will feel guilty. How then can we revenge ourselves?" "I will not live on unless both the wretched nun and the rascal die before my very eyes," swore the lady.

Thinking for awhile, the *xiucai* asked her, "What did you say to the nun when you saw her after you were cheated?" "I was angry," replied the lady, "and left straight for home without saying anything to her." "If that is the case," said the *xiucai*, "we can't seek our revenge in public, or we will have to give an account of the happening to the authorities, and as a result, the truth will come out and your good name will be besmirched. I'll work out a plan for revenge against our misfortune without leaving any trace and at the same time none of the wrong-doers will escape." Lowering his head, he ruminated for a moment. "Here it is!" he exclaimed. "It is a plan that coincides to the words of Avalokitesvara I read in the dream. It's a great idea!" "What is the plan?" asked the lady. "You must obey me, Madam," replied the *xiucai*, "if you want to have revenge and prove yourself innocent. Otherwise, you'll not be able to take revenge, nor can you prove your clear conscience." "How can I disobey you, master?" said the lady, "but the plan must be well-conceived." "Since you said nothing to the nun, and you didn't quarrel with her either, she may believe you were shy at that time, and a female like you might be of easy virtue. Now you can go and lure her out, and I will take care of the rest." Then he whispered in her ear that they would to this and that. "It will be a perfect plan," he added. "It's a good design all right," said the lady,

---

* In ancient China a scholar whose wife lost her chastity would not be promoted in the ranks.

"except that it's embarrassing. But since I want to have revenge, I must cast away hesitance." So they made an agreement.

The next day the *xiucai* hid himself behind a door and Lady Wu bade Chun Hua to invite Nun Zhao from the nunnery. Seeing Chun Hua and learning that the lady had invited her, Nun Zhao thought, "She must be unable to hold on after she tasted the good happening, so she's changed her mind." With a proud gait she flew to Lady Wu, following the servant Chun Hua. Seeing the lady, the nun said, "I offended you the other day, Madam, and I didn't look after you well. Please forgive me." The lady ordered the servant to go away and, grasping the nun's hand, asked, "Who was the man that day?" Realizing what she meant, the nun replied in a low voice, "He was Master Bu, a romantic fellow of our place by the name of Bu Liang. He knows how to please ladies and the young ladies all love him. He admired your beauty so fervently that he pleaded with me day and night for some help. I was moved by his sincerity and could not be cruel enough to let him down. On the other hand, I sympathized with your loneliness at home. If you have one or two lovers while you are young, you'll live a worthy youth. Because of this, I found a way to bring you and him together. As the saying goes, all cats eat meat. I'll look after everything for you. You need not be scrupulous, Madam. Simply enjoy the pleasure while you can. That man worships you as if you were a Bodhisattva and he treats you as the most valuable treasure in the world. What's wrong with that?"

"But you should have talked with me about it beforehand," said the lady, "you shouldn't have played with me like that. Since what's done is done, I'll leave it that way." "Because you don't know him," explained the nun, "if I had discussed it with you beforehand, you could not have said yes. Since you have now met him once, it's better for you to be long time lovers." "I have been made a fool of," said the lady, "but I didn't see him clearly. I don't know what he is like. If he loves me, you may tell him to come to my house and see me. If I find

him to be a lovely man, I think I can be his lover in secret." Believing
that the lady had fallen in her trap, the nun was overjoyed. She was not
suspicious at all, "If so, Madam." the nun said, "I'll tell him to come
here tonight. He is such a man that if you have a close look at him
you'll find him good." "I will wait for him behind my door when the
lamp is lit," said the lady. "At the sign of my cough, you may lead him
into my room."

Beside herself with joy, Nun Zhao returned to the nunnery and
informed Bu Liang about her conversation. Bu Liang lost his head
when he heard this. He wished the sun would set soon and the moon
would rise early. Towards evening he stealthily spied near the door of
the Jias. But as it became dark, he saw the door had been closed with a
bang. He began to suspect that the Nun was playing a trick on him. As
he nervously waited, he heard a cough beyond the door. He echoed
with a cough and a door flap was opened slightly. Bu Liang coughed
again and another cough was heard from inside. Bu Liang slipped in
and, walking a few steps, arrived at the courtyard. In the light of the
moon and the stars he faintly discerned the figure of a lady. He rushed
forward and took hold of her, saying, "You are so kind to me,
Madam!" The lady was indignant, but she deliberately did not resist.
She reached out her hands and held him, purposely to detain him. Bu
Liang rushed to put his lips to hers, sticking his tongue-tip into her
mouth and moving it. The lady embraced him more tightly and sucked
his tongue incessantly. Exalted, Bu Liang stuck his tongue more
deeply into her mouth. Thereupon the lady gave vent to her hatred,
clasped his tongue with her teeth and would not let go. In unbearable
pain Bu Liang let his hands down and tried to struggle to free himself,
only to hear a crunch and a five-to-seven *fen* section of his tongue was
cut away by her. In a flurry he fled out of the courtyard.

Spitting out the tongue tip, Lady Wu immediately bolted the door
and went to the *xiucai* at the back gate, "Here's the tongue of our
enemy," she said. The *xiucai* was overjoyed. Wrapping the tongue-tip

in a handkerchief and with a broadsword in hand, he made straight for the nunnery in the faint starlight. Nun Zhao anticipated that Bu Liang must have achieved his end and was by now sleeping in the house of the Jias, so she bolted the door and went to bed. When a knock at the door was heard, the young disciple who had gone to sleep immediately after she went to bed, could not be awakened no matter how hard one knocked at the door. The old nun, however, could not get to sleep because she was thinking about Bu Liang and Lady Wu, and this aroused her urges. Hearing the knock, she thought this might be Bu Liang who had returned from the Jias. She tried to wake up the young nun, but she couldn't, so she herself went to open the door. No sooner had she opened it than the *xiucai* struck at her with his sword, splitting her head in half. She fell to the ground and met her end in a gush of blood.

The *xiucai* shut the door and, sword in hand, went into the room in search of his enemy, thinking "If Bu Liang is in the nunnery, I'll finish him off, too." He saw a lamp in front of the Buddha statues. He looked around with the lamp, but he saw nobody except the young nun sleeping in the room. He then struck her with his sword and she stopped breathing. He immediately turned the light brighter, and taking the tongue-tip out from his handkerchief, he pried the young nun's mouth open with his sword and inserted the tongue into it. Putting out the lamp and shutting the door, he went directly back home. "I have killed the nun and her disciple," he told his wife. "We have revenged ourselves." "But the villain lost only a part of his tongue," said the lady, "he is not killed yet." "It doesn't matter," said the *xiucai*, "there will be someone who will kill him. From now on simply pretend to know nothing of this and never mention it again."

That next morning when the sun had risen high, the gate of the nunnery remained shut. Seeing nobody go in and out, the neighbors became suspicious. As they went to push on the gate, it opened easily at the slightest push. On seeing the old nun dead inside the gate, they were alarmed. When they entered, they saw the young nun also killed. One of the corpses had its head split and the other had its throat cut. They hurriedly sent for the local street and neighborhood chiefs to have the bodies examined so that the case could be presented to the authorities. When the local chiefs examined the bodies, they found something tightly clamped between the young nun's teeth. They took it out and discovered it to be a human tongue-tip. "Obviously it is a case of adultery," they said, "but we don't know who the murderer is. Let's report this to the county magistrate first." Thereupon they wrote a report. It happened the county magistrate was in court, so they immediately submitted the report to him. The magistrate said, "It is not difficult to find the criminal. Ransack the town and suburbs. The man with his tongue missing is the criminal. Immediately ask subcounties and villages to search for him and you'll find him." Not long after he issued the order, a man was brought in by the local chiefs.

The events happened like this: when Bu Liang's tongue-tip was bitten off, he realized he had fallen into a trap. Running wildly here and there, he lost his way. Yet fearing that somebody might catch him, he entered a back alley and crouched on a porch for a whole night. At dawn he tried to find his way home. But it was his fate to run into ruin. Though he walked to and fro and looked here and there in the alley, he could not find the main road. Yet he could not speak to ask. The people in the street became suspicious at the sight of him. After awhile the events concerning the murder in the nunnery spread throughout the town and the announcement by the magistrate was posted. A few people started to question Bu Liang, only to hear mumbling from a bloody mouth. The people were alarmed and a crowd gathered around him. They shouted, "Who can be the killer if not him?" Before Bu Liang could defend himself, they tied him up and brought him to the magistrate. Many people near the county yamen knew him. "This man is not a good person," they said, "so it is clear he must have done it." As the county magistrate convened court, Bu Liang was brought in.

When the magistrate questioned him, Bu Liang could only gabble and the magistrate could not make out a single word. The magistrate had him slapped on the face and ordered him to stick out his tongue. Seeing the tip-less tongue and fresh blood stain, the magistrate asked the local chiefs, "Who is this rascal?" Some of the people who hated him gave a full account of his name and his history of adultery, robbery and fraud. "So it's clear," said the magistrate, "that this villain must have tried to rape the young nun. When the old nun came to open the door, he struck her down, then he went in to rape the young nun. The young nun hated him and bit off his tongue-tip. The villain burst out in anger and killed her. Can it be otherwise?" Hearing this, Bu Liang made gestures in trying to defend himself, but how could he utter one single full word? In fury the county magistrate shouted, "I don't think we need paper and ink to record the confession of such a villain! Besides, he cannot speak distinctly and we have not found the lethal weapon, so a statement is impossible. Give him a sound flogging and put him to death now!" He ordered that Bu Liang be given a hundred lashings, which was far beyond what Bu Liang, as a dandy, could withstand. Before he was flogged fifty times, he stopped breathing. The county magistrate had the local chiefs inform the relatives of the criminal to come and claim the body, and he had the local chiefs cremate the nuns' bodies. He wrote a memo about the case with the following comment:

> Oh, Bu Liang, where is your tongue? It is gone because of an affair that split it. Oh, nun, how about your neck? It is cut because of an ardent lover. It is enough to beat Bu Liang to death since the case is beyond suspicion. The memorandum is hereby filed for future reference.

Thus the county magistrate put a conclusion to this case. Of this we'll say no more.

As *Xiucai* Jia and Lady Wu heard the news spreading from mouth to mouth in the streets, they were inwardly pleased. In the end nobody found that Lady Wu had been cheated and that *Xiucai* Jia had taken revenge on his enemy. This should be attributed to the wisdom of the *xiucai*, and at the same time credit goes to Avalokitesvara, who seeing they were pious, informed them of a strategy for revenge while keeping their fame immaculate. As Lady Wu found the *xiucai* to be a man of great resolution and *Xiucai* Jia found the lady chaste, they loved each other ever more deeply.

Later some people commented on the story this way: Although they made up their minds to seek revenge and achieved their end with a perfect scheme that was not discovered by others, Lady Wu's clean body was polluted. Despite the fact that other people did not know the truth, she herself felt the pain. All her misfortune came from her contact with a nun. Chaste ladies, take a lesson from this!

Tale 5

General Woolly Pays the Debt of a Dinner;
Chen Dalang Reunites with His Lost Kinfolk

It is said that in recent years there lived a certain Wang, who came from an ordinary family in Suzhou. His father, Wang Sanlang, was a merchant; his mother's name was Li. Yang, who was the wife of his father's brother, was a childless widow. They lived together. Wang had been clever from childhood and for this his aunt loved him dearly. But unfortunately his parents died one after another when he was about eight years old. It was his aunt Yang who helped to bury the remains of his parents and adopted Wang as her own son. By and by he grew up and, almost before one knew it, he turned eighteen. He was well versed in all kinds of trades.

One day his aunt said to him, "You are a grown-up now. Do you want to continue to just stay idle and live off your fortune? I have some capital for you. This together with what your father left should be sufficient for you to run a business. Let me collect about a thousand *liang* of silver for you. You can then go out and do business." Wang gladly replied, "That is exactly what I will do." Yang collected a thousand *liang* of silver and handed it to Wang, and Wang consulted with some merchants and learned that business ran briskly in Nanjing. So he bought some goods in Suzhou with hundreds of *liang* of silver and, on a chosen date, booked passage on a long distance sailing ship. Having packed his luggage and said farewell to his aunt, he went on board, offered a sacrifice and prayed to the gods for blessing. Then he set off. So much for the beginning of his journey.

In a few days he arrived in Jingkou, from where he sailed with the east wind across the river and entered the Huangtian Marsh. Suddenly a strange wind rose up and the white billows ran high, washing the ship toward an unknown place. Dusk had fallen. The people on the ship looked out, but all they could see around them were reeds. Unable to see any other boats, they were terrified. Then, with the sound of a gong, three or four boats, each with seven or eight men in them, rowed up. As the boatmen jumped over, Wang and his traveling companions huddled breathlessly and kowtowed for mercy. The men, however, said nothing, nor did they kill anybody. They just collected all the gold, silver and valuables from the ship and carried them to their boats. With a "Sorry to have disturbed you," they dashed away, rowing their boats at great speed. The panic-stricken people all gaped, while Wang began to wail, "Oh, how unfortunate I am!" After he calmed down, he talked with his companions. "Now we have been left with neither goods nor money," he said, "what's the use of going to Nanjing? We'd better go home and make new plans for the future." As they chatted, the wind fell, the water calmed down and it turned bright. They were then able to turn the ship around and sail to Zhenjiang, where Wang visited a relative and borrowed several *liang* of silver for the journey home.

Seeing him return in such a short time, wearing disheveled clothes and pulling a long face, Yang had a strong inkling as to what had happened. Wang came forward and with a salute threw himself on the ground, breaking into a wail. He related to Yang what had happened. "This is fate, my son," she comforted him. "You didn't waste the money. Why should you be so upset? Stay home for a couple of days, and let me raise an amount. Then you can try to make money to make up for the loss you suffered this time." "I'll do business in nearby places," Wang said, "this will save the risk of traveling." "A man should do business a thousand *li* away!" his aunt retorted. "Don't you behave like a coward!"

After a month or so Wang consulted some local merchants. "Cloth sells well in Yangzhou," they said. "Let's buy cloth from Songjiang and sell it in Yangzhou. Then we'll use some silver to buy rice and beans and bring them home for sale. This will be a profitable business." Nee Yang pooled hundreds *liang* of silver for Wang, who bought one hundred bolts of cloth from Songjiang. Then, he contracted a sailing ship, and brought with him several hundred *liang* of silver laid aside for rice and beans. He located a partner and fixed a date for departure.

When he reached Changzhou, he heard boat people coming from the opposite direction complaining bitterly: "What a jam! What a terrible jam!" He hastened to ask why. One of the boatmen answered, "Countless ships loaded with grain have blocked the way to Danyang. The water passage between Qingyangpu and Lingkou is so packed that no commercial ships can expect to enter it." "What shall we do, then?" Wang asked the owner of his ship. "Shall we sail on and get caught up in the congestion of traffic? No way! We'd better go by way of Menghe River," replied the boatman. "I am afraid the waterway of Menghe is not safe," said Wang. "If we run the risk only during the day," replied the boatman, "there's nothing to be afraid of. Otherwise, we'll have to wait here. You can never know when we'll be able to get past." Thereupon Wang accepted his proposal and the ship sailed into Menghe River. As expected, they passed through the passage in broad daylight. "Thank Heaven! We've come out," Wang said, overjoyed. "If we had waited in the internal river, I don't know when we would have gotten through."

As they were congratulating themselves, they heard the creak of oars behind them. In no time a boat propelled by three sculls and eight oars darted up. As it approached, a hook was slung over the side of Wang's ship, and a dozen gangsters with sharp swords, iron bars and metal rings in hand jumped aboard. Since Menghe was to the west of Yangtse River, it was frequented by pirates even during the day. Only empty ships could pass by safely. No commercial ship was spared. As the pirates were moving everything from Wang's ship to their own boat, the ship owner tried to hold onto a scull. A pirate threw an iron bar at him and he had to let go. As Wang looked on, he realized they were the same pirates who had looted him on the Huangtian Marsh during his previous trip. "Oh, my lord," cried Wang, "we gave you all our money before. Why should you visit us again today? How much did I owe you in the previous life?" A tall man among the robbers said, "If that is so, spare him some money to cover the expense of his travel." Throwing a small pack onto the deck they fled away towards the inner river. Groaning inwardly, Wang opened the pack and found a dozen *liang* of silver pieces in it. He sneered tearfully, "I am fortunate enough that I needn't borrow money this time." Turning to the boatman he said, "I suffer because you chose to go by way of Menghe. Let's go home." "The world is no longer what it was," replied the boatman. "Nobody could expect that pirates would run rampant in broad daylight." He turned the ship around and embarked on the journey to whence he had come.

Yang was surprised to see Wang return quickly again. Wang tearfully told her of what had happened. Fortunately, his aunt was a very reasonable lady who could appreciate talent. She was certain her nephew would be successful sooner or later, so she said nothing in complaint. Instead, she comforted him, bade him pull through this time of bad luck with patience and wait for a new opportunity.

Before long Yang pooled some more silver and urged Wang to set out once again, saying, "It was because of fate that you incurred disaster twice. If you are doomed to lose, the gangsters will visit you even if you stay home. You mustn't abandon the trade handed down by your fathers just because of two failures." Wang, however, was hesitant. "If you are afraid," she told him, "you can consult a fortune teller and ask him to divine your future for you." Wang then summoned a fortune-teller, who made prophecies about several places for him. Every place except Nanjing were ill-omened. "It is not necessary for you to be in Nanjing to hit a big fortune," said the fortune-teller, "only that you start on the road to Nanjing." "Be bold, my son," said Yang, "A brave man tours around the world and an overcautious man dares not make a single step. There is a distance of merely six or seven stations' from Suzhou to Nanjing. Many businessmen come and go along the way. It was a track beaten by your father and uncles. It was just your bad luck that you happened to run into gangsters twice. But will they be there only to seek you out? Since the divination is good, you may set your mind at rest and go there." Wang thus set off as Yang instructed him. Well, this journey, like the previous ones, was predestined.

Two days later, Wang found himself sailing on the Yangtse River. That day he had smooth sailing, seeing the mountains flashing by like galloping horses on either bank. When he arrived at Longjiang Pass, it was dark and he could not go ashore for the night. He had to moor his ship. Badly frightened by his former experience, Wang tied his ship close to a patrol boat. Thinking that his safety was thus assured, he retired. By the third watch, the beat of a gong and bright torches woke him from his dreams. As he opened his eyes, he saw a gang of bandits jumping over and removing his goods from his ship, which was no longer in the place he had tied it, but was adrift on the broad river. He scrutinized the gangsters in the torch light and recognized them as the

---

'A station is about six li (or thirty kilometers). Six or seven stations equal about two hundred km.

same ones who had robbed him twice before.

Wang plucked up his courage, and holding fast to the tall man who had returned the small pack of silver to him on their previous confrontation, he knelt down. "Oh, my lord," he entreated, "please take my life!" "We swore never to kill people," said the bandit chief. "You may go. Why are you importuning me?" "Know, my lord," cried Wang, "that I lost my parents when I was a child. It is my aunt that aids me in business. I have only come out three times, but it is as if I owed you a debt in my former life every time I meet with you. I am too ashamed to face my aunt and I don't know where to find the silver to return to her. Even if you don't kill me, I'll jump into the river and drown myself. Definitely I cannot return to my aunt this way." He could not stop wailing as he spoke of his distress. The chief was a sympathetic man. He took pity on Wang. "I'll not kill you," the chief said, "nor can I return the silver to you. But I have a way to help you. I pillaged another ship last night, and from that ship got many bundles of ramie. That quantity of ramie is useless to me. I've taken your silver, but I'll give you the bundles of ramie in return, and you can use them as a capital to start a business. I think it is a reasonable compensation."

Overjoyed at the unexpected gain, Wang was profuse in his thanks. The bandits threw the ramie onto the deck of Wang's ship. Wang and the ship owner hurriedly piled them up, but had no time to examine the two or three hundred bundles. Having disposed of the ramie, the pirates with a whistle turned their boat around and moved away. The boatman knew the gate to a nearby harbor, so he steered the ship into it and took a rest for the night. Getting up at daybreak, Wang thought to himself, what a good-hearted bandit! I suppose this ramie may be worth about a thousand *liang* of silver. He couldn't find a way to dispose it, so he gave it to me. But if I go and sell it right away, someone may recognize it and I may be in trouble. I'd better go home, re-bind the ramie and sell it somewhere else." So he had the ship steered into mainstream of the river. The ship moved fast down stream and in a short time he reached home by way of Jingkou Sluice gate.

When he saw his aunt, he told her what had happened. "Although you lost the silver," said nee Yang, "you got the ramie. On the whole you didn't suffer a heavy loss." As they untied one of the bundles, unwrapping layer upon layer of ramie, they found in the core of the bundle something hard in a tight package. They unpacked this and found a stack of silver ingots wrapped in cotton paper. The same happened in every bundle. There was altogether five thousand *liang* of silver. The silver had been thus camouflaged in the bundles as a precaution against robbery. Apparently some merchants used to traveling on rivers wrapped their silver in ramie and disguised themselves as ramie-dealers so as to hoodwink the robbers. But the bandits looted indiscriminately, and the booty had finally fallen into Wang's hands. "We are really lucky!" Yang and Wang exclaimed. Despite the frightening experiences they had had previously, this windfall brought in twice as much as what they had lost. Aunt and nephew were beside themselves with joy.

After that, Wang had success every time he went out on business tours. In a few years he became a magnate. While Wang owed all of this to his good luck, the kindness of the pirate chief contributed much. After all, we cannot say there are not some good people among the gangsters.

Now let me tell you about another Suzhou native. Because he unintentionally made friends with a greenwood hero, his family became prosperous and he was reunited with his lost wife.

During the reign of Jingtai [1450-1457] there lived a merchant surnamed Ouyang in Wujiang County, Suzhou Prefecture. His wife Zeng, was from Chongming County in the same prefecture. They had one daughter and one son. The son was sixteen and not yet married, and the daughter was twenty. The family was of no consequence, but the daughter was rather pretty. She was married to Chen Dalang of the same village and, after their marriage, they lived in her parents' house. The family, neither very rich nor very poor, ran a small grocery store in front of their gate. The daily business was attended to by Chen Dalang and his brother-in-law. The parents, the young couple, and the boy respected each other and led a passable life.

On a cold winter day Chen Dalang went to Suzhou to buy some goods. When he walked in the street, snowflakes were falling everywhere. A snowfall has always been regarded as a good sign for the country. As he moved towards a tavern for a cup of warm wine, he saw a man approaching from the distance. Do you know what he looked like? He

> Wore a close-fitting blue blouse and
> carried a knife under his clothes at the waist;
> He had an awesome bearing,
> With a face full of crude muscles.
> His cheeks were covered with whiskers;
> His body was hidden in hair.

The man was seven *chi* tall and his shoulders were three times the width of his head. His big face was covered with long whiskers. Strangely, the parts of his face that the whiskers did not cover were hairy. Hair, one *cun* in length, concealed the entire face except for his eyes. Seeing the man, Chen Dalang thought, this man looks odd. How does he dispose of his whiskers to expose his mouth when he eats? He then had an idea. He would spend some silver and entertain the man at the tavern. Then he could see how the man was able to eat. He wanted to make fun of the queer-looking man. Chen greeted him with a bow. The man returned the courtesy in haste. "Would you mind having a drink together with your humble servant?" Chen Dalang proposed. Coming from afar and feeling cold and hungry on that snowy day, the man was happy to accept the offer. "Isn't it too much of an honor for me as a stranger!" he said, his face beaming. "Your impressive bearing suggests to me that you must be a great hero," Chen Dalang lied, "so it is my honor to have a chance to talk with you." "I feel flattered," the man said in all modesty. Together they entered the tavern. Chen Dalang told a waiter to bring pots of wine, a cooked sheep's leg and dishes of chicken, fish and other tidbits. Keen to see how the man opened his mouth, Chen Dalang raised a cup and proposed a toast. The man took the cup, put it on the table, and taking out a pair of tiny silver hooks from within his sleeve, hung them over his ears to hold his whiskers apart. He then began to carve the meat and drink and eat. Presently he found the cups too small, so he asked the waiter for a big bowl. Using this bowl he imbibed several pots of wine in a stretch. After this, they ordered rice. When the rice was served, the man ate a dozen bowls of it. Chen Dalang gaped at him in astonishment.

Then the man stood up, cupped his hands in courtesy, and said, "Thank you for your generous treat. My I know your name and where you come from?" "My family name is Chen," Chen Dalang replied, "and given name so and so. I am a native of Wujiang County of this prefecture." The strange man committed these to his memory. When Chen Dalang asked his name, the man hedged, but said, "My family name is Wu and I am a native of Zhejiang Province. If in the future you happened to be in my province on business, we may have a chance to meet again. I will never forget your kindness and I will repay it one day." Chen Dalang made a few polite remarks, saying that he did not deserve to be repaid for what he did. As Chen paid the bill, the man left with a profuse expression of thanks. Chen Dalang thought that this was a chance encounter and did not take it seriously. When he returned home and told his family about his experience, some believed it and others dismissed it as so much humbug, but everyone laughed it off. Of this we will say no more.

Chen Dalang and his wife had been married for years but still they had no child, so they discussed making a pilgrimage to the

Putuoluojia* Mountains to pray to Avalokitesvara for a son, but they had not made the final decision yet. One day, when Mr Ouyang was away on an errand, a man came. "Is Mr Ouyang home?" the man asked. When Chen Dalang went to the door to answer him, he found it was Chu Jingqiao from Chongming County. They exchanged greetings and the man asked, "Is your father-in-law home?" "No, he's out," replied Chen Dalang. "Your mother-in-law's mother, Lady Lu, is not well," said Chu Jingqiao. "She asked me to bring the message to you that she wants your mother-in-law to stay with her for some time." Hearing this, Chen Dalang entered the inner room and told his mother-in-law about it. "I'll go," she said, "but your father-in-law is out, so I can't leave now." She then summoned her son and daughter and told them, "Your grandmother is ill. You should go to Chongming County and wait on her for a few days. I'll go to replace you when your father returns home." The matter was thus settled. They kept Chu Jingqiao for lunch and begged him to bring their word to Lady Lu. Two days later, having gotten everything ready for the journey, the sister and brother hired a boat and set out. Before they left home the mother instructed them, "Please tell your grandmother not to worry. She should take care of herself, have a good rest and take good food. Tell her I will come soon. Although the trip takes only a day or two, you are young and should be careful along the way." Saying yes, the two of them left for Chongming County. Their sailing for Chongming led to the result that

The greenwood heroes acquired a lady fair;
A rosy-cheeked woman landed in a pirates' lair.

Ten days later Mr Ouyang returned and received a letter hand-delivered by someone from Chongming County saying, "Chu Jingqiao

---

*Chinese transliteration of Sanskrit Potalaka, which according to Buddhist sutras is residence of Avalokitesvara in South India. Putuoluojia, or Putuo for short, Mountains are in Zhoushan Islands of Putuo County, Zhejiang Province.

came back the other day with the news that my grandchildren would come soon. But why haven't I seen them yet?" Mr Ouyang and his wife and Chen Dalang were shocked. "They left home ten days ago," they said, "how come she hasn't seen them?" The man who had brought the letter told them, "No one has seen a soul. Your mother-in-law has recovered from the illness, but what has happened to your son and daughter?"

Chen Dalang hurried to find the owner of the boat by which his wife and brother-in-law had gone and asked him about it. "When we drew near the shore," the boat owner told him, "the boat could not move forward. The master and lady said, 'It's not far from the bank and we know the way. You may go back.' It was getting dark then. When they hurried away, I turned my boat around and came home. How can they be lost?" Mr Ouyang was worried out of wits. "Let me stay at home," he said to his wife, "you and our son-in-law can go to see your mother and find about the whereabouts of our children." They were so worried that they got ready without a moment's hesitation, hired a boat and arrived at Chongming early the following day. They felt relieved to learn that Lady Lu had recovered from her illness, but when she told them she had not the faintest idea of her grandchildren's whereabouts, Zeng wailed for her "dear children." Lady Lu and the neighboring women who came to inquire about the matter joined her in tears.

Chen Dalang was an impetuous man. Smiting the table with a fist, he shouted, "I know it must be Chu Jingqiao's trick! He brought the fucking letter the other day and he must have used the opportunity to abduct them." Regardless of the consequences, he rushed out to confront Chu Jingqiao. The two of them ran into each other. Chu Jingqiao could hardly ask what was the matter when Chen Dalang seized him by the chest and shouted, "Return my people! Return my people!" And he began to drag him to the authorities. By then the neighbors were aroused and came to look at what was happening. Chu

Jingqiao, his face as pale as earth, cried, "What offense have I done to you? At least you have to tell me clearly." "You are trying to deny it," said Chen Dalang, "I was safe at home, but you brought me that fucking letter. Where have you kidnapped my wife and brother-in-law?" Beating his chest, Chu Jingqiao swore, "What a wrong! I've sowed hatred with my service. I brought the letter to you out of good intentions. Your wife didn't come for her own reasons. Why ask me and bring this unexpected calamity upon me?" "My wife and brother-in-law left home ten days ago, but they have not come yet. why?" asked Chen Dalang. "There you are." said Chu Jingqiao. "Counting from the day I brought you a letter, twelve days have passed. I returned home at dusk the next day and I have not gone away since. By then your wife and brother-in-law had not set off yet. When could I have kidnapped them? Now all the neighbors can be my witnesses. If I had gone anywhere in the last ten days, I would be answerable for your kin." The neighbors said, "He hasn't left home. Your relatives might have come across kidnappers or bandits. You cannot wrong an honest man."

Realizing that Chu Jingqiao was innocent, Chen Dalang had to let him go, and, in low spirits, returned to his father-in-law's. Thereupon he submitted a report about the lost relatives to the magistrate of Chongming County. He then went to Suzhou and submitted another report to the prefect, who wrote comments on the report and turned it over to Chongming County, instructing the local authorities to search for the missing people. Notices were put up on walls everywhere, offering a prize of twenty *liang* of silver to anyone who could provide clues as to their whereabouts. Then he found the owner of the boat by which the brother and sister had been taken, and took him to the security authorities. The boat owner was released on bail in anticipation for further interrogation. Returning to Chongming County, Chen Dalang stayed with Lady Zeng for twenty or so days, but heard nothing about his wife and brother-in-law. Winter came to its end before they knew it, and the new year set in. Chen Dalang and his mother-in-law had no choice but to return home. Mr Ouyang had learned of the results of their efforts. The three of them collapsed crying. They were in a woeful state while other families in the neighborhood were happy celebrating the new year.

Soon the first month of the new year passed and the second month came. Still there was no information about the missing persons. Chen Dalang suddenly remembered that he and his wife had planned to pay homage to the god in the Putuo Mountains the year before in the hopes of having a child. But now even the mother of the child-to-be were nowhere to be seen! What bad luck! he moaned. And then he thought the nineteenth of this month was the birthday of Avalokitesvara. Why don't I offer incense to the god and fulfill my prayer wish? On the one hand I can pray to the god for help, and on the other, by enjoying the landscape of Zhejiang, I may dispel my gloomy mood and do some business by the way. He told his plan to his father-in-law, and entrusting him with the management of the shop, set out for Hangzhou.

In Hangzhou he went aboard an ocean-going ship that carried him to the Putuo Mountains on an island in the sea. He disembarked, went ashore, and, prostrating himself once every third step, proceeded up to the hall of Avalokitesvara. Having lit incense and made obeisance, he silently told the god about the disunion of his family. Kowtowing incessantly, he pleaded, "Immensely merciful and benevolent Bodhisattva, your disciple begs you to use your divine power to bring my family together." Then he returned to the boat and spent the night moored by a huge rock. In his dreams he saw Avalokitesvara, who dictated to him these four lines:

Please set your panicked soul at rest:
In time you'll regain what you've lost.
The food you offered will be dearly paid,
You'll find your kin though the world is vast.

Chen Dalang awoke suddenly. He could remember every word of the poem. He was not a learned man, but he could understand the meaning of these lines. "Bodhisattva is knowing indeed!" he sighed. "His words suggest that reunion is possible, but how can this come true if things go on as they have?" This thought made him even more depressed. He had long ago forgotten the dinner he shared with the strange man in Suzhou.

Next morning the boat sailed for home. When it had gone only a few *li*, a hurricane arose and the sky and water were soon veiled in such darkness that one could not tell the direction. Grasping the helm firmly, the helmsman gave the boat up to the mercy of the wind. After awhile it struck an island. The wind fell and the sun began to shine brightly. On the island hundreds of outlaws were jousting with spears or staves in a show of archery and boxing skills. The boat, drifting into shore, was like a rat approaching the mouth of a cat — the outlaws certainly would not let it go. Swarming aboard the boat, they ransacked it for silver and luggage of the passengers. Because the passengers were mostly pilgrims, they had little with them. Dissatisfied with the lean booty, the bandits raised their swords and made ready to kill them. In desperation, Chen Dalang shouted, "Please spare our lives, heroes!" Discerning an eastern accent in his voice, they asked him, "Where are you from?" "I am a native of Suzhou," he answered, trembling. "If so," they said, "we will need to tie them up and bring them to the king for disposal. We certainly can't kill them here." Thus the passengers' lives were spared.

They were tied up and brought to the assembly hall of the outlaws. Chen Dalang had no idea what was going to happen. All in all, he thought, his life was in the devil's hands. So he closed his tearful eyes and chanted "Oh, immensely merciful and benevolent Bodhisattva Avalokitesvara!" Thereupon the lord of the outlaws paced slowly toward him and, having examined Chen Dalang, let out a cry of surprise, "Here is my old friend!" he said. "Untie him! Be quick!" Hearing this, Chen Dalang plucked up his courage to steal a glance at the lord. He found him to be the hairy man he had invited to a tavern on that snowy day two years before. As the bandits untied him, the lord brought forth a chair and, pushing Chen Dalang into it, made obeisance, saying, "My children are ignorant and offended you by mistake. Please forgive me for this impudence!" Chen Dalang hastily returned the courtesy. "I have intruded into your fortress" he said, "and therefore deserve to be put to death. How dare I say anything other than this?" "How can you say that?" asked the lord, "I always remember the dinner you offered me in the snow. On several occasions I had planned to pay you a visit, but I was held by the routine here. I have instructed my children that they mustn't kill passengers from Suzhou. It is Heaven that has brought you here today!" "Since you do not loathe your humble friend," said Chen Dalang, "I beg you to untie my fellows, give back their belongings and let them go home at the earliest date. I'll repay your kindness sooner or later, in this or the coming life!" "How can you go now," said the lord, "before I express a little of my gratitude? And besides, I need your opinion on one thing." He ordered his men to untie the passengers, returned their money and luggage to them and let them leave. The passengers were overjoyed to escape from this gate of Hell. Like pecking hens they kowtowed to the lord. And having thanked Chen Dalang too, they flew in haste, wishing that their parents had given them more pairs of legs with which to run!

The lord ordered a meal to help Chen Dalang get over the shock. Soon the tables were spread. Among the dishes were rare delicacies from the mountains and seas, as well as human livers and brains. As the lord sat down and drank a few cups, Chen Dalang asked, "The other time we were in a haste and I did not get to know your full name. May I have the pleasure of knowing it now?" "I live by the sea," the lord answered, "my family name is Wu and given name is You. I have

had great strength since childhood, and so they elected me chief and
we hold this island. Because I am hairy, they call me General Woolly.
I went to Chongming County by way of the sea and was fortunate
enough to meet with you in your honorable place. I am not a man who
cares only for food and drink. I have always been grateful to you for
the dinner you offered me. Men like us make light of money but put
great importance on friendship. If you had not appreciated me among
all the people in this rustling-bustling world, why would you have
entertained a stranger? The old saying goes that a man will die for his
appreciator. You are my real appreciator!" Hearing this, Chen Dalang
thought, "I am really lucky! But for the dinner I offered him, I would
not be alive today!"

After more cups of wine, the lord asked Chen Dalang, "How many
people are there in your family, may I ask?" "There are my parents-in-
law, my wife, my wife's brother and myself," replied Chen Dalang.
"How are they?" asked the lord. This question brought Chen Dalang to
tears. "To tell the truth," he said, "last year my wife and her brother
went to Chongming to see a relative but they became lost on the way,
and I haven't had any news about them since." "If you cannot find
your wife," said the lord, "there is a woman here that might suit you.
She is from your native place too, and she matches you well in age and
appearance. I would let her wait on you at your home. What do you
think of this?" Fearing the lord might be annoyed, Chen Dalang dared
not refuse. "Come up, please!" shouted the lord. Soon a man and
woman appeared in the hall. As Chen Dalang fixed his eyes on them,
he recognized them to be none other than his wife and brother-in-law.
They couldn't help throwing themselves into each other's arms and
weeping bitterly.

Now the lord bade his men set more tables and seated Chen Dalang,
his wife and brother-in-law in the positions for guests. "Brother, do
you know how your wife and brother-in-law came here?" asked the
lord. "Last winter my children went to the shore near Chongming to do

some petty business in unfrequented places. They saw a man and woman walking together at dusk and brought them here. I inquired into their background and found that they were your kin. So I housed them in rooms apart from the others and dared not treat them lightly. They have been here for more than two months, but I could not find a way to send them to you. I have thought that if you could come I would be able to let them go home with ease. I didn't expect that you would come today. It's Heaven that has helped us!" The wife and brother-in-law later told Chen Dalang in private, "We walked on the shore and when grandmother's house was in sight, we let the hired boat go back. Suddenly a gang came and tied us up. We thought we were doomed, but when the lord asked about us and we told him the truth, they began to treat us with respect. We didn't know the reason. As we listened to what you said today, we recalled that two years ago you told us about someone you had met in Suzhou. Now we see what you said was not a lie." How lucky I am, thought Chen Dalang. But for the dinner I offered, my wife wouldn't have been alive to this day.

After the feast Chen Dalang stood up, saying, "My wife's father is looking forward to seeing us with eager expectancy. Since you have reunited us, would you let us return home as early as possible?" "If that's your wish, I'll see you off tomorrow," replied the lord. That night the lord arranged a room for Chen Dalang and his wife and another for his brother-in-law.

The next day another feast was given. At their departure Chen Dalang, his wife and brother-in-law expressed their gratitude. The lord had his men present them with three hundred *liang* of gold, one thousand *liang* of silver, bolts of colorful silk and countless other valuable things. Chen Dalang tried several times to decline the bounteous gifts, saying, "Your presents are too heavy for me to carry home." But the lord only replied, "I'll have some people carry them for you." Chen Dalang had to receive the donation with thanks. "From now on you should come to see me once a year," said the lord. Chen

Dalang agreed. The lord accompanied them to the shore where his men were waiting in a ship. Chen Dalang and his relatives bid farewell to the lord and got on the ship with joy. The pirates were familiar with the water in the sea, and hence did not fear the waves and wind. Within two days they were brought to Chongming. As they climbed up the bank, the ship turned around and went away.

Chen Dalang, his wife and brother-in-law went all the way to see his wife's grandmother. Having been told all that had happened to them, the old woman was overjoyed, crying, "My dears!" Chen Dalang then hired a boat and the three of them returned home. Seeing their daughter and son-in-law home at long last, Mr and Mrs Ouyang felt as if they were caught in a dream. As Chen Dalang related his experience, they all felt a mixture of joy and sadness. "General Woolly is indeed a man of obligation!" said Mr Ouyang, "But for the hurricane, how could you have arrived at the island? The god Avalokitesvara in the Putuo Mountains is indeed capable of working miracles!" When Chen Dalang told them about the four lines he had heard in his dream, all were amazed. From then on Chen Dalang and his wife went to the Putuo Mountains to worship the god every year, and every time they went, General Woolly had his men take them there and then to the island. Every time they went to the island, they would be showered with gifts of money, ranging from hundreds to one thousand *liang* of silver. Chen Dalang also went to other prefectures to engage in trade every year. In doing so he always tried to find some rarities to take as gifts to General Woolly. The general, however, would always repay him doublefold. In this way Chen Dalang became a man of great wealth in his native region. His wealth was, in fact, the repayment for one dinner he offered to a stranger.

Tale 6

Scholar Han Acquires a Pretty Wife Amidst the Chaos;
Prefect Wu Confirms a Marriage Contract in Favor of
Talent

It is related that during the Reign of Zhengde [AD 1506-1521] in our
[Ming] Dynasty in Tiantai County, Taizhou Prefecture, Zhejiang
Province, there lived a *xiucai* whose family name was Han, given
name, Shiyu, and style name Ziwen. Having lost both his parents and
having no brother, he lived alone. At age twelve he entered the public
school and obtained profound and extensive knowledge. He

> *Is more quick-witted than the master poet Cao Zhi,*
> *And more handsome than the literary prodigy Pan An.**
> *He has browsed five cartloads of books,*
> *And learned things about past and present ages.*

---

*Cao Zhi (192-232) and Pan An (247-300) were famous poets, one noted for quick-wittedness and the other for his beauty.

No doubt a laurel-winner in imperial examinations,
But he is now just a student.

Although he was a literary talent, he had to eke out a living by tutoring children in a private school under the pressure of his waning family fortune. So by the time he was eighteen years of age, he still was not engaged.

One day before the Duanyang Festival [fifth day of the fifth month], he asked leave to stay home for a few days. During that time an idea sprang into his mind: "It's time for me to consider marriage. With my learning, if a wealthy family agrees to marry their daughter to me, I will not be unworthy of her! But who in the world would want their daughter to marry me?" After brooding over this for awhile he said to himself, "That's true. But would I be an unworthy husband for a daughter of a Confucian student such as myself?" So he obtained a note container, weighed out five *qian* of silver from his remuneration, wrapped it in paper and put it into the container. Then he bid the page boy to carry it, and with the boy he strolled to the home of the match-maker Wang.

As the match-maker greeted the scholar, she saw he was a poor wretch, and so she showed little interest in him. Having offered him a cup of tea, she said, "When did you come home, master? What wind blows you here?" "I've been home for five days," Ziwen answered, "I have come to ask a favor of you." And taking the silver from the page boy he presented it to the match-maker with both hands. "Please kindly accept this paltry gift. After my aim is achieved, I'll pay you a bigger sum." With a show of declining, the match-maker received the silver, saying, "I suppose my master wants me to deliver a proposal for marriage?" "Just so!" replied Ziwen, "I am poor and dare not expect to get a wife from a wealthy house. A daughter of a scholar like me, who can prepare meals for me and extend my family line, will do. I have in the last few years accumulated forty or fifty *liang* of silver. That will make up a betrothal gift. I beg Mother to find me a partner." The match-maker was aware that a poor scholar certainly could not meet the requirement of an exacting partner and yet would not accept one of a lower origin. But she found it difficult to turn him down. "Since you've granted me a handsome gift, you may go home. Let your humble servant at leisure look for a good partner for you. As soon as there is any hope, I will inform you." Thus Ziwen returned home.

He waited for several days. One day the match-maker entered his gate, shouting, "Is the Master in?" Ziwen answered her and asked, "Is there any news about my marriage?" "I have run about on your behalf until my shoes have become worn out," responded Wang. "Finally I found a family — it is the family of *Xiucai* Xu who lives near the county seat. The daughter is seventeen years old. The *xiucai* died two years ago and his wife is now a widow. Though the family is not well-off, they make a passable living. As I told her about you, the mother showed some willingness. But she said, 'It's all right for my daughter to marry a scholar, but I am a woman without any education. The education inspector will be coming to Taizhou to preside over the examinations. When Master Han has passed them with high scores, we'll send him the card of my daughter's birthday and birth hour.'" Ziwen was, of course, quite confident of his learning and so he thought the matter was very likely to end in success. "If she wants to arrange the matter that way," he told Wang, "I think it will be right to talk about this after the examination." He brought out cups of wine and treated the match-maker to it. Then the match-maker left.

Ziwen went back to tutoring children and patiently waited for a month or so until he saw the announcement of the inspector's arrival time. The inspector, with the family name of Liang and the given name of Shifan, was a native of Jiangxi Province. In few days he reached

---

*In ancient China, sending a card containing the daughter's birth time was the signal for approving a marriage proposal.

Taizhou. With a kerchief as ragged as seaweed over his head, a robe as flimsy and crumpled as the skin of soybean milk over his body, a belt as threadbare as a taro root around his waist and a pair of boots as spongy as fungus on his feet, Ziwen went with other students to greet the inspector to the city. Having offered incense at the Confucian temple and given a lecture to the students, the inspector posted a notice that the examinations for the prefecture school and the county schools of Tiantai and Linhai would be held first.

Ziwen wrote his examination paper with ease. He was complacent. As he left the examination room, he made copies of his paper and consulted some veteran scholars and his friends. They all praised it with admiration. Ziwen himself read over the paper time and again and, banging the table, exclaimed, "What good writing! With this paper I may take first place, let alone be one of the most successful examinees!" He put the paper close to his nose and sniffed it. "Indeed it emits the fragrance of a wife!" he declared.

Now I will tell you that the inspector Liang did not know good writing from the bad, but he was extremely avaricious and only too eager to gratify the county officials and his superiors. Days before, when he examined students in Hangzhou, Jiaxing and Huzhou, he was condemned by almost everyone, and was almost beaten up by some students. Someone improvised this doggerel about him:

> Inspector Liang's shop,
> Has the wealth for its board.
> It sells academic degrees
> To all those who can afford.

And an antithetical couplet said:

> All smiling, the noble scions congratulate one another;
> Long-faced, the poor students blame their forefathers.

Someone also wrote a passage parodying phrases from the four classics:

> *When a gentleman studies the doctrine, the people will be pleased if the lord is fair; but when a small man studies the doctrine, he believes everything in the book. How can a man with an influential father or brother fail in the examination even if he does not study the poetry or the ritual? How can a virtuous man of humble origins be successful even if he studies poetry and the rituals well?*

From where could Han Ziwen get the money to acquire recommendations from influential persons since he was a moneyless student? Ten days later the results of the examination were published. At the top of the list were all the students from noble houses or wealthy families. But where was Han Ziwen's name? Well, it stood among that rank which read two plus one or four minus one: i.e., three. A poem to the tune of Yellow Oriole described the miserable state to which the students of class three belonged:

> *Your writing, akin to others', grants you no grace,*
> *Yet suffices to lose your face.* *
> *Drum beat dashes your spring dream for success:*
> *The brilliant minds the Fate does never bless;*
> *But Fortune smiles at empty heads.*
> *The pity is that you are not from the state scions' school*

---

*During the Ming Dynasty, those scholars whose scores were rated in the first and second classes in the pre-examinations for *juren* would be rewarded, while those whose scores were classified in the fourth grade or lower would receive punishments. The third grade ones (Han Ziwen was listed here) could not receive a reward and yet were not to be punished.

Or you could skip over the local pest.*
Now please stand by, relaxed and cool,
To watch the prize-winners pin flowers to breast.

Having gotten a third-class rating, Han Ziwen was dumbstruck with anger. He vehemently cursed the inspector as "a son of a bitch". He dared not mention the marriage proposal any more and the matchmaker didn't come to see him either. He had to console himself with a sigh:

"Don't worry about an able match-maker! —
Beauty nestles in your books."

As he put away his things, he returned to teach school in low spirits. He blushed and felt discredited when he saw the sponsor of the school and the pupils.

A year later Emperor Zhengde passed away, leaving a decree that the new emperor should be the Prince of Xing. The new emperor, Jiajing, mounted the throne at age fifteen, and decided to fill the palace chambers with beautiful girls from good families. Thus a rumor spread throughout Zhejiang Province: "The court will select girls from Zhejiang." The foolish locals all believed this. In great haste, those with daughters began to arrange marriages for them and those with sons found wives for them, neglecting all etiquette and decorum. This benefited only the silk sellers, music players, maid-servants who accompanied brides, bridal sedan-chair bearers and attendants at the wedding ceremonies. Even more ridiculous was another rumor that. "Every ten girls need one widow to escort them to the imperial court".

---

*The students of the state scions' school could directly enter for the national-level examination and thus be free from the trouble posed by local examination inspectors. Ordinary students should pass local examination before entering for the national-level one.

This drove the seventy- or eighty-year old widows to rush into marriage. The situation was:

A teenage boy got a girl in her mid-twenties as his wife;
A girl in her early teens married a middle-aged man.
A crude-skinned blacky was regarded as a rare beauty,
A loose-hipped slut was taken as a tender bud.
Those who had always bragged of their firm chastity
And who preferred death to a second marriage,
Now, before they filled coffins,
Braved the wind of a second spring.

An anonymous poet of that time wrote an amusing verse:

Because of a decree written in cinnabar — all untrue
With three cups of watery wine, nuptials are rushed through.
On moonlit nights I watch on top of my house
The Moon Goddess is the only one without a spouse!

At that time Han Ziwen was at home. Seeing everything in chaos, he walked outside to have a look. Suddenly a man seized him from behind. He turned around and saw that it was Jin, the owner of a pawn shop in Huizhou. With an obeisance Jin said to Han Ziwen, "I have a daughter and she is sixteen this year. If my master doesn't despise her humble origin, please be good enough to take her as your wife." With this he fumbled out a card containing his daughter's birthdate and tucked it into Ziwen's sleeve, as he stood there in bewilderment. Ziwen said, "Please don't joke with me. I am an utterly destitute *xiucai*. How can I marry your daughter?" Jin knitted his brows saying, "How can my master make this perfunctory remark in such a desperate situation? A moment of hesitation and my daughter may be selected by the court. My wife and I have only this one daughter. If she is taken to the distant capital of Beijing, there will never be an opportunity for us to see her again. How can I stand such a permanent departure? If my master would condescend to accept my proposal, you will really be saving a life!" Saying this Jin made of gesture of kneeling down.

Ziwen realized that Jin would not fall on his knees and that a wife was just what he needed, but he did not tell the truth. He pulled Jin up, saying, "I have only forty or fifty *liang* of silver in my pocket. Even if you don't despise my poverty and betroth your daughter to me, I cannot afford the expense of a wedding." "It doesn't matter," said Jin. "As long as my daughter is engaged, the court will not select her. Let's just hold the ceremony of engagement. We can hold the wedding at leisure after the situation has calmed down." Ziwen replied, "That is a practical idea. But what is said cannot be unsaid. You mustn't go back on your word." As Jin was too eager to have the matter settled, he swore to it by Heaven. "If I go back on my word," he said, "let me be tortured in the court of Taizhou Prefecture!" Ziwen said, "It is not necessary to take an oath. But verbal statements are no guarantee. You may go home first. I'll invite a couple of my friends to your shop. There let me see your daughter first. After that, you can write the marriage contract, which will be signed by my friends as witnesses. After I present my betrothal gift, I'll ask for something from your daughter, perhaps a piece of clothing, a wisp of hair or a fingernail. Only with this can I be assured that you'll not break your promise." Jin was only too ready and willing to accept this. "Why so much suspicion?" he asked. "All right, I'll do your bidding. I only hope you will be quick." As he walked away, Jin turned his head from time to time, saying, "I am waiting for your coming. I am waiting!" He went back to his shop.

Han Ziwen then went straight to the county school to see his friends whose names were Zhang Siwei and Li Junqing.* He told them what

---

*Zhang Siwei and Li Junqing are the same persons as Zhang Anguo and Li Wencai in the latter part of this story. In olden times Chinese usually had two names, one of which was given at birth and the other given by an elder of the clan, a superior or teacher.

had happened. Having prepared a visiting card, they together proceeded to Jin's shop. Jin greeted them and offered tea. After they exchanged greetings, he called his daughter, Zhaoxia, into the sitting room. What a girl she was! She

Had eyebrows like tender willow leaves in the spring
And a pair of bright eyes like brimming autumn water;
Fresh peach blossoms glowed on her cheeks,
And two newly-sprung bamboo shoots appeared under her skirt.
Her beauty, if not meant to enchant a whole country,
Had few rivals within the human world.

Seeing the beautiful appearance of the girl, love was immediately kindled in Ziwen's heart. After saluting the guests, the girl returned to her room. Ziwen consulted a fortune-teller about the marriage. The fortune-teller predicted, "You have the auspices for happiness, but before the wedding there will be an unpleasant trifle." Jin, however, was eager to fulfill the matter, and so he said, "It's all right to have an auspicious divination. A trifle is a trifle." He took out a contract written on a full-length folding sheet, which read:

> *This marriage contract is signed by Jin Sheng, a native of Huizhou, whose daughter, Zhaoxia, sixteen years old and heretofore engaged to nobody, is now engaged to Han Ziwen, scholar in the county school of Tiantai County, Taizhou Prefecture. This engagement is arrived at with willingness on both sides. Henceforth both parties are to adhere to this agreement. Mr. Zhang and Li are the witnesses of this engagement.*
>
> > *Jin Sheng, the engaging party*
> > *Zhang Anguo and Li Wencai, the witnesses*
>
> *on such-and-such a day of such-and-such a month, the first year of the reign of Jiajing.*

The three signed their names and presented the contract to Han Ziwen to keep. Because Ziwen was aware of his poverty, he took the preventive measure. He did not anticipate that an attempt would be made to break the agreement. That is the story to come.

An auspicious date was promptly chosen to present the betrothal gifts. On that date Ziwen spent part of the money he had saved from his remuneration for a few pieces of clothing and jewels. To this he added some silver ingots. He wrote a card with these words: "Betrothal gifts presented by son-in-law Han Shiyu with a hundred kowtows", and he gave Zhang and Li each one *liang* of silver, asking them to function as match-makers for him. With the gifts and silver they went to Jin's shop. Jin was a magnate. When he and his wife, nee Cheng, saw that the gifts were slim, they were not pleased, but they accepted them since otherwise they could not tide over the situation. They returned Han Ziwen a handsome present. And, as Ziwen had asked, they delivered him a wisp of black hair from the girl. Ziwen took these as the token, thinking in himself, "But for the clamor, I don't know when I might have obtained a fiancee, let alone the wealth brought by a wife." He was overjoyed. Of this we'll say no more.

Time flew like an arrow and the days and months passed like a shuttle. As the hot season turned into the cold season, the second year of the Jiajing reign began. The rumor about selecting girls from Zhejiang for the imperial court had already died down. Seeing the crisis was over, Jin and his wife began to regret the engagement of their daughter to a poor scholar. At the same time, Han Ziwen had used up all his savings in presenting the betrothal gifts. Therefore he could not talk about the wedding.

One day as Jin was in his shop doing his accounts, a man with a boy of eighteen or so entered, asking, "Is my sister and brother-in-law here?" This was Mr. Cheng from Huizhou, the brother of Jin's wife. Cheng came with his son, Cheng Shou, to run the pawn shop in partnership with Jin. Jin greeted him in a hurry and introduced his wife and daughter, Zhaoxia, to the two arrivals. After exchanging a few words of greeting, warm wine was served. Cheng said, "My niece has grown so lovely! Is she engaged yet? — Excuse me for my blunt question. My son is not yet engaged. If you don't despise me, let's unite our children in marriage." Jin heaved a sigh, saying, "There it is. If my daughter were to become the wife of my nephew, how could I be unwilling? But because of the rumor about selecting girls for the court the last year, I engaged her to a *xiucai* by the name of Han-whatever in haste. He is a poor Confucian student. From the starved look of his face I could see that he would never be prosperous. Two years ago inspector Liang came to hold the examinations, and the *xiucai* was graded class three. I had anticipated he would never succeed. Why should my daughter marry such a person? Oh, my poor daughter is too unfortunate! But what can I do now?"

Cheng meditated for awhile and then asked, "Are you really unwilling to marry your daughter to him?" "How can I lie?" retorted Jin. "If you are willing to give your daughter to him," said Cheng, "let's drop it. But if you are not, we can have the authorities annul the contract by using only a small bit of tact. It's very easy." "What is your stratagem?" asked Jin. "Tomorrow I'll submit a written complaint to the prefect of Taizhou against you," replied Cheng, "saying that our children are cousins and we engaged them when they were small children, but you repudiated the contract and engaged your daughter to another person when I remained in Huizhou during the recent years. I simply beg the prefect to announce that our original contract is valid. Though my son is not very gifted, he is far better than that poor scholar who is doomed to suffer from hunger."

"That is a good idea," Jin said, "but the scholar has the marriage contract written in my own hand and my daughter's hair as testimony of the contract. How can the authorities announce that my daughter should be your son's? Besides, I am guilty before him." "You don't know the things in the yamen, my brother-in-law," said Cheng. "You and I are both natives of Huizhou and we are relatives. If I say our children were engaged when they were small, people will believe us. As the proverb says, 'With money you can make even the devil turn a mill-stone'. We have enough silver and to spare. I am sure we can buy over the superiors and subordinates as well. Then we can beg a local bailiff to intercede with the prefect. What is a marriage contract? A mere scrap of paper. It will be written off. As for the hair, who knows whose it is? The affair will be settled to our satisfaction. After you bribe them with silver, you'll not suffer." Jin clapped his hands saying, "Marvelous! Do it tomorrow." When they finished the food and drink, the two of them retired for the night.

Next morning Cheng got up early, washed and dressed himself and asked for something for breakfast. Consulting an expert he worked out a draft for the indictment. After that he found a Zhao who acted as the witness. Those people together with Jin went to the yamen of Taizhou Prefecture. Because of their coming,

A beauty soon belonged to a brilliant youth
And the tricksters were tortured at once.

As they arrived at the yamen, the newly appointed prefect, Wu Gongbi, was convening court. Shortly thereafter an announcement board for accepting complaints was put up in front of the yamen. Cheng followed the board in. Prefect Wu had a civil litigation clerk pass him the complaint and he read it from the beginning:

To His Excellency in Taizhou Prefecture

Cheng Yuan, the plaintiff, enters a complaint regarding the breach of a marriage contract. Evil-minded Jin Sheng promised to marry his own daughter, Miss Jin, to Cheng Shou, the son of

Cheng Yuan, and all betrothal formalities were fulfilled. Cheng could not have expected that when later the accused Jin moved to Taizhou he would break the agreement unilaterally. In some month last year he re-engaged his daughter to Han Shiyu, a scholar of Tiantai County. Zhao Xiao is a witness to the contract between Cheng and Jin. Considering that this is a matter of morals and ethics, the plaintiff entreats His Excellency to make a fair judgment and thus the marriage defined in the former contract will be reaffirmed.

Cheng Yuan, the plaintiff, from Shexian County, Huizhou
Jin Sheng, the accused, from Shexian County, Huizhou
Han Shiyu, the accused, from Tiantai County, Taizhou
Prefecture
Zhao Xiao, the witness, from Tiantai County, Taizhou
Prefecture

After reading the complaint, Prefect Wu called in Cheng Yuan and asked him, "What is your relationship to Jin Sheng?" "My just lord," answered Cheng, "he is the husband of my own sister. Because we are close relatives and our children are of similar ages, we engaged our children." The prefect asked again, "But why should he have broken the agreement?" "Jin Sheng later moved to Taizhou," Cheng replied, "and your servant stayed in Huizhou, far away from him. Last year the rumor spread that the court would select girls here. Jin was afraid that his daughter might be selected, and so he engaged his daughter to scholar Han. Your servant came to Taizhou recently to visit him and planned to hold the nuptials for my child. Only then did I learn the truth. He made the mistake in a desperate situation. But how can I give up a daughter-in-law to another? How can *Xiucai* Han return her to me without the intervention of the authorities? I beg your Excellency for protection!" Finding that his account was not groundless, Prefect Wu put the complaint on file and told him, "All parties will be interrogated in ten days." Cheng Yuan then kowtowed and left.

When Jin learned that the prefect had accepted the complaint, he came to Mr Zhang and Li the next day. He deliberately put on a scared look, saying, "What can I do? What can I do? When I was in Huizhou, I engaged my daughter to the son of my wife's brother. Later I came to this place at the time when the court was selecting girls. My wife's brother was too far away to help me out of the crisis. In desperation I engaged my daughter to your honorable friend. You two played the match-makers. To my surprise my wife's brother has now come. He has lodged an indictment against me with the prefect. What shall I do?"

Hearing this, Zhang and Li burst out in anger. "You damned old rascal!" they berated him. "You old ass! When you betrothed your daughter to Han, you made many vows. Who signed the contract? You! How can you now talk all this shit nonsense! We can see that you have devised this scheme because you dislike Han on account of his poverty. Han is a talented person and he will not be in that state forever. We and our friends in the county, subprefecture and prefecture schools will jointly bring you to the authorities. Wait and see if the authorities don't break your leg. Your daughter will never be married off!" Jin wanted to explain, but they paid no heed. They went straight to Han's house to tell him what had happened.

Hearing about the matter, Han Ziwen was choked with anger. He could not utter a word. After awhile Zhang and Li, still fuming, asked Han to call all his school friends so that they together could go to the authorities. But Ziwen persuaded them to give in. "Please don't do that," he said. "If the old rascal doesn't want me as his son-in-law, the girl will not be happy with me even if we seize her. If we can make progress, we needn't worry that illustrious families will not unite us with them by matrimonial ties. Jin is a wealthy merchant, far from being a long-standing influential family. Besides, he has enough money to bribe the authorities, so the authorities will naturally be partial to him. I am poor. Where can I get the money to spend on legal procession? The day of revenge will come when I have been promoted. I have to trouble you, my friends, to tell him that since I paid him fifty *liang* of silver as the betrothal gift, if he'd like to pay me double that sum, the marriage contract can be canceled."

Zhang and Li agreed. Ziwen took out the marriage contract and the hair from a box and went to the pawn shop with his friends. As Zhang and Li told Jin what Han's demand was, Jin rejoiced. "So long as the contract can be canceled," he said, "and I can thus get rid of the trouble, I won't mind giving up several dozen *liang* of silver." He promptly weighed on the scales two shoe-shaped silver ingots which equaled one hundred *liang*. Delivering the silver to Zhang and Li, he demanded that Han Ziwen write a declaration to cancel the engagement and return the contract and hair to him right away. Ziwen, however, said, "It is not right to do that until the lawsuit is settled. I should not return them now. Neither will I take the silver right now." Cheng Yuan gave Zhang and Li two *liang* of silver, asking them to act on his behalf in dropping the lawsuit. Zhang and Li ordered a brush and wrote a memo. Then, together with the plaintiff, the accused and the witness, they entered the prefecture yamen. Prefect Wu was in his evening office hour. They submitted the memo. The prefect read it from the beginning:

> *Mediators Zhang Siwei and Li Junqing, natives of the Tiantai County School, state that: Jin Sheng from Huizhou has accepted betrothal gifts to his daughter from Cheng, but later Jin moved to Tiantai County, and due to long distance and inconvenient communication, when his daughter came of age, he did not hear anything from Cheng; thus he promised his daughter to scholar Han. This has given rise to the lawsuit brought by Cheng. Now Jin Sheng is willing to return the betrothal gift to Han and Han*

is willing to cancel the marriage contract so that the contract between Cheng and Jin will not be broken. We, as kin of the concerned party, convey this to the authorities in hopes that the dispute will be settled peacefully.

Prefect Wu came from an illustrious family of Fujian Province. He was upright and just. He did not love taels (of silver), but he loved talent. After he had received the complaint of Jin, some local gentleman wrote letters to him and he had realized that there must be some reason for this case. Now, having read the memo, he raised his head to size up Han. The brilliant appearance of the *xiucai* appealed to him. He commanded that the *xiucai* be brought forward. As Han Ziwen knelt in front of him, Prefect Wu queried, "I see you bear a striking appearance. You will not remain in hardship forever. If I had you as my son-in-law, I am sure you would be worthy. But why were you so light-headed as to be betrothed to Jin's daughter, and why do you so thoughtlessly give up the contract today?" Han Ziwen was quick-witted in grasping the implications of any signs or gestures. He had already given up any hope of justice. But now, as he realized that the prefect was siding with him, he took a turn. "How can I be willing to have the marriage contract canceled?" Ziwen said. "The day when I became engaged, Jin Sheng swore in the name of Heaven. Being afraid that his vow was not believable, I demanded that he write a contract. Zhang and Li were the witnesses. The sentence 'heretofore engaged to nobody' is evidence. After that he handed me a wisp of black hair from his daughter's head, which I have always carried with me, and I look at it from time to time. Seeing it I feel as if I am looking at my future wife. Now this love will become a stranger. How can I bear this? As for the marriage contract between the Jin and Cheng families, I have never heard of it. This dispute has arisen just because my family fortune does not match his." He burst into tears. It so happened that he also brought the girl's birth time card, the marriage contract and the hair in his sleeve, and so he handed them to the prefect.

The prefect examined them and gave an order, "Take Cheng Yuan and Zhao Xiao away from here." Then he asked Jin Sheng first, "Is your daughter engaged to Cheng?" "Yes, my lord, it's true." replied Jin. "If so, you shouldn't have re-engaged her to Han." "Because of the rumor about selecting girls for the court, I did it without considering the consequences," answered Jin. "I had no choice then." "But was the contract signed by yourself?" retorted the prefect. "Yes," said Jin. "How do you explain the phrase 'heretofore engaged to nobody' in it?" "I was too eager to have my daughter engaged, so I did everything he demanded. It is a lie." Hearing his self-contradictory remarks, the prefect looked angry. He added a question, "On what date did you and Cheng become related by agreeing to the marriage of your children?" Jin Sheng could not give an answer off hand. Thinking for awhile, he concocted a reply, "It was on such-and-such a date."

The prefect then ordered him to retreat and summoned Cheng Yuan. "What testimony do you have regarding the engagement to Jin's daughter?" he asked. Cheng Yuan replied, "We held all the ceremonies of engagement. That is my testimony." "Then where is the match-maker?" the prefect asked. "He is in Huizhou. He hasn't come." "Show me the card of your daughter-in-law's birthday and birth hour." Cheng Yuan said, "I did not bring it with me." The prefect sneered: "On what date was the engagement made?" Cheng Yuan, too, thought for awhile before fabricating an answer "It was on such-and-such a date." His date was quite different from that which Jin had given.

By this time the prefect had seen through the matter. He called Zhao Xiao up and asked him, "You are the witness. Where are you from?" Zhao Xiao answered, "I am a native of this prefecture." "How can you know about things in Huizhou, if you are a native of Taizhou?" the prefect asked. "I am a relative to both families, so I know their affairs," was the answer. "If so," said the prefect, "do you remember the date of their engagement?" Zhao Xiao gave an equivocal date, which agreed with neither date given by Cheng or Jin.

When Jin, Cheng and Zhao saw that their memo was delivered, they thought they would achieve their end with ease, so they had not prepared themselves for the answers to the prefect's questions. They had not expected that the prefect would interrogate them one by one on the details. The clerks in the yamen were all bribed, but fearing the strict discipline and severe punishment of the prefect, none dared to speak a word for them. Naturally their words betrayed them.

The prefect was enraged: "How dare you villains defy the law and swindle the authorities! Let's not speak of the fact that the selection of girls for the court was false. Even if it had been true and the foolish people were frightened, Jin did not need to escape the danger by engaging his daughter to Han if he had the betrothal gifts from Cheng as evidence. I can see that the marriage contract and card of Jin's daughter's birthday and birth hour that Han has with him are all authentic, but the words of Cheng Yuan are incredible. Furthermore, if you have come here to hold a wedding ceremony for your son, why did you not bring the match-maker? Besides, each of you gave a different date for the engagement. How do you explain that? Zhao Xiao is a native of Taizhou. Obviously, you need a witness, but you cannot find another Huizhou native, so you bought his collaboration. All this is because scholar Han is poor. You hatched the evil plot to re-engage your daughter to your nephew. You together worked out the scheme, didn't you? What else can you say?" And the prefect pulled out a bamboo slip of warrant from the container and ordered that Jin, Cheng and Zhao be each flogged thirty times. They all wailed in pain.

Han knelt down in front of the prefect saying, "If my lord protects my marriage, Jin Sheng will be my father-in-law. Please don't let hatred be sown between him and me. Please show mercy on him." The prefect said, "To spare the feelings of Han, I'll reduce the punishment for Jin by half. The plaintiff and witness are not spared at all." They then received the spanking right there. Since they had never anticipated this outcome, they had not bribed the runners beforehand for a lighter spanking, so they were both flogged until they were bruised and lacerated, howling and screaming in agony. Han Ziwen, Zhang Anguo and Li Wencai felt joy inwardly while looking on. The punishment Jin had vowed to take was thus administered.

The prefect smeared the memorandum with a brush and wrote a comment:

Scholar Han who has nothing but bare walls in his house
Wants to have a virtuous lady, but he cannot;
Jin Sheng has accumulated thousands of casks of treasure,
But he tried to abandon the talented youth he had acquired.
The chooser of a son-in-law is not keen-eyed enough
To tell a worthy person from an unworthy one;
The greedy man who covets the fair girl
Attempts to gain his end by a lawsuit.
The marital ties between Cheng and Jin
Lack evidence from either side;
But the marriage contract Han proffered
Is as clear as the daylight.
Let the hundred liang be a fund for the wedding
For the new couple: the girl belongs to Han.
Jin Sheng, Cheng Yuan and Zhao Xiao are flogged
For the disturbance they willfully created!

On finishing this, the prefect handed the contract, the card of the girl's birthday and birth hour and her hair to Han Ziwen. As they took leave of the prefect, Cheng Yuan blushed down to his neck because of his failure, while Han Ziwen called him names such as "old ass" all the way. Han Ziwen also teased him. "Great!" he said. "You really deserve the reward for your virtuous deed! What about the flogging? I suppose it does not hurt, eh?" Cheng dared not return even one word.

Since Zhao Xiao suffered for Jin and Cheng's sake, they had to redress him with some money. Zhao, however, was still grumbling. — Indeed, those who go for wool will come back shorn: they lost the case and face. Thus they dispersed.

After this disturbance, Han Ziwen was afraid that something unexpected might happen, so he quickly spent the one hundred *liang* of silver on bridal attire and gifts. He fixed a good date for the wedding. Again Zhang and Li came to talk about the matter with Jin Sheng. Seeing that prefect Wu had sided with Han, Jin Sheng dared not neglect Han's words. Jin and Cheng wanted to play some trick with the higher-up authorities to reverse the verdict, but they realized that if they did so, the procedure would go through the county and prefecture administration and that would betray them. So Jin had to keep his resentment to himself and accept everything Han put forward. On the wedding night, Zhaoxia found that Han had an impressive bearing and a spirited look. Seeing such a good match, she totally forgot his poverty. Attached to each other, they dallied through a blissful night. She even complained about her father for the obstacles he had posed. Indeed, had the father known that things would go this way, he would have saved much ado about nothing! After that everyone was at peace.

A year later another inspector by the name of Tian Hong came to preside at the preparatory examinations at the provincial level. With the recommendation from Prefect Wu, Han Ziwen passed them with excellent scores. Soon afterward he passed the autumnal examination at the provincial level and the spring examination at the national level. Then Jin Sheng's daughter became a lady of rank. Jin Sheng now began to regret his actions. If he had foreseen this outcome, he would have been willing to make his daughter even a concubine to Han! As the following rhyme says:

Don't look at heroes with short-sighted eyes:
Many a hero has lived through plight.
Praise to the prefect wise and upright
Who brings about felicitous ties!

Tale 7

An Evil Boat Owner Takes Money for an Unidentified Corpse;
A Base Servant Files an Accusation about an Alleged Murder

That a murderer should pay for his deed with his own life is the gravest code of law in the world and it is by no means a trifle. That's why a real murderer cannot be taken as a false one, nor can a false one be taken as a real one. A real murderer, even if he is wealthy and can bribe the authorities and thus escape punishment for a time, will not be tolerated by Heaven's law. In the end the truth will be brought to light before he realizes it. A man wrongly accused of murder, however, may confess to false charges under torture, but he will prove himself innocent in the end. If the mistakes in both cases are not corrected, namely, the guilty person dies a natural death while the innocent one dies in prison or under the guillotine, does the Old One* over our heads not have eyes? That's why an old rhyme goes like this:

---

*Euphemism for Heaven.

None can deceive Heaven just
Who knows your intention; all needs must
Receive his reward in due date
Which comes to some early, to others late.

It is related that in our [Ming] dynasty there was a wealthy man by the name of Wang Jia who lived in Suzhou. He had a feud with another native of that city, a man named Li Yi. Wang Jia tried by every means he could think of to frame him, but all his schemings failed. One night there was a storm. At midnight Li Yi and his wife had finished supper and gone to bed, when a dozen bandits, their faces smeared with ink or cinnabar, broke in. Lady Jiang, Li Yi's wife, was so scared she crept under the bed. There she saw a long-bearded, large-faced bandit seize Li Yi by the hair and kill him with one stroke of a sword. Immediately the bandits dispersed without taking anything. Jiang saw all this clearly from under the bed. Now trembling, she crept out and broke into wailing over the corpse of her husband. The neighbors, aroused, came to see what had happened. They all felt sad about her misfortune, and they tried to comfort her.

"The man who killed my husband is my enemy Wang Jia." she declared. "How do you know?" the neighbors asked. "I saw it clearly from under the bed," said Jiang, "and my enemy Wang Jia has a large face and long beard. Though his face was smeared with ink, I knew who he was. Besides, if the killer was not him, why would he have killed my husband without taking anything? Who else can the killer be if not Wang Jia? I am asking all of you to take sides with me!" "We know," the neighbors said, "that he was feuding with your husband. And we will report the murder to the authorities. You can write an indictment tomorrow morning and go to the magistrate with us. We will return home now." When the neighbors departed, the lady sobbed for awhile and could not go to sleep again. Broken-hearted, she waited until daybreak. She had a neighbor buy a form of accusation and fill it in. And then she made her way to the court of Changzhou County.

When she arrived, the magistrate was holding court. Reaching the stair-steps in front of the office, she shouted about her grievances. After reading the indictment, the magistrate inquired into the matter. Realizing this was an important case, he immediately accepted the indictment. Soon the local bailiffs presented a report about the robbery. The magistrate then had the sheriff examine the witness and bade him and yamen runners to go and arrest the criminal.

After he killed Li Yi, Wang Jia was complacent, believing he had not been detected under his disguise. While he was off guard a group of policemen broke into his house and, before he could hide, tied him up with a rope and took him to the county court. "Why did you kill Li Yi?" asked the magistrate. "Li Yi was killed by bandits," Wang Jia replied, "what have I to do with it?" Then the magistrate asked Jiang, "Why do you accuse him of the murder?" "I saw it clearly from under the bed and recognized him," she replied. "Could you see him clearly in the dark?" the magistrate asked. "Not only could I recognize his appearance," said Jiang, "but also I can deduce that he did it for one thing. If those men were mere burglars, why didn't they made away with anything after killing my man? Who would do this but his enemy?" The magistrate summoned the neighbors and asked them, "Was Wang Jia feuding with Li Yi?" "Yes," the neighbors all said, "and it is true that they killed him but took nothing." Thereupon the magistrate ordered that Wang Jia be tortured by cramping and squeezing his legs. Brought up in a wealthy family, Wang Jia could not withstand the pain. He had to confess, "I was feuding with Li Yi and so I dressed myself as a bandit and killed him. That's the truth." Having his confession committed to paper, the magistrate had him put in death row.

Wang Jia had confessed to his crime, but he was now trying to find a way to escape punishment. After he had given the matter much thought, a local legal pettifogger called Old Man Zou came to his mind. Zou is a crafty man and he is on good terms with me, he thought. Whatever unpardonable crime you might perpetrate, if you consult with him, he will find a way of escaping punishment. Why not bid my son to consult him when my son brings food to me?

In awhile Wang Xiao'er, Wang Jia's son, brought food to the prison. Having told his son his plan in detail, Wang Jia added, "If he asks for pay, you must not begrudge him any money, or my life will be finished." Wang Xiao'er went directly to Old Man Zou, told him about his father's condition and asked for his help. "Your father has confessed to the murder," said Zou, "and the magistrate is a new official who personally obtained the confession. Wherever you plead, the result will not be much different from the magistrate's verdict, nor will the magistrate confess he might have made a mistake. Give me two or three hundred *liang* of silver and I'll go to Nanjing. There I'll find a chance to help you." "What plan do you have?" asked Wang Xiao'er. "You needn't worry about that," said Zou. "Simply give me the silver and wait to see what happens. I can't tell you my plans now." Wang Xiao'er went home and returned with three hundred *liang* of silver which he presented at once to Old Man Zou. As Wang Xiao'er urged him to set off for Nanjing immediately, he said, "With this white matter, I'll try to find an opportunity. You may set your fears at rest and wait." Wang Xiao'er thanked him and went home.

That very night Zou got ready and set out for Nanjing. In a few days he arrived. He made inquiries about the Board of Criminal Penalty and found that Mr Xu, the head of Zhejiang Bureau, was hospitable and ready to get around the regulations to accommodate his friends. Zou immediately got a recommendation letter written and, with bumper gifts, visited Mr Xu. Seeing that Zou was talkative, Mr Xu felt he must be a congenial man. After that visit, Zou saw him often and by and by they became intimate friends. One day as Zou was becoming anxious about how to help Wang Jia, twenty pirates were escorted to the Board of Criminal Penalty to be sentenced. When Zou went over and inquired into the matter, he learned there were two culprits from Suzhou. Overjoyed at this he nodded to himself, saying, I've got it now!

Next day he prepared a grand dinner and sent an invitation card to Mr Xu. Before long the dinner was ready and Mr Xu arrived in a sedan chair. Zou greeted him with a smiling face. As they took their seats at the table they exchanged some trifling remarks. They drank until midnight, and then Zou ordered the attendants to retire and presented one hundred *liang* of silver to Mr Xu with both hands. Surprised, Mr Xu asked what this was for. "My relative, Wang, has been framed in a case and is now in the prison of my native county," said Zou, "I beg you to look into his case." "How could I disobey you," said Mr Xu, "if I can do something? But he is in another place and I can find no way to help." "It's easy," said Zou, "Wang had a feud with Li Yi. Now Li Yi has been killed, but the murderer has not been caught. That is why Wang has been wronged and put into prison. I saw twenty pirates were brought to your board yesterday and two of them are natives of Suzhou. You may pressure these two culprits to confess to having committed the murder. This will not worsen their penalty, since they are doomed to die anyway. But my relative Wang will thank you for granting him a new lease of life." Mr Xu agreed to grant his request. He took the silver and carefully put it into his handcase. He then summoned his servant and, having thanked Zou for the dinner, went away in the sedan chair.

Old Man Zou visited the family of the two culprits in secret and, promising them a handsome sum, presented them one hundred *liang* of silver as the first installment of his payment. The pirates agreed to take the blame for the murder. When they were questioned in court, Mr Xu asked them, "How many people have you killed?" They confessed that they killed so-and-so on this-and-that date and that at this-and-that night they broke into Li Yi's house and killed him. Mr Xu committed their confession to paper and put the pirates into prison. Immediately he sorted out the files of this case. Zou had a clerk of the secretariat make a copy of the culprits' confession for the magistrate of Changzhou County. Zou took his leave of Mr Xu, returned to Suzhou with a copy of the confession, and presented it to the magistrate of Changzhou County. After opening the envelope and reading the file, the magistrate concluded that the principal criminals who had killed Li Yi had been confirmed and that Wang Jia had been wronged. As he was going to call Wang Jia from the prison for examination, Wang Xiao'er came to voice his grievance. This strengthened the magistrate's belief. So he immediately had Wang Jia brought from prison and released. Hearing this, Lady Jiang had to admit that she might not have seen the assassin clearly that night and she gave up her lawsuit.

Now Wang Jia, released, went home in proud strides of ecstasy. But no sooner than he stepped inside his gate, than a sudden chilly gale arose. Screaming "Calamity! Here's Brother Li Yi!" he fell down to the ground. No amount of aid could bring him around. Thus he stopped breathing and met his end. As a rhyme says:

Yama is particular about being fair;
A death for a murderer is his rule.
In finding a scapegoat for a culprit,
The crafty Old Man plays the fool.

The above story was about a real murderer mistaken for an innocent man. Now let me tell you a story about an innocent man who, because of a trivial matter, was framed by a base man. But for the Heaven's distinct code he would have been wrongly put to death. Indeed,

Clear and just is Heaven's code:
To punish vile, bless the good.
He who schemes against others
He himself first suffers.

It is related that during the reign of Chenghua [1465-1487] of our [Ming] dynasty in Yongjia County, Wenzhou, Zhejiang Province, there lived a man whose family name was Wang, given name Jie and style name Wenhao. His wife had the name of Liu. The husband and wife had only one two-year-old daughter. He had several servants and maids, but the family was not very rich. Though Wang was a scholar, he had never gone to public school. He taught himself to read books and write at home; sometimes he saw his friends and discussed writings with them. Lady Liu, a genial and devoted wife, was industrious and thrifty in running the household. They lived at peace with each other.

One late spring day a couple of his friends invited Wang to an outing in the outskirts of the town. Seeing the serene nature, Wang was in high spirits. After getting tipsy at the picnic, he returned home. As Wang approached his gate, he saw two servants quarreling with a man with a basket in his hand. The man turned out to be a native of Huzhou by the name of Lu, a seller of ginger. He was arguing with the servants over the price.

As soon as Wang learned the cause for the brawl, he said to the man, "This is not a low price, why are you making such a row about it? You are too unreasonable." The man, who was obviously a straightforward chap, retorted, "I am a petty merchant with a small capital. Why do you want to underpay me? Be broad-minded and not so mean, master, please." Wang, still tipsy, was enraged by this response. "Where are you from, old ass?" he berated him, "How dare you be so insolent as to talk back to me?" He rushed forward, hit him repeatedly with his fist and then gave him a violent shove. He did not realize that the middle-aged man had phlegm-fire*. The push caused the man to fall and lose his consciousness.

---

*Phlegm-fire, a term of traditional Chinese Medicine, usually referring to cases of asthma, mental disturbances such a hysteria, mania, etc. In this story it refers to a shock due to temporary insufficient blood supply in the brain.

The last thing a person should do is lose his temper. Bargaining in such petty business is, after all, a matter of no consequence, for what was at stake was merely one or two coins. Depending on the power of their masters, servants of influential families tend to bully ordinary people on the slightest provocation. When they cause disaster, they bring disgrace on their masters. That's why decent families always discipline their servants. Because Wang lost his temper and struck the man, he was to suffer a great deal for such uncalled-for folly, as the reader will see in the development of this story.

Seeing the man fall in a coma, Wang panicked and his drunkenness disappeared. He had the man brought into the house and laid on a bed. Then he poured some tea down the man's throat. After awhile the man came to. Wang apologized, treated him to food and drink, and gave him a bolt of white silk to cover the expenses for his recuperation. The man eventually cheered up. With "thanks," he left for the ferry. — If Wang could have foreseen what would happen next, he would have rushed forward and held the man back by the waist and nursed him at his home for half a year or two months. In this way he would have avoided disaster. — To let the man leave was as if Wang himself

> Cast a golden-stringed net
> To catch a confusion of truth and falsehood.

Having seen the man off, Wang still felt his heart wildly pounding. Entering the house, he said to his wife, "Thank Heaven! I almost got into big trouble," he said. It was late at night. The wife told a maid to serve dishes and warm wine to help Wang get over his shock. He had drunk only a few cups when he heard an impatient burst of knocks at the front gate. Wang , startled, picked up a lantern and went to answer the door. The man at the gate was Zhou the Fourth, the boat owner from the ferry. With a bolt of white silk and a bamboo basket in hand, Zhou the Fourth hurried in. "A disaster for you, sir," he said to Wang,

"Why did you commit murder?" Blood drained from his face as Wang asked him what he was talking about. The boat owner asked, "Can you recognize this white silk and basket?" Wang looked at the silk and basket and replied, "A ginger-seller from Huzhou came to my house today. The silk is my present to him and the basket is the container of his ginger. How come they have ended up in your hands?" The ship owner said, "This afternoon a man from Huzhou named Lü wanted me to ferry him cross the river, but when he got into my boat, he suddenly had an attack of phlegm-fire and was dying. He told me that you had been beaten him and handed me the white silk and basket as proof. He asked me to lodge a lawsuit on his behalf and go to Huzhou and report it to his family so that his relatives could come and voice his grievance. After that he shut his eyes and died. His body is still on my boat, which is now near your gate. You may go and have a look if you like, so you can decide what to do."

Wang was struck dumb with fear. His limbs went numb and his heart throbbed wildly like a hopping deerlet. Bracing himself he asked, "How can that be possible?" But when the servant he sent in secret to check out the boat reported back that he saw a body, Wang was quite frightened. Running into his house in panic he told his wife about this. "What can we do?" asked Lady Liu. "It's no use talking now," said Wang. "The only way out is to pay off the boat owner and beg him to dispose of the body this very night."

Wang carried a packet of silver pieces that weighed about twenty *liang* or so in his sleeve and came out. "Please keep quiet, master," he said to the boat owner. "Let me talk it over with you. I was to blame for what happened, but I didn't do it on purpose. You and I are fellow Wenzhou natives and we should cherish our friendship as such. Why should you seek revenge for a stranger? And if you do it, what good it will do you? It's better that you keep your mouth shut and let me pay you. You can dispose of the body somewhere on this dark night. Who will know?" "Where can I dispose of it?" asked the boat owner. "If someone finds it tomorrow and investigates, I'll get involved." Wang replied, "A few *li* from here is the grave of my deceased father. It is in a secluded place, and you probably know it. I suggest you take the body over and bury it there. Neither a human nor the devil will see." "You are right," said Zhou the Fourth, "but how will you thank me?" Wang presented him with the silver from his sleeve. The boat owner, however, was hard to please. "Is a life worth so little?" he said. "That he happened to have died in my boat means a small fortune for me. I won't settle for less than one hundred *liang*." Eager to get over the crisis, Wang dared not argue. He nodded and went in. After a while he brought out some silver, clothes and hair ornaments. Presenting them to Zhou the Fourth, he said, "These, I suppose, are worth about sixty *liang* of silver. I am poor and hope you are magnanimous enough to take them." The sight of the money softened Zhou the Fourth's tone, "All right. Let me have them. You are a scholar and so long as you can look after me from time to time, I will not be too exacting."

Wang was in a desperate situation. As the saying goes, "When the man you plead with nods, your luck is in." For the time being he was a little relieved. Having a table set, he invited the boat owner to dinner. Then he ordered two servants to find spades and pickaxes. One of the servants was surnamed Hu, and because he was vicious and rather strong, he was nicknamed Tiger Hu. Tiger Hu and the other servant got ready in no time, got into the boat and set out for the graveyard. There they dug a hole in a clearance and buried the body. After that, they returned by the same boat. This took them the whole night. As the day glimmered in the east. Wang treated the boat owner to breakfast. When he departed, Wang had his servants to close the door and they all retired.

Wang went into his room and told Liu, "I am a decent person from a respectable family. Never could I have imagined I would be subject to extortion by a villain." With this, tears streamed down his cheeks. The lady comforted him saying, "Maybe you were predestined to such a fright and loss of wealth. Don't you be too annoyed. Thank Heaven, we are safe now. You were busy throughout the night, please take a rest." She then ordered some food for Wang and they all went to rest. Of this we will say no more.

A few days later Wang decided the crisis was over. He bought some sacrificial offerings and presented them to the deities and his ancestors. Zhou the Fourth from time to time came to "see" him. Every time he came, he was accorded hospitably because Wang dared not offend him. If he wanted to "borrow" something, Wang was ready to "lend" it. With this, Zhou the Fourth grew quite well off. He sold his boat and opened a shop. After that nothing happened between them.

Know, gentle readers, that Wang was, after all, a scholar and knew little of the world's ways. When he paid off the boat owner in order to hide the body in the graveyard, he should have piled up some firewood and burned it instead, so that the body could not be found again and he would be free from any trouble. Because he lacked the good sense to do so, he failed to stamp out the source of his misfortune and, in due time, the evil root sprouted.

As the old saying goes: "Frost only bites the rootless grass and misfortune only befalls unlucky people." A year later Wang's three-year daughter contracted smallpox. He prayed to the gods and consulted fortune-tellers and doctors, but none of these produced a cure. The daughter was the couple's only child, whom they adored dearly. Wang and his wife shed tears all day beside their bed-ridden child. One day a relative came with a gift to see the child. Wang received him, offered him tea and told him that his daughter had smallpox and might be dying. The relative said, "There is a pediatrician named Feng in our county who has the skill to snatch the dying from the jaws of death. He lives thirty *li* from here. Why not send for him?" "Right! I'll do as you suggest," said Wang. It was getting dark, so he invited the relative for dinner before he left. Wang then told his wife about this and, having written an invitation card, summoned Tiger Hu that very night. "Set off before daybreak with this invitation card," he instructed the servant, "and invite Doctor Feng to come to see my child as soon as possible. I will prepare lunch and be waiting for you." Tiger Hu left with the order and the night passed.

The next day Wang prepared lunch, but by late afternoon the doctor did not turn up. On the third day he found his daughter's condition worsening. By midnight she breathed out without inhaling and after awhile left her parents for the domain of Yama. Wang and his wife swooned crying over the loss of their treasure. They encoffined her body in a most elaborate fashion and cremated it. At noon the ensuing day Tiger Hu returned. "Doctor Feng is not in," he reported. "I waited for him for half a day, that's why I have come back late." "It seems that my daughter was doomed to come to such an end," said Wang. "Don't mention it any more."

Days later Hu's fellow workers leaked the truth that Tiger Hu had lost the invitation card because he got drunk on the way. That was why he hadn't returned until the next day and why he had fabricated such a lie. Wang became enraged. Calling Tiger Hu in he snatched up a split bamboo pole and intended to strike him with it. "I haven't killed a man," Tiger Hu sneered, "why should you be so furious?" Maddened by this remark, Wang had servants haul Tiger Hu away and beat him fifty times at one stretch.

Tiger Hu, bruised and lacerated, limped to his room. "Why should I have to swallow humble pie?" he said in resentment. "Your daughter was taken away by smallpox, not by me. Yet you gave me such a cruel flogging! Damn it!" Then he thought to himself, I've got it! Don't I have a hold on him? Let me nurse my wounds and then I'll show him my resources. Let me see if the bucket falls in the well or the other way around. But I mustn't let him become suspicious of me at present. Indeed

In adversity the slave can bully the master;
In misfortune the devil can cheat the man.

Let me put Tiger Hu, who harbored an evil plot, aside for the moment and turn back to Wang. A month or so after the death of his daughter, some relatives and friends came with food and wine to comfort him. Gradually he got over his grief. One day as he was taking a stroll in the courtyard, a group of policemen broke in and, without offering an explanation, put ropes and iron chains around his neck. Taken aback, Wang asked, "I am a Confucian student, why should you treat me like this?" The policemen spit at him, saying, "What a Confucian scholar! The magistrate may make a mistake but the police cannot. You can explain yourself before his lordship." Hearing this, Lady Liu and the maid servants, all at a loss as to what to do, stared at the men but dared not step forward and intervene.

Overwhelmed by the policemen who were as ferocious as wolves and tigers, Wang was dragged to the court of Yongjia County. As he went down on his knees to the right of the judge, a plaintiff was kneeling on the left. As he raised his head to look at his accuser, he found him to be none other than his servant Tiger Hu. He realized then that it was Tiger Hu who harbored such resentment against him that he had reported him to the authorities. "Tiger Hu has accused you of the murder of a Huzhou native by the name of Lü," said Ming Shizuo, the magistrate of the county. "How do you explain this?" "Oh, my fair lord," replied Wang, "don't believe his lies. Just consider how a feeble scholar like me could kill a man? Tiger Hu is a servant in my house. The other day I punished him severely for a fault he committed. He nurses a hatred for me and for this he has trumped up this case. I wish my lordship would clear this up." Tiger Hu kowtowed, saying "Oh, my wise and upright lordship, don't believe his one-sided explanation. It is only natural for a master to flog his servant. How could I nurse a deep hatred? The body is now on the left side of the tomb. I beg my lord to send somebody there to dig for it. If a body is found there, my accusation is justified; if not, my accusation is false. If a body is not found there, I will admit to an offense of malicious accusation."

Accordingly the magistrate sent some runners to dig for the body. Tiger Hu pointed out the spot and size. After awhile the body was dug up and carried into the court. The magistrate went over and examined it himself. "There is really a body," he said. "How do you explain this?" He was going to have Wang tortured when Wang pleaded, "Oh, my lord, listen to me. The body is rotten and therefore the dead man could not have been killed recently. If I killed a man a long time ago, why hasn't someone testified against me until today? It is obvious that Tiger Hu has framed the case with a body he found somewhere." "Sounds reasonable," said the magistrate. But Tiger Hu then said, "The body is that of a man who was beaten to death a year ago. I have not been able to steel my heart to inform against him because he is my master. Besides, a servant who accuses his master is an offense in itself. That's why I didn't report him until today. I never expected that my master would refuse to mend his ways. I had no alternative but to tell you what had happened, for fear that if he did something stupid once again, I would be implicated. If my lord does not believe me, please call in the neighbors and ask them if a man was not beaten to death on a certain day last year. This will expel all doubts." The magistrate summoned the neighbors as Tiger Hu proposed. When they had come, the magistrate asked them one by one. They all said that on this-and-that day last year a ginger-seller was beaten badly in Wang's house, and that although the man had regained consciousness after first-aid was administered, they did not know what happened to him later on.

Facing these witnesses Wang turned pale and began hemming and hawing. "The crime is confirmed," said the magistrate. "What else can you say about this? I don't think he will confess if he is not tortured." Pulling out a bamboo slip as a warrant, he shouted, "Torture him!"

The yamen runners, roaring, slung Wang to the ground and beat him twenty times. Unable to withstand the pain, the poor, weak scholar had to admit to the murder. After the confession was committed to paper, the magistrate said, "The man was killed, but no relatives of his have come to demand punishment for the felony. So the case is not concluded yet. Let's put Wang in prison. Only when someone comes to claim the body can he be sentenced." Thus Wang was put into prison and the body was buried again. The magistrate ordered that the body not be burned so that it could be examined later. As the witnesses were dismissed, the magistrate retired. Having worked off his hatred, Tiger Hu was complacent. Daring not to return to see his mistress, he moved away.

On hearing from the county court the news that their master had been put in prison, Wang's servants blanched to the ears with fear. Rushing back they reported this to Lady Liu, who, uttering a cry, as if her spirit had been snatched away, collapsed to the ground.

Before you knew if she was alive,
She lay, limbs motionless.

The maid servants were unnerved, and they cried in desperation to awaken her. By and by she came to. With a "My lord!" she broke out in a wail that lasted half a day. Then she dressed herself in black, put together some silver pieces in a hurry, and carried them with her. Having a boy servant leading the way, she proceeded to the prison of Yongjia County with a maid. Seeing each other, the husband and wife were choked up with tears. "It is the villain Tiger Hu," cried Wang, "that did this harm to me." Liu cursed Tiger Hu between clenched teeth. Then, taking out the silver, she gave it to Wang saying, "You may distribute this silver among the prison guards and jailers and ask them to look after you so that you will not suffer from too much torment." Wang took the silver. As it had by now turned dark, Liu took her leave. All the way home she wept. She ate something at hand as supper and went to bed in a gloomy mood. Remembering that the night before she had slept with her husband but that today an unexpected disaster had torn them apart, she cried once again until she fell asleep dolefully. So much about her.

Wang was not scourged in the prison since he had greased the hands of the jailers and prison guards with silver. But in the company of prisoners with disheveled hair, he was far from being happy. Furthermore, he still did not know what sentence awaited him. Although clothes and food were brought to him from time to time, he suffered from hunger and cold now and then. His health waned. The lady tried to bail him out by bribery, but nobody dared set a murder suspect free. So Wang had to stay in jail.

Time flew like an arrow and months and days came and went like shuttles. Half a year had elapsed since the day Wang was jailed. Due to his worries and the hard living conditions, Wang contracted a serious disease. Lady Liu consulted doctors and tried different kinds medicines, but all her efforts were to no avail. It seemed that Wang was dying. One day Wang said to the servant who had brought him food, "Please tell the mistress that I am critically ill with a disease that refuses to go, and I will die soon. Let her come at once and I will bid her a final good-bye." When the servant reported this to the lady, she shivered in fear. Without a minute's delay she hired a sedan chair and dashed to the county prison. When the jail was only a few steps away, she got down from the sedan and went in. Needless to say, tears were gushing from her eyes when she saw Wang. "Your foolish husband is good for nothing," said Wang. "By killing a person by accident I've been shackled and brought disgrace upon you, my virtuous wife. My illness is going from bad to worse. I won't regret dying now that I have seen you. But even in the nether world I will not let that villain Tiger Hu off easily!" "Don't say that," his wife said. "Don't make such ill-boding remarks. Please take it easy and nurse yourself through the illness. Since you didn't kill the person on purpose and nobody has claimed the body, I'll try to get you out of here even if I have to sell all our fields and the estate. Then we can reunite. Heaven will not spare the disloyal slave Tiger Hu. One day we'll get our revenge. You shouldn't worry too much about it at present." "With a caring wife like you working hard to save me, I feel better. But I am afraid my infirm body cannot hold out for long." Liu comforted him and took her leave in tears. At home she sat cheerless and alone in her room while her servants were playing cards in front of the house. Thereupon an elderly man entered the courtyard carrying a box on either end of a pole over his shoulder. Putting down his load, he asked the servants, "Is your master home?" The arrival of this man was to enable the wronged scholar to receive a fair judgment and the vicious schemers to be brought to justice. This is described in the following lines:

> As the boat owner had caused a distress
> A merchant came in time from afar
> Who concluded a framed case for a scholar
> And showed the ascending blest star!

When the servants took a closer look at the newcomer, they scurried in all directions, shouting, "Phantom! Phantom!" Can you guess who the newcomer was? He was the ginger-seller from Huzhou by the name of Lü, who had come the year before. Seizing a servant he said, "I've come to see your master. Why do you say I am a phantom?" Hearing the clamor in the courtyard, Lady Liu went out. Lü walked up to her and with a greeting he said, "Listen, Madam, I am Lü, the ginger-seller from Huzhou. Last year the master entertained me with a dinner and presented me with some white silk. For this I am grateful to him. After I left you, I returned to Huzhou and in the last one and half years have engaged in trade elsewhere. Now I have come all the way to see you with some native products as a gift for the master, but I don't know why your honorable ladies and gentlemen say I am a phantom?" A servant shouted, "Don't believe him, Madam! He must have heard that you are trying to get the master out of prison and so he has emerged to claim the debt for his life." The lady hushed the servant down and said to the guest, "So you are not a phantom. But you have wrecked my husband!" Aghast at what he had heard, the guest asked, "Where is your husband, and how come I have wrecked him?" The Lady told him how Zhou the Fourth had carried a body to the house and showed them the silk and basket as proof, how her husband had paid off the boat owner and had the body buried, how Tiger Hu had brought the master to court, and how her husband had been forced to admit to a murder.

Hearing this, Lü beat his chest, saying, "How pitiable! Why should there be such a wrong in the world? When I left you and got on the ferry, the boatman saw the white silk and asked me where I had gotten it. I should not have told him how the master had beaten me to the brink of death and then treated me to dinner and given me the present. The boat owner offered to buy the white silk. I agreed when I saw that he offered a good price. Then he asked me for the basket and I gave it to him in lieu of the ferry fare. I never realized that with my things he could work out such a heartless plot. I'm to blame for the master's misery because I should have come earlier." "But for your coming," said the lady, "even I myself wouldn't know my husband was falsely charged. The silk and basket were taken by the boat man through trickery, but from where came the corpse?" Lü thought for awhile and said, "Yes, I see. When I talked with him on the boat, there was a body floating near the bank. I saw him watching it, but I didn't realize that a scheme was forming in his mind then and there. He is really outrageous! Now we must lose no time. Please accept my gifts. Then let's go to Yongjia County to lodge our complaint and get the master out of jail. This is the best way." Liu accepted the suggestion. Putting away the boxes of gifts, Lady Liu gave a dinner for her guest.

As the daughter of a scholar, she was good at writing. So she didn't need to ask help from a pettifogger. Having written the petition herself, she hired a sedan chair and arrived at the Yongjia County court with Lü and some servants. They waited for awhile until the magistrate began his afternoon session. Shouting her grievances, Lady Liu and Lü Da submitted the petition. Having read it from beginning to end, the magistrate summoned Liu first. Liu gave a detailed account of how her husband had beaten a ginger-seller because of a dispute over the price, how the boat owner had extorted a sum of money by carrying a corpse to her house, and how a resentful servant had denounced her husband. "I didn't know my husband had been wronged until the ginger-seller revisited us today," she added. Then the magistrate summoned Lü for questioning. Lü retold his story from beginning to end — of how he had been beaten and how he had sold his silk. "Has Lady Liu bribed you to give this testimony?" the magistrate asked with suspicion. Kowtowing, Lü said, "My lord, I am a native of Huzhou, but I have done business here for years so many people here know me. How could I fool Your Lordship? If I had been dying on the boat, why wouldn't I have asked the boatman to call on one of my friends so that he could take revenge for me, instead of entrusting my life to a strange boat owner? Even if we take it as an explanation that in the critical moment I had no time to do this and that I had died, why have none of my relatives in Huzhou, having not seen me back home for a long time, come and ask about me? If they had found that I had been beaten to death, they would have reported it to the authorities immediately. Why would a servant of Wang be the first to report this after an entire year had passed? I came here today and only a short while ago did I learn of this case of injustice. Although Wang Jie was not framed by me, his misery began with me. I cannot bear to see him wronged in this way, so I am here to request exoneration on his behalf. I beg that with Your Lordship's fair judgment his life will be spared."

"If you really have friends here," said the magistrate, "tell me their names." Counting on his fingers, Lü named ten or so people. Committing them to paper, the magistrate selected four from the end of the list. He summoned two runners and told them, "Secretly bring the four together with the neighbors who served as witnesses the other time." The runners went to carry out his order.

After awhile the two parties were brought to the court. Seeing Lü Da in the distance, his four friends said with one voice, "Isn't that Brother Lü Da from Huzhou? How can he be here? He must not have died last year." Then the magistrate brought in the neighbors. They exclaimed, "Are we seeing an illusion? We saw with our own eyes that this ginger-seller was beaten to death at Wang's place. Was he brought back to consciousness, or is this a look-alike?" One of them affirmed, "There cannot be such an exact look-alike! I never forget a man I have seen once. I am certain this is the ginger-seller. There is no mistake!" By then the magistrate was close to a full understanding of the true events. He accepted the petition and told the neighbors and Lu's friends, "You mustn't let anyone know about this when you leave, or I'll punish you severely." With "Yeses!" they departed. Accordingly the magistrate ordered some runners: "Go to Zhou the Fourth, the boat owner, in secret and cajole him into coming here with sweet words. You mustn't tell him the truth. The accuser Tiger Hu has a guarantor. Bring these two here tomorrow afternoon for interrogation." Having received the order, the runners each went his way. The magistrate then bade Lady Liu and Lü to return the next afternoon. With kowtows they left.

The lady then took Lü Da to the prison to see Wang and tell him what had happened. Wang was overjoyed and, as if inspired by superhuman wisdom or nurtured with divine dewdrops, he felt that his illness was almost gone. "I have been blaming Tiger Hu, but I didn't know the boat owner was so wicked. But for this visitor, I would never have known that I had been wronged."

The lady said good-bye to her husband, went out of the county yamen and made directly for home in the sedan chair, with Lü Da and her servants tagging along. As she entered her house, she ordered the servants to keep the guest company at supper and put him up in the sitting room. On the afternoon of the next day the two of them came to the county court where the magistrate had already begun to handle cases.

In awhile Zhou the Fourth was brought in by two runners. With the silver he had extorted from Wang, he had opened a cloth shop in the county town. The policemen had told him, "The magistrate wanted to buy some cloth," as they had been instructed, and thus fooled him into appearing in court. Maybe it was his lot that his plot would come to light. When he raised his head and caught sight of Lü Da, he blushed all over his neck. "Master," cried Lü Da, "has your business been brisk since you bought the white silk and basket from me?" Zhou the Fourth said nothing and his face turned ashened. In no time Tiger Hu was brought in as well. He had moved to somewhere else. But it happened that he had just returned to the county town that day to see a relative and bumped into the runners. The latter told him a lie. They said, "The relative of the dead man has come to claim the body. As soon as the accuser gets there, the case will be concluded. We have been looking for you everywhere." An unsuspecting Tiger Hu gladly followed the runners to the court where he knelt down. Pointing to Lü Da, the magistrate asked him, "Do you know this man?" Tiger Hu was shocked when he took a close look at the man. He was so perplexed he could not find his tongue.

The magistrate clearly discerned the changes of the expressions on the faces of Zhou the Fourth and Tiger Hu. Pointing to Tiger Hu he reprimanded him, "You heartless and ungrateful slave! How did your master ill treat you so that you went so far as to conspire with the boat owner, finding the body and trump up the false accusation?" "My master did kill a man," replied Tiger Hu, "what I said is the truth." "How dare you, talking back like that!" the magistrate flared. "If Lü

Da is dead, who is the man kneeling in this court?" And he ordered the runners to torture Tiger Hu by cramping. "Own up to your scheme before it's too late!" In torment, Tiger Hu screamed in pain. "My lord," he said, "I'd plead guilty of falsely charging my master because I hated him, but I'd rather die than admit that I am an accomplice. My master knocked Lü Da down, and at once brought him back to consciousness with soup. Then he treated him to dinner and gave him white silk before he left for the ferry. At about the second watch that night Zhou the Fourth carried the corpse to the gate and produced the white silk and basket as evidence. All the family believed him. The master paid off the boat owner. The boat owner and I carried the corpse to the graveyard and buried it there. Later on, as the master inflicted a severe flogging on me, I began to nurse a grudge against him and so I came to my lord to denounce him. I really didn't know if the corpse belonged to the ginger-seller or not. If Lü hadn't come today, even I wouldn't know my master had been wronged. As for where the body came from, you will have to inquire of the boat owner about that."

After his statement was recorded on paper, the magistrate ordered him to leave the room and summoned in Zhou the Fourth. At first Zhou the Fourth hemmed and hawed, but as he was confronted with Lü Da and tortured, he had to admit all he had done. He said, "On that day last year Lü Da got on my boat with some white silk. As I happened to ask him from where he had come, I learned that he had gotten a punch. Just then I saw a corpse floating near the bank, so a plan to extort money from Wang formed in my mind. I bought the white silk and cheated him out of his basket. Then I fished the body out of the water and put it on my boat. When I went to Wang's house, he believed me right away. In this way I got the silver and buried the body in a graveyard. That is the truth and there is nothing false."

"This may be true," said the magistrate, "but there is something fishy about your story. From where had the body floated and how could it look like Lü Da? Maybe you had killed a man somewhere else." "No, my lord!" cried Zhou the Fourth, "If I wanted to kill someone, why didn't I kill Lü Da? It was the corpse in the stream that gave me the idea to buy the silk and basket. I was not sure if Wang would believe me, because the dead man did not look like Lü Da. But I was able to take advantage of Wang for several reasons: first, he had a guilty conscience; second, he had seen Lü Da only once by lamplight, and at dim dusk a body might not been seen clearly; and third, the white silk and bamboo basket were things Wang knew the ginger-seller had. So I plucked up my courage to cheat him. I did not expect that he could be taken in so easily and nobody discovered the falsehood. As for the body, I thought it must be that of a man who had fallen in the water by accident. I really don't know who he was." Thereupon Lü Da reported, kneeling, "When I came across the river, I saw a body drifting in water. What he says is true." This, too, was committed to paper by the magistrate.

"My intention was, my lord," entreated Zhou the Fourth, "to extort money from Wang, but not to frame a false accusation against him. I beg my lord's clemency." "You callous villain!" shouted the magistrate, "Because of your greed for money, you have almost torn his family apart. You must have done harm to many others with such tricks. I'll rid the Yongjia people of a pest like you. The ungrateful servant Tiger Hu brought an unwarranted charge against his master. This hateful wretch should receive a severe punishment." The magistrate ordered that Tiger Hu be flogged forty times and Zhou the Fourth be flogged until he stopped breathing. Because Tiger Hu had not yet recovered from a fever and also because Heaven would not pardon an ungrateful slave, he died in the court before he had been flogged the full forty times. Zhou the Fourth did not lose consciousness until he was flogged seventy times. Thus both villains died under the thrashing.

The magistrate then ordered their relatives to come and claim the bodies. Wang was released from prison right away. Cloth confiscated from Zhou the Fourth's shop was evaluated at a hundred *liang* of silver or so. This was what had been cheated from Wang and, according to regulations, confiscated. But considering that Wang, as a scholar, had been in prison for a long time and because of the false charge, the spoils were returned to their former owner as a token of the kindness of the magistrate. The body dug up from near the tomb of Wang's forefathers was carefully examined, and sand was found under its nails. This proved that the man had fallen into the water by accident. As no relative came to claim the body, the magistrate had the coroner bury it in the mass graveyard.

Wang and the other two thanked the magistrate and went home. Holding each other, he and his wife Liu cried bitterly. Then he came to the courtyard and saluted Lü. Lü and Wang expressed apologies and gratitude to each other, Lü for causing Wang's misfortune and Wang for the help Lü had offered in clearing up the frame-up. As an old saying goes, "Out of blows friendship grows." Wang and Lü later became close friends and kept in close contact. Wang became much tempered. Even to a beggar, he was amiable. Thinking of his experiences, he made up his mind to wipe out the disgrace by making progress in his social status. He shut himself up in his studio for a decade until he became a *jinshi*.

From this story one can see that people in power must not regard human life as a trifling matter. In the case of Wang, only the boat owner knew the truth. Had the ginger-seller not come to Wenzhou, Wang's servants would not have known their master was wronged, neither Wang's wife nor Wang himself would not have known it. Besides, can every fabricated charge be cleared up in court? Kind-hearted gentlemen, take a lesson from this!

Tale 8

Zhao the Sixth Dies at the Hand of His Pampered Son; Magistrate Zhang Punishes the Evil with an Irrevocable Death Verdict

Know, gentle reader, that the ultimate good in the world is filial piety. The parents exercise unbelievably painstaking care in breast-feeding a child for three years and bringing it up. In doing so they worry day and night, fearing that the child may contract an illness or be wounded. And as they expect the child to become clever and capable, they spare no effort or care in cultivating his abilities as he grows up. As an ancient song puts it:

> *I pine for my parents far away*
> *Who with pain gave birth to me!*
> ....
> *Their kindness I should repay*
> *Is boundless as the sky!*

Speaking of this, none in the world could repay even one thousandth of their debt of kindness to their parents — neither the man who caught a fish to feed his mother by melting the ice with his body temperature on a winter day; nor the man who cried over bamboo until a bamboo shoot, with which he served his mother, grew; nor the filial son who swung a fan for his parents in summer and warmed the quilt for his parents in winter.* As for those who enjoy delicacies in food and clothing themselves, but leave their parents in hunger and cold, treating them as strangers or worse, as enemies, their behavior, devoid of human nature and moral considerations, is baser than that of beasts!

Now I will tell a story of an unfilial son. You may have never heard of such a story in the past, nor in recent years. During the Reign of Zhengde [AD 1506-1521] a wealthy man named Yan and his wife of Songjiang [present-day Shanghai] had no child when they had reached their thirties. Whenever they prayed to gods or to the Buddha, they supplicated for the birth of a son. One night when Yan's wife was half dreaming she heard a voice in the air above, saying:

> For a son you plead,
> But one ear is in need.
> More heads in the house;
> Less teeth in the mouth.

She distinctly heard these words. The next day she told Mr Yan about this, but they could not decipher their meaning. Soon afterwards the wife felt something queer in her eyes, her breasts grew and her belly swelled. After ten hard months of pregnancy, she gave birth to a boy, who was delicate-featured. The couple was overjoyed. After that nothing in the world mattered except for the easy and fast growth of the boy.

By and by three years passed and the boy turned out to be clever

---

*These refer to anecdotes about filial sons.

and lovely. The couple was obedient to the boy and complied with all his whims. If the boy wished it, they would have climbed to the clouds to pick the stars or dived into the river to fetch the moon mirrored in water, let alone giving him everyday objects. There are too many such stories to tell. As the saying goes, "A rod-disciplined son is filial; a spoiled child is disobedient". Overindulged by Yan and his wife, the child looked down his nose at everybody as he grew up. But because he had plenty of money, he made friends with the cruel and crafty runners in the yamen, and most people were inclined to flatter him and nobody gave him a tit for tat. Besides, he was addicted to gambling and most of his close associates were wizards at that trade. Other gamblers fawned on him just because of his generous pocket, so they baited him by honeyed words. He, on other hand, believing that they really liked him and took sides with him, became quite free with his hand in die-casting. Thus, by and by, uncounted amounts of yellow gold and white silver drained away from him. Mr Yan often pleaded with his son against doing this, but as he was indulgent and the son grew impatient before he had finished even a few sentences, he had to give up. The family wealth, however, was not limitless. In three years it ran out.

Mr Yan had accumulated the family fortune bit by bit. Now seeing the decline of his family fortune he felt his heart bleeding. One day he went out on some business and, as he walked by a casino, he saw many people gathered there. As he approached, he saw that they were demanding payment of the debts his son owed in gambling. Unable to clear himself, the helpless boy was being pushed and shoved. Fearing that his son might be injured, Mr Yan elbowed his way through the crowd and sheltered his son with his own body. He said to the people there, "Your old servant will pay the money on his behalf, brothers. Please return to your homes. I will deliver what he owes you at your house tomorrow." With this, he angrily dragged his son home. He bolted the door to cut off the retreat, grabbed his son by hair and, trying to harden his heart, intended to beat him. The son struggled away. As Mr Yan tried to catch him again and hold him firmly, the son turned around and landed a fist in his father's face. Immediately the old man saw sparks around him and he fell down unconscious. The son was frightened. As he reached out his hands to support the old man, he found that two of his father's incisors had fallen out and that blood was streaking down his chest. The son, realizing that he had caused a disaster, took to his heels.

After a long while, Mr Yan came to. With resentment he said, "I've spent a life of thrift, but my unfilial son has wasted all the family fortune and has almost killed me. Why should I have such a brute in my house!" He directly went to the yamen of the prefect, just as the prefect was convening court. Mr Yan lodged a complaint against his unfilial son and presented the teeth that had been knocked out by his son as evidence. Having placed the script on file for investigation the prefect retired, and the old man returned home.

Then one of the best friends of Mr Yan's son, a person by the name of Qiu San, a crafty yamen clerk, saw that the prefect had accepted the script. He hurried off to report this to Mr Yan's son. As the frightened youth entreated him for help, Qiu pretended to be in a dilemma. The young man said, "I have brought with me three *liang* of silver for gambling. Please take it as a gift. But you must find a way to save my life." Qiu feigned hesitation for awhile before he told the young man, "It's too late to do anything today. Meet me in front of the prefect yamen tomorrow morning and I'll tell you what to do." The young man agreed and went away.

Mr Yan's son and Qiu met in front of the prefecture seat the next morning. The son impatiently asked him, "With what stratagem will you help me? Please help me quickly." Qiu gestured him to a secluded corner. "Come here," he said. "I'll tell you what to do." The son placed his ear close to Qiu's mouth waiting for his word, and then at the sound of a crunch he yelled "ouch!" and covered his ear with his hand. "I implored you for help," he said. "Why have you have bitten my ear off? I won't leave the matter at this!" Qiu sneered. "Is your ear so dear to you and your good man's teeth worthless?" he replied. "Take it easy. Just do this and this and you will be safe." Hearing his words, Mr Yan's son said, "A great idea indeed! Though I suffered a bit, my life will be spared."

In awhile the prefect began to handle cases. Mr Yan's son was brought in. "How unfilial you are!" the prefect rebuked him. "You indulged in gambling but you refused to accept your father's admonishment and even knocked out his teeth! How can you explain that away?" Mr Yan's son replied, tearfully, "Oh, my just-minded lord! How dare I defy propriety? The truth is that the other day I happened to pass by a casino, when I stopped to have a look. I didn't realize that my father was approaching. He suspected that I, too, was involved in gambling, and so he dragged me home and scourged me. As I could not sustain the pain, I straightened my neck. Thereupon my father gave me a vehement bite and tore away my ear. He is old and his teeth are not firm. In his fit of anger he exerted too much effort and so his teeth fell out. How could I have knocked out his teeth? I entreat my lord to clear this up." As the prefect looked closely at him, he found that there was indeed a part missing from one of his ears and the signs of teeth marks could be clearly seen with congealed blood. So the prefect believed his account. "What he said sounds true," he smiled. "I needn't question him further. He aroused suspicion by watching gambling and his father lost his teeth. Spank him ten times and then expel him, and no more processing will be necessary."

Rejoicing that his life had been spared, the son returned home and pleaded with his parents for forgiveness. "I am willing to amend my ways and wait on you," he said. "I have been punished by the authorities. Now I am ready to accept any punishment my father will inflict on me." Mr Yan had in a fury reported his son to the authorities the day before. Now a night had passed and, as he saw his son had been punished by the authorities and was imploring for mercy, his heart softened. The old couple always had a weak spot for their son. Now they recalled that when the mother was pregnant, she had heard a voice in a dream, saying, "For a son you plead, / But one ear is in need. / More heads in the house; / Less teeth in the mouth." "Now that the father lost teeth and the son lost an ear," they said, "the prediction has come true. This must be predestination. So we shouldn't complain about anything." After that the son fulfilled his filial duty to his parents. Later he died a natural death at the end of a peaceful life. This proves that Heaven pardons those who mend their ways.

Now let me tell you a story of another unfilial son who was steeped in all kinds of unfilial behavior, but refused to mend his ways and thus received retribution from Heaven.

In such-and-such a dynasty, a man whose family name was Zhao lived in a certain county of a certain prefecture. He was the sixth among many brothers, and for this he was called Zhao the Sixth. His family enjoyed a good reputation and possessed abundant wealth. He and his wife had one son who had just been weaned. They loved the child as their hearts or flesh on their bodies. Before the child was born, they had prayed to many gods, promising contributions to the temples if the gods would grant them a son. This alone used an untold amount of money. When the child was three years old, he contracted smallpox. The couple nursed him through many a sleepless night. They went everywhere to see renowned doctors and to look for efficacious recipes. So long as the child could be safe, they would gladly do anything, even give their own lives! After a time of fear and trepidation, the smallpox was cured. They felt great joy, as if they had found a brilliant illuminating pearl in a dark night. They took good care of the child until he recovered. In doing so, innumerable medicines were used, immeasurable pains were taken and uncountable money was spent.

When the child was six or seven years old, they hired a reliable and renowned teacher for him. On a chosen auspicious date they held a ceremony for their son to meet the tutor, who gave the child a formal name, Zhao Cong. At first Zhao Cong learned primary textbooks such as *The Poems for Child Prodigies* and *Thousand Poets' Poems* and later he studied the *Great Learning*. Zhao the Sixth and his wife were afraid that their son would work too hard or that if the tutor was too strict their son would contract illness. Every day they would let the child retire before he had finished reading a few lines. Zhao Cong was quite quick in comprehending the parents' concern. He often feigned illness to shirk work. The parents, however, were compliant. Seeing this, the teacher said nothing, but he thought to himself, this is love of animals towards their offspring! It will only ruin the child. Once this becomes a bad habit, it will be too late to repent! The tutor nevertheless took an indifferent attitude and never interfered with the arrangement of the master.

After about half a year, the Yin family sent a match-maker to propose a marriage. The Yins were an official family. Their father had once taken the post of prefect. Eager to claim kinship with a family of higher position, Zhao the Sixth begged the match-maker to acquire the girl's birth-date card for him. Zhao the Sixth chose an auspicious date to offer a handsome betrothal present and thus the daughter of the family Yin was engaged to Zhao Cong. At festivals the two families would exchange gifts and this drained away nobody knows-how-much money.

Time went apace. Because Zhao Cong was pampered, he learned so slowly that he didn't finish reading the elementary classics until he was fourteen. Yet Zhao the Sixth believed that his son was outstanding. When Zhao Cong was fifteen, it was time for him to learn how to write papers. Zhao the Sixth had already wasted eight tenths of his riches on his son. Now, in order to make his son successful, he willingly took out loans and engaged a much-accomplished scholar to guide his son in writing papers. Needless to say, apart from the yearly tuition fee of fifty *liang* of silver, Zhao the Sixth had to offer generous gifts on festivals and provide transportation for the new tutor. Accustomed to an easy life, for nine days out of ten Zhao Cong would be absent from his studies. The tutor was only too glad to get handsome pay for doing little. Shameless and worthless scholars had eyes on his handsome salary. Honest ones would have declined his offer. That is the difference between virtuous and immoral persons. But enough of such chatter.

A year elapsed and an examination for the selection of *xiucai* was to be held. Zhao the Sixth rashly bade Zhao Cong enter the examinations. To acquire a letter of recommendation from an influential person, Zhao the Sixth spent a sum of silver, all, of course, to no avail. After his son's failure in the examination, Zhao the Sixth decided it was time to hold the wedding for his son. But alas, he was by then in want. So he had to find a mediator to write a deed so that he could borrow four hundred *liang* of silver from the Lius, a wealthy family. The mediator was Wang San, who Zhao the Sixth often turned to for help, and who had written several deeds for him. Thus Wang borrowed four hundred *liang* of silver from Liu on behalf of Zhao the Sixth, who immediately spent the silver on gifts. On a chosen date he presented the gifts to the fiancee, whereupon the date for the wedding was determined. Two months later the wedding was at hand, and Zhao the Sixth again found himself in need of funds for the nuptial. He collected a few clothes and some head ornaments, and pawned them to secure a loan of dozen *liang* of silver. The sum, however, was not enough to cover the expenses. So he again had to ask Wang San for help. The mediator wrote a deed with which he borrowed sixty *liang* of silver from Squire Chu. Only then was Zhao the Sixth able to hold the wedding for his son. The bride's brother escorted his sister to Zhao's house, where Zhao the Sixth received them with humble hospitality. The feast went on for seven days before the guests were dismissed.

The new couple loved each other deeply. They lived happily in a small courtyard next door to Zhao the Sixth's house. The new wife possessed many virtues with the exception of the shortcoming that she, because of her conceit over her high origin, was quite arrogant towards her parents-in-law. She was also very mean. She often abetted her husband to exploit other people. Had the young wife been virtuous and one who admonished her husband to do good, the disaster that eventually befell them would have been avoided! Indeed:

A virtuous wife is a blessing to her husband;
A filial son is a consolation for his father.

Of this we'll say no more. The family Yin endowed the girl with a bountiful dowry of about three thousand *liang* of silver. The young wife kept the dowry safely and never gave away even a little bit. Zhao the Sixth supported his daughter-in-law carefully, always being afraid that he might neglect something. Yet the son and daughter-in-law always complained about this or that.

Soon three years passed. The wife of Zhao the Sixth was confined to bed by phlegm-fire.* The management of the household was commissioned to the daughter-in-law. The daughter-in-law promised to wait on her parents-in-law, and at first she waited on them not so badly. But after several months she stopped supplying them even with food and water. Sometimes the old couple had to ask for food or drink when they could not stand their hunger or thirst any longer. The daughter-in-law expressed her discontent, saying, "What a big family fortune have you entrusted to me? And you are always asking for this or that. Wouldn't you save trouble if you looked after the family yourselves? I don't want to take such hard labor upon myself. I'm

---

*Phlegm-fire, a term of traditional Chinese medicine that refers to a wide range of diseases including asthma, mental disorders such as histeria, etc.

bored enough these days." Hearing this, Zhao the Sixth had to swallow his humility. He could not refute her because he really did not have much to entrust her with. Sighing, he told this to his old wife, who had been sick for a long time. Now, hearing the daughter-in-law's remarks and feeling her cold attitude, she realized this was because they were hard up, not as well-off as they had been three years before. The house was besieged by creditors demanding payment of debts. Most of her clothes and jewelry had been used to cover the interest on loans. Even their scrap of land had been mortgaged to other people.

Having lived a life that knew no want, the old wife saw that when her family fortune declined even her own daughter-in-law treated her coldly, as did strangers. Thinking of this, she could not help feeling annoyed. Being angered to dizziness, she took no food or water. The son and daughter-in-law did not visit her in bed, nor did they administer medicine. The meals they served were but bowls of rice with pickles. After half a month of such endurance the asthma worsened and, alas, she went to the west.

The son and daughter-in-law uttered tearless cries and left for their own house. Zhao the Sixth wailed, beating his breast and stamping his feet. Then he went over to the next house and said to his son, "Now your mother has died. To tell you the truth I have nothing left. I have prepared nothing for her funeral. If you cherish her love, buy a good coffin for her and choose a piece of land to bury her the day after tomorrow. This will manifest your filialty." "Where can I get the money for a coffin?" the son asked. "Not only does a good coffin cost far more than I can afford, but even an inferior one, pieced together with odds and ends of miscellaneous wood, costs two or three *liang* of silver, and that is beyond my means. Carpenter Li of the neighboring village has an inferior coffin. Why not go and buy it on credit? I'll see to the matter tomorrow." Tears collecting in his eyes, Zhao the Sixth dared not say anything more. He stepped out of the house and went to find Carpenter Li.

Zhao Cong entered his house and told his wife, "The old man really knows no content! He asked me for a coffin to bury my mother. My answer was, 'even an inferior coffin costs two or three *liang* of silver, not to speak of a good one.' I told him to get a cheap coffin on credit from Carpenter Li and the credit can be settled tomorrow." "But who will settle the accounts?" she asked. "To dismiss the nuisance," said Zhao Cong, "let's pay the debt for him." The wife went into a rage. "Where can you find money to buy a coffin for him?" she demanded. "It's a disaster to buy a coffin! You may pay for it if you like, but I have no money for that. I've never gotten any benefit from your parents, why should I take this trouble? If you give in once, he will pester you ten times. Don't you dare give him a thousand and one nos?" Zhao Cong was numb. He said, "You are right. I will not pay for it." Zhao the Sixth engaged two men to carry the coffin home and put the remains of his wife in it. A mourning ceremony was held, with a cup of watered wine as sacrifice. The coffin was placed in a room. The son and daughter-in-law did not stand by the coffin, nor did they prepare any delicious food. The daily meals were still cooked rice with chopped pickles. During the night, Zhao the Sixth kept company with the coffin alone. The woebegone old man would give a cry whenever he felt a surge of grief.

Twice seven days* after the death of the old wife, Carpenter Li came for the price of the coffin. Zhao the Sixth told him, "You may ask my son for it." Accordingly Carpenter Li went to Zhao Cong and said, "I wish you would pay for the coffin you bought from me on credit." Zhao Cong glared and shouted, "Are you out of your mind? You are not blind, and should have clearly seen who bought the coffin from you the other day. You should settle accounts with the buyer. Why ask me?" "It was your old gentleman who bought the coffin on

---

*A traditional mourning period in China was divided into seven parts, each having seven days.

credit," said Carpenter Li. "And it was he who told me a moment ago that I might ask you for the credit." "Don't listen to his shit nonsense!" roared Zhao Cong. "Shame on him! He had the money for the coffin. Why should he shift the liability? Get away at once, or I will be angry!" With his hands clasped behind his back, he turned around and went into his room. When Carpenter Li told Zhao the Sixth, the old man could not help crying, tears streaming down his cheeks. "Hold yourself please, Mr Zhao," the carpenter comforted him, "If you have no silver, you may give me something to cover the price — anything you can give me will do." Zhao the Sixth had to ransack his boxes and chests for something. Having found three pieces of winter clothing and a silver hairpin, he delivered these to Carpenter Li to cover the price of the coffin.

Seven times seven days passed after the death of the old wife. By now Zhao the Sixth was out of his senses. From the purchase of the coffin he should have learned a lesson that under no circumstances should he ask his son for help. But he forgot the lesson. As the mourning period of forty-nine days was up, he said to his son, "I want to find a piece of land to bury your mother. You make the decision." "Why should I make the decision?" retorted Zhao Cong. "I am no geomancer. How can I know where to dig a grave? Even if I could locate a spot, can I have it for nothing? In my opinion, you'd better choose a date to burn the corpse to the east of the village." This left Zhao the Sixth speechless. Tears welled up in his eyes. Zhao Cong left without saying anything more. Zhao the Sixth thought to himself, "She was the wife of a rich family all her life. It's beyond my expectation that she should have nowhere to be buried. Let it pass. Why should I turn to such an unfilial son for help?" Again he searched his boxes for something to mortgage for a loan with which to buy a spot of land and cover the expense of a burial ceremony. Finally he found two suits of clothes and a gold hairpin. He mortgaged these for six *liang* of silver. He spent four *liang* of silver for two *fen* of land and two *liang* of silver for four Buddhist monks who prayed for the soul of the deceased and several men who carried the remains to the graveyard. All this finished, Zhao the Sixth felt relieved. He returned to his home to live a life in accordance with his resources.

Soon freezing winter arrived. Zhao the Sixth was cold. He bought one *jin* of silk wadding on credit, but he had no money to settle the account. He took one piece of unlined clothing to his son and said, "This is a piece of my clothing. If you like it, buy it. If not, I'd like to mortgage it with you for some money." Zhao Cong replied, "It is ridicules to buy summer clothes in winter. I have no money to spare. Won't it eventually be mine if I leave it there? Why should I buy it now? No, I won't buy it, nor will I take it as a mortgage." Zhao the Sixth said, "If that's the case, I'll say nothing." And he put away the clothing.

After Zhao Cong told his wife, the latter said, "It's foolish of you to say that to him. If you don't take the clothes as a mortgage, he will certainly go to a pawnshop. That means you will lose them. If you take them and give him a price you think fit, you'll have a good bargain." So Zhao Cong came out and said to Zhao the Sixth, "My wife wants to have a look at the clothing. Perhaps she'll give you a mortgage on them." "You may take them, if you like," said Zhao the Sixth. "I want to mortgage them for a loan of seven *qian* of silver." When Zhao Cong showed the clothing to his wife, she said, "Give him four *qian* of silver and tell him that, if he agrees, we'll take out the loan, or he may keep his clothes." As Zhao Cong delivered the silver to Zhao the Sixth, the old man gladly took it. Zhao Cong wrote a contract for a term of five months and delivered it to Zhao the Sixth. Seeing the contract, Zhao the Sixth was enraged, and his face darkened. Tearing the contract to pieces, he heaved a long sigh and said, "I must have committed some sin in my previous life so that Heaven requites me with my own son. It's fate! It's fate!" He grumbled for a long while.

After a long night, he rose and washed himself. Then he suddenly saw Wang San enter his house. His heart thumped and his face turned as pale as dust. Wang San greeted him and said, "Excuse me for disturbing you, Zhao the Sixth. I am here for the loan of sixty *liang* of silver due to Squire Chu. Though you have paid the interest every year, you have paid in kind, and not always readily. He has decided to clear the loan, the capital and interest together this year. I could not say no to him. I think it's wise to find a way to pay off the debt. You will save your breath in talking about the loan, and your house will be free from debt collectors." Zhao the Sixth sighed, saying, "It was to hold the wedding for my disobedient son that I raised this heavy loan. Since then I have paid the interest every year. Now I have nothing left. I wanted to borrow some from my son to pay the debt, but he and his wife were too stingy to give me anything. I don't even have enough for daily food and clothing. How can I pay back the loan? I beg you, Mr Wang, speak for me to the debtor. I will be grateful to you if the debtor can give me more days of grace."

Wang San soured. "What are you saying, Zhao the Sixth! To speak for you I've dried my saliva. You don't know how many times Squire Chu's men have come to my house to press me because I was the mediator. I didn't take any fee from you. Why should I have this trouble? I regret that I made a mistake when I offered you help. Squire Chu sends his men time and again to demand the return of the loan, and you are asking for mercy! If you are hard up, why not turn to your son? It was for his wedding that you raised the loan. What's wrong if you borrow some from him? I really can't go like this. I will have to sit here until I get an answer." Hearing this, Zhao the Sixth was full of tears. He said with polite gravity, "You are right, Brother Wang. Let me talk it over with my son. You may go home now and I will certainly see you tomorrow morning." "That's all right," said Wang San, "but you mustn't relax after I leave. I have never received any reward for the trouble I've taken to help you, not even a cup of tea or half cup of wine! Why should I come to your place time and again?"

With this, he stalked away without even saying a good-bye.

Zhao the Sixth was utterly helpless. He thought to himself, if I ask Zhao Cong for help, I am afraid I will be humiliated by him. But if not, I really can't find any way out. Mr Wang is right. Since I raised the loan for my son's sake, perhaps he will lend me some money. In hesitation he went towards Zhao Cong's house. When he reached it, he saw there were many people there and food was being cooked. He asked somebody, "What is all this for?" The man told him, "Family Yin's first son has come. He was invited to stay for dinner. Because of this we are busy." Hearing this, Zhao the Sixth was distressed. He could do nothing but turn back. But then he hit upon an idea. His brother-in-law was having dinner in his house, why couldn't he, the father, take this chance? He decided to find out how he would be treated. He stopped and waited for awhile, only to be given the same two bowls of rice as usual. Choked with anger, he could not swallow the rice. That day Zhao Cong and his brother-in-law held a day-long feast. Finding it was inappropriate to interrupt them, Zhao the Sixth retired.

Early next morning Zhao the Sixth went to his son's house again, only to be told that Zhao Cong had not gotten up yet. The old man woodenly waited for a long while before Zhao Cong came out. Zhao Cong asked, "What do you want to say to me this early in the morning?" With an obsequious smile the old man said, "It isn't early. I want to talk about an important thing with you, but I am afraid you'll not listen to me." "If you think I'll listen," replied Zhao Cong, "speak out; or you needn't say it at all. What the hell do you mean?" Zhao the Sixth faltered and stammered, and then said, "The other year I borrowed sixty *liang* of silver from Chu to hold the wedding for you. I have paid him the interest every year. This year he wants me to pay back the principal. How can I pay him such a big sum? Surely I can't pay the principal. So again I have to deliver the yearly interest. I really haven't a single coin left. I would not bother you if it was for other matters. But because I raised the loan for your sake, I need to borrow some from you to cover the interest." Zhao Cong changed his countenance, and spreading his hands said, "What nonsense are you talking about! It seems that weddings in other houses are paid for by the sons. Let me ask some people and see if that is the case. If it is, I will pay the interest on your behalf." "It's not that I want you to pay the debt," said Zhao the Sixth, "I mean to borrow some for the time being." "You are talking about lending, eh?" said his son. "If you can pay the debt in the future, they shouldn't have come to press you. I have five *qian* of silver with me, a gift from my brother-in-law yesterday. Let me ask my wife's opinion. If she agrees, I will spend the money on a dinner for the mediator and let him beg the debtor for an extended limit." With these words, he returned to his room. Zhao the Sixth thought to himself, what can I do with five *qian* of silver? And he wants his wife's opinion! Obviously it is as hopeless as scooping up the moon mirrored in water.

After waiting for some moments, as he didn't see Zhao Cong come out, Zhao the Sixth had to go home where he saw Wang San waiting for him. Wang saw Zhao the Sixth before the latter could dodge. "How about what we agreed on yesterday?" Wang San asked. "Chu has sent his men to my house to urge repayment three or five times." Blushing to the roots of his hair, Zhao the Sixth replied, "My unfilial son would not give even a single coin. It's impossible for me to repay the capital. I will find something to pay this year's interest in kind. But let me have more time to find some way to pay the capital. Please grant me that favor." Saying this, the old man knelt down before Wang San. Tilting his head, Wang San extended his hands to lift him up, "If you can pay in kind, I'll take it. It will be a good excuse for me to put the lender off. I may then be at peace for a time." Zhao the Sixth entered his room, opened his box and took out some clothes and jewelry in addition to his own clothes and handed them to Wang San. Wang San made a generous calculation of the value of those items and in this way the twenty percent interest of sixteen *liang* of silver was covered. As Wang San took these together with the box away, Zhao the Sixth was now utterly deprived of any extra goods.

Let's make a long story short. Two days later Wang San came to ask for the interest on the four hundred *liang* of silver borrowed from Squire Liu. The situation was indeed desperate. Zhao the Sixth was at his wits' end. He fell down on his knees. "I have borrowed two ingots of silver," he said, "Let me convert it into small pieces of silver. Please go home. I will deliver the owed money to your house tomorrow morning." Knowing that Zhao was an honest man and besides, the old man could not escape even if he wanted to, Wang San returned home. Zhao the Sixth thought to himself, I have put him off for the time being. But any boil will sooner or later fester. What shall I do when he comes again? Under the pressure of the situation, he went to Zhao Cong again. "Wang San has come to demand the interest on Liu's loan today. The only thing I have left is my life. Have a heart and help your own father!" Zhao Cong said, "Do you think I will pay the debt on your behalf if you scare me with that kind of bluff? You may die if you like. What does your life mean to me!"

Hearing this, Zhao the Sixth grabbed Zhao Cong and broke into wailing. Zhao Cong struggled to get away from him and entered his house. Comforted by a neighbor, Zhao the Sixth went home. Over and over he thought about what he might do when Wang San came again. In desperation he hit upon a way out: "I've got it! This is the only way out of the difficult situation! I'll try it, even at the risk of my life!" As the evening fell, he ate supper and went to bed.

As for Zhao Cong and his wife, they had their supper, washed their feet, put out the light and went to bed. Zhao Cong couldn't get to sleep that night. Hearing steps in the house, he suspected there was a thief. But he remained silent. Because he owned riches, he was often on guard against theft. After awhile he heard the door faintly creak and a rustling sound approaching his bed. He made no sound, but as the sound was quite near, he picked up an ax which he always hid under the bed and struck at the intruder. With a thump the man fell by the bed. Zhao Cong got up quickly and keeping the man under his foot he dealt him two more blows. Hearing no sound from the fallen man, he realized he must be dead. In a hurry he woke his wife. "There's a thief in our house," he said. "I've chopped him." They lit a lamp. Fearing there might be some accomplice outside, they cried for help. As many neighbors came to their aid, they saw a large hole in the wall to the left of the gate and heard Zhao Cong shouting, "I've hacked a thief in the house!"

As the people thronged in, they saw a body lying there. A quick-sighted man gave out a cry: "Isn't this Zhao the Sixth?" When they moved closer and examined the body, they said, "Yes, yes, it is him. But why should he have committed robbery in his own son's house and be killed by his son? It's odd." "Maybe this shameless old man did not come to steal, but to seduce his daughter-in-law, and his enraged son killed him in the name of stopping thieves." But an experienced man said, "Don't talk such nonsense. Zhao the Sixth was not such a person." Zhao Cong and his wife could not make out what had happened. Though they were a treacherous couple, they were stunned. They cried as if they were really sad. "I really did not know it was my old dad," said Zhao Cong. "I thought it was a thief and killed him bluntly. Look at the hole in the wall and you'll see I didn't kill him on purpose." The neighbors said, "Since he came to steal and you couldn't make out who he was in the dark, you are not guilty. But this is an important matter and it should be reported to the authorities." Dawn broke after a whole night of confusion. The neighbors escorted Zhao Cong to the county yamen. His wife was frightened. She prepared a gift of some valued things which she meant to present to the people in the yamen in secret.

The county magistrate, a man by the name of Zhang Jin, was upright and incorruptible, and besides, he was quick-witted. As he convened court, he saw the people bring Zhao Cong in. Having questioned them about what happened and having the corpse examined, he declared, "A son who kills his father commits one of the ten unpardonable crimes!"* A clerk came forward and said, "Zhao Cong committed the crime of killing his father, but he did this to stop a thief in the darkness and he didn't realize the man was his father. So he should not be inflicted with the extreme penalty." The neighbors said the same. Regardless of their defense, Zhang Jin took up a brush and wrote the verdict:

Even if Zhao Cong is pardonable for stopping a thief, he is not forgivable for his unfilial behavior. A son who possesses enough wealth to spare and drives the father to theft in utter destitution is obviously an unfilial one. How can he be exempted from death!

With this, he had Zhao Cong flogged forty times and then shackled and put into prison. Nobody there dared speak a good word for Zhao Cong. And furthermore, everyone knew of Zhao's unfilial behavior. Now seeing the right verdict, they were convinced. Zhang Jin ordered that a coffin be bought for Zhao the Sixth and the old man be buried by converting some of Zhao Cong's property. Able and wealthy as the wife was, she could find no way out. All she could do was to spend more money to acquire permission to see Zhao Cong in prison from time to time. Unexpectedly, as she went to prison frequently, she caught a contagious illness from some of the other prisoners. In no more than a month, she died. Being used to a life of abundance, Zhao Cong couldn't stand prison life. After the death of his wife, nobody

---

*The ten unpardonable crimes are: conspiracy against the state, conspiracy to revolt, conspiracy to betray, plotting the murder of elder members of the family, disobedience toward a sovereign, slaughtering of innocent people, unfiliality, breach of propriety toward superiors, disharmony, and incest.

served him any food. After three days of hunger, he died in the cell. His corpse was dragged out of the cell and put into a mass burial pit. This was the due retribution for his unfilialty.

Zhang Jin confiscated Zhao Cong's family fortune. When the Squires Liu and Chu and Zhao the Sixth's other debtors presented the deeds to the magistrate, Zhang Jin paid their debt from Zhao Cong's property. The rest went into the state treasury. The two misers, who had exploited others all their lives and had begrudged even giving a single coin to their parents, had meant to secure an eternal fortune for their descendants. They could not have expected that their assets one day to turn to null. And they, themselves, came to such a miserable end that they couldn't even be buried decently. Indeed, Heaven's judgment and requital is the fairest!

Tale 9

To Steal Money, Yu Dajiao Murders a Drunk Man; To Confront his Enemy, Yang Hua Haunts a Living Lady

When a man ceases to be, his soul will not go;
So a vengeful ghost will not let off his foe.
Hearing my story of a ghost witness you'll know
    That justice governs Hell
    And the human world as well.

Do you know, readers, why I cite this? Because some people in the world, having done something against their conscience, think nobody will ever know what they have done in absolute secret. Believing that a dead man cannot give witness against them, they feel they are out of the woods as they watch their victim die. They don't understand that in the dark world the spirits know everything with accuracy. Thinking of the stories about people who tell of their previous lives or how the ghosts who possess living bodies retaliate against their foes — as if the victims were still alive and appearing in front of you — any hardened and audacious person will be so scared his hair will stand on end. It is a well-known fact that a dead man becomes another man in the next incarnation; equally well known is the fact that a ghost will revenge himself on his murderer by attaching himself to a living person. Since ancient times there have been many such tales to tell.

What I'll tell you now is a far stranger story about the soul of a man who had been slain and who served as a witness in court by clinging to a living person. He didn't stop until the verdict was reached, after going through a succession of yamens. Such a story is seldom heard.

In Yujia Village, Jimo County, Shandong Province there once lived an ex-soldier by the name of Yu Dajiao. The Yus had inherited a soldier's position in the Right Garrison at Xingzhou [present-day Xinghua County, Hebei Province]. The man of the family now serving in that garrison was Yu Shouzong. The post had been instituted during the Reign of Hongwu [1368-1398]. Although it was filled by the soldier's direct descendants, expenses on the soldier's food and clothing were covered by all the families of the clan. According to an established rule, the money was collected once every several years. It was the twenty-first year of the Reign of Wanli [1593] when Yu Shouzong in the garrison sent his family retainer to his native village to get the silver. The retainer by the name of Yang Hua was a native of Jizhen [the region from present-day Beijing to Shanhaiguan], an honest and straight-forward man. Yu Shouzong chose him because he had been to Jimo before and thus was familiar with the area. Having bid farewell to his wife, Yang Hua set out on a lame donkey he had raised himself. In a few days he arrived at Jimo and put up for the night in the house of Yu Dajiao. He then went from house to house to collect money. The money collected bit by bit from different branches of the clan — ranging from several *fen* to a few *qian* — amounted to two *liang* and eight *qian*. Yang Hua carefully carried the silver on his person.

On the twenty-sixth day of the first month, Yu Dajiao came to Yang Hua and told him, "A fair is being held at Aoshan Station today. There will be a lot of fun there. Let's go and have a good time." Yang Hua replied, "I am not used to staying at home, so let's go." Tying the money sack around his waist, Yang Hua mounted his donkey and headed for Aoshan with Yu Dajiao. Well, his going there set the stage for a hero from the frontier to become a wronged ghost and a poor village woman to play the victim's mouthpiece for a time. Indeed, his going there was like a pig or sheep entering a butcher's house and meeting its death step by step.

After Yang Hua and Yu Dajiao had browsed the fair for awhile, they became hungry. Yang Hua said to Yu Dajao, "Let's have a drink in a tavern." Yu Dajiao responded by showing him to a wineshop in the town run by a certain Yin San. Wineshops in Shandong at that time served few dishes to go with wine except for some plates of garlic and a few pastries. Being a poor soldier from the north frontier, Yang Hua was fond of spirits, and the liquor in Yin San's shop, reputedly the most potent brew in town, was quite to his taste. With Yu Dajiao abetting him insistently, Yang Hua downed one big bowl of the wine after another until he was stewed to the gills. By evening Yang's legs were too weak to take a single step. Supporting him onto the back of his donkey, Yu Dajiao steadied him as they went on their way. Tottering, Yang Hua almost fell from the donkey on several occasions. When they arrived at the Shiqiaozi Valley north of a post station, Yang Hua dozed off and with an "Ouch!" dropped to the ground. "Since you cannot ride the donkey," said Yu Dajiao, "you may as well sleep here for awhile." After turning his body over on the grassy slope, Yang Hua went to sleep, snoring thunderously, unaware of where he was.

The knowledge that Yang Hua had collected packs of silver pieces had set Yu Dajiao's heart on fire, although he did not know how much there was. He wanted to take the silver from him. He reasoned that a poor single soldier like Yang Hua was a stranger whose whereabouts nobody would know, and besides, members of Yu's clan were eager to see Yang Hua go away. With Yang Hua out of sight, everybody would be only too happy to inquire into his whereabouts, and the money would belong to Yu. That's why he had purposefully gotten Yang Hua drunk. Yu Dajiao waited by the sleeping Yang Hua until the first watch of the night. If a tender-hearted man wanted to take the silver, he could seize upon his drunkenness to simply take it from his belt and run away. Then, when Yang Hua found the silver missing after he woke up the next day, he might think he had lost it while he was drunk. Even if he was suspicious of Yu Dajiao, he would have no evidence and Yu Dajiao could deny it. He would not go so far as to murder him. As a cruel and ruthless Northerner, however, Yu preferred to go the whole hog. They called this "beating before talking." It made little difference how much money was involved. Even a petty robber who went after a hat or a piece of clothing would kill the victim first. Such was the practice in this part of the world that a man's life was often seen as no better than that of a louse. Seeing that Yang Hua was asleep and nobody was around, Yu Dajiao untied the reins from the donkey and made a loop. Putting the loop around Yang's neck and stopping his mouth with his hat, Yu Dajiao tread on his face with one foot and tightened the loop with his both hands. Thus the poor soldier with such a pittance of silver came to a miserable end.

Yu Dajiao put his hand close to Yang Hua's nostrils and found that he had stopped breathing. He then took the pouch of silver from Yang's waist and tied it around his own. If the body stays here, he thought, it will turn foul and someone may discover it in the morning. So, putting the body on the back of the donkey, he made for the sea shore three *li* from Yujia Village. There he threw the corpse into the sea with a splash. As he led the donkey back, he thought to himself, "The donkey belonged to Yang Hua. There may be somebody who knows that. If I keep it at my home, they may ask about it and then I will be in an awkward position. I must get rid of it." So he led the donkey to Huangpushe Village and left it to roam about a slope. Free from its reins, the donkey rolled on the ground happily. It was led away by nobody-knows-whom the next day. Yu Dajiao sneaked home that night without being seen by anybody.

On the eighth day of the second month, namely twelve days after Yang Hua's death, Yu Dajiao was sure that the body must have by now drifted many thousand *li* away. But strangely enough, the body, having floated for days, was washed ashore by the evening tide and stopped right near Yujia Village. Yu Liang, head of the neighborhood, found the body and reported it to the magistrate of Jimo County. Having no clue as to the name or background of the dead man and how he had fallen into the water, Magistrate Li could do nothing. But the trace of a rope on the neck suggested an unnatural death. So he bade the local bailiffs to keep the body and investigate the cause of the man's death. At the same time, he abstained from meat for a period of time, went to the Temple of the City God, and prayed to the god for a divine revelation. So much for the Magistrate.

On the thirteenth day of that month, Lady Li, the wife of Yu Deshui in the same clan as Yu Dajiao, suddenly fell down while pestling rice with her husband. Yu Deshui held onto her and called to her. After about an hour, she sprang to her feet and, with her eyes closed, cried, "Give back my life, Yu Dajiao!" Astonished, Yu Deshui responded, "You must be a spirit. Where are you from and why do you cause me such trouble?" A strange voice came from within her mouth, "I am Yang Hua who came to fetch the allowance for the frontier soldier. I was made drunk by Yu Dajiao at the Aoshan Fair. He took me to the Shiqiaozi Valley and strangled me with the reins of my own donkey. My body was cast in the sea. Fearing that if Yu Dajiao escapes, the authorities might involve innocent people in the case, I am here to inform you of this. I have a brother by the name of Yang Da.

My wife is called Zhang and we have two sons and two daughters. But they are far away in Jizhou, and none of them can come to avenge my death. How pitiable they are! So I have come myself to confront Yu Dajiao in court. I won't give up until the authorities avenge me."

"But my family has nothing to do with your case," said Yu Deshui. "Why do you come and harass us?" The voice from the woman's mouth said, "I am attaching myself to your virtuous wife's body for the time being so that I can confront my enemy in court. When my case is settled, I will leave and will never trouble you again. I beg you to report this to the authorities. Otherwise, I will not leave your house." Yu Deshui had no alternative but to inform Yu Liang of this. In doubt, Yu Liang came to Yu's house to see for himself, and no mistake, the woman repeated every word in Yang Hua's voice. Yu Liang ran to tell an elderly man by name of Shao Qiang, who came along with some yamen runners to Yu Deshui's house, only to hear the same words retold.

Yu Liang and Shao Qiang, together with other local villagers, rushed to Yu Dajiao's house and called him out, saying, "What a charitable deed you've done! Now the ghost of your victim is in Yu Deshui's house. Go and confront it." With a guilty conscience, Yu Dajiao was astounded by what he heard, but he replied, "How can there be a ghost? Let me go and see. I have nothing to fear." Because he could not defy the people, he had to follow them to Yu Deshui's house. There he heard the woman shout, "Here you are, Yu Dajiao! What wrong have I done you? Why should you have laid murderous hands on me and made away with my property? You have made me suffer so much!" Thinking that nobody could testify to his crime, Yu Dajiao was stubborn, "My eye! Who's taken your things? How absurd!"

"You are denying it!" cried the voice from the woman's mouth. "You strangled me with the reins, carried me to the sea shore by donkey and threw me into the sea. You took my two *liang* and eight *qian* of silver and planned to spend it for your own happiness. Hand over my silver now, or I'll beat you and bite your flesh to vent my anger." Hearing the precise amount of silver announced, Yu Dajiao realized that this was the spirit of Yang Hua that had entered the woman's body. He dared not deny the fact. He admitted to the people that what she said was true. He had never expected that a spirit could possess a person and tell the truth with such accuracy. He had no choice but to wait for his death as a punishment.

Having heard this, Yu Liang escorted Yu Dajiao home, where he found Yang's pouch with two *liang* and eight *qian* of silver in it from the stove chimney. "Good!" he said. "With these spoils, we can report the case and let the authorities convict him. Otherwise, the only evidence we have for this case of a corpse from the sea is the utterance of a spirit; if the spirit goes away and the haunted woman comes to her senses, we will have to take responsibility for a false accusation." So they lost no time in taking Yu Dajiao together with the spoils to the county magistrate.

Yu Dajiao thought to himself, "There is no escaping the punishment now! And no one will bring food to me while I'm in prison. I will make a false confession so as to implicate two or three men from my clan. When their relatives bring food to them, they'll somehow let me share it. So thinking he said to Yu Liang, "Three men from our clan, Yu Dabao, Yu Da'ao and Yu Dajie, collaborated with me. Why should you put all the responsibility only on me?" Thereupon Yu Liang and his men arrested the three, who pleaded innocence. But no one listened, so they were also hauled to the county court.

Having accepted the statement, the magistrate wrote a comment on it, "The report sounds plausible, but the evidence comes from a spirit. So Lady Li must testify in court." Accordingly, Li was summoned to court and there she was confronted by Yu Dajiao. Every word from her mouth, in Yang Hua's accent, made it categorically clear that Yu was the murderer. Seeing other names on the statement, the county magistrate asked, "What are Yu Dabao and others?" The voice answered, "Yu Dajiao is the only culprit. The others are innocent. Because I was afraid that innocent people might be involved, I risked transgressing the boundary between man's world and the spirit's, and came to clarify the truth." Raising his voice the magistrate called Yu Dajiao to account. Scared out of his wits by the woman's accurate account, Yu Dajiao had no choice but to plead guilty. "Your Lordship," he said, kowtowing, "until today did I not know that a spirit could not be deceived. The truth is that I strangled Yang Hua and took his money, and nobody else had anything to do with it. What a damned wretch I am!"

Realizing that such an important case concerning a murder had not been examined yet, the magistrate himself took Yu Dajiao to the seashore where Yang Hua's body lay. The coroners examined the body, and found wounds caused by looped ropes. They thus confirmed that the man had been strangled to death. After the coroners had written the autopsy report, the magistrate returned to the county court. There he had all parties' testimonies recorded and sentenced Yu Dajiao to death. The witnesses, including Lady Li, signed their names to the statement. The magistrate enjoined her, "This case will be submitted to higher authorities. You mustn't retract your statement." "I won't," replied the woman. "I'll make the same statement again." The magistrate had said this to her because he feared that Yang Hua's spirit might take leave of her body and then the woman would speak otherwise. He did not know it was Yang Hua's spirit itself that was talking. The magistrate put the papers in a file and handed them over to the prefecture together with the culprit and concerned parties.

Having read the records, the prefect found it to be a queer case. Suspicious, he questioned the culprit and the others at once, but what he heard was exactly the same as what he had read. So he wrote his comment:

Yang Hua was a poor frontier soldier who had come from a thousand li away. The money he raised amounted to less than three liang, but this was enough to incur Yu Dajiao's malice. Making Yang Hua drunk with wine first, he strangled him with a rope, carried his body by donkey back to the shore and threw it into the sea. He thought that with the body swallowed by fish, no one would testify against him and thus he could possess the money and get away with it. But the heavenly law is fair and the spirits are all knowing. The body refused to sink into the sea and the spirit of the victim made itself heard through a living person. Thus the evil was exposed and the wicked man was stricken with terror. The statement "I'll ... bite your flesh to vent my anger" is as sharp as an ax; the remark that he was "fearing that ... the authorities might involve innocent people" speaks volumes of his fair-mindedness. Indeed, Yang Hua's spirit is epiphanic and upright that even death cannot obliterate this quality. Who says one can kill a man and get away with murder? The county magistrate had prayed the god for revelation and his call was answered; his meritorious performance is worthy of commendation. The death sentence he announced is a right decision since the statement came directly from the mouth of the culprit. The murder and the haunting spirit are real, so the case should be submitted to the higher-up authorities for examination. The final decision lies with the provincial governor.

So the prefect wrote a report and sent it with the culprit to Governor Sun.

Having read the details of the case, the governor was not convinced. "How can a verdict on murder be made according to the statement of a woman such as Li talking in the tune of a ghost? How can I be sure there is no falsehood in all this?" So the governor called in the people who had been sent, and, questioned them one by one, circling a name with a writing brush before each round of questioning began. After he had called the name of Lady Li, he stopped his brush and asked, "Where are you from?" "I am from Jizhou," she replied. Then he summoned the local bailiff and asked, "Where is Lady Li from?" "She is a native of Jimo County," answered the local bailiff. "But why did she say she's from Jizhou?" asked the governor. "She is a native of Jimo, but the dead soldier, Yang Hua, is a native of Jizhou," came the answer. Then the governor asked Li, "What's your name?" "Your servant's name is Yang Hua. I am a soldier under Yu Shouzong in the right garrison troop in Xingzhou." Then she related in detail how Yang Hua had come to raise the allowance and how he had been murdered, with the accent of a northerner but not the voice of a woman or a Shandong native. Having got clear answers to his questions, Governor Sun nodded with a smile. "This is indeed a strange happening!" So he wrote a note on the report:

> The spirit of Yang Hua attached itself to a woman and voiced his grievances through her mouth. As I questioned her, she spoke with the accent of a Jizhou native. This is indeed very strange. Therefore I am referring this case to the Surveillance Commission for further investigation.

The Surveillance Commission, in turn, referred the case to Deputy Prefect Liu, who was in charge of the criminal court for re-trial. As the culprit and those concerned were brought under guard to the prefecture court, a receipt was immediately issued. Yu Deshui, Li's husband, tearfully pleaded with the prefect, "My wife Li has been haunted by the spirit of Yang Hua for a long time and she's forgotten her own identity. As she has been involved in this case, she has been repeatedly questioned for months. Our baby cannot be breast fed and so both the mother and the baby suffer. I beg Your Lordship for mercy!" Hearing this pitiable plea, the prefect nodded, "It is not normal for a woman to stay away from home for long. But it's difficult for me to handle problems concerning a ghost." So he called her before his desk and asked, "Are you Lady Li or Yang Hua?" "I am Yang Hua," replied Li. "Your wrong has been redressed," said the prefect. "I am much obliged to my lord for this immense kindness," she said. "Though you are Yang Hua, your body belongs to Lady Li, do you understand?" asked the prefect. "This I know. But though my wrong has been redressed, I have no home to go back to. So I prefer to stay here." "Nonsense!" the prefect said, flying into a rage, "Since your wrong has been redressed, you should go back to the corpse. How can you trouble a man's wife for so long? Go at once, or I'll give you a sound flogging!" Hearing this the woman seemed to be scared. She kowtowed repeatedly, and told him, "I'll go." And then she stood up and began to leave. The prefect had her pulled back, saying, "I bade Yang Hua to go. You are Lady Li. Where are you going?" The woman replied, still in the voice of Yang Hua, "I'll go myself." And she stood up to go again. Pounding the table, the prefect ordered her back, shouting, "Why are you so stupid! Yang Hua should go but the body of Li should remain here. Why have you disobeyed my order once and again? Runners, give her a sound drubbing!"

The runners, roaring, threw their bamboo flogs onto the ground so that they made a cracking sound. The woman fell down in a swoon. When the runners called her by name, she didn't answer; then they called her "Yang Hua," but she didn't respond either. Her eyes were tightly shut and her face was pale as ash. Scared out of his wits, Yu Deshui called into her ears, but heard no answer. He broke into a wail, forgetting he was in court. The prefect didn't know what to do. Holding Li in his arms, Yu Deshui saw her limbs were trembling, dripping with sweat. After a long while, she opened her eyes. Seeing the spacious court and the crowd of strangers there, she asked in surprise, "I am a daughter of the Lis. How have I come here?" And she covered her face with her sleeve. Realizing that she had become herself once again, the prefect asked if she knew what she had undergone these past days. She answered, "I was pestling rice at home, but I don't know how I came here." And she did not know how many days she had been away from home. The prefect wrote four big characters in cinnabar "Lady Li being herself" as a talisman, pasted it on her back, sealed it with his stamp, and bade Yu Deshui take her home and nurse her back to health.

The next day Deputy Prefect Liu summoned the concerned persons to the court. Li's name had not been canceled from the list of people to be summoned. Having seen his wife so often in court, Yu Deshui did not take the matter to heart any more. But to his surprise, this time she was too shy to show up in the yamen. When Yu Deshui told her what had happened, she wailed, "I have been made a fool of, as if I was in a dream. It is too late for me to repent, but since I have become myself again, how can a woman such as me appear in court?" "The case has been settled," said Yu Deshui. "The prefect permitted you to return home yesterday. The case will be reviewed today and then it will be concluded." "Reviewed or not," she replied, "what have I to do with it?" "If you don't go," said Yu Deshui, "I'll be in trouble." Thereupon she had to appear in court with Yu Deshui. When she was questioned, however, she said nothing and only cried. When the deputy prefect asked Yu Deshui about this, Yu related how she had been haunted by Yang Hua's spirit and testified on his behalf, how the prefect had released her and how, since Yang Hua's spirit had left her, she had become herself again. And he showed the prefect's talisman pasted on her back and the seal imprinted on it. Amazed at this story, Deputy Prefect Liu gathered all the documents about this case and submitted them to the higher authorities for examination with a note that said, "Since Yang Hua's spirit has gone, Lady Li is released and can go home. I will exempt her from further interrogation. We've collected credible evidence for Yu Dajiao's crime, and so collateral evidence is not necessary. He will be executed in late autumn."

One night Yu Deshui had a dream in which he saw Yang Hua come to express thanks. "I have troubled your virtuous wife for a long time," said Yang Hua, "but I have nothing to repay your kindness. A male donkey, my only possession, has gotten lost and fallen into someone's hands. Now I will let it go to your gate. Please receive it as a token of my gratitude." When Yu Deshui opened his gate the next day, he saw the donkey there and so he saddled it for riding. Only then did he realize that the spirit of Yang Hua had not died yet. People all know that a spirit is not to be deceived, yet no story is as authentic and appalling as this one.

> *The ghost, a man murdered by a man,*
> *By way of a living person testifies a crime.*
> *When both the murderer and murdered got their due,*
> *The haunting spirit vanquishes in time.*

Tale 10

Zhang the Lucky Makes Easy Money by Setting Beauty Traps;
Lu Huiniang Seeks Happiness by Dissolving a Loveless Bond

This story is about a *xiucai* of Tongxiang County, Jiaxing Prefecture, Zhejiang Province. Surnamed Shen and named Canruo, the twenty-year-old *xiucai* was a famous scholar of his native prefecture. He had an imposing bearing and was broad-minded. His wife nee Wang, extremely beautiful, was a good match for him. His immense family fortune was managed by his wife. The couple of talent and beauty was a happy pair. They were mutually attached like glue or turpentine. The pity was that Wang, of weak constitution, was always pestered by an illness. Shen Canruo had entered the public school at twelve and at fifteen he became a stipend student. Quite proud of his talent, the ready-witted young student regarded acquisition of a scholarly honor as easy as picking up a grass leaf. Usually he and his friends, young and of unrestrained nature, gathered for the delight of drinking and chanting, or sightseeing. Among them were four *xiucais*, who were his best friends — as the old saying goes, "Bright heads appreciate each other." They were Huang Pingzhi of Jiashan County, He Cheng of Xiushui County, Yue Erjia of Haiyan County and Fang Chang of his native county. Apart from these friends from his native prefecture, countless students from other prefectures kept contact with Shen Canruo. They were all bright minds of the time.

The county magistrate, Ji Qing by name, was a native of Jiangyin County of Changzhou Prefecture. He respected learning and knowledge and appreciated talents. Believing that Shen Canruo was a sure winner in the imperial examination, he adopted him as his student. The two of them were in close association. It was the year of province-level examinations for scholarly honors. Shen Canruo returned home and dressed himself up for the journey to Hangzhou where he was to participate in the examinations. As he said good-bye to his wife, Wang, despite her illness, packed up the luggage for him and said in tears, "You have a bright future ahead of you. Please go and come back early. I don't know if I will be fortunate enough to share your success and prosperity." "What are you saying?" Shen Canruo said. "You are ill. After my going away, you should take good care of yourself." Despite himself tears ran down his cheeks. When the moment for departure came, they grasped each other's hands. Wang saw him off at the gate. Wang did not turn back with her hand on her tearful face until Shen Canruo was out of sight.

All the way Shen Canruo sulked. In a few days he arrived in Hangzhou and stopped in an inn. As he hurried through the three rounds of examinations, he was satisfied with his papers. One day he and some friends visited a scenic lake and returned drunken. At midnight he heard a knock at the door. As he got up with a piece of clothing over his shoulder to answer the door, he saw a man in high hat and broad-sleeved robe. The man seemed to be a Taoist. "What will you teach me, sir," asked Shen Canruo, "since you come here at such a late hour?" "I can observe the breath of Nature," said the Taoist, "and divine a man's fate. I happened to come from the Southeast, and finding nowhere to spend the night, I knocked at your door. Please excuse me for bothering you." "If you want to live here, I would not mind your sleeping in the same bed with me. The result of the examinations is to be announced. Since you are skilled in divination, will you foretell according to my humble birth hour if I have access to a scholarly honor?" "It is not necessary to calculate. I can tell your fortune just by observing your complexion. You have a full appearance; this means you needn't worry about honors, but you will be successful only after the expiration of your lady's term. I have two lines to describe your life experience. Please commit them to your memory:

When the great roc spreads its wings the six-canto dirge* is heard;
As a broken string is renewed,** a pair of mandarin ducks flirt.

Unable to get the meaning of the two lines, Shen Canruo meant to ask him for an explanation when he heard a cat outside throw itself upon a rat with a thump. Alerted, Shen Canruo found he had been dreaming. "This is a strange dream indeed," he said to himself, "The Taoist said clearly that I would acquire an honor only after my wife's death. I would rather be a student without any scholarly honor all my life than lose my beloved wife!" As the two lines resounded in his mind, he kept tossing and turning in bed. Then he said to himself, "Why should I believe what I heard in a dream? If my name is not on the list of succeeding students tomorrow, I'll return at once."

While he was so thinking, he heard a hubbub of voices mixed with gongs. Some people snatched Shen Canruo and demanded tips: they came to deliver the news that Shen Canruo had won the third place

---

*"Six-canto Dirge" is a poem in memory of a deceased person.
**To renew a string (as for a musical instrument) is an often-used metaphor for remarriage after the death of the first wife.

among the successful examinees on the Confucian classics. Shen Canruo wrote a bill immediately, and when the visitors dispersed, he dressed himself and went in a sedan chair to see the chief examiner and his fellows. The chief examiner was none other than Ji Qing, the magistrate of his native county. The student who had topped the list was his close friend He Cheng. Huang Pingzhi, Yue Erjia and Fang Chang, all among the foremost successful candidates, were very happy too.

It was dark when Shen Canruo arranged everything and went to his inn. There he saw the inn-owner hurrying towards his sedan chair and crying, "Mr Shen! A man came from your house with an urgent letter! He has waited for you half a day." Hearing the words "urgent letter", Shen Canruo suddenly thought of the words he had heard in the dream. He felt unsettled. Upon entering the inn he saw Shen Wen, one of his servants, in white and plain clothes. "Is my wife well at home?" he asked. "Who has sent you here?" "I can't answer your question, sir," Shen Wen replied. "It is Butler Li who has sent me here to deliver a letter. You'll know everything after you have read it." Taking the letter into his hand and seeing the envelope sealed with the flap tucked inside,* he felt his heart was being pierced. The letter said thât Wang had passed away on the twenty-sixth of the month. Stupefied, Shen Canruo could not utter a word for a long time, then he swooned down on the ground. Awoken and held up by the people there, he was choked in tears. Calling his wife's name, he cried endlessly. The people in the inn were all moved to tears. "Had I known this," Shen Canruo said, "I wouldn't have come to enter the examinations. I never imagined that she would part from me forever." And to Shen Wen he asked, "Why didn't you come earlier if her illness was so serious?" "After you left," replied Shen Wen, "her illness was the same as before.

---

*An envelope with the flap tucked inside was the container for news of somebody's death.

Who would have thought that she would lose consciousness on the twenty-sixth. So I came here to report this in the night." Sobbing for awhile, Shen Canruo bade Shen Wen to hire a boat for home. He could attend to nothing else. He thought to himself that the dream was extraordinary indeed: the result of the examinations was issued on the twenty-seventh and his wife died on the twenty-sixth. This realized the line: "When the great roc spreads its wings the six-canto dirge is heard".

When he packed up his things and left the inn, he came across Huang Pingzhi, his schoolmate, in a sedan chair. After a courtesy greeting, Huang Pingzhi asked, "I saw sadness on your face. What has happened to you?" With tears in his eyes, Shen Canruo told Huang Pingzhi everything from his dream to the letter and his journey home. Huang Pingzhi sighed again and again, "Please restrain your grief and don't carry your grief to excess. Let me tell this to the chief examiner and our fellows. You may go home." And they parted.

Hurrying back home, Shen Canruo entered the room and wailed over the corpse. Once again he fell into a coma. On a chosen hour the body was encoffined and the bier laid in the hall. During the night Shen Canruo kept company with the coffin. After three or four seven-day mourning terms, his friends paid condolence visits to him. Some of them mentioned the metropolitan examination. To this Shen Canruo was indifferent, "For this meaningless fame, I have my undoable knot cut. Even if a first candidate honor was on the ground today, I would not pick it up!" This was what he said when his wife had just died.

Soon seven seven-day mourning periods were over. His friends and relatives came to persuade him, "Your wife has been dead, and obviously you cannot bring her back to life. What's the good if you lose ambition because of her? Besides, if you stay home, you will feel lonely. If you go to the capital with your friends, you will be able to enjoy the sights and thus you will feel better, and at the same time, talking with your fellows your heart will be less loaded with grief.

How can you give up your ambition for life because of the grief?" Unable to resist the persuasion, Shen Canruo said, "Thank you for your kindness. I will go there." Then, in parting with the coffin of Wang, he instructed Butler Li to look after the sacrificial offerings to the deceased. Then he set off with his friends Huang, He, Fang and Yue.

It was mid-winter. Traveling during the day and resting at night the five of them arrived at the capital city in a few days. All day they talked or chanted poems together, and from time to time they would amuse themselves in parlor houses. But none of the girls attracted the attention of Shen Canruo.

As time flew by, a new year set in. After the lantern festival in the middle of the first month, streams turned warm and the peaches put out fragrant blossoms. Then the yellow announcement for imperial examinations was posted and the examinations were held. Shen Canruo and his four friends went through the examinations for three subjects. They were all satisfied with their papers and boasted of their prowess, except Shen Canruo, who in low spirits finished his papers carelessly and hastily. Before long the result of the examination was announced. Shen Canruo's name alone was not found on the list of successful candidates. Shen Canruo, however, did not care about it. Huang, He, Fang and Yue went to participate in the ceremony for announcing the candidates' names in the order of their scores. There they learned that He Cheng's place was among the second dozens, and he was positioned in a branch of the Warfare Ministry and would live in the capital with his family; Huang Pingzhi was selected as a member of the imperial academy; Yue Erjia was named an official in charge of the ritual ceremony and Fang Chang was assigned to an official in charge of the publication of decrees. The county magistrate, Ji Qing, was promoted to the head of the criminal department in the capital because of his outstanding performance in Tongxiang County. They all proceeded to their new posts.

After enjoying himself for some time in recreation places, Shen Canruo went back to Tongxiang. When he entered his house, he paid homage to Wang's coffin, cried and offered sacrifices to her. Two months later he consulted with a geomancer and selected a good spot to bury her. After that some people began to offer proposals about marriage. I am a man of excellent bearings, Shen Canruo thought, yet I was so ill fated as to lose a beautiful wife like Wang. Where could I find another match? He decided that only the lady whom he saw with his own eyes and found satisfactory could be taken into consideration. He paid little attention to that matter.

Time flies like an arrow and months and days come and go like a shuttle. Let me cut the long story short to tell you that three years later Shen Canruo was to go to the capital to sit for the imperial examinations again. Then he found his house wanted a care-taker. As the saying goes, "A house without a hostess is turned upside down." Since the death of his wife, the day-to-day affairs of his household were poorly managed. He thought, "I had better have a wife to manage the house. But I can't find a match." For this he was unhappy. He had to entrust the house to Butler Li before he set out. It was the eighth month when the west wind brought fresh coolness and it was a good time for travel. During the night a bright moon shed its light upon the immense expanse of waves, and the sky and the earth were fused into a blue color. Drinking by himself, Shen Canruo felt lonely. When he was soused, he slept in the boat.

After twenty or so days he arrived at the capital. Having rented a room to the east of the examination place, he put his things there and settled down. One day he was drinking with several friends at the Qihua Gate when he saw a lady in white riding on a lame donkey, with a porter carrying food boxes in tow. It seemed that she had just returned from a visit to someone's tomb. As Shen Canruo fixed his eyes on the lady, he found she was:

Fair-skinned that if she was powdered, she would be too white; her cheeks were so rosy that with cinnabar applied, they would be too red. She would be too tall if she was one fen *taller and she would be too short if she was one* fen *shorter. All her features were perfect and everything about her was charming. She was so gentle that nothing about her could be different. Her smile was so charming that everyone who looked at her was conquered. Her glance was so enchanting that the world was bewitched.*

Seeing this lady, Shen Canruo felt his soul escape from his head, and vigor fled his feet. Having left his friends there, he hired a donkey and riding on it, he began stalking her step by step. Mesmerized, he fixed his eyes on her. The lady on the donkey from time to time turned her head around and cast a bewitching glance toward him. After going a *li* or so, they arrived at a tranquil place and there the lady entered a house. Getting down from the donkey, Shen Canruo, unwilling to go, stood rooted to the ground, and, not knowing what he was doing, he peeped in through the gate. But the lady never appeared again.

When he was at a loss as to what to do, a man came out, asking, "Why are you looking in the gate, sir?" "I have just come this way and saw a woman in white enter this gate," replied Shen Canruo, "and I'm wondering whose house this is and who the woman is. I find no one to ask." "She is none other than Lu Huiniang, my newly-widowed cousin," said the man. "She has just visited her deceased husband's tomb. She is trying to find a new spouse. I am playing the matchmaker." "May I know your honorable name, please?" asked Shen Canruo. "My family name," replied the man, "is Zhang. Because I am successful in everything I set my hand to, I am known by a nickname Zhang the Lucky." "What kind of man does your cousin want to marry? Will a man from another place do?" "She wants to marry a young student, either a local or nonlocal." "To tell the truth," said Shen Canruo, "I got the title of *juren* in the former imperial examinations and now I am here to participate in the metropolitan examinations. I have seen your cousin's rare beauty and I've fallen in love with her. If you'll serve as the matchmaker, I'll thank you generously." "That'll be easy," replied the man, "I don't think my cousin will say no once she sees your impressive bearing. You may leave it all to me and success is guaranteed." Overjoyed to hear this, Shen Canruo said, "If so, I will ask you to tell her what I wish." And taking out a silver ingot from within his sleeve, he handed it to Zhang the Lucky. "Please take this paltry gift. I will pay you a handsome reward." After making a modest show of declining the gift, Zhang accepted the silver. Seeing Shen Canruo pay such a handsome sum without hesitation, Zhang believed that he must have a fat purse. So he said, "You'll have my answer tomorrow." Shen Canruo returned to his lodging exalted.

The next day Shen Canruo went to the house and waited for the answer at the gate. There he saw Zhang the Lucky smiling as he approached. "You are blessed, sir!" he said. "You came here very early. Yesterday I did what you asked me to do, telling my cousin what you wished. My cousin has taken a fancy to you. So with little effort I talked her into agreeing to such a marriage. You may go and prepare the betrothal gifts. My cousin is entitled to make her own decisions, so she does not care how much you are willing to pay. You may pay any sum you please." Accordingly, Shen Canruo spent thirty *liang* of silver on jewelry and clothes and sent them to the woman. Her side agreed on a date to hold the wedding, without asking for more gifts.

Seeing that the agreement for marriage was so easily settled, Shen Canruo became a little suspicious. But on second thought, he explained away his own fears. A widow on second marriage, he said to himself, is called by the northerners the wife of a ghost, so the matter is settled this way. On the chosen date, Shen Canruo hired a band of musicians and a sedan chair and went to greet his bride. Lu Huiniang was thus installed in the sedan chair and borne to Shen Canruo's lodging. When he looked at his bride in the lamp light, he found her to be the very girl he had seen the other day. He was transported with joy and set his fear at rest. He and the bride made obeisance to Heaven and earth, and then drank the wedding toasts. Before long the guests all left.

When the couple entered the bedroom, Lu Huiniang sat in a chair. After the first watch was beaten the night set in. Having not slept with a woman for a long time, Shen Canruo felt his urges inflamed. "Please go to bed," he said to her. Lu Huiniang replied in a crystal voice, "You may go to bed first." Shen Canruo thought she said this because she was shy, so he did not force her. But he could not go to sleep. After about half a watch, he urged her again, "You must be tired after the day's traveling. Why don't you retire? Why are you sitting there alone?" "You may sleep by yourself," said Lu Huiniang, her eyes fixed on Shen Canruo. For fear of offending his bride, Shen Canruo had to try to sleep for awhile. Then he asked her in a soft voice, "Why don't you lie down?" Sizing up Shen Canruo from tip to toe for awhile, Lu Huiniang asked, "Do you know any influential or powerful friends in the capital?" "I have a large circle of friends," replied Shen Canruo, "and there are many, many schoolmates here, not to mention ordinary acquaintances." "If that is the case," said Lu Huiniang, "I will marry you in a real sense."

"You are being funny!" laughed Shen Canruo, "I came from afar and saw you. I was able to hold this nuptial ceremony after I found a matchmaker and sent betrothal gifts. Why are you talking about a real marriage at this moment?" "There's something you don't know, sir," replied Lu Huiniang. "Zhang the Lucky is a well-known swindler. Do you think I am his cousin? I am in fact his wife. Because I am pretty, he uses me as bait, saying that I am newly-widowed and want to marry somebody and that he is the matchmaker. Many people admire my beauty and willingly propose marriage. He does not demand high gifts.

Instead, as long as the marriage is agreed to, he sends me to the bridegroom. He instructs me to pretend to be shy and refuse to sleep with the man. That way I won't be defiled. The next day he arrives with a group of villains, accusing the man of seducing a woman from a family of good reputation. In this way he is able to take me away together with the man's boxes and suitcases. The victims are strangers and so they are afraid of becoming implicated in a lawsuit. So they have to swallow their humiliation. Quite a few men have fallen prey to this plot. Yesterday I saw you on my way back from visiting my mother's tomb; I am not a new widow. The wretch saw you and schemed to entrap you by his old trick. I often wonder how I can live in this way. If one day his trick is exposed, I will be ruined. Besides, how can I with a spotless body continually greet a new man and part with an old one in secret? Although I am not tainted yet, I cannot bear this emotionally any longer. I have admonished him several times against doing this, but he does not listen. So I decided to make use of his plot to find a worthy man. Once I've found such a man, I plan to elope with him. I see that you have impressive bearings and are honest and gentle, and so I've taken a liking to you. But I am afraid that if I go away with you, he may be able to catch us and you will suffer. Since you have many friends in the capital, I will entrust myself to you. You can move to a secret place of one of your good friends this very night. Only in this way can you have me in peace. This means that I offer myself to you. Please don't forget my sincerity in the future."

Hearing this Shen Canruo was struck dumb. After a long pause he said, "I am much obliged to you. But for your advice, I would have suffered from his plot." He then opened the door in a haste and woke up his servants. Having packed his things, he put Lu Huiniang on his donkey, had a servant carry the cases and he himself walked on foot. At the gate he told the inn-keeper, "I have something urgent to do and have to go home." Knowing that He Cheng lived in the capital with his family, he went there and knocked on the door. After he entered, he told He Cheng what had happened from beginning to end and brought Lu Huiniang and his luggage into He's place. He Cheng had many empty houses, so a two-yard compound was assigned to Shen Canruo for his lodging.

Now let's turn to Zhang the Lucky. The next day he and a mob of villains came to seize the bride. What they saw was an empty room without a soul in it. When they asked the inn-keeper, "Where is the *juren* who got married yesterday?" the answer was, "He left for home during the night." Stunned for a moment, the gang shouted, "Let's go after them!" They rushed to Zhangjiawan in a great hubbub. But the capital city, Beijing, was too vast for them to be able to locate the woman. Houses in Beijing were often rented out. Guests kept coming and going, and so the owners seldom took notice of where their tenants went. So no one could tell the whereabouts of a tenant who moved away.

Shen Canruo stayed two months at He Cheng's place, reading. Then the spring imperial examinations were announced. Believing that he had acquitted himself well in the examinations for all the three subjects, Shen Canruo awaited the publication of the list of candidates that he hoped to top. As he had expected, he was among the top candidates on the list. He was appointed to be the magistrate of Jiangyin County, the native county of Ji Qing. In a few days he proceeded to his post with a mandate and with Lu Huiniang. It so happened that Fang Chang was on an errand in Suzhou, so Shen Canruo made the trip aboard Fang Chang's ship. Lu Huiniang became the lady of a county magistrate. Thus the line from his dreams, "As a broken string is renewed, a pair of mandarin ducks flirt," came true. Shen Canruo got promotions later until he reached the rank of provincial governor. Lu Huiniang gave birth to a son, who later passed the imperial examinations and became an official. This prosperous family line continues to this day. As a poem says:

Praise to Lu Huiniang,
    who, wandering like a drifting patch,
Can discern her perfect match:
Oh, with what tactics, what wit
She beats the scheme of a cheat!

Tale 11

A Soul is Redeemed in West Mountain Monastery; A Breathing Body is Encoffined in Kaifeng Prefecture Court

Let me tell you another story. It is about a Taoist who, having seduced a woman by taking advantage of the opportunity of a praying ceremony, finally died a violent death. From this story Taoists should take warning.

The present story begins with a woman surnamed Wu in Kaifeng Prefecture of (present-day) Henan (Province) during the Song Dynasty. At fifteen she was married to a certain Liu of the same city and gave birth to a son named Liu Dasheng. When Dasheng was twelve, the father died of an illness. The mother, Wu, who was very beautiful and had an elegant bearing, was still in her twenties when she became a widow. Without any parents-in-law or clanspersons, she managed to live by herself and look after the son. Remembering her deceased husband's kindness, she planned to redeem his soul by some religious ceremonies.

In the vicinity of the city was a West Mountain Monastery where Taoists preached and practiced their doctrines. One of these Taoists, by the name of Huang Miaoxiu, excelled in weaving spells, and besides, his bearing was impressive. He was therefore elected the abbot. One day while he was transcribing some documents for a client, he saw a young lady in white coming to the monastery with a boy of twelve years of age or so. As the old saying goes, "White mourning attire makes a beauty shine". This woman had pretty looks. With the white dress and white head-ornaments she appeared even more graceful. If she had been seen in a Buddhist temple instead of this Taoist monastery, she would have been mistaken for the white-robed goddess Avalokitesvara, who provides sons to women's wombs. When the woman approached the abbot, as if she were planting a candle, she bowed to him twice. Casting a glance at her, the abbot felt his soul snatched away. Returning a salute in hurry, he asked, "Whose relative are you, may I ask? And for what are you here?" "I am Wu, a widow of Liu. My husband died not long ago and I want to have his soul redeemed. That's why my child and I have come to beseech you to display your immense power and do a favor for the deceased." Hearing this, the abbot had an evil idea. "If you want to redeem your husband's soul," he replied, "you will have to set up a mourning hall at home. Only in such a hall can magic figures drawn and a ceremony performed do good. The services performed in the monastery will not be very effective. What's your opinion, Madam?" "If my master will kindly condescend to visit my humble house," she replied, "it will be my glory. My child and I will be obliged to you. I'll go back and prepare the mourning hall and wait for your coming." "When shall I go to your place?" asked the abbot. "In eight days my husband will have been dead for a hundred days," said Wu. "I intend to hold a seven-day service. If the service starts tomorrow, it will end coincidentally on the hundredth day of my husband's death. It would be better if you come early tomorrow morning." "What's said cannot be unsaid," said the abbot. "I will not be late in arriving at your house tomorrow." Taking out one *liang* of silver from her sleeve, Wu handed it to the abbot to cover the expense for paper* and took her leave. When she got home, she cleaned a house for the Taoist to perform his art.

When Wu had come to ask the Taoist to perform rites to redeem her husband, she was in earnest and did not harbor anything evil. But the abbot was a hungry lecher. Upon seeing Wu's beauty, while he was speaking to her, he would have liked to carry on with her right away. Wu, on the other hand, did not know what was on the abbot's mind; impressed by his unusual bearing and alacrity, she was praising him inwardly. "Why would such a handsome man have become a Taoist?" she thought to herself. "I love his unfeigned manner. When I asked him to perform rites, he promised to come to my house. He is certainly a warm-hearted man." She began to take a liking to him.

The next morning the abbot Huang, with two young disciples and a lay brother carrying boxes of canons and scrolls, went straight to Wu's house. Because the son, Dasheng, was very young, Wu herself administered all the house affairs. She greeted the abbot and ushered him into the mourning hall. The abbot, together with his disciples and lay brother, hung up the portraits of the Deities of the Three Purities**, laid out the instruments and began to apply magic incantations. The routine included no other than proclaiming a decree, praying for the deities' arrival, conjuring up the spirit, announcing amnesty and summoning the migrant soul. Wu came forward to pay her respect to the deities. Catching sight of her, the abbot put on a more enthusiastic show. When he and his disciples finished chanting the canons, they knelt down on the carpet before the deity portraits and made a

---

*Paper was used to make images of deities and demons in a religious ceremony.

**The three purities are believed by Taoists to be the three pure realms in the universe. The Deities of Three Purities point to all the Taoist gods.

statement. He bade her to convey her sincere intention to the spirit on her knees. All the while Wu and the abbot were next to each other by half a *chi*. Smelling the perfume exuding from his clothes, she could not help casting a little squint in his direction. Having sensed this, the abbot turned his head to look at her from time to time while he chanted. Thus they made eyes at each other, itching to move closer and fall into each other's arms. Upon finishing this ceremony, Wu stood up and, while lighting incense in front of the deities and kowtowing to them, she stole a look at the altar. There she saw that the two young disciples wearing long dark hair over their shoulders and small hats on their heads. They had delicate skin, white teeth and red lips. These priests are leading such a pleasant life, she thought to herself. How beautiful the two will be when they are fully grown! And she felt passion begin to kindle in her heart. Unable to suppress such urges, she kept peeping out from behind the curtain.

Know, readers, what really counts in a love affair is the look of fascination in the eye. Once you are fascinated by what you see, you'll derive grace from one who is tall, strength from one who is short, muscularity from one who is robust, and elegance from one who is slim. A woman tends to be consistent in love. Once she takes a fancy to a man, she will never forget him. Wu looked at the abbot again and again. The more she looked at him, the more lovely she found him to be. She was a newly-widowed young woman and had a strong lust. As her thoughts turned to this aspect of her life, her face became now flushed and now pale. She kept pacing to and fro in front of the drape, exposing now half a face, and now her whole body as if she wanted him to understand her intention. How could the abbot, with a ready mind for women, fail to take the hint? What prevented him from acting impetuously was the fact that this was his first visit. All he could do was to return her attention with meaningful eyes, but this was short of getting anywhere. Liu Dasheng, Wu's son, was too young to understand all this. When he entered to see the pictures of deities, he toyed with the bells and drums, entirely ignorant of his mother's covert desire. At the lamp-lighting hour they had supper. Wu prepared a clean side room for the abbot and his disciples. The abbot sent the lay brother back to the monastery and he and the disciples slept in the same bed. They retired for the next morning's audience with the deities.

Let's turn to Wu who slept with her son in her room. She could not get to sleep. The Taoist is doing "it" with the two beautiful children in his arms, she thought, but I have to sleep in loneliness. When she thought about this over and over again, she felt her private parts burning unbearably. To get over this uncomfortable feeling, she gnashed her teeth noisily and perspired profusely. As she dozed off she heard steps by her bed. Raising her head she saw someone pull aside the curtain and slip under her quilt. From the voice she knew this was the abbot. "Much obliged to you for your winks at me," the abbot told her. "Your servant could not fail to get your meaning. Please seize this opportunity of the deep night and do me a favor, Madam." Saying this, he stuck out his enormous organ. She readily accepted it. Just as she was about to reach her orgasm, a disciple drew the curtain open to look for his master. Seeing what his master was doing, the disciple said aloud, "Are you a virtuous woman really? See what you are doing, seducing a priest like that? Let me have a share and I'll keep my mouth shut." He reached out his hand and began to grope for her waist. "Don't be so impertinent in front of me!" said the abbot angrily. Wu had been taking her sensual pleasure with the Taoist, but her ecstasy was about to reach its peak when she awakened with a start. She had just been dreaming. When she felt her private parts, she found both her thighs were wet and even the mat was soaked by her secretion. She wiped it up with a handkerchief in haste and sighed, "What a dream! How can I be so lucky?" For the rest of the night she could not sleep well.

When she arose the next morning, she heard bells and drums from outside. She bade her maid servants carry hot and cold water to the abbot. The two young disciples, taking advantage of their youth, came into the mourning hall asking for this and that and, by and by, became familiar with Wu. As Wu sat in the mourning hall a young disciple came in for tea. She stopped him and asked, "What's your name?" "My humble name is Tai Qing." he replied. "And the elder one?" she asked. "He is Tai Su," the youth answered. "Which one of you slept with your master last night?" Wu asked. "What difference does it make if any of us slept with him?" the disciple asked back. "I am afraid your master was not well-behaved," she said. The disciple grinned, "You're joking, Madam." After he went out, he let his master in on this in private. The abbot, his desire aroused once again, thought to himself, "From the way she put it, she must have a heart for me. We are side by side in the same mourning hall, but, after all, I am an outsider. How can I flirt with her?" Then he hit upon an idea. "I have it!" he mused aloud. Soon Wu came forward to offer incense to the deities. With a bell-stick in one hand and a tablet in the other, he hurried up, stood by her side, and began to chant a song to the melody of "Lang Tao Sha":

I kowtow to the deities at the utmost height
And pray for a divine matrimonial tie.
How can a girl in her prime lie
In an empty draped bed through the lonely night!

The pious lady builds an altar to redeem
Her deceased spouse. Now soul saved, she may forget him!
I hope at the Blue Bridge she and I will make a date
To quench my thirst, and she will be my divine mate.

The abbot chanted this with the clear implication that Wu might volunteer to give herself to him. Wu, hearing him, naturally understood his intention. "Why are your words mixed with irrelevant phrases?" she asked, smiling. "All I said is the correct approach to our doctrine," the abbot replied. "The predecessor deities left behind them romances that serve as examples for us." Wu was fully aware then that he was infatuated with her. She entered her inner room, shelled half a bowl of fine nuts, made a pot of refined tea and had a maid bring them to the abbot with this message: "My hostess hopes these will quench your thirst." This message echoed with what he had sung and suggested a "yes" to him, and it set the abbot in a rapture. He began to fling his arms and swing his feet, entirely forgetting his *Canons for Divine Treasures* or *Secrets from the Seventh Heaven*, while brooding over Gimmicks for Lovers or Pleasures in Bed. He secretly bade his disciples to inquire about Wu's lodging room. Upon learning that she shared the same room with her son and a maid servant, he thought it would not be convenient for him to break in.

That night he went to bed with his disciples. Recalling Wu's words and actions during the day, he released his desires upon Tai Qing, making the bed creak. Hugging him from his back, the abbot said, "My dear children, I have something important to talk to you about. I see the hostess has settled on me. If I can have her, it's probable that you too will benefit. But she and I are separated by partition walls and she has her son and the servant, and I have you two. It's quite inconvenient. What shall I do?" "We'll not disturb you," said Tai Qing. "But at the beginning she wants to shun strangers." "I saw a bed for the soul in the mourning hall," said Tai Su. "It is draped with nice curtains and covered with fine bedding. It stands between the outer and inner quarters, a good place to carry on a secret affair." "You are right, my child!" cried the abbot. "I now know what to do tomorrow." He then whispered to them conspiratorially. Clapping their hands, Tai Qing and Tai Su said, "Great!" At this point the abbot felt excited and finished his game with Tai Qing. The two boy's desires were aroused, but, having nowhere to release them, they abused themselves. Thus passed the night.

Meeting Wu the next morning, the abbot said, "Today is the third day of the ceremony. I have a method to summon your husband's soul to see you. Would you like to see him?" "Certainly, if you can!" replied Wu, "but I have no idea how you will perform your art." "Build a bridge with white silk in the hall," the abbot said, "and I'll let the soul come across the bridge. Leave only one relative there on guard. If there are too many people, the strong breath of the living will keep the soul at bay. The hall should be tightly shut and nobody should be permitted to peep in, or the heavenly secret will be divulged." "There are only two relatives of the dead," Wu said, "me and my son. My son is too young and it isn't urgent for him to see his father. But I do want to see my husband. Let me stay in the hall and watch you perform the ritual." "That's a great idea," remarked the abbot. Wu then went into her inner room, took out two bolts of white silk from her box and handed these to the abbot. Holding one end of the silk, the abbot asked Wu to take the other end into her hand. Thus doubling back the silk they measured it again and again. Seizing the opportunity, the abbot made eyes at Wu. When he crossed hands with her, he tapped her wrist lightly, and she remained silent. Then he instructed her to pile the tables up to mock a bridge which blocked the way to the mourning hall, so that the people on the other side of the curtain could not see inside.

The abbot then came out and told his disciples, "I'll shut the mourning hall to summon the soul of the deceased man. You must keep guard at the door and not allow anybody to steal a look inside, or my magic will be ruined." "We see," they replied in tacit understanding. Wu, on her part, told her son and the maid servant, "The priest will summon the soul of the dead to meet with me. The art must be practiced in secret and tranquillity. You'd better stay in your room and not come out and make noise." Hearing that his father would come, Dasheng shouted, "I want to see Dad, too." "My son," said Wu, "the priest said if there are two people, our breath will be too strong and the soul will not be summoned. So only your mother can stay there. If your father does not come because of your presence, our efforts will be wasted. If we succeed this time, you will be able to see your father in the future." Wu knew only too well that the abbot was using this pretext to cover up his scheme. She comforted her son with honeyed words and gave him some fruit. Locking her son and maid servant in her room, Wu came into the mourning hall and sat down.

The abbot closed the door with a bang and bolted it. Putting on a show he beat the warrant board on the table and mumbled something. Then, all smiles, he turned to Wu, "Please sit on the bed to await the soul, Madam. But I'd remind you of one thing. The soul may be called in, but it's an indistinct image as if seen in a dream and can do no good for you." "All I hope," said Wu, "is to see him and tell him of my longing for him. I don't care if it does me any good or not." "You can see him but you cannot relive the pleasure you used to enjoy in bed. That's why I said it will do you no good." "There you go," said Wu. "It's enough for me to see the soul. Why do you say this?" The abbot replied, "I have the power to make you happy again." "How can that be?" Wu asked in surprise. "The soul is intangible," said the abbot. "Only when it attaches itself to my body can I make you happy." "A soul is a soul and a priest is a priest," said Wu. "How can the two substitute for each other?" "We Taoists have mastered this art over a long time," he replied. "Many souls have seen their kin by attaching themselves to our bodies." "But how can we do that here?" she asked. "If I can't act the way your husband did, you may choose not to believe me," the abbot replied. "What a honey-tongued rascal you are, Taoist!" Wu rebuked him, "and a swindler at that!" The abbot came forward, gathered her into his arms and pushed her down on the bed. "Let me act as your spouse," he grinned. By that time Wu had been turned on. They began to dally in the bed —

One was a handsome youth from the metaphysical school who had seldom tasted a chaste lady; the other, a beauty in an abandoned room who had been neglected in bed. His power to conjure up wind and thunder was exercised on bringing about clouds and rain, while her pride in chastity fell off like the petals of a blossom. The deities in the portraits in the hall were unreal and the soul of the dead was in the netherworld once and for good. The one who held incessantly sucked the nectar, while the one who plugged continually probed in the obscure nest. Along the slippery path a solitary bird came to have an audience with god; among flowers a bald monk went home. The taste was .sweet and yet mysterious; when exhausted, the bodies lay numb.

When they finished, both felt satisfied. The abbot asked Wu, "Is my capacity inferior to that of your husband?" Wu retorted with a tush: "You beast! Why ask such an embarrassing question?" The Taoist thanked her, "I'm much obliged to you for your favor. I wouldn't be able to repay your kindness even if I were to give up my life." "Since you've taken me," said Wu, "I want to continue with you for a long time." "Let's claim a relationship as cousins," said the abbot, "so that we can keep contact without arousing suspicions." "Sounds like a good idea," answered Wu. "May I know your age, Madam?" he asked. "Twenty-six," answered Wu. "I am one year older," he said. "You may call me elder brother. I'll manage it." So he rose from the bed, and striking the warrant board once or twice, opened the door and told his disciples, "I conjured up the soul of the dead a moment ago. I did not realize that the madam was my cousin until the soul told me so. As I have been given the details, I am sure there's no mistake. So she and I are close relatives." "Of course," smirked the disciples, "close kin." Wu called her son out and repeated the abbot's lie to him. She told him, "This is what your father said. Come and see your uncle." Her son was too young to see through the ruse, and so the boy began to call the abbot uncle.

From then on they did it every day on the pretext of summoning the soul. At night Wu came from her room and the abbot entered the hall. They used the bed in the hall to make love and they became more and more intimate. Having been told that the spirit would be called back, the son insisted on seeing his father. She kept putting him off saying, "You belong to the human world. So you can't see him." The son had to give up, but he got suspicious. "Why only I not?" he wondered.

Seven days and nights later the ceremony came to an end and the hundred-day mourning period expired. Wu thanked the Taoist and his disciples and closed the mourning hall, while making a date with him in secret. Instructing her to avoid being noticed, the abbot returned to the monastery. Wu entrusted her son to the tutor of a free school, so the child left home in the morning and returned in the evening as he had done before. During the day the disciples would bring her a message or the abbot himself would come. After her son went to bed at night, Wu would open the door and let the abbot in. Then they would make merry to their heart's content. Only the maid servant knew what was going on, but she had been paid off. In this way they met every day for three years running.

Then Liu Dasheng was old enough to understand the secrets between men and women. He also found some traces of his mother's secret life. Being a clever boy who was knowledgeable and knew propriety, he was not happy about his mother's behavior. But he dared not expose it. One day in school his schoolmates mocked him as a "Taoist's son". Blushing, he went home and said, "Mother, I have something to tell you: better not let that uncle come again. Somebody called me 'Taoist's son'. I don't like to be ridiculed that way." At these words the blush of shame spread from the roots of his mother's hair to her cheeks. Knocking twice on her son's head with her knuckles, she scolded him, "What an ignorant child you are," she said. "Your uncle is your mother's cousin. Who can stop him from coming to see us? If any short-lived wretch says something irreverent to you, I'll go and give him a rating!" "I heard nothing about this uncle before the prayers two years ago." Dasheng said. "If he is really my uncle, it's only right for you to treat him like a cousin. Why is there so much talk about this?" Seeing that her son had hit the point, Wu was enraged, "Oh, you heartless boy! Who has brought you up? How can you believe other's remarks and ridicule your mother? What's the use of having such an ungrateful and disobedient son like you!" Smiting the table, she broke into a wail. Frightened, Dasheng knelt down in front of her. "It's my fault," he said. "Please forgive your son." Seeing him beg mercy, Wu stopped crying. "From now on you should not believe such idle talk," she said. Dasheng had to swallow the insult and he dared not say anything more, but he thought to himself, Mother denies it too stubbornly. She will not give up unless she's caught in the act. I'll keep a watchful eye and look on coldly.

One night Dasheng slept in his mother's room. When he awoke at midnight, he heard the door creak and someone seemed to be going out. Now fully alert, he threw a piece of clothing over his shoulders, sat up and observed. The door was open. He realized that his mother had gone out of it. He turned around and felt his mother's quilt, but she was gone. He did not go out to look for her, but hit upon another idea. He bolted the door, propped a stool against it and returned to bed.

The truth was that Wu had made an appointment with the abbot that night for the hour after dusk. The bier had been removed from the mourning hall, but the bed was retained for their secret affair. The bed was tightly curtained. The abbot had lain there and Wu came from her room to meet him. Billing and cooing they spent an acrobatic night. Usually when day broke, Wu would let him go and she would return to her own room. But this time she found the door bolted. She could not push it open. Realizing that her son must have discovered something, she sat down there in embarrassment until morning. She clenched her teeth in hatred, but she had nowhere to give vent to her anger.

Only in broad daylight did Dasheng open the door. Seeing his mother, he pretended to be surprised, "Why are you sitting on the ground outside of the door, Mother?" he asked. "Last night I heard steps outside," Wu answered, concocting a story. "I suspected it might be a thief. So I opened the door and came out to look. Why did you lock the door?" "When I saw the door open," said Dasheng, "I feared that there might be a thief. So I locked the door and placed a stool against it to make sure that it couldn't be opened. I thought you were in bed. But why were you out? And why didn't you call me to open it? Why did you sit here all night?" Wu searched her brain for an answer, but she couldn't find one. I cannot keep this nuisance in my room any more, she thought to herself.

One day she said to her son, "You are grown up now. It's not appropriate for you to sleep in the same room with your mother. The bed in the parlor is made, you may sleep on that tonight." She meant to send him away so that she could sleep with the abbot in her room comfortably without being disturbed. The son, however, was smart enough to see through this ploy. Saying yes, he went to school during the day, and he became even more vigilant at night when he retired to the parlor.

A disciple came that day. Wu asked him to tell the abbot how she had been shut out of her room the previous night. "So I've told my son to sleep in another room," she said. "This evening the abbot may come directly into my room through the back gate." That night the abbot came. Dasheng, in the parlor, did not go to bed. Instead, he hung around to see if anything was out of order. Hearing a sound at the back gate, he hid himself in the dark. He clearly saw the abbot come and, as the maid shut the gate, go into Wu's room and close the door.

"A son is not meant to catch the adulterer of his mother," he mused, "but I can shake them up a little bit." After a while he heard the sound die down in his mother's room. Finding a thick rope, he fastened the door knockers together tightly. When the abbot can't open the door, he thought to himself, he will try to get out through the window. I'll make him suffer. In the front yard, he brought out a pail full of urine and a half-broken jar of night soil, and put them where he reckoned was the spot that the abbot would jump to. After that he went to his room and slept.

After a night of debauchery, the abbot heard roosters crow twice. Fearing that it would be too late to leave after daybreak, he threw his clothes over his shoulders and went to open the door. As he could not pull it open, he told this to Wu. Wu came to his aid. They pulled the door until it cracked loudly, but it seemed to be tied with something. "Strange, said the mother, "Maybe it is the young devil up to some mischief! Since you cannot go through the door, you may leave through the window. I'll take care of it tomorrow morning. It is turning bright and you can't stay any longer." Eyes still fogged with sleepiness, Wu opened the window and the abbot jumped down. There was a "thud" as he stuck his right foot in the pail of urine, leaving his left foot flailing in the air. So he lost his balance and stamped it in the night-soil jar. As he hastened to pull his right foot out of the urine pail and run, the deep pail toppled and he stumbled, half of his body soaked with urine and feces. His lips were slit open, but he dared not utter a sound. Sustaining the pain and covering his nose with his hand, he ran to the back gate and scooted through it.

When Wu found she could not open the door, sae was quite annoyed. As the abbot went out through the window and she had heard a thump, she looked out to see what had happened, but it was still dark. She smelled an offensive odor, which she could not make out. She returned to her bed fretfully and slept.

Early the next morning Dasheng got up and removed the rope from the door. Seeing the ground covered with feces and the pail turned upside down near the window, he could not help feeling angry and at the same time amused. Before his mother awoke, he softly removed the urine pail and night-soil jar. When Wu arose and pulled at the door, it opened without a hitch. Then she wondered why she had not been able to open it during the night. Perhaps she had been in a hurry, she thought. By the window she saw urine and feces and wet shoe prints leading all the way to the gate. She called Dasheng in and asked him, "From where did the night soil come?" "I don't know," he answered, "but the prints suggest there was a man. I think maybe he pissed and shitted in desperation." Speechless, Wu blushed and then became pale. She began to harbor a deep hatred toward her son. She would get rid of this thorn in her flesh as soon as possible.

Having suffered that night, the abbot found his perfumed clothes were now all soiled. He washed sullenly at the monastery. And because of the wound on his lips, he did not return to Wu for some days. Wu was in a sulky mood too. She wanted to see him and talk to him, but he didn't come. The more she missed him, the more ruffled she became.

Days later the abbot sent his disciple, Tai Su, for information. "Your master hasn't come for days. He must be angry," she said. "He is afraid of your ruthless young master. So he just wants to avoid him for a few days." "My son is at school during the day, " Wu said. "It is better for your master to come during the day. I want to discuss something with him." Tai Su, now eighteen or so, understood what kind of a woman Wu was. He made eyes at her and dropped a hint, "My master can't find time. It will be all right if his young disciple comes in his stead." "Young slave," Wu rebuked him, "are you also taking liberties with me? If I report this to your master, he will strike you on your lower part." Tai Su grinned, "My lower part is as good as yours. It is of use for any master and so he won't steel his heart to strike it." "Shameless slave," she chided him, "you are very cheeky to say that!" Wu had been infatuated for some time by this handsome youth, but in previous years she had found him too young. Now he had grown up. At his amorous words, she became excited. Holding him by one arm, she gave him a kiss. As she reached a hand to touch his private part, she found it erected. The moment she was pulling him into the bed and doing it with him, Tai Qing came in. The abbot, wanting Tai Su back after waiting for a long time, dispatched Tai Qing to look for him. Hearing Tai Qing's voice in the parlor, Tai Su feared that the abbot would blame him if he knew what had happened. So he stopped abruptly and returned with Tai Qing to the monastery to report back to the master.

The next day the abbot visited Wu during the day as she had instructed him. Shutting up the gate, she ushered him into the parlor and seated him. "Why didn't you send me a message after you left the other night and only yesterday sent a disciple to me?" she asked. "Your son is extremely crafty," replied the abbot. "He is growing up and becoming hard to deal with. It's inconvenient for me to see you. It seems that we have to break up." Eager to keep on with the Taoist, and even to capture his two young and handsome Taoist disciples, Wu was irritated to hear this. "I have no seniors to hinder me," she said, "but the little beast is in the way. I'll have to get rid of him. Then I will be free. I really can't endure him anymore." "He is your own son," said the abbot, "how can you be so hard-hearted as to finish him off?" "A son of one's own should be kind and considerate to his mother," she replied. "A disobedient and vexatious son is worse than none at all." "It is up to you to make up your mind," the abbot said. "We won't encourage you. You may regret it." Wu replied, "I will put up with him for one or two days. Don't be afraid and just come to enjoy ourselves tonight. I don't care even if he finds out. Let him do what he pleases. He can do nothing against me." Their conversation lasted for half a day before the abbot left. He was to return that night.

The very same day Liu Dasheng left school earlier than usual because the teacher wanted to go home. When the young man ran into the Taoist on the may, he reckoned that the Taoist must have been to his house and so he perfunctorily addressed his "uncle" with a cup-handed salute. Taken aback, the abbot returned a salute and went straight away without saying anything. Dasheng thought to himself, he suffered the other night and so my house has been at peace for the last few nights. Now that he has come to my house today, he will surely come again tonight. But I cannot catch him again. I will take preventive measures. When he got home, Wu asked him, "Why have you come back so early today?" "The teacher went on a home visit," replied Dasheng. "I'll not go to school for a few days." Wu was disappointed, but asked mechanically, "Would you like to have a snack?" "Sure. I will go to bed after having a snack. I am tired after working hard for days. I'll go to bed early this evening." This was precisely what his mother hoped. She gave him a snack. As she expected, Dasheng went to the parlor and fell asleep. Wu, her heart set at ease, had supper, ordered the house and had a short rest. Then she told the maid to leave the gate ajar and awaited the arrival of the abbot.

Without her realizing it, Dasheng was feigning sleep. When all was calm, he got up quietly and went out to examine all the gates. He found the front gate was locked and the gate between the front and back yards was bolted from the other side. He pried it open and went to the back gate. There he found it had been left ajar. He gently bolted it, fetched a stool and sat there waiting. After beating of the first watch he heard someone pushing against the gate. The push sounded timid. Now and then he heard a finger tap on the door. In hushed silence he waited to see what would happen next. Suddenly a voice came through the seams in the gate: "It's me. Why is the gate bolted? Please open it." Knowing who this was, Dasheng assumed a high-pitched voice, "You can't come tonight. You should go, or you are asking for trouble." The sound died down outside.

Now Wu, waiting in her room for her paramour with burning desire, did not see a soul come after the watch passed. She had to ask her maid to go to the back gate and see what had happened. The maid went there in the dark and, groping around, touched Dasheng. She was startled. "You witch!" Dasheng shouted in a stern voice. "What are you up to here at this hour?" Frightened, the maid gave out a scream and ran away. "I didn't see the priest," she reported to Wu, "but the young master sat there. I was almost scared to death." "The beast is too abominable indeed!" Wu said clenching her fists. "Why should he be so calculating, spoiling my plan like that?" She wanted to give her son a talking to, but since justice was not on her side, she had to swallow her defeat. At the same time she was uneasy, fearing that the abbot might have come in vain. Thus in restlessness she could not sleep.

Hearing no sound for awhile, Dasheng knew that the abbot had gone. Only then did he go back to his room and go to bed. Wu sent the maid to the gate for a second time, but the maid could not find the abbot there. She opened the gate and went out and looked about in the street. She did not see a single soul. When she reported back to Wu, the woman was devoured by impotent rage. She stayed up with wide-open eyes until morning. Seeing Dasheng the next day, she could not help but give way to her anger. "Why should a small child like you sit at the back gate and not go to bed?" she asked. "I did nothing bad," retorted Dasheng. "What's wrong with me sitting there?" Blushing, Wu scolded him, "You short-lived wretch! You did nothing evil, did I do anything wrong?" "Who said you did anything wrong?" her son replied. "I went there just to lock the gate and, since I had nothing to do in the night, I sat there for awhile. This cannot be a serious mistake." Although she resented his actions, Wu had no reason to rebuke him. "Mother will not run away," she said. "Why should you keep guard on me?" Tearfully she disappeared into her room. She expected a disciple would soon come and ask about the night's occurrences.

That day Dasheng did not go to school. In the parlor he opened books to read. From time to time he went to the front and back yards.

Seeing the Taoist disciple Tai Qing come, he stopped him and asked, "What are you up to?" "I want to see the madam," Tai Qing replied. "I will pass on your message," Dasheng said. Hearing the Taoist disciple's voice, Wu had the maid bring him in. Dasheng, however, closely followed. In the presence of Dasheng, the disciple could say nothing in private. All he could say was, "Master asks if the madam and the young master are all well." "We are all very well," said Dasheng, "Your master needn't worry. You may go back." The helpless Tai Qing stared at Dasheng, who was staring at him, and then he went away disappointed. Wu hated Dasheng even more bitterly after that. During the ensuing ten days or so she heard nothing from the abbot.

One day a schoolmate brought word that the teacher was back. Dasheng took leave of his mother and returned to school. Wu felt as if she was receiving a decree of amnesty from the ninth heaven. The Taoist disciples Tai Qing and Tai Su not only served as messengers for their master, they themselves craved savoring the sweetness of the woman. So they went there frequently like shuttles. Having been humiliated by Dasheng a few days before, however, they would never enter if they learned that he was home. Now Dasheng was out. As Wu was going to send a message to the abbot, Tai Qing came. Having been spied on by her son several times, Wu should have been more prudent from now on. But bewitched by her lust and wishing to make light of her young son, she remained reckless. She asked the abbot to come that night. She enjoined him to enter through the front gate where her son might not have taken any precaution — but that he should come in late hours. Thus an appointment was made.

It was late when Dasheng returned home. After he and his mother had supper, Wu with her maid ostensibly lit a torch and locked the front and back gates. Then she bade Dasheng go to bed. She, herself, also retired to her room. Dasheng considered the situation, saying to himself, "I was not home today. Something will certainly take place tonight." But why, he wondered, did she lock the gates? Suddenly he said, "I see! She did this to dispel my suspicions. I won't sleep. Something will happen." He sat up until midnight, then stole out. Seeing the gate between the front yard and the back yard not bolted and the back gate locked, he thought to himself, "He will surely come through the front gate." Dasheng stealthily moved to the front of the parlor and squatted in the dark. In the glimmering starlight he saw his mother and the maid came out. His mother stood in front of the door, meaning to prevent Dasheng from coming through it if he tried to do so. The maid went over to the gate and, hearing a tap, unlocked it and opened it. Then a figure slipped in. As the maid shut the gate, the three sneaked into the house together. Opening the gate wide immediately, Dasheng snatched an alarm gong and began to beat it, crying, "Stop thief!"

Kaifeng was the capital that covered a vast area and there were many thieves. So the authorities had ordered that every household should have a gong. If one family encountered a thief, they were to beat the gong and the people from the group of ten neighboring houses would come to help. If the victim suffered any loss, the whole neighborhood took responsibility and covered the loss. The order was strictly practiced.

Now the abbot was about to enter the room when he heard the gong. Frightened out of his wits, he hurried out without uttering a word. He tried to open the side gate, only to find it locked. So he dashed to the front gate. Fortunately, it was open. He ran out in such haste that he wished he had another pair of legs so he could go faster. Dasheng ran after him, but to save his mother's face, he did not mean to catch him. He, however, picked up a stone and slung it at the abbot. The stone hit the abbot's leg. The abbot drew back his leg and his shoe fell off, but he was too flurried to pick it up. So he ran with one foot wearing only a sock. When the neighbors came and asked what had happened, Dasheng told them the thief had escaped. The shoe in hand, he shut the gate and went back inside.

Wu was greatly frightened at the turn of events as she waited to enjoy her meeting with the abbot. She and the maid trembled in utter confusion. When the beats of the gong had died down and the front gate was shut, she somewhat regained her composure at the realization that the abbot had left. Dasheng came in and, knowing the answer, asked, "Are you frightened, Mother? I was stopping a thief." "Where is the thief?" his mother asked. "Why did you cause such an upheaval?" "I didn't catch the thief," replied Dasheng, showing her the shoe, "but I have one of his shoes. We may find out to whom it belongs to tomorrow." Wu understood that her son had deliberately unsettled her and her lover. She became even more hostile toward her son, but she could find no excuse to berate him. After this, the abbot dared not come. Thinking of the fright the abbot had taken, Wu was uneasy. Nursing enmity against her son, she wanted to conspire with the abbot to get even with her son, but she did not have the courage to make an appointment, for she had to be cautious as long as her son was around.

Two days later was the first anniversary of her husband's death. With a plan forming in her mind, Wu told Dasheng, "You may take some paper coins to your father's tomb and offer the first sacrifice. I'll prepare some food offerings and get there later in a sedan chair." Dasheng wondered to himself, is it really necessary to go to the tomb on my father's death anniversary? And why does she want me to go there first? She must want to send me ahead so that she can go to the monastery by herself. Let me show obedience and not reveal to her that I've seen through her intention. He said to his mother, "Yes, I'll go and wait for you there." Actually he did not go to the tomb, but instead went directly to the West Mountain Monastery. When he entered the monastery, the abbot was greatly surprised and dismayed. — Do you know why the abbot was in dismay? He was terrified because of the events of the other night. As he calmed down, he asked,

"What's up, my good nephew?" "My mother is coming," replied Dasheng. The abbot was flustered. When, he mused in perplexity, did she begin to stand by her son's side? How can she send her son here first if she wants to come? It's most odd!

As he stood there in doubt, he saw a sedan chair approach the monastery. When it arrived and a woman got down from the sedan chair, he saw this was none other than Wu. And as she stepped out, Lady Wu saw that her son was standing there. He greeted her, saying, "You've come, too, Mother!" Startled, she wondered how her jinx could have come too. She had to fabricate a lie. "I thought that since today is the anniversary of your father's death," she said, "it is necessary to redeem his soul with magic figures. So I've come here to see your uncle." "I, too, thought so," said Dasheng. "It is rather useless to visit the tomb on an anniversary. Better ask my uncle for help. So I came here first." Despite her bitter hatred for the youth, she could do nothing. The abbot, too, had to make tea for them and inscribe magic figures, which he burned after announcing his will — all this was done only for show. And there was nothing else he could do about this awkward situation. After much ado, Wu ordered Dasheng to go home first, but he refused, saying, "I'll go after Mother's sedan chair has left." The helpless woman had to get into the sedan chair and leave. She had gone to the monastery in vain — unable to share a private moment with her lover. With each step on the way home her abhorrence for her son increased and finally she made up her mind to get rid of him.

The sedan chair traveled fast. Dasheng was too young to keep pace. Besides, he had to relieve himself. The way ahead is to our home, he reasoned, so I don't think there can be any problem. I needn't follow her too closely. So thinking, he let himself trail behind. Perhaps he was fated to have trouble. At this point Tai Su bumped into Wu's sedan chair from the opposite direction. Wu asked the sedan carriers, "Is the young master following me?" "No," replied a carrier, "he's far behind us, out of sight." Rejoiced, Wu beckoned Tai Su to the sedan chair and whispered to him, "I'll send off the young devil with a scheme tonight. Your master must come and I'll have something important to discuss with him." "Master's been frightened many times," replied Tai Su. "He dares not enter Madam's house again." "If that's the case," said Wu, "he doesn't need to enter the gate. He may stay outside and make a signal by throwing a brick over the wall. I will go out of the gate and have a talk with him. He can come in when I am sure the coast is clear. There will be no danger." As she said this, she made eyes at the disciple. Tai Su, infatuated, wished to have her right there on the grassland, and would have if there had been no sedan carriers around. Wu whispered into Tai Su's ear, "You come too and I'm sure it will be good for you." Tai Su trotted away, his head swinging.

When Wu returned home, she paid off the bearers. Then Dasheng arrived. Towards evening Wu prepared some food and had dinner with her son in her room. She comforted him in a sweet voice, "My son, your father has died and I have only you to look after. Why are you recalcitrant toward me?" "It is because my father has died," replied Dasheng, "that you have made up your mind to support the family. How dare I, as your son, to disobey you? But I have heard talk about you that I don't like." Wu turned her angry look into a smile. "To tell the truth, I did something immature when I was young. Now in my thirties, I repent for what I did in those years. I am determined to lead a straight life and look after you." Dasheng was all smiles at his repentant mother. "If so, I will be blessed all my life," he said. Filling a cup of wine for Dasheng, Wu said, "If you can forgive your mother, please take this cup of wine." Dasheng was apprehensive. Is she trying to poison me? he wondered. Cup in hand, he hesitated. Wu realized he was suspicious of her intentions. "Can your mother be scheming against you?" She took the cup of wine from him and finished it in one gulp. Realizing he had misunderstood his mother, Dasheng felt guilty. He took up the pot and poured wine for himself, "Your son should be forfeited by this drink," he said as he downed three cups at one go. "I am penitent, so I have told you the truth," Wu said. "If you understand me and forget my misconduct, let's drink to our content." Dasheng was happy to hear this. He took every toast she offered to him without hesitation. Wu was a good drinker, while Dasheng was too young to drink much. So Wu deliberately soused him. Soon he began to yawn and was about to fall down in sleep. With more cups forced on him, his head turned and he collapsed. Getting the maid to put him to bed, Wu went out and locked the door. "Thank Heaven!" she said, "He fell into my trap at last."

She went out and waited. When she heard a clatter on the roof, she realized it was the brick thrown by the abbot from outside. She immediately asked the maid servant to open the back gate. There Tai Su entered, saying, "Master is outside of the gate. He dares not come in. You may go out to see him, Madam." Wu had the maid keep guard at the door to her room and went with Tai Su towards the front yard in the dark. Tai Su suddenly seized Wu in his arms. Wu turned around and held him, saying, "Oh, you little slave! I have been in love with you for a long time. We didn't make it the other day, but today let me pay off the debt first." They moved to the empty bed where her son used to sleep and began to make love.

When they finished, they ordered their clothes and opened the front gate to see the abbot waiting outside. Wu stepped out and let him in. But the abbot hesitated. "The little beast has fallen in drunkenness in my room," said Wu. "I want to talk with you about how to seize this moment to finish him off. Be quick and come in." Following her in, the abbot said, "It will not do. How can you end the life of your own son like that?" "I'll do anything for your sake," she said, "and I can't endure the annoyance anymore." "But if you do this," said the abbot, "you'll have to bear the consequences if someone discovers it." "I am his mother," said Wu. "Even if I kill him, it's not a felony." But the abbot replied, "There must be someone who knows our affair. If you put your son away, you'll merely take the responsibility of intentionally killing your own child. And if an enemy accuses me of being the accomplice, I'll have to pay for his life!" "If you are so timid," said Wu, "and will keep him around us, we'll never get anywhere. How can I live a happy life?"

"Why not get him a wife," the abbot suggested, "and drown him in pleasure? Then he will not be able to steel his heart to supervise you." "That would be still less desirable!" exclaimed Wu. "I cannot foresee what woman we could get him. If such a woman is not of one mind with me, I'll have another overseer and I'll have an even harder time. The only good way is to get rid of him. Without him around, although I can't marry a priest like you, nobody will prevent us from keeping in contact as cousins. In this way we will have a long and happy time together."

"If that is the case," the abbot offered, "I have an idea: let the authorities do it for us." "How can it be done that way?" asked Wu. "The magistrate of the Kaifeng Prefecture loathes disobedient sons," said the abbot. "Accused disobedient sons are either flogged to death or punished heavily and sentenced to imprisonment. If you file a complaint against since your son for being unfilial, he will not be able to plead for himself. Since you are his mother and not a stepmother or a surrogate one, nobody will doubt what you say. Even if he is not put to death, he will be thrown into prison and will not able to come out for a long time. In this way we will remove the obstacle. And if you can harden your heart and insist that he should be put to death, the authorities will certainly do what a mother demands." "But what will we do if the devil lays bare our affair when he is desperate?" asked Wu. "How can a son be a witness to his mother's adultery?" the abbot replied. "If he talks about it, you may say that the unworthy son is slandering you. Then the authorities will be more convinced that he is unfilial. Furthermore, if one accuses adulterers, he has to catch them in the act. But no one has hard evidence for our relationship. What he may say, the authorities will take as his excuse to cover up his own fault. The authority will certainly not investigate into the secret affairs of a mother on behalf of a son. You may set your fears at rest."

"Today I told him to visit his father's tomb," said Wu, "but he didn't go there. That can serve as evidence, and with it I can charge him with being unfilial. But we must not let him know our plan." "He is living with you," said the abbot, "so it's inconvenient for you to carry out the design. I am familiar with some yamen runners. Let me lodge the complaint in secret and try to get the authorities to accept the case and send runners to arrest him. Then you may appear in court as the witness. Neither a human being nor a ghost will discover our plan." "This is the way to achieve our end," said Wu, "but after my son dies, you must treat me kindly and satisfy my every need. After all, if something goes wrong, won't I have lost a son for nothing?" "What should I do to make you happy?" the abbot asked. "Sleep with me every night," Wu replied. "You mustn't let me sleep alone." "But I have business to attend to in the monastery," said the abbot. "How can I accompany you every night?" "If you can't find time," said Wu, "you may send one of your two disciples in your place. I can't stand loneliness at night." "I will do just that," the abbot answered readily, "My two disciples are confidants. They are interesting fellows. If you like, we may make merry two or three together, even if I am here, not to mention when I am absent. Isn't that a good idea?" These remarks turned Wu on. So they climbed into the bed in the parlor and played an intense game to her heart's content. Then Wu said in a sweet voice. "For your sake I will give up my son. You mustn't forget me." "If I betray Madam," the abbot replied, taking an oath, "let me be left unburied and unencoffined after death!"

After their heated love making the abbot was exhausted, but the woman was not satisfied yet. "Why not let Tai Su come and have a try?" she said. "Wonderful!" replied the abbot. He got up, went out to Tai Su and pulled him by the hand, saying softly, "Madam Wu wants you." As Tai Su followed him into the room, the abbot said, "Be quick to get into the bed and keep Madam company!" Although Tai Su had done it once already that night, he was young and so it was no problem for him to get an erection for a second time. There he jumped onto her and began to dally. Sitting on the bed rand, the abbot said, "I have offered you this good opportunity," but he didn't know that this was the second time for Tai Su to be at it with the woman. Only after both men had mounted her was Wu gratified. "Without the young devil," Wu said to the abbot, "no one will keep us from having this enjoyment." Then, fearing that her son might awake, she sent them off. "I will be waiting for good news in the next couple of days," she added. "Be sure to make it a success." With repeated injunctions she saw them to the gate. The abbot went ahead, Wu seized Tai Su's hands in the dark and they embraced and kissed before she let him go. Having locked the gate and returning to her room, she found the maid dozing off at the door. She opened the door, only to see her son asleep. She went to the bed in the parlor and slept.

When Dasheng awoke the next morning, he was surprised to find himself in his mother's bed. I must have been badly drunk yesterday evening! he mused. Then, recalling what his mother had said the night before, he wondered if she was sincere, and whether she had done something while he was drunk. Seeing Dasheng, Wu deliberately found fault with him. "You were drunk and lost consciousness in my bed," she said, scolding him, "so I had nowhere to sleep all night!" Dasheng felt guilty and dared not talk back.

In the early morning two days later someone knocked loudly at the door. Dasheng was suspicious. When he opened it, two runners rushed in and threw a rope around his neck. Dasheng was astounded. "What's the matter, sir?" he asked. "You short-lived prisoner!" the runners brawled out. "Your mother has accused you of unfilial behavior. The authorities will beat you to death. And you are asking what the matter is!" Flurried, Dasheng cried, "Allow me to see my mother once more."

"Your mother will go to court to testify for sure," said the runners. One of them escorted him to Wu's room. The knock at the gate, the roar outside, and her son's crying revealed to Wu what was happening. When she hurried out, Dasheng held onto her crying, "Mother, I am not a good son, but it was you who gave birth to me. How can you be so cruel to me?" "Why should you have been disobedient?" retorted Wu. "Now I'll teach you a lesson!" "In what way was I disobedient to you?" the son asked. "The other day I asked you to visit your father's tomb," said Wu, "why didn't you go?" "You didn't go either," Dasheng replied. "Why blame me?" Not knowing what the argument was about, the runners put in, "It's your duty to pay homage to your father's tomb, how can you blame your mother? At first we thought she might be your step-mother or a surrogate mother, but now we know that she is your real mother. It's obvious you are unfilial. There is no way for you to justify yourself. Now let's go to the court!" Together with Wu they hauled the young man to the court of the Kaifeng Prefecture.

They got there just as Prefect Li Jie was taking his seat in court. A wise and incorruptible man, Prefect Li Jie bitterly hated unfilial sons. Seeing the complaint was about an unfilial son, he scowled as the culprit was brought in. But he became suspicious when the culprit turned out to be a child fifteen or so years of age. "In what way could such a little child have so offended his mother that she accused him of being unfilial?" Rapping his gavel on the desk he said to Dasheng, "Your mother accused you of being unfilial. How will you plead your innocence?" "I am young," replied Dasheng, "but I've read some books. How could I dare to be unfilial? I have been unfortunate ever since I was born. I have lost my father and now I have incurred my mother's disfavor so that she has sent me here. This alone is my unpardonable sin. You may beat me to death to please my mother, but I will not explain for myself." As he said this, tears ran down his cheeks like rain.

The young man aroused the prefect's compassion for him. He thought to himself, if a son speaks this way, can he be unfilial? There must be some reason behind this. Then he had second thoughts. "Maybe the boy just has the gift of gab." Then he summoned in the mother, who came in with her hair tied up in a handkerchief. As she approached with graceful steps, she removed the handkerchief. When the prefect bade her to raise her head, he saw she was a young woman and quite pretty. He became even more suspicious. "In what way is your son unfilial?" he asked her. "My husband died," she replied, "and my son doesn't obey me. He makes his own decisions in whatever he does. When I admonish him, he calls me names. At first I thought he is just a child and so I did not treat him tit for tat. But now he is becoming more and more disobedient. Since I cannot manage him, I have had to resort to law to discipline him." The prefect then said to Dasheng, "That's your mother's accusation. What will you say to defend yourself?" "How dare I argue with my mother?" Dasheng answered. "What she said is right." "Is your mother partial to any of your brothers?" the prefect asked again. "My mother is very kind and she has me as her only one child. How can she be partial?" replied Dasheng. Thereupon the prefect beckoned him to the table and said to him in private, "There must be some reason in all this. You may tell me what it is and I will make the decision for you." Kowtowing, Dasheng said, "There is no reason at all. It is my fault." "If so," said the prefect, "no parent in the world can be wrong. Since she has accused you, I will punish you." "I deserve to be punished," said Dasheng.

This made the prefect still more skeptical. But for the sake of his own prestige, he shouted, "Give him a flogging!" Accordingly Dasheng was laid down on the floor and flogged ten times with bamboo poles. The prefect calmly observed Wu, and found no sign of uneasiness on her face. She even fell on her knees and entreated, "Oh my lord, I beg you to beat him to death right now!" The prefect was furious, "You shrew! This must be a child from your husband's former wife or his concubine. You are so virtueless that you want to have him killed!" "My lord," replied Wu, "he is my own child. You may ask him." "Is this your own mother?" the prefect asked the son. "She is my own mother and it cannot be otherwise," he cried. "But why does she hate you so bitterly?" the prefect questioned again. "Even I myself don't know," replied Dasheng, "but you may put me to death as my mother demands." This increased the prefect's doubts, but he deliberately put on a angry look and shouted at Dasheng, "You are indeed an unfilial son, and no question about it. You'll certainly be put to death!" At this stern statement Wu kowtowed repeatedly, "Oh, my lord, please finish him off as soon as possible, and free me from trouble." "Do you have another son or an adopted one?" the prefect asked her. "No," she replied. "Since you have only one son," said the prefect, "I'll give him an admonishment and spare his life so that he may take care of you in your later years." "I'd rather live by myself," said Wu, "than have this son." "A dead person cannot be revived," said the prefect. "You must not regret it." Wu replied between clenched teeth, "I'll not regret it." "All right," said the prefect, "you may buy a coffin tomorrow and come to pick up his body. I'll put him in prison for today." Thereupon Dasheng was put into prison and Wu was dismissed.

Wu went away, her face glowing. Gazing at her until she was out of the gate, the prefect thought to himself, her manner shows she is not a virtuous woman. There must be something hidden behind this case. The child doesn't want to tell; he is a filial son. I must make the matter straight. He summoned a deft and keen-eyed runner and bade him, "When the woman goes out, no matter how far she goes, there must be someone she talks with. Note who he is and report every detail to me. If you make an accurate report, I will award you with a high prize; if you provide false information or cover something up, I'll punish you with death once I find out!" Since the prefect was rigorous with discipline, the runner never dared to defy his order. He went out and tagged along behind Wu.

Only a few steps out of the yamen, he saw a Taoist greet Wu and ask her, "How did it turn out?" Smiling, Wu said, "Settled. Just buy me a coffin and tomorrow I'll come to take his body away." The Taoist clapped his hands, "Great! A coffin is no problem. I'll have it carried here tomorrow." Together they went away, talking and laughing all the way. The runner recognized the Taoist as the abbot of the West Mountain Monastery. When he reported this to the prefect, the prefect said, "There is an affair! That's why she wants to kill her own son scrupulously. It's really outrageous!" He wrote something on a piece of paper, sealed it and handed it to the runner, "When the woman comes tomorrow, I'll order the coffin to be brought in. Then open the envelope and act as I have written."

When the court was held into the next day, Wu was the first to appear. "According to your order yesterday, I have prepared a coffin," she said, and here I am claiming my unfilial son's body." The prefect told her, "Your son was beaten to death last night." Without the slightest trace of sadness on her face, Wu kowtowed, "Thank you for your justice, my lord." Thereupon the prefect declared, "Carry in the coffin!" At the order the runner opened the envelope that had been sealed the day before and found it to be a warrant written in cinnabar which read, "Arrest Wu's adulterer, that is, the Taoist who looks after the coffin, and don't let him escape." The runner had committed the Taoist to memory the day before, so he would not catch the wrong man. When the abbot was bossing around the carriers of the coffin, the runner collared him and showed him the warrant in red. Unable to struggle free, the abbot had to follow the runner into the yamen to see the prefect. The prefect asked him, "You are a Taoist. Why did you buy the coffin for a woman and hire the carriers?" Finding no excuse, the abbot had to admit, "The woman is my cousin. Since she asked me for help, I lent her a hand." "So you are the child's uncle, but you are helping her to kill your nephew!" said the prefect. "That is her own business and I have nothing to do with it," said the abbot. "As her relative you did nothing to intermediate the matter when she accused her son, but when she needed a coffin, you offered assistance readily enough. Isn't that proof that you are having an affair with her and that you are her collaborator in this plot? You base slave! Even death can not expiate your crime!" The prefect commanded that the abbot be cramped and tortured for a confession. Unable to sustain the pain, the abbot confessed everything. The prefect then had the abbot sign his statement that said, "Huang Miaoxiu, a Taoist from the West Mountain Monastery, abetted Wu to kill her son because he was committing adultery with her." Seeing this, Wu moaned inwardly.

Promptly the prefect had Dasheng brought from prison. When Dasheng had been put into prison, he thought to himself that the prefect is amiable and might not go as far as to take my life. But as he approached the court and saw the new coffin, he was quite frightened. He now wondered, "Will he really have me flogged to death today?" Trembling, he knelt down. Then he heard the prefect ask him, "Do you know Huang Miaoxiu, the Taoist from the West Mountain Monastery?" Realizing the question touched the point, Dasheng feigned ignorance. "No, I don't know him," he answered. "You don't know your enemy?" asked the prefect. As Dasheng turned his head, he saw that the abbot, crippled from the torture, was groaning on the ground. Dasheng was surprised and could not make out what had happened. He kowtowed to the prefect saying, "My lord, you are just and insightful. How dare I say anything!" The prefect then said, "I asked you repeatedly yesterday what was the problem, but you didn't tell me the truth. This proves that you are filial. However, I have found out all the details." Then he summoned Wu and told her, "You'll have a coffin with a body in it!" Wu thought the prefect would beat her son, but what she heard was, "Pull down Huang Miaoxiu and put forth all your strength to flog him!" Soon the abbot was dying, bruised and lacerated. The prefect had some of his runners put Huang, still breathing, into the coffin and nail it shut. Her face ashen pail, Wu quivered in fear, her teeth crackling.

As the coffin was nailed, the prefect shouted at Wu, "You wanton bitch! For the sake of adultery, you can bring yourself to kill your own son. What's the use of letting you remain in the world? You should be thrashed to death, too. — Runners, pull her down in the court and give her a sound spanking!" The runners picked Wu up like hawks pouncing upon a sparrow, threw her down on the ground in front of the stairs and were about to torture her. But Liu Dasheng dashed forward and lay down on her back, crying, "Let me take the punishment on her behalf!" The runners thus could not administer the flogging, and some of them came and tried to pull him away, but he clung to his mother tightly, crying. The prefect beckoned the runners to stop. He bade Dasheng to come closer, and said to him, "Your mother wanted to kill you. If I flog her you can vent your anger. Why do you protect her?" "How dare I bear a grudge against my own mother?" replied the son. And my lord does not blame me, but instead blames my mother. I cannot set my mind at ease this way. I plead my lord to consider my sincerity!" And he kowtowed repeatedly.

The prefect ordered Wu to rise, saying, "You should have been put to death. With a view of your son's feelings, I will now spare your life. You must mend your ways from now on. If you commit sin again, I'll not spare you any more!" Wu had thought she was finished when she saw the Taoist put to death. When her son persisted in taking the torture on her behalf and pleaded mercy for her, she was moved, but made no expression of it. Now, hearing the prefect's warning, she was aware of her son's consideration for her. Tears ran down her cheeks. "I betrayed my own son," she said, "and thus I deserve death. From now on I will look after my son and dare not commit any outrage." "Obviously, your son is a promising child," the prefect told her. "I will commend his filial deeds." Upon hearing this Dasheng kowtowed and implored, "Oh, my lord, if you do this, it will mean that you are eulogizing me at the expense of my mother. I wouldn't venture to go that far all my life." Hearing this, Wu embraced her son and burst into crying right in the court. The prefect let her go home.

Accordingly, the prefect sent a summons to Taoists of Abbot Huang Miaoxiu's sect at the West Mountain Monastery, telling them to claim the corpse and coffin. By the time the Taoists had learned what had happened in court, they dispatched Tai Su and Tai Qing. When the disciples were brought in by runners, the prefect scrutinized them and found them to be handsome youths. Those priests deceive young people to satisfy their lust, he thought to himself. One day these two handsome youth will also bring ill repute to good women. So he instructed the runners to make sure that the young Taoists were returned to their parents as soon as they claimed the coffin and buried it, and they were never permitted to enter a monastery again. The runners were ordered to obtain a receipt from their homes and report back to the prefect. The other Taoists in the monastery were to be warned separately.

As for Wu, after she returned home, she was so grateful to her son that she treated him kindly. The son, on his part, was meek and docile. Thus no discord between them occurred again. Furthermore, since the abbot had died and the young disciples were dismissed, Wu had to set her mind on leading an honest life. But whenever she thought of her former experiences, she was disconsolate. The fright she suffered developed into some illness. Before long she died. Liu Dasheng buried her remains together with those of his father, and when the mourning period expired, he got married. The couple respected each other and the family enjoyed a reputation for moral discipline. Later he attempted to acquire a scholarly degree and, with the recommendation of Prefect Li Jie, became an official.

Let's turn to Tai Su and Tai Qing. After they were dismissed, on their way home they talked about what had happened. Tai Qing said,

"I dreamed last night that the Supreme Deity told me, 'Your master has achieved tremendous attainments in self-cultivation. I will make him a holder. You may claim this on his behalf.' I wondered how it was that our master, who ran so wildly, could have achieved any attainments? And why should he become a holder of an official post and how can we claim it for him? Today we were ordered to take his coffin. Now I see that the 'holder' meant this holder of his body." "Our master enjoyed a great deal of sensual pleasure," said Tai Su, "and so his death was worthy of him. But without him, our road to such bliss is cut off too." "Even if the master were alive, we would be salivating in vain," retorted Tai Qing. "Not really," said Tai Su, "I have tasted it." And he then related his experience to Tai Qing. "We were under the same tutor," said Tai Qing, "but you were favored. Fortunately we have returned to the secular world and we can both marry a wife to quench our thirst." They buried their master in the graveyard of the ancestor Taoists and they returned home.

After some time Tai Su recalled his relation with Wu. Unable to forget her, he went to the Lius to ask about her. Having learned of her death, he was grief-stricken, and drifted into a trance. Whenever he shut his eyes, he saw Wu coming to make love with him. Sometimes he dreamed that his master had come to struggle with him over her. He soon contracted nocturnal emissions and consumption. Before long he died. By that time Tai Qing had married. Hearing about Tai Su's death, he said, "I never realized that a Taoist must never violate the commandments until today. The master was killed because of his lecherous behavior, and Tai Su died of diseases because he, too, was infected. Fortunately I never did anything wrong, or I would have become a ghost together with them." After that he lived an honest life until he died. From this story we can see that either the good or the evil will eventually receive their due retribution. All Taoists must wake up to this truth!

Tale 12

The Soul of Elder Sister Keeps Her Love Company; Younger Sister, Recovered from Illness, Fulfills the Union

This story is about a wealthy man surnamed Wu who lived in Yangzhou during the reign of Dade [1297-1307] of the Yuan Dynasty. Since he once had been a garrison commander, he was called Commander Wu. Living near the Spring Breeze Chamber, he had two baby daughters. One was Xingniang and the other, two years younger, was Qingniang. Wu's neighbor, a prefect named Cui, was his close friend. Cui had a son named Xingge who had been born in the same year as Xingniang. When Cui asked Wu for his daughter to be wed to his son, Wu gladly accepted the proposal. Cui presented a gold hair pin as the betrothal gift. After the engagement, Cui moved with his family to a distant place because he was taking a position in the government there. In the ensuing fifteen years, however, Wu never heard from the Cuis. By this time Xingniang had become nineteen. Seeing that the daughter had grown up, the mother said to Commander Wu, "Xingge of the Cuis has been gone for fifteen years and we have heard nothing at all from him. Now Xingniang has grown up. How can we stick to the engagement and waste her youth?" "A promise is a promise," replied Commander Wu, "we cannot take it back even if we are offered a thousand *liang* of gold. I have promised to give my daughter to my friend's son. I cannot go back on my word simply because we have heard no news about them." The mother, after all, was a woman. Seeing her daughter without a spouse, she was worried. Every day she importuned Commander Wu, trying to persuade him into agreeing to find another spouse for the daughter.

Xingniang, however, was waiting for Cui's return and she never wavered. Although her father was adamant on his decision, hearing her mother's grumbling made her groan inwardly about her fate. Because of this she often shed tears. She was also afraid that her father might succumb to her mother's pestering and eventually change his mind. Her only hope was that the young man Cui would return as soon as possible. But despite her eager expectancy, she heard nothing from him. By and by she lost her appetite and became ill. She lay in bed for half a year and died. Her parents, sister and the entire family cried their eyes out. During the encoffinment, her mother, with the hair pin presented by the Cuis in her hand, wailed over her body: "This is the gift from your husband to-be. Now that you have died, why should I keep it? I will feel sad at the sight of it. Better you wear it." With this, she stuck it in Xingniang's hair and had the coffin nailed. Three days later Xingniang's body was carried out of town and buried. A memorial tablet was set for her in the house, and before it relatives tearfully offered sacrifices from morning till night.

Two months later, Cui returned. Commander Wu ushered the young man into the house and asked him, "Where have you been these years? How are your father and mother?" "My father," replied Cui, "took the position of judge in Xuande Prefecture, but he died in his post. My mother also died several years ago. I observed the period of mourning for them there. Now that the period of mourning has expired, I have

come to fulfill my engagement." The reply brought tears to
Commander Wu's eyes. "My unfortunate daughter Xingniang," he said,
"became ill pining for you. Two months ago she passed away with
grievance in her heart. She was buried out of town. If you had come
back half a year earlier, she might not have become so ill as to die. It is
too late for you to come now." Then he resumed crying. Although Cui
only knew Xingniang by name, he was touched too. "My daughter was
buried," said Commander Wu, "but the memorial tablet for her is there
in the room. You may see it so that her spirit will know you are here."
The tearful father led Cui into the inner room. As Cui raised his head,
he saw:

> *Streamers of white paper fluttering and figures of virgin boy
> and girl serving as guides to the nether world. On the streamers
> were sutra passages written in gold; the child guides, one
> holding a silver basin and the other an embroidered
> handkerchief, stood facing each other. Smoke curled up from an
> incense burner; flames shimmered on the wicks of lamps. A
> picture showed a rare beauty and the white wooden tablet bore
> the words, "Our newly-deceased daughter".*

Cui prostrated himself before the tablet. Smiting the table, Commander
Wu said loudly, "Oh Xingniang, my poor daughter! Here is your
husband. Your spirit mustn't be gone so far away. Do you know what
is going on now?" Saying this, he started wailing. At those broken-
hearted words, members of his family cried themselves half dead.
Even Cui shed a lot of tears.

Then Commander Wu burned some paper coins and led Cui in to
see the mother, who, still sobbing, returned with a half courtesy. When
the two men returned to the front hall, Commander Wu said to Cui,
"Since your parents are deceased and you have come a long way here,
you may stay in my house. Even if there have not been the engagement,

I would take my friend's son as my own. Don't regard yourself as a stranger just because of Xingniang's death." He had Cui's luggage carried in and put him up in a small study. Commander Wu went to see him every morning and evening and they became quite intimate.

Half a month later Pure Brightness Day* arrived. Thinking of his newly deceased daughter, Xingniang, Commander Wu went with the whole family to visit her tomb. Qingniang, Xingniang's sister, now seventeen years old, went to the tomb in a sedan chair behind her mother. Cui was left alone at home. Because the female members of a well-reputed family seldom went out, whenever a festival arrived in the bright spring, they would find an excuse to go on an outing. Although they were depressed when they visited the tomb of Xingniang, the wilderness with red peach flowers in blossom and willow trees putting forth green leaves was a good place for them to go. They strolled here and there and didn't go home until dusk. Cui came out of the gate to await their return. Seeing two sedan chairs for ladies approaching, he moved to the left of the gate to greet them. The first sedan chair soon entered the gate. When the second one followed close behind and moved past him, he saw an object fall from it with a "clang" on the brick-paved ground. When the chair was through the gate, Cui hurried over to pick up the object and found it to be a gold hair pin. Realizing that it belonged to some female member of the family, Cui hastened in to return it. But the gate to the inner quarters was bolted. The whole family had become tired after the day's outing and mellow from the day's drinking, so when they had entered their rooms, they had locked the doors and gone to sleep. Understanding that they were sleeping, Cui refrained from knocking at the door, and thought it better to return the object the next day.

After Cui retired to the study and put the hair pin on a book case, he

---

*Pure Brightness Day falls on April 5. It is a traditional festival when Chinese people visit their ancestral tombs.

sat down lost in reverie under the candlelight. Why, he wondered, was the marriage aborted, and he ended up as a lonely man under another's roof. Though for the time being he was treated like a son, he knew this was not a solution, and he did not know what would finally become of him. A cloud of melancholy hung over his heart. Heaving a sigh, he went to bed. Just as he was lying down, he heard a knock at the door. "Who is it?" he asked. But there was no answer. He dismissed the sound as an illusion. But as he lay down again, the sound became a hasty "rat-tat-tat". He raised his voice and asked who it was, but again there was no answer. Bewildered, Cui sat up to put on his shoes, when the knocking was heard again. But he heard no voice. Unable to overcome his curiosity, he stood up. Seeing the lamp was not out, he trimmed the wick to make it brighter. Holding the lamp in his hand, he opened the door. In the bright lamplight he clearly saw a beautiful girl of eighteen or so standing by the door. With the door open, she drew aside the curtain and walked in.

Cui retreated a couple of steps in consternation. The girl, beaming with sweet smiles, asked in a low voice, "Don't you recognize me, master? I am Qingniang, Xingniang's sister. When I entered the gate a moment ago, my hair pin slipped from the sedan chair. So I came to look for it. Have you seen it?" Hearing that this was his sister-in-law, Cui reverently answered, "When your sedan chair followed another one into the gate, a hair pin did fall on the ground. I picked it up. I wanted to return it to you, but I saw the doors were shut. Not wanting to disturb you, I decided to wait until tomorrow. Now that you've come for it, I'll return it to you." Taking the pin from his book case, he put it on the table, saying, "Here you are." The girl reached out a delicate hand to pick it up and pin it into her hair. All smiles, she said to Cui, "Had I known you saved it for me, I wouldn't have come to take it in the night. But it is now midnight. I cannot return to my room. May I share your pillow and mat and stay for the night?" Frightened, Cui answered, "What are you saying! Your parents treat me as their flesh-and-blood. How could I dare to be so impudent as to defile your chastity? Please go back. I dare not obey you!" The girl, however, insisted, "Now everyone is sound asleep. Nobody knows I am here. Why don't we profit from this good opportunity and fulfill our wishes? The two of us may see each other in secret. We'll be dearer to each other because we are relatives. Why not?" "No," said Cui, "If you don't want others to know it, simply don't do it. I am obliged to you for your kindness, but if someone got wind of what's going on between us, I wouldn't be able to look your parents in the eye, and furthermore, if outsiders learned of it, how could I acquit myself as a man? Wouldn't that ruin my reputation for the rest of my life?" "This is a pleasant night," said the girl, "In the dead of night I am lonely and you, too, are in solitude. It seems we are predestined to be together in the same room. Simply enjoy this blissful moment and don't worry whether or not we'll be discovered. Besides, I will try to keep our contact from being discovered. Please don't hesitate, master, or we'll let this opportunity slip by."

Impressed by her sweet words and extreme beauty, Cui could not help becoming infatuated. But when he thought of the Commander's kindness to him, he could not give himself over. Like a child letting off a fire cracker, he was timid about something he loved to do. He wanted to grant her request, but on second thought he shook his head. "No, that won't do," he said. He implored the girl, "Please allow me to keep my personal integrity for the sake of your sister, Xingniang." His repeated refusal threw the ashamed girl into a fury. She scowled at him, "My father treats you as if you were his nephew and puts you up in this study. How dare you lure me here in this late hour of the night? What are you up to? If I make it public and tell my father, he will report you to the authorities. Let me see how you'll defend yourself! Certainly you'll not be spared." She was stern in voice and countenance. Seeing her turn the blame on him, Cui was scared. She is tough indeed, he thought to himself. Now that she is in my room, I have no way of clearing the matter up. If she makes a false accusation against me, how will I be able to prove my innocence? I'd better obey her. At least the affair will not be discovered for the time being. Then I'll find a way out at my leisure. Indeed, he was like a ram butting at a hedge, only to have its horns entangled in the hedge so that it was torn between the choices of advance and withdrawal. He said with an obsequious smile, "Please don't be so loud. Since you're so kind to me. I'll do your bidding." Thereupon the girl became happy. "It's so timid of you," she told him. Cui closed the door and the two of them took off the clothes and went to bed. A song to the tune of Xi Jiang Yue intones their union:

A solitary youth all around roaming
And a girl with teeth glistening and cheeks blooming
On brocaded bedding lie double
Like a passionate phoenix couple.

This seems a union fortunate.
Who knows the mystery in it?
When with his new love he swims in bliss
He tastes his former love's tenderness.

When the clouds expended the rains in indescribable joy, they found themselves burning with love for each other. At daybreak she got up, said good-bye to Cui and sneaked back to her boudoir.

Though Cui had got her first taste of the pleasure of the union, he felt guilty, always fearing that it might be discovered by other people. Fortunately the girl came and went in secret and she walked with light steps. Every morning she would sneak back to her boudoir and in the evening she would sneak out again to frolic in the study by the side of the gate. Everybody was kept in the dark about the carryings-on.

One night a month later the girl said to Cui, "I am a girl in a boudoir and you a traveler away from home. Fortunately no one has seen us together. But I am afraid that the road to happiness cannot be smooth and our meetings cannot always go on this way. Once our affair is laid bare, my parents will blame us. Then I will be confined to my room and you will be driven out. Even though I'm willing to take the consequences, I will feel guilty for damaging your good name. We'd better make a long-term plan." Cui replied, "That was precisely why I dared not comply with you the first night you came. Otherwise how could I, a man and not a vegetable, be apathetic to affection? But what can we do now?" "In my opinion," said the girl, "we can elope to another place before it is too late. Hiding ourselves in a strange county, we could accompany each other in happiness till death. What do you think of my plan?" "That's a good idea indeed," said Cui, "but I am a lonely traveler with no friends or kin here. Where can we go?" After a pause, he hit upon an idea. "Now I remember," he said, "that my late father once said he had a loyal servant by the name of Jin Rong who lived in Lücheng Town of the city of Zhenjiang. He is a rich farmer. If we go to him, he may cherish his former master's feelings and certainly will not refuse us. And we can reach him easily by water." "If so," said the girl, "we'd better be quick. Let's go this very night."

So settled, they rose before daybreak and got everything ready. Since the study was at the side of the gate, it provided easy access to the outside world. Immediately outside of it was a small river and a ferry crossing. There Cui called a rowboat to the gate and helped the girl on board. They made directly to Guazhou, where Cui paid the boatman and hired a ship for the long journey. Then they sailed across a larger river, reached Runzhou [present-day Zhenjiang, Jiangsu Province], journeyed by way of Danyang, for forty more *li*, and arrived at Lücheng. Having moored the ship, Cui climbed onto the bank and asked a villager, "Is there a Jin Rong living here?" "He is the neighborhood chief here," replied the villager, "and he is well-off and honest and kind. Everyone knows him. Why do you ask about him?"

"I am his relative," said Cui, "and I have come to see him. Would you mind showing me the direction?" Pointing to a house the villager said, "See the large brew-house there? He lives next door to it."

Pleased with the answer, Cui went back to the ship and comforted the girl. Then he entered the gate to Jin Rong's house and walked directly in. Hearing steps, Jin came out to ask, "Who is this honorable guest?" Cui moved forward and bowed. "Where are you from, scholar?" asked Jin. "I am the son of Lord Cui from Yangzhou," replied Cui. The mention of "Cui from Yangzhou" obviously surprised Jin, who asked, "What is the rank of Lord Cui?" "He was a judge of Xuande Prefecture. He has passed away," replied Cui. "What's your relationship to him?" asked Jin. "He was my father." "Then you are the young master! Do you remember your infant name?" "My infant name was Xingge," "Then you are my young master!" Pushing his guest into a seat, Jin prostrated himself before Cui. "When did the old master pass away?" he asked. "Three years ago," Cui answered. Thereupon Jin arranged a table, set up a memorial tablet for the old master on it and kowtowed before it, crying all the time as he did all this.

Then Jin asked, "Why are you here, young master?" "When my father was alive," Cui replied, "he arranged a marriage between me and Xingniang, the daughter of Commander Wu ..." "This I know," Jin broke in. "Have you held the wedding ceremony?" "No," said Cui. "Unexpectedly, Xingniang fell ill when she heard no news from my family. By the time I got there, she had been dead for two months. Commander Wu had not forgotten the former agreement and so he put me up in his home. Fortunately Qingniang, Xingniang's sister, had an eye for me and we became man and wife in secret. For fear that we might be discovered, I am trying to find a place for settlement. I have no one else to turn to for help. I remember my late father once said you were a loyal man and that you lived in Lücheng. So here I am, along with Qingniang. If you still cherish the memory of your former master, please help us." Hearing this, Jin said, "There's no problem. I'm duty bound to share my young master's worries." He called out his wife to salute the young master and bade her to go with maid servants to the ship and pick up Qingniang. The old couple personally cleaned the main room and arranged bedding in the same way as they had for their late master. They provided the couple with food and clothing, so Cui and the girl settled down with ease of mind.

About a year later the girl said to Cui, "We are comfortable here, but we are separated from my loving parents to whom I feel indebted for bringing me into this world. This is simply not a good ending, and I feel guilty about this." "Since we've come this far," Cui said, "there is no way for us to account for what we did. Can we just go back to them like this?" "At first we came together in haste," the girl answered. "At that time, had our union been exposed, my parents would certainly have blamed us and it would have been doubtful if we could have stayed together. In that situation escape was the only way out if we were to stick together for the rest of our lives. Now one year has gone by. I think all parents love their children. During my departure, my parents must have missed me. If I return home with you to see them, they will be so happy as to forget about our past rash actions. That is to be expected. Why don't we go together to see them even though we may run the risk of being embarrassed?" "A man has the whole world on his mind," said Cui. "To hide ourselves here is at best an expedient. Now that you have made up your mind, I'll gladly take the blame from Father-in-Law for your sake. Since we have been man and wife for a year, I think your family, which is a reputed one, will not tear us apart and marry you off to another man. Besides, your sister's engagement with me has not been fulfilled and it is only right that you should take her place. If we behave with great caution, I think we can handle all this when we go to see them."

So decided, they asked Jin Rong to hire a ship for them, bade farewell to him, and set off. Having crossed the Yangtse River and arriving at Guazhou, they moved towards Yangzhou. As they were drawing near the house of Commander Wu, the girl said to Cui, "Let's moor the ship here. Don't row it directly to the gate of my family. Besides, I wish to have a word with you." Cui asked the boatman to moor the ship, and said to the girl, "What is it you want to tell me?" She replied, "You and I eloped and have been away from home for a year. All will be well if they forgive us when we go together to see them. But if they become angry, it will be tough for us to handle. I think it would be best for you to go first, see if they are happy or angry, and make a clear explanation. When you are sure the coast is clear, come and pick me up. Isn't that a face-saving way of doing things? And I will feel less embarrassed. I will stay here waiting for you." "You are right," said Cui, "I will go first." He jumped onto the bank, and was about to leave when the girl beckoned him back. "One more thing," she said, "For a girl, elopement is no proper conduct. Very likely my family will hold this against me and deny our relationship. We must be prepared against this." At these words, she pulled the gold hair pin from her head and handed it to him, "If the talk turns out to be disagreeable, show them this hair pin and they will not be able to deny our relationship." "It's so thoughtful of you!" claimed Cui. Taking the hair pin, he put it in his sleeve and made for Commander Wu's house.

When Cui entered the hall, he was ushered in. Rejoiced by Cui's arrival, Commander Wu came out to see him. Before Cui could say anything, Commander Wu said to him, "I did not look after you well, so that you felt it inconvenient to stay here. It was my fault. Please don't blame me for the sake of my friendship with your late father!" Prostrating himself, Cui dared not look his father-in-law in the eye. Finding it too embarrassing to own up to the truth, he kowtowed repeatedly, saying, "Your guilty son-in-law deserves death!" Astounded, Commander Wu asked, "Guilty of what, my son? Why do you say this? Please tell me clearly to dispel my doubts." "Only when you promise to forgive me do I dare tell you the story," Cui replied.

"Please be frank," said Commander Wu. "You are my old friend's son and you needn't feel any misgivings." Seeing the old man in a good mood, Cui said, "Thanks to the kindness of your daughter, Qingniang, she and your humble son-in-law united in secret. Since then we have indulged ourselves in merriment and love, but in doing so I have borne ill fame for being ungrateful and committing an illicit relationship. For fear of being punished for this felony, she and I escaped in the deep of night and have since hidden ourselves in a village. Now one year has passed. During this period we were unable to see you, neither could we send letters to you. Although we are in love with each other, how can we forget our indebtedness to our parents? So I am here with your daughter today to see you. I hope you can understand our affection, forgive our sin and grant us the leave to stay together forever as a loving couple. In this way you will be regarded as a loving father and I will be fortunate to have a happy family. I only hope you will forgive me!"

Commander Wu was astonished, "What are you talking about! Qingniang has been bed-ridden for a year without eating or drinking. She cannot even turn herself without the help of others. She has never left her bed. How can your story be true if you didn't see ghosts!" Cui thought to himself, "Qingniang is foresighted indeed! He is afraid that the reputation of the family will be sullied. That's why he is trying to cover up the truth under the pretext that his daughter is ill in bed." Then he said to the Commander, "How can I lie to you as your humble son-in-law? Qingniang is staying on the ship. You may send for her and everything will be clear." Sneering in disbelief, the Commander said to a servant, "Go to Cui's ship and see who is with him and claiming to be my daughter Qingniang!"

When the servant went to the ship and looked, he found nobody in the silent cabin. He asked the boatman, who was hanging his head and having dinner on the prow, "Where is the woman who was on your ship?" "A scholar went up the bank and left behind a girl in the cabin," replied the boatman. "A moment ago she went away, too." The servant returned to report the matter to the master, "I didn't see anyone in the cabin. I asked the ship owner, and he told me there was a girl, but that she went ashore and disappeared." Realizing that he had been lied to, the Commander was beside himself. He reprimanded Cui. "A young man like you should be honest. Why should you make up such an absurd story to abuse a good girl's honor!" Desperate, Cui rummaged in his sleeve and produced the gold hair pin. Presenting it to the Commander, he said, "This belongs to your daughter Qingniang. It will serve as evidence. How could I fabricate the story?"

The Commander took the object and was astonished, "This is the hair pin that was pinned on the head of my deceased daughter, Xingniang, when she was encoffined. It has been entombed with her for a long time. How can it be in your hand? It's strange!" Thereupon Cui told him in detail how he had picked up a hair pin from under the sedan chair when the family came back from their visit to the tomb the previous year, how Qingniang had come to his room to look for the hair pin and thus they became man and wife, how fearing that their relationship would be discovered they had escaped to the home of the former servant Jin Rong, and had stayed there for a year before returning together. The Commander was dumbfounded. "Qingniang is in bed in her room," he said to Cui, "If you don't believe me, you may go and see for yourself. But your tale in vivid detail sounds real! And how has the hair pin appeared? There must be some reason!" Holding Cui by the hand, he led him into the room to see the sick girl so as to clear up the facts.

Now let's turn to Qingniang. She had been ill and had never been able to leave her bed. That day when the whole family was in perplexity, she sprang up from her bed and dashed straight out into the parlor. Seeing this strange happening, the servants and the mother followed her in a clamor. "She has not been able to move about," they said. "How come she can suddenly walk?" When Qingniang entered the parlor, she prostrated herself before the Commander. Seeing it was Qingniang, the Commander was even more surprised, "When did you begin to be able to walk?" he asked. Cui, on the other hand, believed that the girl had come from the ship. Let me see what she will say, he thought to himself. Qingniang said, "I am your daughter Xingniang. I left you, my parents, and was buried in the wild. But my affections for Cui were not diminished. Today I've come for no purpose other than to speak for Cui. Please marry my sister Qingniang to Cui. If you listen to me, my sister will recover at once; otherwise she will die after I go." The whole family was horrified. Judging from her body and face, she was none other than Qingniang but her voice and carriage belonged unmistakably to Xingniang. Then they realized that it was the spirit of the dead girl who had attached herself to the living body of Qingniang and spoke through her mouth. The Commander put on a grave look and scolded her, "Why should you plague living people and make trouble in the human world since you are dead?" Again in Xingniang's voice, the girl said, "When I went to the nether world after my death, the governor of the nether world said because I was innocent I should not be confined. Instead, I was sent to the Queen of Earth and my duty was to transfer reports to her. Finding that I could not shake myself free from my bonds of love with my destined spouse in the human world, I asked the Queen for one year's leave so that I could fulfill my commitment to Mr Cui. My sister's disease was caused by me because in my union with Cui I borrowed her soul. Now that my leave is expiring, I have to go. How can I leave Cui a stranger to our family? So I've come to plead with Father and Mother to marry my sister to Cui so that his matrimony will continue. If you grant my demand, I will feel relieved in the underworld."

Hearing her earnest entreaty, the Commander and his wife granted her request, saying, "We'll do what you ask and marry Qingniang to him. Please set your mind at rest." Seeing her parents had thus consented, her face lit up and she thanked the Commander with obeisance. "Thank you, father and mother, for granting my plea," she said. "I'll go feeling satisfied." Then she walked up to Cui, grasped his hand and sobbed, "You and I have spent a year in love, but we must say good-bye now. My parents have promised to marry Qingniang to you. You will become a bridegroom. When you enjoy marital felicity with your new love, don't forget me, your old love." Having said this she began wailing. Only when Cui heard her narration about their past year, did he realize that it was the spirit of Xingniang who had been with him. Now, having heard her plea, he felt a deep regret. But knowing that the body belonged to his sister-in-law, he could not express his affection in the presence of other people.

When the spirit's instruction in the voice of Xingniang was finished, several cries were heard and the body of Qingniang fell to the ground. When the alarmed people hurried forward to help her, they found her breath had ceased. But they felt her breast was still warm. They immediately poured some ginger soup down her throat. After a long while she came to. Her disease had disappeared and she could walk as a healthy person again. Being asked about what had happened to her during the past year, she said she knew nothing about it. Raising her head, she caught a glance of Cui among the onlookers. Covering her face she ran through the middle gate and entered the inner quarters. As if awakening from a dream, Cui remained there in a trance for half a day.

The Commander chose an auspicious date and held the nuptial for Qingniang and Cui. On the wedding night Cui was intimate to Qingniang since he had been familiar with her, but Qingniang, on her part, was shy because Cui was a stranger to her. The situation was:

> One was a fragile girl in the boudoir who had never exchanged a word with the bridegroom; the other, a traveler who had been together with the beauty for a year. He found a nuance of difference in the voice but the face was exactly the

*same; she was a little timid seeing her new partner in front of
her. He was reliving an experience with an old love, while she
was testing the first red bud on a crabapple bough.*

That night Cui found Qingniang's maidenhood intact and he knew she
was a virgin. He whispered to her, "Your sister accompanied me for a
whole year with your body. Why is your body so intact?" Qingniang
scowled. "It is you who did it with the spirit of my sister," she said. "I
had nothing to do with it. Why should you involve me in it?" "But for
your loving sister," said Cui, "how could I have become your husband?
We mustn't forget her kindness." "You are right," said Qingniang.
"Had she not come to bring about our union, how could I face the
people since she made me a fool for so long a time? Then you would
believe it was I that had eloped with you. I would be ashamed to death!
Fortunately her spirit came to put us together. This is her great
kindness towards us."

The next day Cui wanted to redeem the soul of Xingniang for he
was greatly obliged to her. But he had nothing on him. So he sold the
gold hair pin at the fair for bills worth twenty silver ingots. He spent
all the money on incense, candles and paper coins. He came to the
Jade Flower Monastery and hired Taoists to hold a three-day-and-
three-night redeeming ceremony for her soul.

When the ceremony was finished, Cui in his dream saw a girl whom
he did not know. The girl said, "I am Xingniang. I used to stay with
you assuming the form of my sister, that's why you don't know me
now. It was my spirit that accompanied you for a year. Now that you
and my sister have gotten married, I am showing you my own
appearance." Then she thanked him, "I am much obliged to you for the
redeeming ceremony you held for me. Although we are separated, one
in the nether realm and the other in the human world, I am deeply
moved by your sincerity. My sister Qingniang is gentle. Please look
after her well. I must say good-bye to you forever!" Cui could not help

crying and awoke.

Hearing Cui cry at the other end of the pillow, Qingniang asked him what it was. Cui told her what Xingniang had said to him in the dream. "What did she look like?" Qingniang asked him. As Cui described in detail the features of the girl he had seen in the dream, Qingniang said, "It's true. She is my sister." She couldn't refrain from tears either. Then Qingniang asked Cui about his experiences of the past year, Cui told her everything from beginning to end. Qingniang found these details tallied with Xingniang's nature. Both Cui and Qingniang found the story amazing. They became even more intimate with each other. After that they saw no trace of Xingniang. It was because Xingniang, in deep love, could not forget Cui that she made so many extraordinary things happen. Now that her wish was fulfilled, she put an end to all her adventures. After that, Cui and Qingniang visited Xingniang's tomb every year to cherish her memory. When Cui later became an official, he asked the superior for an honorary title for Xingniang. He also made a testament that he, Qingniang and her sister should be buried in the same grave after their deaths.

Somebody improvised four lines to highlight this story:

> *The younger sister's body*
> *And elder sister's soul*
> *For hearts' mutual devotion*
> *Become a perfect whole.*

Tale 13

Fighting for Affection a Village Woman Gives Her Life; Conversing with Heaven an Assistant Governor Settles a Case

It is told that there was a *juren* surnamed Zheng in Lin'an [present-day Hangzhou, Zhejiang Province] who studied by himself in the Qingfu Temple. A room in the northwest of a temple was named Clean Clouds Studio. Guang Ming, a monk in the temple, was a handsome, refined and tasteful man and had many friends among officials and scholars. Besides, he was wealthy and so gentlemen loved to associate with him. Having stayed in the temple longer than anyone else, Scholar Zheng found his talk with Guang Ming to be most congenial and so they became intimate friends. Guang Ming took him to see all the fine meditating cells and rooms nestled in remote corners, except for one small room in a most reclused corner. That room was locked and unlocked by Guang Ming himself when he went in and out of it, but even he seldom entered the room. It was always locked and nobody else ever set foot in it. Scholar Zheng, though a good friend of Guang Ming, had no access to it. Zheng thought it might be a treasure house for the monks and for this reason people were sensible enough not to look into it.

One day the bell clanged in the front hall, signaling the arrival of an important official. Guang Ming was in that small room then. He hurried to the gate to greet the visitor. Zheng, strolling by himself, happened to pass by the room at that moment, and saw that the door had been left open. This room has always been locked before, Zheng thought to himself, and I have never been allowed to see what is in it. Why is it not locked today? As he stepped in, he found the room had a wooden floor. Looking around, he saw nothing rare or extraordinary except for the refined furniture. Zheng thought, those people who have renounced the world are really strange. Why should Guang Ming always lock the door immediately after he goes out of the room since there is no secret here? Then Zheng caught a glimpse of a pretty fish made of red sandalwood hanging from the curtain hook of a small bed. The wooden fish, with a beater attached to it, looked delicate and lustrous. Zheng, a man fond of fun, took the fish down, felt it and beat it twice. Immediately the clang of a bell was heard from underneath the floor, a piece of the wood was pushed up and there emerged the head of a beautiful young woman, who, at sight of Zheng, drew back in fright. Zheng, of course, was surprised too. As he had gotten a close look, he realized that she was one of his cousins.

The floor boards had been skillfully constructed so that when this particular board was pushed open it became a door, and when closed it looked just like a floor board. It could be pushed open only from beneath and it could not be opened from above. Upon hearing the wooden fish as a signal, a bell would clang in echo and the person inside would come out. Under the floor was a cellar with windows that opened elsewhere and contained a secret pathway that led to the kitchen. Even a god could not find such a secret place. Zheng said to himself, no wonder the bald villain has the door tightly locked. I should not have discovered it. This might mean disaster for me!

Flurried, he hung the wooden fish back in its original place and made for the door, where he ran square into Guang Ming.

Finding the door unlocked, Guang Ming was nervous. He saw Zheng come out in a fluster and that he was blushing. As he glanced at the wooden fish, he saw it swinging on the curtain hook. He thus realized that his secret had leaked out. "What did you see?" he asked Zheng. "Nothing," replied Zheng. "Why don't we have a chat in the room?" he said. Holding Zheng by the hand he dragged him into the room. Then, having bolted the door, he drew out a knife at the bed.

"Though you are my good friend," Guang Ming said, "you and I cannot both survive today. I cannot afford to let my secret be brought to light and die at another man's hand. It is your ill fate that has led you to this room. Now please take your own life at once and don't blame me." "I am too unfortunate to meet with this disaster," Zheng cried. "I know you will not spare me and I cannot escape death. But I hope you will allow me to drink until I am tipsy so that when you cut my head off, in drunkenness I will feel no pain. You and I have been friends for a long time and I hope you will take pity on me." This reminded Guang Ming of their friendship and, somewhat touched by his pitiable plea, he granted his entreaties. Having locked the scholar in, he went to the kitchen with the knife in hand, and returned with a large tin pot of wine. As he was about to pour it out, Zheng said, "The wine alone is unpalatable. You've got to give me a little pickled vegetable." Again Guang Ming went to the kitchen for pickles. Zheng thought, "Since I can't run away, I must find an object and attack him in surprise!" But instead of bricks, stones or bars, all he could find in the room were light utensils. As his eyes fell on the bulky wine pot, he hit upon a scheme. Immediately he tore a piece of cloth from his robe and with it he stopped the pot spout, so the pot with the wine in it amounted to about six *jin*. Holding the pot in one hand, he hid himself behind the door.

When Guang Ming came in, his body leaning against the door,

Zheng, with all his might, hit the bald head of the monk with the pot. As Guang Ming, going black, felt his head with his hand, Zheng struck his head two or three more times. Guang Ming fell to the ground unconscious. Thereupon Zheng pestled Guang Ming's head several dozen times until his skull split open and his brains dashed out. It was clear the monk was done for.

Zheng locked the monk's body in and went out. Nobody had yet discovered what had happened. He hurried to the county magistrate and reported on the matter. The magistrate dispatched some runners and soldiers to the temple, who laid siege to the room. After they broke into it, they saw the monk lying in a pool of blood on the floor with his skull broken. But they could not find the woman. Zheng smiled. "I have a way to make her appear right here." He took the wooden fish from the curtain hook, and rattled it twice. With a tinkling of the bell, a board on the floor was pushed up and a woman climbed out. The runners uttered an alarm, seized the board before the woman could retreat, and stormed into the cellar below. It was walled with bricks and fortified with bars. A window opened on one side onto a stone-walled yard where nobody ever went.

Five or six women were ferreted out of the cellar. Asked where they had come from, they said they were abducted from nearby villages. When Zheng's cousin had come to pray to the gods for the birth of a son, the monk got the carriers of her sedan chair drunk with wine and stealthily took her into the temple. Her family had reported her missing to the authorities, and the two sedan carriers were still in prison. Guang Ming had many friends and he had not left any traces of his conduct, so he had not been involved in the case. Nobody had thought the woman would be in his place. The county magistrate had all the monks in the temple slaughtered.

As you know, gentle readers, monks need not worry about food or clothing since they are supported by patrons from everywhere. They have clean rooms and refined bedding. When they lie in bed at leisure, they think of nothing but affairs. Although from time to time they can give vent to their desires on young disciples, as the old saying goes, "Nibbles don't allay hunger." On the other hand, women come from all places to the temples to pray. Thus they move to and fro in front of the monks. How can the monks refrain from thinking of the beautiful women during the night whom they have seen during the day? So the monks stop at nothing to seduce them. Seduction itself is an unpardonable felony, not to mention the fact that no bald-pate is not vicious and no vicious man is not a bald-pate and that on the other hand, all bald-pates are vicious and all vicious persons are bald-pates. They don't cringe at committing murder or arson to gratify their salacious desires. As to the above-mentioned monk of the temple in Lin'an, he was a good friend of Zheng's. He should have paid Zheng off to keep his mouth shut after his secret was out. Why did he go so far as to try to kill him and in the end get killed himself? The reason is that Heaven cannot tolerate such an outrage and the monks were unreasonably cruel.

Now let me tell you another story about an extraordinarily wicked monk.

In Wenchuan County of Chengdu Prefecture, Sichuan Province, there lived a farmer by the name of Jing Qing. His wife, Du, was pretty and amorous. She disliked him because she thought he was crude and slow-witted. Since they did not get along, she found faults with him and squabbled with him every day. One day because of petty bickering she went back to her mother. Ten days or so later, persuaded by others, she swallowed her pride and decided to return to him. Her husband's house and her mother's were but three *li* away and in those years Du was used to coming and going by herself. Maybe she was fated to meet trouble. She was well on her way when it started raining heavily. She did not bring rain gear, and there was no shelter for her in the wild. Hearing bells beating in a distance, she looked about and saw a temple along a path. She braved the rain and made for it along a detour, intending to continue her journey after the rain stopped.

The Buddhist temple, named the Peace Temple, was situated in a desolate place. A dozen monks lived there. Three of them lodged in a room at the gate. The oldest one, by the name of Da Jue, was the master. One of his disciples, Zhi Yuan, a delicate-featured and romantic young man was tenderly loved by the old monk; and the other, Hui Guan, was a young novice eleven years old or so. Da Jue, though in his late fifties, was no less lecherous than a young man. Every night he would sleep with Zhi Yuan in his embrace. Whenever they talked about the sweetness of women, they would be aroused, and would resort to "it" — the obscenity was beyond description.

That day they were chatting at the gate when they saw a beautiful woman come in to take shelter from the rain. Like a cat that sees a rat approaching, how could they remain unstirred? The old monk, seeing the woman, signaled to Zhi Yuan, "Here comes the Bodhisattva. Receive her the best you can." Zhi Yuan reeled up and greeted her, "Finding shelter from rain, Madam?" he asked. "Right," replied Du. "It started raining when I was on my way. So I've come here to take shelter." Grinning, Zhi Yuan said, "It seems the rain won't stop for awhile. It isn't right to let you just stand here. Would you like to come to my room for a cup of tea? You may go after the rain lets up." Well, if Du had been a proper woman, she would have stood there until the rain stopped and not have listened to whatever the monk said. How could a woman easily enter a monk's room? Du, however, was a wanton woman. Seeing the fair complexion of the young monk and hearing his clever remarks, she took a liking to him. The rain is heavy, she thought to herself, why should I stand here? It won't do me any harm if I go in and sit for awhile as he asks. So she followed him in.

Seeing the woman moving her steps, the old monk hastened to enter their quarters, opened the bedchamber and waited for her. As the young monk escorted Du through the gate he kept exchanging glances with her all the way. There Du sat down. The novice presented tea on a tray. Picking up a fine porcelain cup, Zhi Yuan spread his sleeve and presented the cup to her. As Du hurried to take the cup, she found his full figure even more lovable than she had previously thought. When she, in a trance, stole a glance at him the cup toppled and tea spilled on her sleeve. "Your sleeve is wet with tea, Madam," said Zhi Yuan, "Please come into my room and dry it over the brazier." Du had an eight-tenth inkling of what he was up to by asking her in, and decided to let the matter take its own course. Instead of declining him, she asked him which room to enter. Zhi Yuan led her to the room of his master, knowing that he was there. He meant to let his master have her first, because he dared not preempt. When Du entered the room, Zhi Yuan pointed to a brazier saying, "You may dry your sleeve there. There's fire burning in it." And then he retreated.

Du was perplexed when she saw that the young monk did not follow her in. She guessed that he might be too timid to take her. She was about to dry her sleeve over the brazier when an old monk jumped out from behind the bed and gathered her into his arms. Du screamed like a pig being butchered. "It's useless to shout," said the old monk, "since there is no one else here. Who let you come in my room?" Du wanted to run away, but the door had been tied by the sensible young monk. Held tightly in the old monk's grip, she could feel his rampant manhood hard against her body from outside of her clothes. Having struggled for a moment Du was somewhat aroused too. "Where is the young priest I saw a moment ago? Why have you come in his stead?" she asked. "Are you infatuated with my disciple?" asked the old monk. "He is my treasure! When you have satisfied me, I'll let him join you." I do have eyes for the young monk, thought Du, and I never expected that I would be pestered by this old nuisance. I don't think I'll get free from this situation. It's better to let him finish off and then his disciple will surely come. So, with reluctance, she let the old monk take her into his bed and clouds gathered for a rainfall:

*One of them was ardent but in a haste; the other however,
languid, reacted perfunctorily. One found the meeting a chance
to find an easy prey; the other thought the encounter unexpected.
The impassioned one got breathless like a billow; the listless one
lay as a bag of flesh. The union, though rude and tasteless,
might be taken as a short romance after all.*

Although the old monk was very lustful, his strength failed him.
When he embraced Du, he had already lost some seminal fluid, so the
intercourse had hardly begun when he was spent. His impotent
performance utterly disappointed the woman, who had been impatient
with him all along. Rising to tie up her skirt, she grumbled, "Why
should a good-for-nothing like you pester me!" Realizing that he had
failed her, the old monk, abashed, hastily ordered the disciple to open
the door. As the door opened, Zhi Yuan asked the master, "Had a good
time?" "Very tasteful indeed!" the man said. "The pity is that my vigor
betrayed me, so I made a fool of myself." "Let me make up for it,"
said Zhi Yuan. Hurrying into the room and shutting the door behind
him, he hugged Du. "My dear, you must have been tormented by the
old fellow!" "Why did you lure me into the room and leave me at the
mercy of the old nuisance?" Du asked. "He is my master," replied Zhi
Yuan, "I could do nothing until he was served. Now let me make good
for your loss." Seizing her in his arms, he made for the bed. Having
been disappointed by the old monk, Du put on airs. "Your master and
you, as his disciple, are really very cheeky to pester me in turn," she
said. "My master always fights in the van," replied Zhi Yuan. "That's
why he was sacrificed first. You and I are of about the same age. Don't
lose this opportunity!" He knelt down in front of her. Helping him up,
she said, "It's all because the old nuisance failed me that I put it that
way. Actually I'm in love with you." Making use of the momentum,
Zhi Yuan embraced her, kissed her, pushed her into the bed and

started the game. The pleasure she got this time was quite different from what it had been previously:

One, seeing a beauty, was like a hungry tiger preying on a sheep; the other, eager to have a young love, was like a thirsty dragon at the edge of water. The village woman, lewd by nature, was fond of the play; the youth in the monastery, endowed with skills, showed his valor in engagement. Neither the giver nor the taker would admit defeat; both the attacker and the defender exerted their utmost might. The old monk forced the gate open, but it was the young Buddhist that swam in an expanse of the water of supreme wisdom.

The monk in his prime of youth was strong and energetic; and Du found him handsome. They made love to each other tenderly. They did not give up until two hours later. Du, fully satiated, said, "I've always heard that Buddhist monks were well endowed with this. The old nuisance really abashed me, but you are so bewitching. I'll sleep with you tonight." "Much obliged to you for your kindness," said Zhi Yuan, "but may I know from whose family you come and can you stay here?" "My family name is Du," she replied, "and I am married to a Jing in a nearby place. The other day I quarreled with my husband, and so I went back to my mother's house. I was returning to my husband's house when I was caught in the rain. When I came into the temple to take shelter, I ran into you, my destined lover. My husband does not know I am returning and he will probably not ask my mother about it. So nobody will discover it if I stay here for a couple of days." "If that is the case," said Zhi Yuan, "I will be lucky to be with you for a whole night. But my master will sleep in the same bed with us." "I don't want that old nuisance," said Du. "He is the master here," said Zhi Yuan, "so I cannot decline him. Please go through with it and send him off one way or another." "Isn't it embarrassing for the three of us to sleep together?" asked Du. "The old monk is a lecher," said Zhi Yuan, "but he is not strong. Let us, you and me, together deal with him. Either you or I can serve him once and he will then be effortless. Thus we can leave him alone and enjoy ourselves."

As they found their talk congenial, they talked on, unaware of the old monk outside of the door. Hearing the bed creaking for a long while, he regretted having finished too quickly and failing to enjoy her to the full. The thought that he had left them to dally to their hearts' content caused jealousy to surge through his body. Having waited for them to come out of the room for a long time, he lost his patience and broke in, only to see the two lovers holding onto each other tightly and sucking each other's tongues. He was a little irritated, thinking to himself, why didn't she treat me as tenderly as that? Unable to hold back his jealousy, he shouted, "You should work out a plan since you have tasted it. How brazen you are to sleep in a closed room in broad daylight!" Seeing that the master was angry, Zhi Yuan smiled, and said, "Know, my master, we'll have the gusto for a long time." "How's that?" asked the old monk. "The woman will not go home tonight," Zhi Yuan replied. The old monk smiled. "Of course we'll not let her go," he said. "If we detain her," said, Zhi Yuan, "we'll have to take the consequences. It is the woman herself who said she would stay here. Thus we can set our fears at rest." "Which family does the woman come from?" asked the old monk. Zhi Yuan repeated Du's account to him. Overjoyed, the old monk prepared supper in haste, laid it out, and the three of them shared the meal at the same table. Du was not much of a drinker. When the old monk proposed a toast to her, she declined, but when Zhi Yuan proposed a cup, she took it. She and Zhi Yuan made passes at each other, and they became extremely ardent. The old monk teased the woman by putting in some amorous remarks, but to no avail. He felt he was being neglected, but he hung on like a dog licking a hot plate.

When the supper was finished and the table put away, he had the woman and Zhi Yuan sleep in one bed with him. Lying down, Du hugged the young monk tightly, paying no heed to the old monk. The old monk kept pestering them. The young monk had to let go of the woman and give her over to his master. Du, annoyed, of course could not receive him tenderly. The old monk was desperate, so he soon began gasping and became listless. "Why should you make a fool of yourself?" Du sneered. Abashed, the old monk silently turned himself to the inner side of the bed. The young monk and woman resumed their prolonged fight, interrupting it only occasionally to catch a moment of sleep. The old monk, swallowing saliva, could do nothing but pester them endlessly.

In the morning Du got up and dressed herself. "I'll go today," she told Zhi Yuan. "Yesterday you said that it wouldn't matter if you were to stay for a few days," Zhi Yuan said. "This is an outlying place. Nobody will know you are here. How can you have the heart to say this when we are just tasting the sweet of our union?" "It's not that I have the heart to part with you," she said, "but the old man is giving me a hard time. If you want me to stay, you must sleep with me in one bed without that old man." "But he will never agree to that," said Zhi Yuan. "In that case," she insisted, "I won't stay." Helplessly, Zhi Yuan went to his master, "Lady Du is leaving," he said. "What shall we do?" "I can see she is intimate with you," said the old monk, "so how can she part with you?" "She's from a good family," replied Zhi Yuan, "so she is too shy to sleep with two men in one bed. In my opinion, it will be better if I make another bed in the opposite room and sleep with her there one or two nights, thus to cajole her into staying. You may seize opportunities to act. When she becomes familiar with both of us, the three of us can sleep together again. Otherwise, she will be offended and leave us, then neither you nor I will have access to her." These remarks reminded the old monk of what had happened the previous night, a night of little pleasure and a lot of loathing for him. On the other hand, he feared that if she was gone, he would lose even that little pleasure. So he thought it better to let them stay together in privacy and then he could ask her to come to his bed and enjoy her exclusively for a night. Why should I stay beside them and be loathed? So he said to Zhi Yuan, "I think you are right. So long as we can make her stay, we both can benefit. And you are my heart. It's my pleasure to help you." But despite what he said, the old monk was jealous. He made the arrangement only to wait for an opportunity. When Zhi Yuan told Du that they would sleep in another room, she rejoiced, and settled down waiting for the blissful night.

In the evening the old monk instructed Zhi Yuan, "I'll rest this night to recover my strength. You and she may have your good time. You should soothe her with sweet words. Tomorrow night you must give her to me." "Certainly," replied Zhi Yuan. "If I don't accompany her this evening but we muddle together as last night, we can't keep her. When I get intimate with her, I will lead her to you and then you'll surely be gratified." "You are indeed my understanding child!" said the old monk. Zhi Yuan went over to Du, bolted the door and slept with her. This night they were free to enjoy their sensual union to the full.

As for the old monk, he granted his disciple's demand because he feared that the woman might go. When he was left alone in his bed that night, he found his lacking of a woman compounded by the absence of his disciple. He slept miserably. And imagining how happy they might be, he could not go to sleep. All night through he beat the bed, his head off the pillow. When he got up the next morning he said to Zhi Yuan, "You had a good night but I was left all alone." "That is the only way to make her stay," replied Zhi Yuan, Then the old monk said, "Tonight I should enjoy her to my heart's content."

By evening Zhi Yuan, who dared not to defy his master, tried to persuade Du to go to the master's bed, but Du obstinately refused: "I stay here because I am convinced by you. Why do you ask me to accompany that old nuisance?" "Because he is my master," said Zhi

Yuan. "But I am not married to him," retorted Du, "why should I be afraid of him? If you pressure me, I will go home this very night!" Realizing that she would not go to the old monk, Zhi Yuan came to his master and said, "She is a bit shy, so she doesn't want to come on her own. You may go to her room." Accordingly the old monk groped his way into her room.

Du was in bed waiting for Zhi Yuan. She did not know it was the old monk who had come and jumped into her bed. Believing it was Zhi Yuan, she hugged him and gave him a kiss, whereupon the old monk was mesmerized. Only when they began to make love did she realize that it was not Zhi Yuan. "You old nuisance again!" she cursed, "Why do you always bother me?" The old monk, overestimating himself, employed all his might to thrust in and out of her, hoping to win her favor this way. But he soon began to puff and blow due to his over-exertion. Du was about to come, only to realize he was retreating from the battle. Disappointed, she turned aside and with a hard shove pushed him out of the bed. Pulling himself to his feet, the old monk thought to himself, this slut is too vicious! In resentment he went back to his room.

Seeing the master come out, Zhi Yuan went to fill in the blank. The old monk had aroused Du's concupiscent urges but left her unfulfilled. Zhi Yuan came at the right moment to quench her thirst. Before they had time to speak, they enfolded into each other and went at it with vehemence. The old monk was still fretting when he returned to his room. Now that I am out, he thought to himself, they are enjoying themselves again. Let me go and listen. As the old monk reached their door, he heard them wrestling boisterously in the bed. Clenching his fist, the old monk said, "This wanton woman is so discriminating! If you let me have a share of the fun, we all will benefit. I am giving the night to you two. Tomorrow I'll have my revenge at the risk that none of us will have any more pleasure." He went to bed in a gloomy mood.

When he awoke next morning, he thought to himself in resentment,

I have suffered much from that crone! But when Du got up, the old monk cheekily tried to tease her. She didn't answer, giving him a snub. Then seeing her and Zhi Yuan whisper in each other's ears and laugh and giggle, his resentment grew into vehement hatred.

As night fell Zhi Yuan said to Du, "Let me go and fell the old monk, so that he will not come to bother us." "Be quick," said Du, "I will be waiting for you in bed." Coming into the room of the old monk, Zhi Yuan put on his usual seductive airs, saying, "I am sorry I have not accompanied my master for two nights. I'll sleep with you this night." "Why should I eat from my store while a cunt is here?" said the old monk. "Go and wheedle her into keeping me company for the night." "I can't," said Zhi Yuan. "You can go and try to entreat her." To this the old monk said, resentfully, "I'll see if she will come or not this night." Then he went to the kitchen to fetch a knife. Entering the room in which Du was staying, he thought to himself, if she is not sensible, I'll finish her off! Not seeing Zhi Yuan come for a long time, Du thought he must have settled the affair with the master. Now hearing steps near the bed, she believed Zhi Yuan had at last come. "My dear brother," she urged, "please shut the door, or the old nuisance will come and harass me." Hearing this clearly, the old monk's anger grew to malice. "The old nuisance wants you to sleep with him tonight!" he shouted stridently, dragging her from the bed with one hand. Seeing that he was so ferocious, she struggled, clinging to the bed. "Are you forcing me?" she asked. "I won't go with you anyway!" As the old monk exerted himself to tear her away from the bed, she yelled, "I won't go with you even if you kill me!" "If you don't, I'll give you a cut!" he shouted. "That will be no good to any of us." Pressing her on the neck he thrust the knife down on her. Since the old monk was mad with anger, he struck with so great a force that her throat was slit open. Following one or two bounces she met her end.

After the master had left the room, Zhi Yuan had lain in bed waiting. As he heard a scream in the opposite room and the sound of a thud, he became suspicious. He ran out to have a look, and bumped into the old monk emerging from the room with a knife in his hand. Seeing Zhi Yuan, the old monk said, "The witch was too hideous! I have killed her." Zhi Yuan was shocked. "Really?" "Why not?" the monk replied. "Should I let you monopolize her?" Lamp in hand, Zhi Yuan went into the room to have a look. He groaned inwardly, thinking to himself, "Oh, how could the master bring himself to do this!" "The witch despised me." said the old monk. "I lost control of my temper. Don't blame me. Now that I have done this, we mustn't hesitate. Put the body away. Tomorrow I'll acquire a good one to satisfy your needs."

Zhi Yuan could not utter his grief. He had to go with the old monk, spade in hand and the body on his back, to a rear yard and bury her there. Zhi Yuan shed tears in secret. He moaned inwardly, saying to himself, had I known this would happen, I would have let her go. Why did she have to be killed? The old monk feared that Zhi Yuan might be annoyed so he tried every means to please him. Thus the truth was kept an absolute secret. Only the novice was surprised by the absence of the woman. But he was a child, after all, and he did not inquire about her whereabouts. So nobody knew of the murder. Of this we'll say no more.

Let's turn to the Du's family. Two or three days after she left, her parents began to wonder if she and her husband had become reconciled. They sent a man to the Jing's house to see what the situation was. The Jings, on the other hand, had sent a man to the Dus to pick her up. Both sides failed to see Du. The Jings claimed that the Dus must have married her to another man since she was not on good terms with Jing; the Dus said she must have been murdered because the husband and wife had fallen out. Thus the two families made charges against each other. In time they filed complaints with the county court.

The position for county magistrate at that time was vacant and an assistant from the provincial military commission served as the acting

governor. He was surnamed Lin and named Dahe and he was from Fujian Province. Though he had been trained in the Imperial College, *
he was quick-witted in handling cases and insightful in making judgments. When he questioned the two families, Jing Qing said, "My wife quarreled with me and went home in a fit of pique. My father-in-law hid her and doesn't want to return her to me. That's why I have turned to the law!" Du's father said, "It is because of the discord between her and her husband that she returned to my house and stayed for a few days. Three days ago her anger melted under the persuasion of my wife and me. We let her go back to her husband. I don't know what discord happened after that, and I'm sure they have tormented her to death. Yet they are accusing me! I plead my lord to back us!" With this, tears poured down his cheeks.

Assistant Lin found that Jing Qing's appearance suggested he was a honest man and not a vicious one. "Why were you and your wife not on good terms?" he asked Jing Qing. "She disliked me for my crudeness and thought me a mismatch to her." Jing answered. "So she often nagged me over trifles. But there's no other reason." "What does your wife look like?" Lin asked again. "She's quite pretty," Jing answered. The judge nodded and said to Mr Du, "Your daughter finds the marriage a mismatch and she loathes her husband. You, as her parent, may have shielded her fault. Maybe you have hidden her and are trying to marry her to another man. It is quite possible." "My house is quite close to her husband's," replied Mr Du. "How could I be able to keep the secret if I married her to another? Could I be so hard-hearted as to send her to a strange prefecture and cut our relationship? If she had a new spouse, people would know it. How could there be such a marriage? And what's the use of our hiding her? She must have

---

*In ancient China, children of officials of the seventh rank or above studied in the national college for state scions, and children of officials of the eighth rank and below entered the imperial college. That Lin studied in the imperial college suggests that he was from a low origin.

been put to death by her husband's family. That is why we couldn't find any trace of her."

After thinking for awhile, Assistant Lin said, "None of you are right. The situation may be that when she decided to go back to her husband, neither of you knew where she was. In the meantime she might have encountered trouble by coming across evil people on her way. You may post surety bonds and wait for the results of a search." Thereupon he had a search announcement posted and sent his runners out to investigate everywhere. A long time elapsed but no news was forthcoming.

Now I will tell you of a twenty-year old doorman of the county yamen by the name of Yu. He was handsome and witty. As men from Fujian were addicted to homosexuality, he was loved by Assistant Lin. With the Assistant as his protection, Yu tended to act unlawfully. One day he was exposed in the presence of the staff. Although Lin intended to shield him, he had no way of justifying his leniency toward him. So Lin thought out a plan to let the doorman redeem his fault with good deeds. He called in the doorman in private and said to him, "Your crime deserves the punishment of expulsion from your post. If I pardon you, people here may talk. I therefore will remove your name from the list and announce the punishment on a wall poster. In this way I may silence the people." Hearing that his name would be canceled, the doorman kowtowed over and over again, saying that he was willing to take this punishment.

"That's not all," said Lin. "I have a plan to help you. There must be some reason behind the disappearance of the woman belonging to the Jings and the Dus. You may pretend to flee from the yamen because you have offended me, and then you can investigate the case for me in secret. Don't miss any corner in the area between the two families, be it a village, a town, a Buddhist temple or a Taoist monastery. I am sure if you try hard enough you will find a clue. If you can get some information, I will not only restore you to your job, but will reward

you handsomely. Then nobody will gossip about me." The doorman
had no choice but to accept the order before he left. Thereupon he
went everywhere inquiring about the woman. As a youngster,
wherever he talked to people and observed their expressions, he was
not suspected. But he found out nothing.

One day some people were talking together when the doorman
approached them to listen. One of the chatterers raised his eyes and
caught sight of him. He whispered to the other, "What a beautiful
boy!" Another said, "Even more beautiful is the young monk at the
Peace Temple. But the old monk is lustful and jealous. He is good-for-
nothing." The doorman pretended he did not hear anything and
strolled away. He wondered who was the young monk they were
praising, and decided to go to the temple to see for himself. He made
the decision because he had a thing for men of good looks, and the
mention of the handsome young monk aroused his interest. Having
found the way to the temple, he made for it. When he went through the
gate, he saw a delicate-featured young monk sitting on the threshold.
This must be that young monk they were talking about, he thought to
himself. The young monk, seeing such a handsome boy arrive, stood
up to greet him. "What has brought you here, my brother?" the monk
asked. "I am idle, so I've come for fun," said the doorman. When the
young monk hospitably asked him to enter for a cup of tea, the
doorman, having taken a liking to the lovely young monk, gladly
followed him in.

The old monk saw his disciple lead the boy into the temple, and he
thought a delicious treat had come his way. All smiles, he asked his
name and address. The doorman told him, "I was a doorman in the
yamen, but for some fault I was expelled. Now I have no place to live,
so I wander about." The old monk was elated by what he had heard.
"Our little rooms are lodgeable," he said. "It will be alright for you to
stay here for a few days." The old and young monk kept the doorman
there by serving him tea and wine. Buoyant with elation from the wine,

the old monk dragged him into his room and pulled down his trousers for a round of pleasure ride. The doorman was an old hand in such business, and he did not mind doing it with an old monk. He was not like the village woman who was particular about her lovers. The old monk went into rapture.

After this, Zhi Yuan came and said to the master, "The boy was led in by me, but you have been served first. Tonight I should have him in my bed." "Of course," said the old monk, smiling. The doorman intended to stay, so he slept with Zhi Yuan that night. As a rhyme goes:

None of the youth in prime,
Would their partner spare.
Though Zhi Yuan was served first,
He must serve; the game is fair.

The two pretty young men enjoyed each other that night and slept in each other's arms.

The next day the old monk came to seduce the doorman and try to lure him into his room for another tryst. Zhi Yuan, who had suffered at the hand of the old monk, was jealous. "According to the Heavenly principle and our conscience," he said, "this boy should belong to me! You shouldn't rob me of him." "Why not?" asked the old monk. "You use me every day," replied Zhi Yuan, "but I have never been rewarded. I always suffer from the absence of a place to work off my desires. Fortunately I came to know a good lay the other day, but you made trouble and screwed our relation up! This boy was brought in by me. I don't think I'm asking for too much to possess him." The old monk was displeased by his disciple's stubbornness, but he dared not challenge him. Lips pursed, both were cheerless.

All this was not lost on the doorman. That night, when he and Zhi Yuan were in high spirits, he asked Zhi Yuan, "What was the relation you said during the day the old monk had screwed up?" In the climax of his zest, Zhi Yuan let his tongue slip. "The other day a woman from the neighborhood came and we kept her for fun," he said. "I had a wonderful time. But when the old fool saw she was intimate with me, he became jealous. Later he made a mess of it and the affair came to an abrupt end. I always feel regret when I think of it!" "Where is the woman?" asked the doorman. "Why don't you look for her and ask her to come again?" "Where can I see her?" Zhi Yuan sighed. Sensing there was something not being said, the doorman asked more probing questions, but Zhi Yuan refused to divulge any further details.

The next day when the doorman found the twelve-year-old novice alone, he asked him in a low voice, "Was there a woman in the temple?" "Yes," replied the novice. When the doorman asked how long the woman had stayed, the answer was, "A few days." "Where is she now?" he asked again. "Nowhere," the novice replied. "She's gone. She disappeared overnight." "What did she do here?" the door-man asked. "I don't know," said the novice. "I saw her staying with the old master and young master for couple of nights and then she vanished. They often nagged each other after that, but I can't make out the cause." Though the doorman did not find out the whereabouts of the woman, he surmised that she was the root of their discord. Assuming a casual air, he went to the old and young monks and said, "I have been here for a couple of days. Today I will go out for a walk. I'll return in time." "Please do come back," said the old monk. "Don't leave us for good." Grimacing, Zhi Yuan said, "He won't. Perhaps he can part with you, but he can't part with me." The doorman made eyes at Zhi Yuan, and said, "I'll come back soon."

After the doorman left the temple, he made straight to Lin and told him what Zhi Yuan and the novice had said. Lin nodded, "There we have it! It seems that the woman has died at the hands of the evil monks. Or why didn't she go home three days after she left the temple? Where can she be? The lawsuit has lasted half a year and yet no trace has been found of her." He enjoined the doorman to keep his mouth shut about his findings.

The next morning Lin went to the temple in a sedan chair with his retinue. He bade a forerunner to inform the monks that Lord Lin had a strange dream last night and was coming to the temple to pray. Thus the whole temple gathered to greet him. When Lin dismounted the sedan chair, he lit incense and showed obeisance to the gods. The abbot served him tea and the monks stood on either side. Stepping down the stairs from the temple hall, Lin looked up as if he was listening to someone. After awhile he bowed to the sky and said, "Your servant has learned of this matter." Then he looked up and bowed again, "Yes, your servant understands who he is." Thereupon he hurried into the hall and shouted, "Runners, come and arrest the murderer at once!" The runners responded in chorus. As Lin stole a glance at the monks, he found that almost all of them were standing there reverently. They were a little surprised but not scared; only one elderly monk was ashen faced, his teeth rattling. Pointing his finger at this monk, Lin commanded the runners to tie him up. He then said to the other monks, "Didn't you see? Heaven told me 'It is Da Jue who has killed Lady Du of the Jings'. — Be quick to tell the truth!" The monks, ignorant of what had happened, said among themselves, "This lord has never before come to our temple. How can he know his name is Da Jue? Obviously Heaven has spoken to him." They did not know that the doorman had informed him in advance.

The old monk, taken by surprise, was caught unawares. Besides, believing that the all-knowing Heaven had shown its power, he was paralyzed and unable to hide his dismay. He kowtowed, unable to utter one single word. Lin ordered that he be cramped with sticks and, as expected, the old monk confessed in detail how he and Zhi Yuan seduced the woman and how in a fight for her love he killed her. Lin had Zhi Yuan cramped too. This young monk was even more fragile and the pain was too much for him. Before the torturers exerted their strength, he was already telling it all: how his master had killed the woman and how her body was buried in the rear garden. Lin ordered the runners to escort the monks to the place. They dug into the earth and a woman's body was exposed. Her neck was cut open and the body was covered with congested blood. Lin had the two monks brought back to the county court and had their statements recorded. He condemned Da Jue to death on charges of rape and murder. Zhi Yuan, who had participated in the seduction but had not reported the case to the authorities, was sentenced three years in prison, and when the imprisonment term was concluded, he was to resume secular life and perform servitude. Then Lin called in the Jings and Dus to claim the body and have it buried. Thus the feud between the two families was resolved.

Awarding doorman Yu a high prize, Lin reinstalled him in his former post. All the people of the county praised Lin for his wisdom and condemned the vicious and lecherous monk. Later, with the approval of the superior administration, the old monk was executed at the end of autumn. The public felt satisfaction. The fame that Lin was a wise man who could communicate with Heaven and settle an intricate case void of any clue is still told from mouth to mouth in the Shu* region even today.

---

*Shu is another name for Sichuan Province, because in antiquity that region was the State of Shu.

Tale 14

**Faithful Lamplight Conducts to a Boudoir;
Glad Tidings Break into a Cell**

This story takes place in the years of Duanping [1234-1236] of the Song Dynasty. There was a learned *xiucai* in Zhedong [east of the Zhejiang River in present-day Zhejiang Province] surnamed Zhang and named Zhongfu. Although he was a man of official origin, because of deficient financial resources he had to make a living as a secretary for officials or as a family tutor. Luo Renqing, his neighbor, came from a poor family, but had recently become wealthy. It happened the two families gave birth to children on the same day: Zhang had a boy and gave him the name Youqian; Luo had a girl and gave her the name Xixi. The Zhangs were running a private school. When the children were old enough to begin reading, Luo sent his daughter to Zhang's school. Seeing that the two children were well matched in both looks and age, someone teased them, saying, "Since you were born on the same day, you are to become husband and wife." The children, however, were too young to understand this joke. But hearing people say this, they began to believe it. In secret they promised to live together until death tore them apart, and each wrote a vow to be the other's life-long companion. Their parents, of course, knew nothing of this.

After four or five years at school the two children turned fourteen and reached the age of puberty. Hearing about what man and wife do, they talked about it, saying, "Since we are husband and wife, let's learn how to do it." Because they had a liking for each other and did not know the serious consequences, they readily agreed. In front of the classroom was a pomegranate tree with a stone stool under it. Luo Xixi sat on the stool with her back against the tree, while Zhang Youqian lifted her feet and made love to her. Although they were very young and found little pleasure in this, they loved the fun. By and by they came to know the pleasure, and so unable to hold themselves back, they did it every day.

In winter school was over. Luo Xixi returned to her home. The next year she was fifteen years old. Her parents thought it improper for a girl of fifteen to read in their neighbor's home, so they did not send her back to the school. Zhang Youqian often stopped by Luo's house hoping to meet her, but the Luos were a wealthy family, whose daughters lived in seclusion and could not come out easily. Xixi had a maid servant by the name of Fei Ying who had often kept her company at the school. Now that Xixi no longer went to school, Fei Ying was absent too. She came out of the door only when she was asked to pluck flowers in the morning for Xixi to pin on her head. By the next winter Youqian, unable to contain his longing for Xixi, wrote two stanzas to the tune of "Yi Jian Mei" which he intended to deliver to Xixi via Fei Ying when the servant came out. The stanzas read:

We are schoolmates born on the same date.
If we are not a perfect pair,
Who in the world can be a pair?

From the hasty tryst by a pomegranate
In fear we've been torn apart,
In fright we've been torn apart!

You've been absent from school over a year.
How can I help thinking of you!
How can I help pining for you!
Every dawn and dusk I say a prayer:
Let us become a happy match,
If we are a destined match!

After he finished the poem, he didn't see Fei Ying come, so he composed a quatrain:

Yearning for their beloveds, people used to send
Bloomed boughs to the land's remotest end.*
Alas! The blossom's in your reach, why don't you come?
Know a man pines alone by a plum!

When he finished this poem, Fei Ying chanced to come by his study to pluck plum-blossoms. Youqian picked a bough of plum-blossoms and handed it to her together with the poems. He instructed her to take it to Xixi, telling her, "Now the plum is in full bloom. Please bring her reply to me on the pretext of plucking flowers." Agreeing to do this, Fei Ying brought the poems to Xixi. On reading them, Xixi shed tears. She wanted to write verses in reply following his rhyme sequence, but it was the end of year and she was too busy to do this.

---

*The first two lines refer to an old poem:
    As I pluck a bough of blossoms a post comes by.
    I asked him to hand it to my distant friend
    With a message: There is nothing in South land,
    But a bough with the hue of the spring.

Early next year the prefect of Yuezhou [around present-day Shaoxing City] invited Zhang Zhongfu, Youqian's father, to be his secretary. Zhang Zhongfu took his son with him so that he could continue teaching him how to read and write. Two years later they returned on a home visit. On hearing of Youqian's return, Xixi, remembering the poems she failed to write two years before, had Fei Ying hand-deliver a small box to him. Youqian opened it to see ten coins and one love pea* in it. Youqian realized those objects were riddles pose by Xixi: the round coins symbolized union, and the meaning of the love pea, of course, was obvious. Transported with joy, he said to Fei Ying, "I am much obliged to her for her kindness. It would be better if we could have a meeting again." "She does not come out of her room," said Fei Ying, "and you cannot get in. How can you see each other? All I can do is to deliver a message." Youqian then wrote a poem and handed it to Fei Ying as his reply to Xixi. The poem read:

A day apart seems to me like three years;
How can I stand three years' living apart?
The coins are not a substitute for your hearty smile;
Our love will last until death does us part!

After Fei Ying left, Youqian tied the coins into the lace of his shirt. Whenever he thought of Xixi, he would unloosen them and toss them for divination and fun. When his mother saw this, she asked Youqian, "Where did you get those coins? I haven't seen you with them since your childhood." "I dare not hide the truth from you, Mother," replied Youqian. "These were a gift the Luos' daughter, my schoolmate, gave me recently." The mother understood. She thought to herself, my son is approaching his twenties, the age for marriage. He and the young

---

*A love pea or red bean (*Abrus precatovius*) is a token of love or friendship.

daughter of the Luos were schoolmates when they were children and they exchange gifts even today. They must be in love. Besides I did find their daughter both beautiful and virtuous when she was reading in my house. Wouldn't it be a perfect idea to have someone to talk to them about a proposal for marriage?

Zhang's next door neighbor was an old flower seller by the name of Yang. She played the match-maker for other people. She also often went between the Zhangs and the Luos. Zhang's mother invited the woman to her home and said to her, "My family is poor and shouldn't aspire to an affinity with the rich. But Luo's daughter often came to my house in her childhood and she was my son's schoolmate. Besides, the two children have the same birthday. Perhaps for this reason the Luos may condescend to grant our petition for a marriage between them." "What are you saying, Madam?" asked Yang, "You are not wealthy, but yours is an official's family. The Luos are rich, but they are of low origin. If a match is made between the two families, they are the inferior part! Let your servant go and give them your proposal." "I am much obliged for your thoughtful service," said Zhang's mother. Youqian then talked to Yang in private, begging her to give Xixi his regards. After Yang agreed, she left the Zhangs and made directly for the Luos.

When Luo Renqing and his wife asked Yang about the intention of her visit, she answered, "I am here as a go-between for your daughter." "Which family do you mean?" Luo Renqing asked. Yang replied, "They needn't ask for your daughter's birth-card; the youth was born on the same day as your daughter." "So you mean Zhang Zhongfu's son?" asked Luo Renqing. "Quite right!" replied Yang. "His son is nice." "His family is from a line of Confucian scholars and enjoys a good reputation," said Luo Renqing, "but they are in adversity now. He has to support his family by tutoring school-children all year. Can he be expected to make any significant improvement?" "The young man is handsome and intelligent," said Yang. "He will surely amount to something someday." "But people put great importance on the present situation," said Luo Renqing, "Who knows what the future holds? I can see the young man is good, but one's prosperity is in the hands of Fate. Who can tell if he will be favored by Fate? Unless he wins scholarly honors and becomes an official, I won't give my daughter to him." "In my opinion," replied Yang, "the young man will have that in time." "If so," said Luo Renqing, "I will not go back on my word!" Luo's wife chimed in. "Let me report this to Lady Zhang," said Yang, "and I'll instruct the young man to study hard so as to acquire a degree." "That's the right thing to do," said Luo's wife. "I'd like to go to your daughter's house to see her," said Yang. "Please do so," said Luo's wife, "she is in. You may go and have a cup of tea with her."

Since Yang was no stranger to Luo's house, she needed no guidance. Seeing Yang enter her room, Xixi seated her and had Fei Ying fetch tea. "What are you doing here, Auntie?" she asked. "I am here to propose for your marriage on behalf of the son of Zhang, your nextdoor neighbor. The young man asked me to give you his regards. He said he has been missing you as a schoolmate from childhood, all the time he and you have been separated. He wanted me to ask your honorable father and mother for their consent to the marriage. He wants you to make up your mind and help bring about the union." "This is a matter for the parents' decision," said Xixi. "How can a daughter voice her opinion? What have my father and mother said about it?" "From their words I guess they despise the destitute circumstances the Zhangs are in," said Yang. "They said the young man may gain the marriage only if he wins a scholarly honor." "He will surely have that some day," said Xixi, "but I am afraid my parents are not patient enough to wait for that to happen and they will break their promise. Since my parents have said so, please take the trouble to bring the message to him. Tell him he should work hard for an early success and that I am waiting for it."

In order to secure Yang's help, Xixi took out two golden rings and presented them to her, saying, "If he has any message for me in the future, bring it to me in secret. I will reward you, but don't let my father and mother know." — You should know, gentle readers, that the old woman was a champion to happy unions between men and women, and she could not fail to get the meaning. Perceiving the affection in the words from both sides, she knew that even if the marriage would not be a success, she could gain a large profit by bringing the couple together in private. At the sight of the two golden rings she smiled and said, "Leave to me, your old servant, whatever you want me to do. I will not fail you."

From the Luos' house she returned to the Zhangs, and related what she had heard to Zhang Youqian's mother. Zhang Youqian, who on hearing the report, sneered, "To gain a scholarly honor is a man's job. Can it pose an obstacle? I will have her as my wife for sure!" "The girl also said that the young master will certainly get a scholarly honor some day," said Yang, "but she is afraid her parents are not patient enough and may go back on their word. She is determined to wait for you and you must work hard." Lady Zhang said to her son, "These are good words. You mustn't disappoint her!" Then Yang told Youqian in private, "Luo's daughter is really very affectionate toward you. When I took leave, she told me that if you have any message for her, I should deliver it in secret. She gave me two golden rings. She is a very sedate and virtuous girl." "If one day I ask you to bring her a message, please don't decline me," Youqian said. "Certainly not," Yang replied and took her leave.

The next year Zhang Zhongfu sent a servant from Yuezhou to his home with the message that he and the prefect of Yuezhou would be proceeding to the capital for new appointments, and that he had decided to bring his son along so that his studies would not be interrupted. Youqian had no alternative but to obey. Of this we'll say no more.

As for Luo Renqing, he had intended to decline the proposal from the Zhangs from the beginning, since he loathed their poverty. His remark that if Zhang's son could become an official he would give his daughter to him was a far-fetched one. It is hard to predict when someone can become an official. His daughter was getting older with each passing year. If Zhang's son ended up like the Grand Duke Jiang,* who had not met an appreciative sovereign until he reached his eighties, his daughter would be an old granny by the time she got married. And seeing the Zhangs always going on a distant journey, he presumed they would never make good. At the time an extremely wealthy neighbor named Xin had an eighteen-year old son. Hearing of the talent and beauty of Luo's daughter, the Xins sent a match-maker to visit the Luos. Luo Renqing was delighted by the immense fortune of the Xins. He thought to himself that the Zhangs had offered a marriage only by word and given no gift, so it would not be counted as a breach of contract if he accepted Xin's proposal. So, consigning the Zhangs to the remotest corner of his mind, he promptly assented to the Xins' request. A day was then chosen for the exchange of betrothal gifts.

When Xixi learned of this, she groaned inwardly. Too shy to tell her parents the secrets in her mind, she had to keep her distress to herself. "Zhang's young master and I were born on the same day and we were schoolmates," she told Fei Ying in private. "Who can say we are not a natural pair? We have been dear to each other like brother and sister and our love is like that between a husband and wife. Now they are going to marry me off to another man. How can I bear this? I would be free from this misfortune if I took my own life. But I can't bring myself to commit suicide yet because I wish to see him once more." "The other day Zhang said he wanted to see you," said Fei

---

*Grand Duke Jiang, a premier of the Zhou-dynasty founder. He remained in poverty and obscurity until he became a premier in his eighties.

Ying, "I told him that he had to give up the idea since I could not find a way. Now Zhang is no longer at home. Even if he was at home, you couldn't see him." "I've thought of a way to meet him," said Xixi, "if only he could come! You may go out from time to time and inquire about him." From then on Fei Ying kept this in mind.

One year later Zhang Youqian returned from the capital. When he heard that Luo Xixi had been promised to the Xins and that Xixi had said nothing against the engagement, Youqian was exasperated. He said, "I cannot blame her parents. But can Xixi be so obedient to them that she didn't say no?" In anger he took up his brush and wrote a conventional poem to the tune of "Chang Xiang Si":

The gods in Heaven know
The gods on the earth know
Every word in our vow —
The ink is still wet!

Elapsed one springtime
Elapsed another springtime,
The coins have lost their golden shine.
You have forgotten me!

Slipping the poem into his sleeve, he hurried to Yang's house. Yang greeted him, asking, "What do you want me to do, master?" "Did you know that Luo's daughter has become engaged?" he inquired. "Yes," replied Yang, "but the match-maker was not me. What a good girl! Her heart was for you, but she missed the opportunity." "I don't blame her parents," said Youqian, "but I blame her. How could she have let her parents arrange her marriage without a word of protest?" "How would a girl like her be bold enough to reveal her intentions?" said Yang. "I think she must have her own opinion. You shouldn't blame her wrongly." Thereupon Youqian told her, "I am asking you to inform her of my arrival. I have written a small poem to sound out her attitude. Would you please deliver it to her?" He fished the poem from within his sleeve along with one *liang* of silver, which had been presented to him by the prefect of Yuezhou at their parting. He gave the silver to Yang as a tip. Seeing the silver, Yang was like a fly seeing blood. Only too ready to do his bidding, she went away pleased.

On the pretext of selling flowers, she made directly to the Luo's house and entered Xixi's room. "I haven't seen you for a long time, Madam," Xixi greeted her. "I have not dared to trouble you without a special reason," Yang replied. "Now young master Zhang has returned home and he wanted me to deliver a message, so I came." Hearing that Youqian had returned, Xixi said, "I have asked Fei Ying to inquire about him, but he has come home before I knew it!" "When he heard that you were engaged to one of the Xins, he was sad. He asked me to bring a letter to you." Taking out the letter from her sleeve, Yang presented it to Xixi.

Xixi took the letter with a sigh. As she read the poem from beginning to end, tears streamed from her eyes. She said, "He has wronged me." "I can't read," said Yang. "What has he written in the letter?" "He said I've forgotten him," answered Xixi. "He doesn't realize it was my parents' decision to accept the proposal. How could I have a choice?" "How will you reply to him, Miss?" asked Yang. "Since you were willing to deliver Master Zhang's letter," replied Xixi, "he must have confidence in you. Can I tell you my innermost thoughts?" "I haven't done anything for you since you gave me that handsome gift last year. And furthermore, I am entrusted by Master Zhang. I will do whatever you bid me, even at the risk of my own old life. Let me assure you that not even half a word will leak out." "I am much obliged to you for your kindness," said Xixi. "The first thing I want you to do is to tell Master Zhang about my feelings. I have lived in humiliation till today because I haven't seen him. If I can see him once, I will gladly die together with him rather than live an unworthy life as another man's wife."

"I can tell him what you think," said Yang, "but a meeting with him is impossible. Your residence is large and tightly guarded. How can he come here if he cannot fly and I cannot hide him in my sleeves?" "I have a stratagem for him to come," said Xixi. "If you can help, a meeting is sure to be realized." "I've just said that I'll do whatever you want me to do," replied Yang. "I'll do my best as long as you have a brilliant scheme." "My bed-chamber," said Xixi, "is in the last row of the compound and entirely isolated from the front quarters. Under my chamber there is a gate that leads to a small garden. The garden is surrounded by low walls and beyond those walls are open fields. In the garden by the wall are four or five tall camellia trees. Climbing up one of the trees will allow a person to get over the wall. Tell Zhang to wait outside. At night I will have my maid servant climb to the top of the wall by way of the tree branches and put down a bamboo ladder on the other side of the wall. Zhang can then mount the wall by the ladder and get down into the garden by way of the tree. Then he can make straight for my chamber. I beseech you, if you are sympathetic for our love, to notify Zhang of my plan in detail." She then entered her inner room, found a silver ingot worth four or five *liang* and tucked it into Yang's sleeve, saying, "You may use this to buy snacks." "I haven't done anything for you," Yang protested, putting on a show of declination, "how can I accept this high reward? — But if I don't take it, you may suspect I am not being sincere with you. So I'd better make bold to take it." Having taken her leave with an expression of gratitude, she went to Zhang Youqian and told him of Xixi's plan exactly as Yang was told.

When Zhang Youqian learned this, he wished that the evening would set in immediately. His house was not very far from hers. During the day he went to inspect the outside walls of her residence. As he peeped in, he could see four or five camellia boughs sticking out over the wall top. Having committed this to memory, he went there in the night. For what seemed an eternity no sound could be heard from beyond the walls, and there was no sign of a ladder. In the latter half of the night before the beat of the watch-drum, he went home in disconsolation. Nothing happened the second and third nights. Having waited for three nights in vain, he thought to himself, is she playing a joke on me? Or have I misinterpreted something in the message? Maybe, as a very young girl, she's sleeping too heavily to keep the appointment in mind, without realizing how I have suffered waiting in the open. He decided to ask Yang to inquire about the situation. He wrote this poem on a piece of paper:

Like countless mountains in the way
Camellia trees block the vernal breeze!
While you enjoy cozy dreams on a golden draped bed,
In dewy moonlight I suffer a freeze.

When he had finished the poem, he went to Yang's house, and asked her to deliver it to Xixi and see why she had broken the appointment.

The truth was that Xixi was an able member of the Luos who ran all the household affairs. One of her aunts arrived the day she had fixed for the meeting through Yang. Xixi had to receive and accompany her aunt, and during the night her aunt slept in Xixi's room, ruling out any maneuver. The day her aunt left, Yang arrived to deliver her the poem. Having read it, Xixi said, "Master Zhang blames me wrongly. My aunt slept in my room for the past three nights and I haven't slept a wink. It is not that I didn't want to see him, but that I couldn't get the chance. Now my aunt has left. Tell him to come tonight after the lamp is lighted. I won't fail to keep the appointment!" Yang left to report her promise to Zhang Youqian. "She has not been able to get a chance during the last three days. She's appointed a meeting for this evening when the lamps are lit."

At the fixed hour, Youqian arrived at the scene, and, as arranged in advance, found a ladder against the wall. Enraptured, Youqian climbed it step by step. On the wall top a dark figure in the shadow of camellia branches gave him a start. It turned out to be Fei Ying who was waiting for him. A cough was enough for them to identify each other. They climbed down the boughs and landed on the ground. When Fei Ying led him to the chamber door, Xixi was already there. Hand in hand they went upstairs. Scrutinizing each other by lamp light, they each found the other to have grown more lovely. In ecstasy they said in chorus, "Fancy we can meet today!" And then they fell into a firm embrace, totally forgetting Fei Ying's presence. Taking the cue, Fei Ying moved with the lamp to the outer room. In the moonlight that came through the window, the two lovers held each other tightly and fell into bed.

Having experienced four years' separation they savored every second of their union. Recalling their good old days, they felt as if they were in a dream. In the past what went on between them was nothing more than mere skirmishes; now the war was waged with full powers. The bud was nipped leaving stains of red; the club grew tremendously huge yet was a bit timid in its first action. For the sake of heart-felt love for each other, they ran the risk behind the parents' backs.

When the cloud expended its rain, they poured out their hearts to each other. "Our merriment is short," said Youqian. "One day another man will come in my stead." "Don't you know my heart, Brother?" asked Xixi. "Ever since I was betrothed, I have always been prepared to die. But the wedding day has not arrived yet and I have been anxious to be with you. If I give myself over to another man, I will be no better than a sow or a dog. You'll see what a woman I am." Thus they murmured the night through. At dawn Xixi urged Youqian to dress himself and leave. When Youqian asked her about her plan for the next night, Xixi replied, "There is often something going on in my house and it is not convenient that we meet every night. I'll make a sign for you. The west chamber of my house is visible from the distance. If you see three lamps lit in that chamber, then you will know that I will let you in with a ladder; if you see only one lamp, it means you can't come. Then you need not wait in vain and suffer as you did." With this agreement made, Youqian took his leave. Again he climbed up the camellia tree and down the ladder. Fei Ying, on the wall-top, pulled up the ladder after he was gone. All this was done in complete secrecy.

After that Youqian would go each night and watch from a distance. Whenever he saw three lamps lit, he would go to the outside of the wall and there would find a ladder ready for him. He could then enter for a sensual union with his lover. Usually they would have a sweet time for four or five nights running. If there was a break, it would be just for one or two nights. Thus for more than a month, they were at the climax of their pleasure.

But alas! The road to happiness is strewn with setbacks. Because of Zhang Zhongfu's reputation, he was engaged as a secretary by the marshal of Hubei. Having resigned his tutorship in the Yuezhou prefect's house, Zhang Zhongfu returned home, ordered his affairs, and decided to take Youqian along with him. He wanted his son to sit for the provincial-level examination. Youqian was quite unhappy about the news. He was reluctant to leave Xixi. He was vexed, but dared not defy his father's order. He told Xixi about this and tearfully said good-bye to her. Taking out many valuables, Xixi presented them to him for his expenses on the journey. "If I am fortunate not to be married off," she sobbed, "I'll meet with you when you come back. But if, before your return, the wedding date is due and I am forced to marry, I'll drown myself in the well in front of my chamber. Then I'll be your mate in the coming life, but for this life we'll be parted forever." Whimpering and whining half the night, they felt their enthusiasm dampened even when they slept together. Before Youqian's departure, Xixi held him by the hand and enjoined him, "Don't forget our love. Find an opportunity to come back — I'll be happy if you can return earlier by even a single day." "You needn't warn me about this," said Youqian. "Were it not for the examination, I would surely be able to find an excuse not to go. Now, because of the examination, I cannot find any pretext. It is not what I want at all. I will come back as soon as possible. I'll be happy if I can see you one day earlier!" They held each other for a long while, unable to bear the idea of separation. Then they parted, eyes brimming with tears.

Needless to say, everything that came in sight aroused Youqian's sorrow on his way to Hubei with his father. They arrived just in time for the examination. If I come first among the successful candidates, Youqian thought wishfully, perhaps my marriage will be salvaged. So he exerted his learning and talent to the utmost when he wrote his paper. As soon as he stepped out of the examination room, he said to his father, "I'm going home because I am worried about my mother." "Why not wait until the results of the examination are announced?" asked Zhang Zhongfu. "If I fail," replied Youqian, "won't I be ashamed? Mother is lonely at home. She must be eagerly looking forward to my return. This place is far from home and unlike Yuezhou, where we could often hear from her. How can I set my mind at rest about her? The academic honor is an external matter and is predestined by Fate. What's the use of seeing the honor-list?" After he importuned his father for several days, his father granted his leave. In a few days he arrived home.

By that time the Xins had chosen a date in the coming winter for the nuptials. Burning with anxiety, Luo Xixi longed for Youqian to return with eager expectancy. From time to time she would find a pretext for Fei Ying to go to Youqian's home and inquire about him. When Fei Ying learned that Youqian had come back, she hurried to report this to Xixi. "Go to him immediately," said Xixi, "and tell him to come this very night. He may enter as he did before." She also composed a poem, sealed it in an envelope and gave it to Fei Ying to pass on to him. Upon her instructions Fei Ying went to Zhang's house and at the gate ran into Youqian. "Great!" exclaimed Youqian, "You came at the moment I was just going to Lady Yang to ask her to deliver a message." "As my sister has not seen you, she has often shed tears and had me come to ask about you every day. Today, when she heard of your return, she at once sent me to arrange a meeting. You may come to see her this evening by way of the bamboo ladder. Here's her letter for you." When Youqian opened the letter, he saw a poem written to the tune of "Bu Suan Zi":

> *I am blessed that you have come!*
> *But how can I make you come?*
> *I am pining for you all day, every day —*
> *My heart is your home!*

> *You and I are a good match.*
> *Yet I dread the match is untrue.*
> *If I am forced to follow another*
> *In the nether world I'll wait for you!*

Having read the poem, Youqian said to Faiying, "I see." When the maid left, he put the poem away in a safe place.

At night, seeing three lamps lit in the west chamber in the distance, Youqian hurried to the outside of the wall and there found the ladder. He entered the chamber to see Xixi. As if she was finding a treasure, she held him tightly with both arms, complaining, "How could you put off your return until now! My wedding day has been fixed. Even if I can be with you every night, we have little more than two months left. Our time is limited. If I can enjoy the union with you to my heart's content before I take my own life, I'll feel no regrets. You are young and talented, and will have boundless prospects. I dare not force you to die with me, but if you have a new spouse in the future, don't forget me!" With this she broke into tears. Youqian cried too. "If you die, we'll die together. How could you talk this nonsense?" he said. "Since I saw you last time, what day did I spend without thinking of you? That's why I came back without waiting for the honor-list to be published. I delayed a few days because I could not defy my father. I'm sorry for my delay. Please forgive me. Now that I have read your new poem, let me write one in response upon your rhyme pattern just to show my feelings." Setting Xixi's brush to paper, he wrote:

I had to leave you against my will;
Nor could I decide when to go home.
An oath has tied us, in life or death;
I won't leave you alone!

My feelings are genuine;
Nothing in my heart is untrue.
If you complain of my late coming, give me
A thousand spanks, I entreat you!

The poem made Xixi realize that there was nothing he could do about his belated arrival and so he was not to blame. Together they fell into the curtained bed for a prolonged round of sensual union. As the old saying goes, "A reunited pair is sweeter than newly-weds." Besides, they were aware of the limited time they had to spend together. So every moment together was as dear as gold to them. They were desperate in their love making.

Thus half a month passed. Youqian grew increasingly apprehensive. "I come here every night," he said to Xixi, "and you go to bed early and get up late. Aren't we being too carried away? What if somebody gets wind of this?" "I will die sooner or later," replied Xixi. "Let's enjoy our good time the best we can. Even if we are exposed, the worst thing will be nothing other than death. So what should we fear?" True to her words, Xixi became more daring.

Seeing that her daughter was listless all the day, yawning from time to time, and that sometimes her eyelids were swollen in the early morning, the mother became suspicious. "She is not what she used to be," she thought. "Is she doing anything improper?" So she kept a watchful eye on her daughter. When the world died down at night, she stole to the front door of her daughter's room. Hearing her daughter speak with somebody in a low voice, she said to herself, "Here it is. Does she have anything to talk with Fei Ying about at this late hour? And even if she does, why should she speak in such an indiscernible faint voice?" As she listened more carefully, she heard someone snoring downstairs. This surprised her even more. She thought to herself, someone is talking upstairs and someone else is sleeping downstairs. So there are three people all together? If the sleeping one is Fei Ying, then who is the one talking with my daughter? It is strange! She hurried to tell her husband about this.

Luo Renqing was taken aback. "The wedding is coming," he said to his wife. "We mustn't let anything disrespectable happen! Don't hesitate. Break in and we'll see what's going on. He cannot hide in the chamber." Thereupon the mother woke up two maid servants and had them light two lamps. With the maids leading the way, and Luo Renqing following behind with a rod in hand, she rushed to her daughter's chamber. Finding the door tightly bolted from within, she shouted, "Fei Ying, you slave girl!" Fei Ying, sound asleep, did not answer, but Xixi, who lived upstairs, heard the shout. "My mother is calling," Xixi said. "There must be something she needs." Youqian hurried to get dressed. "There's no hurry," said Xixi. "Be quiet. Let me go down to meet her. She doesn't come upstairs at night." She put on her clothes and went down to open the door. Zhang Youqian felt a bit apprehensive. He put on his clothes too, but finding no exit, had to hide himself in a corner and listen.

Thinking that her mother had come to ask her something, Xixi believed she could stop her by a greeting downstairs. But to her surprise, she had no sooner opened the door than she saw two bright lamps and her father. Before she could utter a word, her mother snatched the lamps from the maid servants and with her father, rod in hand, dashed upstairs. Realizing the disastrous situation, Xixi dashed out of the chamber and headed for the well. Seeing her run in that direction one of the maids lit the way for her with a torch. The other servant, with nothing in hand, and realizing that she was about to jump into the well, seized her, shouting, "Why are you doing this?" The servant then screamed, "Sister is drowning herself in the well!" By that time Fei Ying had awakened from her sleep. As she got up and went out, she saw Xixi being held by two maid servants and struggling. Fei Ying walked up and, leaning against the railing of the well, shouted faintly, "No, you mustn't do this, sister!"

Let's put the chaos aside and turn to Luo Renqing and his wife who searched out the man from his hiding. As Luo Renqing was raising the rod to hit him, his wife moved forward and shone the lamp on him. Luo Renqing recognized him to be Youqian, Zhang Zhongfu's son. Luo Renqing put down the rod and reprimanded him: "You bastard! You beast! You are my friend's son. How could you do this shameless thing and defile the reputation of my family!" Youqian knelt down. "Please forgive your child for his impunity, Uncle," he implored, "and listen to his explanation. Since your daughter and I were schoolmates and born on the same day, we long ago reached an agreement in our hearts. Years ago I sent a match-maker to you, and you personally promised to marry her to me if I could win an academic degree. For this purpose I have studied hard in the hope that my wish would come true. I never imagined that you would marry her to another suitor. In resentment, your daughter had me come in secret. We have pledged to live and die together. Now that our affair is exposed, your daughter will surely die. I don't want to live without her. I entreat you, my uncle, beat me to death." "I did make that promise once," retorted Luo Renqing, "but when did you acquire a degree? Yet you are blaming me for betrothing her to another man! A bestial man like you cannot be blessed with scholarly honors. Your crime is not light and you will be punished according to law. I won't torture you in my house." And he grabbed Youqian to pull him out of the house.

Hearing the clamor outside, the mother feared that her daughter might commit suicide, so she urged Luo Renqing to go downstairs. Dragging Youqian to a parlor, Renqing tied him with a rope. He shut him in the study and had it guarded by his servants. He planned to take him to court next morning. As he turned around and entered the inner room, he saw that his daughter, hair disheveled, was struggling with her mother and the maids, yelling. Luo Renqing was fuming, "What a worthless puss she is! Let her die! Why should you stop her?" And raising the rod he was going to strike at her when the mother and the maids, half supporting and half pushing, brought her upstairs. Luo Renqing was left alone. As he raised his head he saw Fei Ying at the well. Finding nowhere else to give vent to his anger, he went over and snatched her by the hair, and hauling her up he gave her a thrashing. "You are the go-between who led her astray!" he shouted. "Tell me the truth about how it began!" At first Fei Ying said that since she had slept downstairs, she did not know what happened upstairs. But, as she could not stand the beating, she had to relate the story in detail from beginning to end. "Sister often cried. She wishes to die together with Master Zhang," she added. Hearing this, Luo Renqing ordered Fei Ying to leave. He was a little remorseful, "If I had accepted his proposal, she would not have come to this. But now with the Xins as the other party, I cannot settle the matter easily. I have to submit this to the authorities."

After almost a whole night of commotion the day broke — as a rule people who have trouble during the night find the day always breaks early. While the mother and maid servants stayed with the daughter to prevent her from committing suicide, Luo Renqing escorted Zhang Youqian to the county court. The county magistrate convened court and received the indictment. Finding it was a case regarding adulterers who had been caught on the spot, he knew the evidence was reliable. And, as he read in the file that Zhang Youqian was a *xiucai*, he called him in, asking, "You are a student and should know propriety. Why did you act so as to offend public decency?" "I dare not hide the truth from you, my lord," replied Youqian. "There is a reason for this, and it is not the lascivious activity of a lecherous man and woman." "What is it then?" asked the magistrate. "Luo's daughter and I," responded Zhang Youqian, "were born on the same day and same month of the same year. As a child she studied in the school run by my house. When we were schoolmates we found our feeling congenial. So we secretly took an oath to keep company the rest of our lives. Later I sent my proposal through a match-maker, but the Luos replied that I would be promised the marriage only if I got a degree. I studied in another city where my father held a post for two years. When I returned, I learned that the Luos had gone back on their promise and had betrothed her to the Xins. Luo's daughter didn't have the heart to betray me so she risked death threats before the wedding and invited me to her place to bid me farewell for good. Because we failed to keep our relationship a strict secret, I was caught. Luo's daughter will surely die if she is forced to marry another man, and I won't live alone in the world. Now that our relationship is exposed, I will not shirk my responsibility." Seeing him to be a person of imposing bearing and hearing him speak so eloquently, the magistrate decided to help him. He turned to Luo Renqing and asked, "Is what he said true?" "Yes," answered Luo Renqing, "but he shouldn't have done that." The magistrate wanted to know Youqian's talent, so he said, "If so, an oral confession cannot be taken as testimony. You will have to commit your statement to paper." Youqian took up the brush and finished writing his statement at one go.

It read:

> *Your humble servant thinks:*
>
> *Love is deep in the hearts of both of us, her and me; sincere feelings are not against rightfulness, so why should we fear idle talk? Luo's daughter was born on the same day as I, and she was my classmate in school; I am her close and faithful friend, and not a seducer of good girls.*
>
> *When the writer Sima Xiangru* plucked strings, he meant more than just music; though the poet Song Yu** wrote candid songs for beauties, shall we say they are obscene expressions?*
>
> *Because I was promised a marriage if I acquired a degree, I have never been impatient; but the Luos accepted the proposal of another suitor — they have the heart to cast me into eternal solitude! Luo's daughter bade me an eternal farewell before the wedding's arrival — her chastity is good because she hasn't been engaged in the ten years. I fulfilled the appointment at the risk of my own life — my faith hasn't betrayed our yearning in separation.*
>
> *Now that I am entrapped, I will gladly take the consequence of imprisonment. Still I wish you would be sympathetic for our fidelity and grant us a chance to renew our beautiful past, and that you would feel pity for our genuine affection and find an excuse to set me free. Then, as a cold valley bathing in the fresh spring, our extinguished hope would be rekindled. Your kindness is as great as that of the planter of jade*** and our gratitude*

---

*Sima Xiangru (179-117 BC), a writer, once expressed his love for a girl (who later became his wife) by playing a musical instrument.

**Song Yu, a poet living between the fourth and third centuries BC, praised beautiful goddesses in his works.

***An anecdote says that a man once received a stone from a passer-by. The donator told him if he planted the stone in good field it would yield jade. Later the man got a wife with the jade harvested from the stone as betrothal gifts.

towards you will be cherished in this and coming lives.
That is all I confess.

Having read the statement, the magistrate gasped in admiration. He said to Luo Renqing, "Such a brilliant talent is a worthy son-in-law for you. Since what your daughter has done cannot be undone, why don't you help them in a roundabout way?" "I have received Xin's bride-price," replied Luo Renqing, "so I cannot make the decision myself." "If the Xins learn of this," said the magistrate, "they may not be willing to keep the engagement."

While the county magistrate was admonishing Luo Renqing, the Xins, having learned of the matter, filed a lawsuit. They demanded the authorities to punish the adulterer. The Xins were extremely wealthy and on friendly terms with the magistrate, and furthermore, they were in the right, so the magistrate could not neglect their demand. On the other hand, he feared that if Youqian was set free, he might be badly beaten by the two furious families. What he could do, however, was to put Youqian in prison and place the case on file. He would then summon Luo's daughter and question her for more details.

As for Zhang Youqian's mother, because she did not see him turn up for breakfast, she went to his study. But she did not see him there either. At this juncture Lady Yang arrived in a hurry to tell her, "Do you know, Madam, that the young master was caught in adultery by the Luos and has been put into prison!" Mother Zhang was shocked, "That's why he has not been himself recently!" "The Luos and Xins are both wealthy," said Yang, "I am afraid the authorities will give harsh treatment to the young master. How can we help him out?" "The only way," said Mother Zhang, "is to send someone to inform his father of what has happened and ask his advice. I am a woman and cannot do anything significant. All I can do is to bring food to the prison." Accordingly Mother Zhang called in a servant, wrote a detailed letter and sent the servant to Hubei to report to Zhang

Zhongfu about Youqian's trouble and to ask him to find a way out. The servant set off that very evening.

In prison, Zhang Youqian thought to himself, the county magistrate is very kind and maybe he will spare me. But I don't know if Xixi has survived the night. I am afraid she and I will never meet again in this life. His yearning for her brought tears to his eyes. At this point the jailers came to extort the so-called regular tribute and expense for the lamp-oil. Thanks to the magistrate's order that they mustn't trouble Youqian, they didn't go so far as to beat him, but their nagging was quite displeasing. How could Youqian, a student who was in bad mood, stand such impudence?

But as he and the jailers were haggling, there was a peal of gongs from outside and a band of people broke through the door. The whole prison was startled. Youqian looked at the man in the front and could see that he had a banner on his shoulders with bells attached to the tassels and the words "Good News from the Marshal's House" written on it. "Who is the *xiucai* named Zhang Youqian?" the man shouted. People there pointed to Zhang Youqian saying, "This is he. Who are you?" The intruders, however, gave no reply. They mobbed Zhang Youqian and said loudly, "We've come from the Marshal's headquarters in Hubei to deliver the glad tidings of your success in the examination. Be quick to tip us with a bill!" One of them took out a brush and ink and grasped him by the hand. They boisterously demanded that he write a bill for five hundred or three hundred strings of coins. "There is no hurry," said Youqian, "Show me the announcement and let me see what place I've taken. Then I will reward you." "A good place!" said the messengers. As they took out a red sheet, Youqian saw that he was listed in the third place. "I am a culprit in confinement," said Youqian, "why don't you report this to my home rather than make so much noise here? If the county magistrate learns of this, you may have trouble." "We did go to your house," they replied, "but when we heard that you were here, we came.

We have sent a man to report the matter to the county magistrate and ask for his permission. This is a good thing. We don't think the magistrate will blame us." "I don't know my future yet," said Youqian. "It all depends on the decision of the magistrate. Why should I write you a bill?" The group, however, did not give up, and as the jailers joined in abetting them, the prison was in turmoil.

Then came the shouts, "Clear the passage!" and the jailers fled in panic, saying, "Here comes the magistrate!" Soon the magistrate paced into the prison smiling. Seeing Zhang Youqian being surrounded, he asked, "What are you doing?" The people replied, "We are waiting for you, our lord. *Xiucai* Zhang refuses to write us a bill on the excuse that he is in prison. We plead that you give a fair judgment." "Please stop haggling," the magistrate said, smilingly comforting them. "For the success of *Xiucai* Zhang there is a public fund. The reward is fifty strings of coins. You may get it from my coffers." Taking up the brush he wrote a bill. The intruders thought the tip was not generous enough, and so they went away only after the magistrate added ten more strings. Then the magistrate asked Zhang Youqian to come over, had him change his clothes and headgear, and with a salute seated him in the office. "Congratulations on your success!" the magistrate said. "I am much obliged for your protection," replied Zhang Youqian, "Although I passed the examination by luck, I rely on your lordship to help me out of the trouble because of the sin I committed." "That's a trifle," said the magistrate, "and you needn't worry about it. I will find a way out for you." By then the runners who had gone to summon Luo Xixi had not returned yet. The county magistrate immediately wrote out a warrant in these words: "Zhang's son, fresh from success in the examination, should be escorted home to the accompaniment of music. Luo's daughter is exempted from interrogation and the case is to be submitted to the prefecture court." Having finished writing this, he ordered his subordinates to prepare flowers, musical instruments and horses. The magistrate himself toasted Youqian with three cups of wine, pinned a flower on his chest, put red drapes on his shoulders as a token of honor and mounted him on a horse. With the band going ahead, he escorted Zhang Youqian out of the county yamen. As a rhyme says:

Yesterday a convict jailed;
Today a bridegroom hailed —
Thus an episode in a romantic affair
Is opened in a buoyant air.

As for Zhang Youqian, on his way home he came across the two runners who were escorting a lady's sedan chair toward the county yamen. A faint sobbing could be heard from within the covered sedan chair. Realizing that the sedan chair held Luo Xixi, the runners who accompanied Zhang Youqian shouted, "Don't go any further! *Xiucai* Zhang has won a degree and the interrogation is annulled!" They showed the warrant to other runners. Hearing this clearly from inside the sedan chair, Luo Xixi pushed aside the curtain and peeped out. She saw Zhang Youqian on horseback, all smiles and full of mettle. She felt joy in her heart. Zhang Youqian cast a glance at the sedan chair and saw Luo Xixi in it. Discovering that she had not committed suicide the night before, he felt great relief. They exchanged glances and a mixed feeling of happiness and grief welled up in their hearts. The carriers of the sedan chair turned around to bring Luo Xixi closer to Youqian's horse. So the sedan chair and the horse began to move in the same direction, in the same way a bridegroom greets his bride, but for the absence of drapes and flowers over the sedan chair. At a fork of the road they made eyes at each other and parted.

When Youqian arrived home, he paid his respect to his mother and rewarded the runners who had escorted him. After they left, the mother said, "You acted too carelessly. I was almost worried to death. But for the help from Heaven, how would we have put an end to the lawsuit?

When the band of people broke in here, I took them to be policemen from the yamen and was too frightened to hide. Only after they had explained why they had come, did I set my fears at rest. I told them you were in prison, so they went there. But how come the county authorities set you free?" "For love's sake," said Zhang Youqian, "your unworthy son has incurred trouble on himself and at same time implicated his mother. Fortunately the county magistrate is very kind. He tried to salvage my marriage, but he could not defy the opposition from the Xins. Today, because I am lucky to have won the honor, the county magistrate is happy. He sent me home and even exempted Luo's daughter from interrogation. I wishfully hope that I might not only be exempted from punishment, but that there might be a chance for my marriage as well." "Though the magistrate is considerate," said the mother, "I heard the Xins will not give up and they will appeal to higher authorities. I am afraid we will lose in court. I have sent a man to talk to your father. I don't know yet if he can find someone who can intervene." "The county magistrate will send a memorial to the prefecture," said her son. "Let's wait until the prefect makes a decision. You may take it easy for now, mother." In a while the neighbors came to extend their congratulations. Lady Yang was among them. The mother was pleased. Of this we'll say no more.

As the prefect began to hold trials, he received a letter from the marshal of Hubei. He opened it and found it was about Zhang Youqian and Luo's daughter. The addresser entreated him to mediate it so that the marriage could be secured. The letter was written by the marshal at Zhang Zhongfu's request, after the latter had read the letter that came from his home. Since the letter to the prefect was ghost-written by Zhang Zhongfu, it was naturally composed in an earnest voice. Because the marshal had great power, the prefect wanted to do everything he could, but he was ignorant of the details of the case. While he was waiting for the county magistrate's arrival, he received the document from the county. After reading it, he learned what the case was about. And realizing that Zhang Youqian had just passed the imperial examination, he was quite willing to help him.

Then the Xins came to submit their complaint, saying, "Zhang Youqian committed a crime, but the county magistrate released him without investigation and affixing of the responsibility. This is malfeasance." The prefect called up Xin and admonished him, "According to your accusation, Luo's daughter is a woman of loose morals. What's the use in claiming her? Even if I were to announce that she should belong to your family, such a daughter-in-law will spoil your reputation. So isn't it better to get the betrothal money back and marry your son to a better and immaculate girl? Your family has been of good repute, not like the Luos. Why should you hold to this meaningless lawsuit?" Xin was dumb for a moment. Then he kowtowed and said, "I will rely on my lord for a decision." The prefect had a secretary bring in a brush and paper and asked Xin to write a bill of divorcement, which was to be transferred to the court of his native county where the betrothal gifts would be re-claimed from Luo Renqing. Daring not say anything against the prefect's arrangement, Xin kowtowed and took his leave. The prefect at once wrote a confidential letter to the county magistrate and sealed it in an envelope with the transferal files. The letter read:

Zhang and Luo are a nice match. You may help them to fulfill the matrimonial tie. This is according to the bidding of the Marshal and so you should not think light of it.

When the county magistrate had received the papers from the prefecture and read the letter, he wrote two invitation cards. He then dispatched a runner to invite Luo Renqing and another to invite Zhang Youqian to his office. Seeing the card from the magistrate, Luo Renqing, a magnate of humble origins, dared not lose a minute in getting to the county office. He put on his melon-shaped skullcap and a broad-sashed pleated gown in a hurry before proceeding to the prefecture office. The county magistrate, intending to bring about a good match, received him hospitably. "Zhang Youqian would be a good son-in-law," he said to Luo Renqing, "I advised you the other day to accept him. Now that he has gained a degree, it will be a good thing if you accept my proposal." "How dare I defy my lord's bidding?" replied Luo Renqing. "But I have promised the Xins. They will insist on taking my daughter. How can I decline them? So I am in a dilemma. I wish my lordship would understand my situation." "If you consent," said the magistrate, "the Xins' claim is no problem." Smilingly he took out the Xins' proclamation on divorce and showed it to Luo Renqing. "Since the Xins have disclaimed the bond, I can now congratulate you upon the acquisition of a good son-in-law!" Luo Renqing seemed a bit hesitant. "But how can the Xins have written such a paper?" "You don't know, my friend," smiled the magistrate, "it is the prefect's order. He let Xin write it so as to help your son-in-law." And feeling in his sleeve, he showed the prefect's letter to Luo Renqing. Luo Renqing dared not decline what the prefect and county magistrate had done for him. "Since the trifle of my child has troubled my lords," said Luo Renqing, "how dare I disobey?" Then Zhang Youqian arrived too. The magistrate admitted him in and said with a smile, "Your father-in-law has personally expressed his consent to your marriage a moment ago." He showed him the confidential letter from the prefect and the Xins' statement of divorce, and told him in detail what had happened. Overjoyed, Youqian was profuse in thanks. The magistrate had Youqian make a reverence to his father-in-law right there, to the great delight of Luo. The magistrate ushered him and his father-in-law to a back hall and there a feast was spread for them. To show his reverence Luo Renqing politely said he dared not take a seat. "Together with your son-in-law," said the magistrate, "what's wrong if you take a seat?" The feast ended in everyone's enjoyment.

Upon returning home Zhang Youqian related to his mother how his father had asked the Marshal of Hubei for help, how the Marshal had asked the prefect to mediate and how the prefect had bid the county magistrate to arrange the matter. The mother was very happy to hear this. Luo Renqing, on the other hand, felt himself heartier since he was treated to a feast by the magistrate. Realizing he had enjoyed due respect because of Zhang Youqian, he looked upon him with more respect. Being always partial to her daughter, Luo's wife was exultant to hear of the favor from the prefect and county magistrate and to have a son-in-law with a newly gained degree. Since the next day was an auspicious one, they asked Lady Yang to serve as the match-maker. On the excuse that they couldn't part with their daughter, they had Zhang Youqian live in their house.

In the nuptial night, the newly weds, who had been long sweethearts and who had lived in fears and tears and just escaped death, felt an unspeakable felicity.

After the wedding, the couple paid a visit to Zhang's mother. Seeing the beautiful, happy pair, the mother told them, "You mustn't forget the kindness of the prefect and the county magistrate. Now you've gotten married, you should go and express your gratitude." "That's exactly what I am going to do," said Zhang Youqian. Accordingly, Luo Xixi remained home in company with her mother-in-law while Youqian went to express his gratitude to the prefect and magistrate. — Having known the daughter-in-law since her infancy, the mother was even more affectionate towards her. As Youqian returned home, both the prefect and the magistrate sent gifts to him. When the porters took leave, Youqian returned to his father-in-law's home.

The next spring Youqian sat for the national imperial examination held by the Ritual Ministry and became a candidate at one go. Later he was promoted to the rank of assistant prefect. The couple stayed together all their lives. As a poem says:

The prison turns out a blessing room!
From it comes out a bridegroom.
But for the bone-nipping chill,
How can the plum fragrantly bloom?

Tale 15

By Exchanging Wives, Mr Hu Indulges in Debauchery;
To Expound Retribution a Prelate Sinks into Meditation

Now your humble servant will tell you a story about some men who seduced others' wives and, as retribution, their wives were seduced by others. During the Yuan Dynasty there was a man surnamed Tie and named Rong from an influential family in Yuanshang of Mianzhou [present-day Mianxian, Shaanxi Province]. One of his ancestors had been an imperial supervisor of important legal cases. Tie Rong's wife, Di, was famous as a rare beauty in town.

Conventionally, Mianzhou's women were sociable. Noble and influential families vied with one another in showing off their beauties. Once a man married a beautiful woman, he was only too eager to let other people know, and so he would go everywhere to show off his wife. In delightful seasons people would enjoy the sight of flowers or the moonlight, when men and women gathered in boisterous crowds, their shoulders and backs rubbing against each other. They also made amorous eyes and dropped hints to one another. Such behavior was regarded as normal. On their way home at dusk they would appraise each and every woman they had seen, saying so-and-so was the most beautiful, so-and-so was the second most, and so on. They would admire the good ones in loud voices, heedless of whether the husbands were listening. And even if the husbands heard such comments, they would take them as compliments to their wives and feel pleased, and they would not take offense at derisive remarks. During the reigns of Zhiyuan [1335-1340] and Zhizheng [1341-1368], this custom was the most prevalent.

Since Tie had married a dazzling girl, he was only too eager to parade her beauty. Everywhere he went he heard compliments. His acquaintances, needless to say, would tease him with jests or extol his good luck. Even strangers came to play up to Tie when they learned that Di was his wife. They either gratified him with sweet words or treated him to food and drink, claiming him to be a blessed man who deserved flattery. That's why when Tie went out, he never needed to take money with him — there were always people who would entertain him with a feast and he always returned home tipsy and full. People within and without the town all knew him and many harbored evil schemes to seduce his wife. But since Tie was from an influential family and an atrocious man, they dared not offend him rashly. So they had to keep their wanton fancy to themselves. All they could do was to feast their eyes on her and crack a joke or two about her.

Since Di was so charming and the local customs were such, how could she be left alone to live a clean life? Something inevitably would befall her. As the saying goes, "Without coincidences there can be no stories." It so happened that in the same neighborhood lived a certain Hu Sui, whose wife, Men, was also very attractive. Though she compared slightly unfavorably with Di, she was still among the top beauties in town. In Di's absence there would be no rival for her. Hu Sui was a philanderer. Although he had a beautiful wife, he was not content just to have a belle next to Di. Tie, on the other hand, was captivated by Men's radiance the moment he saw her. He decided he would be happy only when he possessed the two beauties at the same time. So each with an intention of deceiving the other, Tie and Hu became close friends. They hoped to exchange their wives for temporary use. Tie was candid by nature but Hu was crafty. As Tie often revealed his intention to seduce Hu's wife, Hu decided to make use of the opportunity. He tried in every way to ingratiate himself with Tie. Tie believed that Hu could be persuaded and that he could take advantage of him. He did not know that Hu was profiting from his intention by baiting a hook for Di — a scheme he was hatching in a most undetectable way.

Tie said to his wife, Di, "People tell me that you are the greatest beauty, but in my opinion Hu's wife is no less attractive. How can I find a way to take her? If I can monopolize two beauties, my life will be worthy and I will feel no regrets at death." "You are so friendly with him," said Di, "can't you tell him frankly what you want?" "I have made suggestions to him about it," answered Tie, "and he didn't take offense. But how can I be candid about this? I won't achieve my end unless you act as bait. But I am afraid you will be jealous." "I am never jealous," said Di, "I will help you wherever I can. But you must realize that this involves women each having her own household. How can we lure her here? The only way is that our family befriend Hu's so that the wives and children will be in close contact. Invite him together with his wife to our house from time to time. Only then will you get a chance to achieve your end." "Oh, my virtuous wife," Tie exclaimed, "you are right!" After that he became more intimate with Hu. He often invited Hu to his house to dine and wine. In doing so he always asked that Hu's wife come to keep Di company. He solicited famous prostitutes and whore-mongers to make merry. His first purpose was to please Hu, and the second was to arouse Men's passions. Whenever they enjoyed themselves at a feast, Di and Men, in the inner chamber, would peek at them from behind a curtain. Seeing the obscene scenes at the feast, even a woman made of stone would eventually become infatuated.

The two men, each harboring his own wicked plan, did everything they could to show off their handsomeness, meaning to stir the beauties. One woman in the inner chamber was the first to be stirred up. Do you know who this was? The situation was like this: Although Men and Di were both peeping from behind the curtain, Men was, after all, a guest and thus was a little constrained. Di, however, was at home and so she watched the bawdy men and women to her heart's content. Thus her libidinous desires were stimulated. Hu was not only more handsome than Tie, he was far more graceful in manners, far gentler in temperament and much more impressive in bearing. Di, taking a liking to him, often emerged from behind the curtain to flirt, and was more enthusiastic in offering wine and food, never showing any signs of fatigue. Believing his wife to be a good assistant, Tie was very glad to see this, being entirely ignorant of her aim.

In drunkenness, Tie said to Hu, "You and I both have beautiful wives and we are good friends. People seldom have such a friendship." "My wife is commonplace," Hu said, putting on a show of modesty. "She is no match for your noble spouse." "In my opinion," Tie insisted, "they are more or less equally attractive. But it is boring for each of us to have only one woman. May I venture to suggest that we exchange our wives for temporary use, so we can both taste something fresh? What do you say?" This was exactly what Hu desired, but he put on a modest tone. "My humble wife is very crude," Hu said. "Though you praise her, how dare I take liberties with your lady? No, it is not right!" "We can banter about anything when drunk," said Tie. "We are really free spirits!" In loud laughter they parted.

Entering the inner chamber, Tie cast an inebriated glance at Di and, stroking her chin, said to her, "I mean to exchange Hu's wife for you. Will you agree?" Feigning anger, Di scolded him, "You muddle-headed cuckold! You are from a decent family. How can you seduce another's wife at the expense of your own wife's body? You are really brazen to say this!" "Since his family and ours are good friends," said Tie, "why not act as I see fit?" "I may help you to achieve your aim by adding humor to your play," said Di, "but I won't do anything at my own expense." "I was just joking," said Tie, "do you think I would have the heart to give you up? What I mean is that I want to seduce her." "But you mustn't be impatient," said Di. "If you please Hu in every way, maybe he will not be as petty as you are and will yield his wife." Holding Di, Tie said, "Oh, my wise girl! You are right!" Saying this he went into bed with her.

Now let's see what Di actually thought. Although she had a desire to go with Hu, she knew Tie was ill-tempered. He is talking nonsense, she thought, because at this moment he is in good mood and because he wants to lure Men. If I really have an affair with Hu and he learns about it, he may become jealous and get in our way. Then we'll be in a vulnerable situation. It's better to work out a plan to keep the affair from him and then Hu and I will feel safe. By and by she worked out a plan.

One day Hu came to Tie's house again for a drink. That day no other guests were invited. Di went to and fro behind the curtain and made signs to Hu. Taking the hint, Hu purposefully sipped little but proffered large cups to Tie. "I am much obliged for the fraternal love you've extended to me," he said, coaxing Tie. "It's so kind of you to be concerned with my humble wife, and she admires you too. I have tried to persuade her, and she seems somewhat willing. So long as you look after me well, there will be no problem. But you must first treat me to a hundred prostitutes. Then I will help you to achieve your end." Hearing Hu's promise, Tie was elated. "So long as you'll show me a favor, I will gladly entertain you with even a thousand prostitutes, not to speak a hundred!" Tie then downed one large bowl of wine after another. Hu, on the other hand, coaxed him into drinking even more. In a while Tie was as full as a tick. Hu, pretending to help him to bed, took him through the curtain into the inner room. Di, who never stayed away during a feast, was behind the curtain. She reached her hands to support Tie who was by now unconscious. As Hu pursed his lips close to Di's cheek in a kissing fashion, she touched his feet with her toes. She called the maid servants, Yan Xue and Qing Yun, to carry the master in. This left her and Hu alone behind at the curtain. Hu seized her tightly in his arms and she, turning around, melted into his embrace. "I have been yearning for you," Hu told her. "The fact that I can enjoy the heavenly blessing today is a predestination for my former, current and future lives!" "I have been in love with you for a long time," responded Di, "you needn't say more." She let down her trousers, sat down in the chair with her legs raised up, and allowed Hu a free rein. — It was ridiculous for Tie, who had coveted Hu's wife, only to have his own wife ravished first by Hu.

Hu was an expert in making love. He exhibited all his skills to satisfy Di. Overjoyed, Di enjoyed him and asked him to keep their relationship. "I am grateful to you, Madam, for this happy union," said Hu, "but your husband has promised you to me for quite some time. Even if he learns of our affairs, I don't think he will pose hindrance to us." "My husband said that simply because he was infatuated with your wife," said Di. "Although he is very lecherous, he is of strong character. We mustn't offend him. We will have to cheat him and enjoy ourselves in secret. Only in this way can we keep our relations going for a long time." "But how can we cheat him?" asked Hu. "He is a debauchee," replied Di. "Find some well-known prostitutes and take him to drink and whore. He may then stay out and I can make merry with you for the whole night through." "What you say is insightful," said Hu, "He has just promised to take me to a brothel a hundred times in order to lure my wife. I'll seize this opportunity and let one or two nice girls hold him there. He will certainly indulge in the pleasure. But where can I get the money to cover the cost of the girls?" "You may leave that to me," said Di. "If you are so generous," said Hu, "I'll gratify your lust at the risk of my own life!" Having worked out the scheme they parted.

I am telling you that the Hus were poor and the Ties were rich. That's why Tie made friends with Hu by way of food and drink. Hu, while flattering Tie, took advantage of him. On the other hand, though Tie had an enormous family fortune, a good part of it had been drained away in parties attended by girls. Besides, since Di was carrying on with Hu, she always abetted her husband to debauch outside while she and Hu held a bountiful feast at home, enjoying various delicacies and never calculating the daily expenditures. Di, only too happy to have Hu, was quite generous. Taking advantage of Tie's desperate need, she and Hu in collaboration wheedled him into selling his estate at a low price. Di put part of the money aside for her expenses with Hu. Whenever Hu found a noted prostitute, he would bring Tie to her and there he would entertain Tie with a feast. Thus Tie would stay with the prostitute for days and nights. Di, from time to time, sent some of her private savings to her husband to cover his expenses for food and girls. So long as Tie stayed away from home, she and Hu were able to dally to their hearts' content. Believing that his virtuous wife was not jealous, Tie gloated and became even more unbridled. When he occasionally went home, Di would be pleased to see him and never complained. Tie was very grateful to her. Even in his dreams he thought she was a good lady.

One day, just as Di was setting a table for Hu, Tie returned home. "Why have you spread the table?" he asked. "I knew you would come back today," replied Di, "I was afraid you might feel lonely, so I prepared food for you. I have sent for Hu so he can come to keep company with you." "It is my wife," said Tie, "who best understands my feelings." After a while Hu came. Tie and Hu enjoyed the feast to the full. What they talked about were all the brothels. When drunk, Tie mentioned Men. "You have associated with so many beautiful girls," said Hu, "why do you still have your eye on my crude wife? If you don't detest her ugliness, I will let you have her." Tie was deeply grateful to Hu. But despite his promise, Hu continued to entice Tie to more brothels, where he whiled away his time in drunkenness and wanton dreams for days on end. While he was busy with prostitutes, he scarcely found time to flirt with Men.

Hu and Di, on the other hand, became so ardent with each other that they never let one night pass idle. When Tie was at home, they found it inconvenient. So Hu gave Di an intoxicant recipe. Anyone who took dozen or so cups of wine laced with this drug would soon become limp and fall asleep. After Di got this recipe, she would use the drug in Tie's wine when he was at home, and Tie would fall into sleep after taking a few cups with Di or Hu. Then Hu would emerge. He and Di would change the liquor and spend the night in obscene conversation and licentious play. Yet Tie never discovered this. On the few occasions when Tie returned home and found Di and Hu drinking together, Hu would quickly slide away but there would not be time enough to put away the disordered dishes. When Tie asked Di about this, Di would reply that a relative had come and she had entertained him with a feast, but the relative had departed fearing that Tie would force him to drink more. Tie would not probe into the matter any further. Because Di had said that she would not serve as an exchange for Men, Tie believed she was a chaste lady. Besides, Hu flattered and fawned upon him in every way and accompanied him to brothels or at table so that Tie would not become suspicious. Furthermore, two well-prepared minds certainly could outwit an unwatchful one. The maid servants were co-conspirators. Even if a trace was left, they would help to cover it up or explain it away. Taking Hu as his trusted friend and Di as his virtuous spouse, Tie was not aware of the real situation. By and by his neighbors learned of it. They composed a doggerel to the tune of "Shan Po Yang" to ridicule him:

With erotic women
Who is not infatuated?

Having married a beauty
You should be satiated.
Why should you hunt all day
Everywhere for an easy prey?
Before you trespass another's domain,
Your dear has become another's gain!
While you mean to have not one, but two,
Your wife has betrayed you!
She has offered herself first,
Yet nowhere have you quenched your thirst.
As one may feed a cat with its own tail cooked
So by the bait of your money you are hooked!
Oh, boy! You may take your loss
As sacrifice to the gods for bless!
Oh, boy! This transaction is
In no way a fair business!

Indulging in booze and women, Tie whiled away his days as if in a dream. Thus his health began to decline and in time illness confined him to bed at home. Hu, finding it now inconvenient to visit Di, ceased coming. Di sent a message to him saying, "My husband cannot get up, and my servants will watch out for us. You may feel free to come as usual." Thus Hu resumed his visits. As he had no scruples about moving around the house, Hu soon forgot his situation and walked past Tie's bed. Catching sight of him, Tie was surprised. "Why did Hu come from within the house?" he asked. "We didn't see a soul pass by," Di and two maids said in chorus. "Where on earth is Hu?" "I just saw Hu clearly," said Tie, "but you said you saw nobody pass by. Maybe I have dim sight because of my illness and saw a phantom?" "No," said Di, "you didn't see a phantom. Because you think of his wife all day long, you are in a trance, so when you opened your eyes you saw an illusion."

The next day Hu learned of this. "We've put it over on him," said Hu, "but when he feels himself again he will think about the matter again. Won't he become suspicious then? Since he took me to be a phantom, I have an idea. Let me show him a phantom so he will be sure that he was hallucinating. Otherwise he may suspect me." Di laughed. "You are kidding," she said. "Where can you find a ghost?" "Let me hide myself in your back room tonight," said Hu, "so you and I will have a pleasant time. Tomorrow morning I will make myself up like ghost and go to his room. Isn't that a plan that will kill two birds with one stone?" Accordingly, that night Di arranged a bed in a room for Hu and bade two maid servants to keep company with the master. Making an excuse that she was tired and wanted to have a peaceful sleep in another room, she left Tie and slept with Hu for the night.

The next day, learning that Tie had just woken up, eyes still fogged, Hu smeared his face with indigo, dyed his hair red, wrapped his feet with wadding so that they would not make noise and dashed towards Tie's room. Being weak from illness, Tie was shocked by what he saw. "Phantom! Phantom!" Tie shouted, burying his head in his quilt and trembling all over. Di hurried in to ask, "Why the jitters?" "I said I thought I saw a phantom yesterday," Tie cried. "Today I really did see a phantom. It seems my condition is fraught with grim possibilities. You must invite a master priest at once and ask him to pray to the gods to redeem me." After this, Tie's illness became worse. Feeling a bit guilty, Di had to seek a prelate.

At that time a hundred *li* away from Yuanshang there was a Buddhist prelate named Liao Wo and styled Empty Valley. His attainments were the highest among Buddhists. Tie cordially invited him to his house and pleaded with him to set up an altar so that he could pray to the Buddha for a blessing. That day the prelate sank into a prolonged deep meditation and did not wake up until evening. Then he inquired of Tie, "Was there an imperial supervisor among your forefathers?" "He was my grandfather," replied Tie. "Is there a Hu among your friends?" asked the priest. "He is my good friend," Tie answered. Hearing them mention Hu, Di felt somewhat apprehensive and so she began to eavesdrop. "What I have just seen is very strange," said the prelate. "What was it?" asked Tie. "As I came here," replied the prelate, "I met with the earth god of this residence. Your ancestor, the imperial supervisor, was complaining to the earth god saying that his grandson had been ruined by Hu. On the excuse that his rank was too lowly to handle such a case, the earth god advised him, 'The gods of the Big Dipper and the Southern Dipper will meet under the Jade Basket Peak today. You may go to them and they will certainly handle your case.' The imperial supervisor asked me to go there together with him. As we arrived, we saw two old men, one in red and the other in green, playing chess. The imperial supervisor kowtowed and voiced his grievances, but the old men did not answer. So the supervisor repeated his complaints. Only after the game ended did the old men say, 'To bring fortune to the good and calamity to the lecherous is the eternal law of Heaven. Why should you, an enlightened Confucian scholar, ignore the fact that weal and woe root in one's deeds and instead pray in vain? Your grandson is unworthy so he deserves death. But considering that you are a famous scholar, your family line should not become extinct. So your grandson can be exempted from death. Hu is licentious and has tempted your grandson to go astray. He will be duly requited, either on earth or in Hell. You may go now. Hu has his punisher. You needn't hate him, nor complain to us.' Then they turned to me saying, 'You are providential in coming to see us. Since you have learned the Heavenly principle, you should propagate it among the people and let them know all good and evil deeds are duly paid for.' After that they left. That's what I saw during my meditation. Now I have found out that an imperial supervisor and a Hu do exist. Isn't it marvelous?" Hearing this, Di was astounded. Tie thought his grandfather accused Hu because Hu had lured him into whoring. He did not know that Di was a factor in this case. Anyway, he felt easy knowing that he could live on. As he became better, Di, on the other hand, fell ill due to her secret worries over Hu.

In time Tie recovered but Hu began to feel a pain in his waist. In less than ten days a huge boil appeared. The physician said there was no cure for the illness which was caused by exhaustion of the water element in his body due to excessive sex and drinking. Tie went to his bedroom to see him every day. Since the two families had been friends, none of their family members avoided seeing each other. While Men was waiting on her husband at his bedside, she made ambiguous signs to Tie. Seeing Tie come to help them from time to time, she was grateful to him. By and by she talked to him intimately and even made eyes at him. Having been thirsting for her for a long time, Tie went all out to draw her in. As her passion was aroused, they began carryings-on behind Hu's back. Tie, who had sacrificed his wife for so long, was at last repaid. This proves that:

One must reap what one has sowed;
God grants no exemption.
For a defaulted debt
There will be redemption.

When Men and Tie became lovers, they, too, became closely attached to each other like Di and Hu had been. Realizing that there was little time left for Hu, they swore to be a loving couple the rest of their lives. "My wife is virtuous indeed," Tie told Men. "Since she permitted me to take you to my house and was willing to help me fulfill my wish in the past, it would be marvelous if I marry you and the three of us live together." Men sneered, saying, "Since she was ready to offer help, she has helped herself!" "What do you mean by saying she 'helped herself'?" asked Tie. "You have known my husband for a long time," answered Men. "He often spends nights away from home. When you were out, he would stay in your home.

Haven't you discovered any traces of this?"

Only then did Tie, as if awaking from a dream, realize that Hu had deceived him. That explained his ancestor's complaint that the prelate had heard in meditation. That Men became his mistress was a retribution for the actions of Hu. "When I was ill I saw Hu at my home," Tie told Men, "but they covered it up with a story. If you had not told me, I would have never known the truth." "But you mustn't tell your wife," said Men, "or she will blame me." "Since I have you," said Tie, "my hatred is released. And your husband is dying. Why should I make this public?" He took his leave of Men secretly, and returned home without revealing the humiliation he had suffered.

In a couple of days Hu died. When Tie returned home from his condolence visit, Di, who was thinking of the bygone days with Hu, couldn't help shedding tears. Tie, now knowing the situation, easily saw through her frame of mind. "For what reason are you crying?" he said leering. Abashed, Di could not respond. "I know everything," said Tie, "and you needn't try to hide the facts from me." Blushing purple, Di was stubborn. She told him, "It's because *your* good friend has gone that I shed tears. What is it that you know and what am I hiding from you?" "You shouldn't be so stubborn," said Tie. "When I spent nights away from home, did Hu sleep at his home? And who was the man I saw when I was ill? It's because *your* lover has gone that you shed tears!" Seeing the truth laid bare, Di dared not refute it anymore. She had to suffer the pain in silence. Because she missed Hu, whenever she closed her eyes she would see him. In time she contracted a disease and, unable to take food, eventually died.

Half a year later Tie married Men. Tie found Men to be the wife of his heart's desire. Thinking of the prelate's warning about requital, he became vigilant. "Because I coveted your beauty," he said to Men, "and harbored an evil plot, my wife was seduced by Hu first. That's retribution for me. Hu and my wife conducted adultery behind my back and, as a result, they both died and you belong to me. That's the payment for them. This may serve as an admonishment for wanton and lewd people. The prelate revealed everything. Now I am set to mend my ways. Although I have wasted my family fortune, I can make it again. I will lead an honest life with you." Thereupon Tie became a disciple of the prelate, pledged to abide by the Five Commandments,* abstained from lascivious practices, and never allowed Men to go about by herself.

As this story spread in and around Mianzhou, it drove home to people that heavenly retribution is no hearsay. The prelate, on his part, went everywhere and admonished people with what he had learned during his meditation. Thus the behavior of the local people was greatly improved.

---

*The Five Commandments of Buddhism are: No slaughtering, no stealing, no adultery, no falsehood and no drinking.

Tale 16

Charitable Squire Zhang Fosters an Orphan;
Witty Prefect Bao Extracts a Contract

Now readers, let your servant tell you another story entitled "Witty Perfect Bao Extracts a Contract". Do you know where this story comes from? It took place in Yidingfang on the western outskirts of Bianliang [present-day Kaifeng, Henan Province] during the Song Dynasty [960-1279]. There lived a Liu Tianxiang and his wife Yang. His younger brother, Liu Tianrui, had a wife named Zhang. The brothers lived together. They had never divided the family property between themselves. Tianxiang had no child of his own. His wife Yang was a remarried woman and had brought over a daughter by a previous marriage. Tianrui had a son named Liu Anzhu. The village chief by the name of Li had a daughter Dingnu who was born on the same day as Anzhu. Since Li and the Lius were good friends, he had promised his daughter to Liu Tianrui's son before she was born. When Liu Anzhu was two years old, the two families exchanged betrothal gifts. Yang, not a virtuous woman, intended to get a son-in-law to live in her house so that when her daughter was grown up a large share of the family fortune would go to her. So the sisters-in-law often squabbled, but thanks to the harmonious relationship between the brothers and good-naturedness of lady Zhang, no discord arose among them.

Unexpectedly a famine year befell and there was no harvest of food crops. The authorities issued a decree ordering local residents to divide big households into small ones and settle some of them in places of good harvest to make a living. As Liu Tianxiang and his brother discussed the matter, Tianxiang said, "You are old, Brother, and mustn't go out. Let me go elsewhere with my wife and child." Tianxiang agreed. Then, having invited Village Chief Li to his home, Tianxiang said, "You know, because of this lean year, we can hardly support ourselves. The government instructs us to divide up families and go out to make a living. Now my brother, his wife and child will leave for a distant place. Our family fortune has never been divided between us. I mean to write a contract in duplicate and to list all the fields, houses, and other objects on it. My brother and I will each hold one copy. If my brother returns in one or two years, let's drop it. If, however, he doesn't come back in five or ten years, and if something unexpected happens during this time, the contract will serve as evidence of his claim to the property. So I have invited you here to be a witness and to sign your name on the contract." "It's my pleasure," said the Chief. Thereupon Liu Tianxiang took out two sheets of blank paper and wrote the following words on them:

Considering that the crops were not harvested, according to the superior's decree that the local people should divide up extended families and make a living in places of good harvest, Liu Tianxiang, his brother Liu Tianrui and his nephew Liu Anzhu, local residents of Yidingfang on the western outskirts of

the Eastern Capital, *agree to this: Tianrui, the younger brother,*
leaves home of his own accord with his wife and son. The family
belongings have not been split up between the brothers. This
contract, in duplicate, is held by the brothers, one copy by each.

On this-and-that day of this-and-that month of this-and-that
year

    Signed by

        Liu Tianxiang

        Liu Tianrui, the younger brother

        Village Chief Li, the witness

Then the three signed their initials to the contract. The brothers each
held one copy and they dismissed after entertaining the Chief at
dinner.

Liu Tianrui chose an auspicious date to leave. He collect his things,
and bade farewell to his brother and sister-in-law. The brothers both
shed tears. Only Yang, who was eager to see Liu Tianrui and his
family go, was pleased. A song to the tune of "Xian Lü Shang Hua
Shi" describes this episode:

Each collecting a contract, getting things packed,
The blood kin departed, both broken-hearted.
Leaving their home
The world at large to roam,
Woebegone they left their native earth
To outlive the time of dearth.

I will now tell you about Tianrui and his wife who struggled all the
way, taking meals in the wind and spending nights by the water. Now
riding over bridges, then boating across rivers, they arrived, in time, at

---

*The Eastern Capital during the Northern Song Dynasty was Bianliang.

Xiama Village in Gaoping County, Luzhou Prefecture of the Shanxi Region. The harvest there was good and commerce was lively. So Tianrui settled down in a house rented from a rich family. The master of the family was Squire Zhang with the given name of Bingyi; his wife was Guo. The rich couple was generous in aiding the needy. With vast farms and estates, they found life unsatisfactory because of their lack of a child. Finding Liu and wife to be amiable and congenial and their three-year-old boy, Liu Anzhu, to have delicate features and to be clever, Zhang took a particular liking to the boy. So he discussed with his wife the possibility of making the child his adopted son. This was exactly what Guo herself wanted. So the Squire sent this message to Liu and wife through a go-between: "Squire Zhang has taken a special liking to your child. He wants to make him his adopted son so your whole family and his will become close relatives. What do you two think of this?" Seeing that the rich family wanted to adopt their son, Liu Tianrui and lady Zhang found no reason to decline. "We are too poor and of too humble an origin," they replied, "to deserve such kinship. If his lordship is kind enough to adopt him, it will be our honor to live here!" As the go-between passed these words to Zhang, Zhang and his wife were most pleased. Having fixed an auspicious date they proclaimed that Liu Anzhu had been adopted by them and his family name changed to Zhang. Because Liu's wife and the Squire had the same family name, Zhang, she took him as her adopted brother. After that the Squire regarded Liu Tianrui as his brother-in-law. The two families became quite intimate, and Liu was exempted from paying for lodging, food and clothing.

Nearly half a year later, however, when the good life had hardly begun, misfortune befell Liu and his wife. They contracted an epidemic illness and were confined to bed. Squire Zhang engaged doctors and administered medicines to them as if they were his blood kindred. Despite his endeavors, their condition worsened from day to day. After a few days Lady Zhang died. Liu Tianrui cried his heart out.

Again it was Squire Zhang that bought a coffin and buried her. Days later Liu Tianrui's conditions further deteriorated. Realizing his illness was incurable, he sent for Squire Zhang. "My benefactor," he said to the Squire, "may I tell you of the worries that lie deep in my heart?" "We are as close as brothers," replied the Squire, "I will undertake everything you bid me and I will in no way betray your trust. Please tell me what is on your mind." "I have a flesh-and-blood brother and sister-in-law at home," said Tianrui. "When I left home, my brother had two copies of a contract written and signed. My brother keeps one copy and I keep another. If anything unexpected happens, the contract will serve as a testimony. I am much obliged to you for your special treatment, but I am ill-fated and realize that I am about to become a ghost in a strange place. My child Anzhu is too young to know these things. Since he is your adopted child, I hope you will accumulate merit for your future life by bringing him up. When he grows up, give him the contract and let him bury me and my wife's bodies in the ancestral graveyard. I cannot repay your kindness in this life, but in the coming life I will become your donkey or horse to repay your benevolence! The most important thing is not to let the child forget his own ancestors!" With this, tears streamed down his cheeks. The Squire tearfully promised to fulfill his bidding and comforted him with soothing words. Tianrui took out the contract and handed it to the Squire. By that evening Liu had shut his eyes forever. Squire Zhang bought a coffin and shrouded him. He buried Liu and his wife temporarily at the side of Zhang's ancestral graveyard.

After that they looked after Anzhu as their own child. As Anzhu grew older, they kept the knowledge of his parents' deaths from him, and sent him to school. A gifted boy, Anzhu had a retentive memory and, by the time he was ten or so, he become well-versed in the classics, history books and many literary works. He was also good-tempered, and filial to his foster parents. The old couple treated him as a treasure. On festivals every spring and autumn they would take him to the tombs of his parents and have him pay reverence to the deceased. But they did not tell him why they had him do so.

As time flew like an arrow and the days and months shuttled to and fro, fifteen years elapsed and Anzhu entered his eighteenth year. The Squire and his wife, Guo, talked about how to let Anzhu know his parents' story so he could bury them where they belonged. Then the day of Pure Brightness arrived, so the couple took him to the grave. There Anzhu pointed to the mound at the side of the tomb, asking the Squire, "You take me to worship this tomb every year, Dad, but I have never asked about what relative the deceased was. Can you tell your child now?" The Squire replied, "I will tell you about this, my child, and let you visit your home place. But I am afraid that once you realize who your own parents were, you might make light of our love for you. Your family name is not Zhang and you are not a local. Your family name is Liu and you are the son of Liu Tianrui of Yidingfang on the western outskirts of the Eastern Capital. Your uncle is Liu Tianxiang. During a famine in your native place your parents came here to make a living. Unexpectedly both your parents died. They are buried here. At his death your father entrusted me with a contract that records all your family property. He requested that when you were grown up I should tell you about this, and let you go with the contract to see your uncle and aunt, and to bury your parents' remains in your ancestral grave site. Oh, my son! I have to tell you this today. Although we didn't breast-feed you, we have reared you for fifteen years. You shouldn't forget us."

Hearing this, Anzhu let out a cry, collapsed to the ground and passed out. As the Squire and his wife brought him to, Anzhu tearfully prostrated himself before the tomb of his parents. "I never knew who my parents were until today," he said to the Squire and Lady Guo. "Since I have learned this, I won't delay any more. I beg you to give me the contract. I will carry my parents' bones to the Eastern Capital. When I have buried them there, I will return to attend you. What do you think about this?" "That is the practice of filial piety," said the Squire. "How can we stop you? But you should return as early as possible or we will be anxious about you." Thereupon they returned home together.

After Anzhu had packed up for the journey, he bade farewell to the old couple. The Squire took out the contract and gave it to him. Then he had the remains of Anzhu's parents dug up and let him carry them to his native place. When the time for departure came, the Squire enjoined him, "Don't forget your adoptive parents out of your love for your native place." "How can your son be so ungrateful?" responded Anzhu. "I will come back to wait upon you when I have finished my commitment." The three all shed tears at the parting.

Anzhu lost no time in completing the journey and before long he reached Yidingfang on the western outskirts of the Eastern Capital. Asking directions, he came to the gate of the Lius where he saw an old woman standing. Anzhu approached and with a salute asked: "May I bother you, Madam, to announce me? I am Liu Anzhu, son of Liu Tianrui. I heard that this is the house of my uncle and aunt. So I am here to pay my respects to my kin and to identify myself as Liu's descendant." Hearing this, the old woman scowled a bit. "Where are my brother and sister-in-law?" she asked Anzhu. "If you are Liu Anzhu, you should produce the contract as evidence. Otherwise how can I believe an utter stranger?" "My parents died in Luzhou fifteen years ago," replied Anzhu, "I have been fortunate enough to be brought up by my foster father. The contract is in my pack." "I am the wife of Liu Tianxiang," said the woman. "If you have the contract, you are genuinely my nephew. Give the contract to me and wait here for a moment. Let me show it to your uncle and he will come to take you in." "Forgive me for my impunity," said Anzhu, "I didn't know you were my aunt." Unpacking his luggage, Anzhu proffered the contract with both hands to her. Lady Yang went in with the contract. There Anzhu waited for a long while, but nobody came out.

The reason was that Lady Yang's daughter and son-in-law now lived in the house. She was set on handing the whole family fortune down to her son-in-law and day and night she guarded against the return of the brother, sister-in-law and nephew. Now, hearing that the brother and his wife had both died, she saw an opportunity to trick her nephew, since the nephew and uncle did not know each other. After she got the contract by trick, she hid it under her clothing. If Anzhu was to ask for it, she was ready to deny ever seeing it. Well, Liu Anzhu encountered tough going by meeting her first. Had he run into Liu Tianxiang initially, he would not have been stuck in this situation.

Now let's turn to Liu Anzhu who had been waiting outside of the gate until he was quite thirsty. Not a soul came his way, but he thought it improper to break in. As he was beginning to suspect that the woman would not return, he saw an old man approaching. "Where are you from, young man," asked the man, "and why are you standing by my gate?" "Are you my uncle?" inquired Liu Anzhu. "I am Liu Anzhu, who was brought to Luzhou fifteen years ago when my parents went there to make a living." "If so," the man said, "then you are my nephew. But where is your contract?" "My aunt took it and went in awhile ago." replied Anzhu. Liu Tianxiang, all smiles, grasped his hand and conducted him into the hall. As Anzhu prostrated himself to make obeisance to his uncle, the uncle said, "You needn't do that, my child, after your fatiguing journey. As our age advances, we two are ailing like candles fluttering in the wind. After you three left, I haven't received any news from you for the past fifteen years. My brother and I have only you as the successor to our family line. Thinking that such an enormous family fortune would go without an inheritor, I have been so vexed that I am now hard of hearing and dim-sighted. Fortunately you've come back. Great! But may I know if your parents are well? Why haven't they come with you?" With tears dripping, Anzhu related, in detail, how his parents had both died and he had been brought up by his adoptive father.

Hearing this, Liu Tianxiang cried too. Calling out to his wife he said to her, "Sister, our nephew is here to see you." "What nephew?" asked Yang. "He is Liu Anzhu who left fifteen years ago," Tianxiang answered. "Who is Liu Anzhu?" responded Yang. "There are many swindlers here. Probably he covets our wealth, so he has come for it under Liu Anzhu's name. When his father and mother left, they took with them a contract. If this young man has the contract, he is the genuine nephew, otherwise he is a false one." "The child said he just handed it to you." said Tianxiang. "I didn't see it," asserted Yang. "I gave it to you with my own hand!" said Anzhu. "How can you say this, Aunt?" "You are joking, aren't you?" said Tianxiang. "The child said you've taken it from him." But Yang kept shaking her head and insisted that she hadn't. Then Tianxiang asked Anzhu, "Where is the contract? Please tell me the truth." "How would your child dare deceive you?" replied Anzhu. "It is in Aunt's hand. How can she deny it against her conscience and Heaven's law?" Yang scolded him. "You lying son of a bitch! When have I seen the contract?" "Please don't be so angry," said Tianxiang. "If you do have it, why not let me have a look at it?" "You old fool!" she said, flying into a rage, "I am your wife, yet you don't believe me. He is a complete stranger, yet you don't suspect him! What use is the paper to me? Can I use it to patch windows? If our nephew comes, I will be happy too. Why should I have detained it? This honey-mouthed wretch is trying to defraud us of our belongings!" "Your child is willing to give up the inheritance, Uncle," said Anzhu. "All I want to do is to bury my parents' bones in the ancestral graveyard. Once I have buried them, I will return to Luzhou. There I have my means of living." "Who can believe your sweet words?" rebuked Yang. Taking up a rod, she gave blows on Anzhu's face and caused his head to bleed. Tianxiang tried to reconcile them, saying, "You should get to the bottom of the matter first." But since he did not know his nephew, and his wife stubbornly refused to recognize him, he could not really tell if the young man was his nephew or not. Yang pushed Anzhu out of the gate and shut it in his face.

Anzhu fell into a swoon for anger, and it took a long time before he came to. Seeing the bones of his parents there, he broke into loud crying. "Oh Aunt, how can you be so heartless?" Then a man came up. "Boy," the man asked, "where are you from and why are you weeping here?" "I am Liu Anzhu who left home with my parents to make a living fifteen years ago," he replied. The man was surprised by what he heard. Taking a close look at him, the man asked, "Who wounded you on the head?" "It's nothing to do with my uncle," said Anzhu, "it's my Aunt who refused to recognize me. She took my contract and denies that she did. It's she who hit me on my head." "I am none other than Chief Li," said the man, "so you are my engaged son-in-law. Tell me about your experiences over the past fifteen years and I will stand behind you."

Hearing that this man was his father-in-law, Anzhu obeisantly saluted him and tearfully told him, "Please listen, my father-in-law, when my father and mother took me away to make a living, we stopped at an inn run by Zhang Bingyi at Xiama Village in Gaoping County, Luzhou, of the Shanxi Region. Later my parents died in an epidemic. Squire Zhang adopted me as his son and has brought me up. Now that I am eighteen years old, my foster father told me my true history. So I have brought the bones of my parents and come to visit my uncle. I never expected that my aunt would extract my contract from me by trickery and hit me on my head. Oh, where can I give vent to my grievance?" Tears rushed out of his eyes. Chief Li, his face darkened in anger, asked Anzhu, "Now that the contract has been taken from you, do you remember its content?" "Of course, I do," replied Anzhu. "If so, recite it," said Chief Li. Thereupon Anzhu recited the contract from the beginning to end without missing a single word. "You are my son-in-law-to-be, no mistake about it," said Chief Li. "The slut, your aunt, is unreasonable indeed. Let me break into the

Liu's house. If I can talk her around, all will be fine. If not, the prefect of the Kaifeng Prefecture is Lord Bao. He is wise and insightful. I will go with you and submit an accusation against her. The lord will surely return the property to you!" "I will rely on you in everything," said Anzhu.

Knocking at Liu Tianxiang's gate, Li and Liu Anzhu entered his house. "My dear in-laws," Li asked them, "what is all this about? Why don't you recognize your own nephew but instead injure his head?" "Chief Li," retorted Yang, "you don't seem to realize that he is a swindler who purposefully came to our house to make trouble. If he is my nephew, he should have the contract that bears your signature. If he has it, he is Liu Anzhu." "He said you took the contract away with you," Chief Li said, "Why do you deny it?" "How ridiculous you are, Chief Li!" said Yang. "When and where did I see his contract? You act as if I am a thief! You'd better not poke your nose into other people's business!" Then she took up the rod and was about to attack Liu Anzhu again.

Fearing that Anzhu might be seriously wounded, Chief Li stepped forward and shielded him with his own body. Taking Anzhu out of the gate, Li said, "The slut is really atrocious. Shall we give up? Nothing doing! Don't be annoyed, my child. Take the bones and your luggage and stay at my house for the night. Tomorrow we'll lodge a complaint with the Kaifeng court." Liu Anzhu obeyed, following his father-in-law to his house. Introducing Anzhu to his mother-in-law, the Chief treated him to food and drink, bandaged the wound on his head and applied medicine to it.

Early the next morning the Chief wrote an indictment and went to the Kaifeng court with his son-in-law. They waited for awhile before the prefect convened court. In front of the court, Chief Li and Anzhu expressed their grievance. Then having taken the indictment, Lord Bao read it. He summoned Chief Li first and questioned him. As Chief Li related the story from the beginning, Lord Bao said, "Perhaps you abetted him to do so in order to manipulate the case for your own gain?" "He is my future son-in-law, my lord," explained Li. "The contract has my signature. I sympathize with him because of his young age and the wrong he suffered, so I've come to seek justice on his behalf. How could I dare deceive my lord?" "Do you recognize your son-in-law-to-be?" asked Bao. "He left home at the age of three," said Li, "and returned today. I don't know him." "Since you don't know him and he has lost his contract," said Bao, "how can you believe he is your son-in-law?" "None except Liu's brother and myself have ever seen the contract," the Chief answered, "but he can recite its contents from beginning to end without missing a single word. Isn't that convincing evidence?" Calling Liu Anzhu in, Lord Bao asked him some questions, which Anzhu answered readily. Lord Bao examined his wound. "Maybe you are not Liu's son, but have assumed his name to practice fraud." "My lord," said Anzhu, "the false in this world cannot be easily passed as genuine. How can I take the risk? Besides, my foster father Zhang Bingyi has enough land and houses for my life-long consumption. I have even said that I am willing to give up my claim to the property, and as soon as I have buried my parent's bones in my ancestral graveyard I will return to Luzhou to live with my foster father. I hope my just lord will make a thorough investigation into this." Hearing both of them give such a reasonable explanation, Lord Bao put the indictment on file for further investigation. Promptly he had Liu Tianxiang and his wife brought to court.

Calling Liu Tianxiang forward, Lord Bao asked him, "Since you are the master of the house, why don't you make your own judgments instead of listening to your wife in everything? First, please tell me, if that young man is your nephew." "My lord," replied Tianxiang, "I don't know my nephew and the contract is the only proof. Now the young man insists that he had the contract, but my wife insists that he did not. I don't have a third eye, so I can't tell what is what." Then summoning Yang, Lord Bao asked her once again if she had the contract. She was adamant that she had never seen it. Lord Bao said to Anzhu, "Your uncle and aunt are really heartless. I permit you to beat them up so as to vent your anger." Tears streaming down his face, Anzhu said, "That won't do. My father was his brother. There is absolutely no reason for a nephew to beat his uncle! I've come here to fulfill my filial duty by burying my parents and visiting my relatives, not to claim a share of the family wealth. I would never be so audacious as to violate proper human relationship."

Hearing this, Lord Bao had a good idea of the facts. Having asked Yang a few more questions, Bao said in assumed seriousness, "I see this young man is a swindler! He is not ruled by common sense or any code of conduct. You, Liu and wife and Li may go home now. Put the young man in prison and I will conduct a closer interrogation of him some other day." Liu Tianxiang, his wife and Li kowtowed and went out of the court, while Anzhu was taken to prison. Yang exulted inwardly. Chief Li and Anzhu were on tenterhooks. Lord Bao was reputed for his insightfulness, they wondered, but why did he put the plaintiff into prison?

Lord Bao covertly warned the jailers against tormenting Liu Anzhu. In the meantime he had his subordinates spread the rumor that Liu Anzhu had come down with tetanus and was dying. He also sent for Zhang Bingyi, who arrived from Luzhou in a few days. By interrogating the Squire in detail, Lord Bao learned the whole truth. He let Zhang see Anzhu at the prison door so as to comfort him. The next day he signed a warrant for questioning the concerned parties. He also stealthily commanded the jailers to do this and that at such and such a moment. All the parties were promptly escorted into court.

First Bao confronted Zhang Bingyi with Yang. Yang remained stubborn and would not give up her claim that she never saw the contract. Thereupon Lord Bao ordered that Liu Anzhu be brought from prison. The jailers came up and reported, "He is dying and cannot be moved." There Chief Li met Zhang Bingyi and got the precise facts straight. Angry, he argued with Yang for some time. Again the jailers emerged reporting, "Liu Anzhu died from the serious illness." Ignorant of the consequences, Yang said to herself, "Thank Heaven! If he has died, my family is rid of a nuisance!" Lord Bao asked, "From what disease did Liu Anzhu die? Tell the coroner to examine the body at once and deliver a report." The coroner then came to say, "After observing the body, I found the dead to be about eighteen years old. He died from an injury to his temple caused by a foreign object. Black bruises are clearly discernible around the wound." "What shall we do?" said Lord Bao. "The case has become more complicated since it now involves a life. Tell me, Lady Yang, what Liu Anzhu was. Was he your relative?" "My lord," responded Yang, "he was not my relative." "If he were your relative," said Lord Bao, "you were his senior and he, a junior, so even if you caused his death, it was an accidental slaughter of a descendant, for which you would have to pay some copper coins, but you would not necessarily pay with your life. Now that he was not your relative, haven't you heard that 'a life is paid for with a life and a debt is paid for with coins'? If he was an irrelevant man, it's right that you refused to recognize him. But why should you have hit his head with some object that led to the tetanus that caused his death? The legal code says: 'He who beats a commoner and causes the latter's death is to be put to death.' Runners, chain this woman and shut her in death row in anticipation of her execution at the end of the coming autumn to pay for the murder of the young man." The runners, echoing with a thunder-like roar, immediately fetched a cangue. Yang, her face ashened in fear, yelled, "Oh my lord, he was my nephew." "Do you have any evidence to prove that?" asked Lord Bao. "The contract is the evidence," she answered. She rummaged in her clothes and produced the contract for Lord Bao.

Having read the contract, Lord Bao said to Yang, "If Liu Anzhu was your nephew, I will have his body carried out and you should take the body and bury it. You mustn't refuse." "Your humble servant is willing to bury her nephew," she answered. Thereupon Lord Bao had Liu Anzhu brought in from the prison and said to him, "Liu Anzhu, I've retrieved the contract through trickery." Kowtowing, Anzhu thanked him. "But for your clean and upright lordship," Anzhu said, "I would have been utterly wronged!" As Yang raised her head to look at Liu Anzhu, she saw that his face was normal and even the wound had healed. Blushing, she couldn't utter one word. Lord Bao took up a brush and wrote this verdict:

> Both Liu Anzhu's filial virtue and Zhang Bingyi's good-heartedness are rare, so honors are conferred upon their families. Chief Li is to wed his daughter and son-in-law on a chosen date. The remains of Liu Tianrui and his wife are to be buried in their ancestral graveyard. Liu Tianxiang lacks a good sense of judgment, but considering his advanced age, he is pardoned. His wife, Yang, who should have been punished severely, is permitted to gain her ransom by paying a sum. Yang's son-in-law is not one of Liu's offspring, so he is to be expelled from Liu's house and must not embezzle any of Liu's property.

After the verdict was pronounced, all were ordered to go home. They kowtowed and took their leave.

Squire Zhang prepared a visiting card and visited Liu Tianxiang and Chief Li before he returned to Luzhou. When Liu Tianxiang returned home, he blamed his wife for all the trouble. He and his nephew brought the remains of his brother and sister-in-law to the ancestral graveyard and buried them there. On an auspicious date Chief Li held the wedding ceremony for his daughter and son-in-law.

A month later Liu Anzhu and his wife went to Luzhou to see Squire Zhang and his wife Guo. Later on, Liu Anzhu was appointed to be an official and he became an aristocrat. Neither Liu Tianxiang nor Zhang Bingyi had any descendants, so the property of both families went to Liu Anzhu. — This shows that prosperity or predicament is predestined by Fate and one mustn't make futile efforts to thwart it. What is more, fraudulence between kin badly undermines the vitality of a family. That's why I have told this story; you people in the world should never hurt the feelings of your flesh-and-blood relatives just for trifling gains.

Tale 17

In Laxity the Monk of the East Veranda Encounters a Monster; During an Elopement a Knave in Black Commits a Murder

This story took place during the Tang Dynasty. To the east of Yizhou of (present-day) Shandong (Province) there is Gongshan Mountain that towers above the other peaks. At that time not a single soul could be found there within a circumference of thirty *li*. At the beginning of the Reign of Zhenyuan [785-804] two Buddhist monks arrived and took delight in the tranquillity and secludedness of the mountain. They found it a good place for their austere practices. So they gathered withered branches from the side of the mountain and built a shed among the huge trees. Having furnished the shed with seats they intermittently recited sutras day and night. As people in nearby villages heard of this, they raised money to build houses for them. In a month or so a courtyard had been completed whereupon the monks practiced their religion even more diligently. Because of this, people from far and near came to admire them and supplied food to them on a daily basis. The two monks, each sitting on one of the verandas, resolved to concentrate on reciting sutras and never to leave the mountain until they attained enlightenment. Thus they practiced their faith for over twenty years.

One winter night during the Reign of Yuanhe [806-820], while the two monks were reciting sutras on their verandas, one of them faintly heard bitter weeping coming from the foot of the silent and empty mountain. The sound seemed to be approaching. Soon it reached their gate. Hearing this in the tranquil night, the monk of the eastern veranda was stirred. He thought to himself, for many years I have been living on this lonely mountain, yet I don't know what kind of world lies underneath it. The mournful weeping has made me sad. Then, as the weeping stopped, he saw a figure jump down with a thump from the top of the wall and head for the western veranda. From a distance he could see that the figure was of gigantic build and looked grotesque. The monk was aghast. With bated breath he was trembling as he observed what was happening. After the figure entered the western veranda, the reciting of sutras abruptly stopped and there was the sound of fighting. After awhile he heard a loud crunching and gnawing sound. The monk of the eastern veranda was very frightened. He thought to himself, there is no one else in the yard. After eating him, it will surely turn to me. I had better escape. So the monk opened the gate in haste and dashed out in panic. Because he had not been outside of the temple for a long time, he could not find the path. Tumbling along, he was all but exhausted. As he looked over his shoulder, he could see the figure staggering along in big strides after him. At this he was frightened out of his wits and began to dart and dash aimlessly. Suddenly he came to a stream. Holding the hem of his cassock in his hands, he waded across the stream. The figure now arrived at the bank. "But for the stream," it shouted across the water, "I would have eaten you as well." The monk ran on, terror stricken. Not knowing where he was, he had to just let his legs carry him along.

Soon it began to snow. It was so dark he could hardly see more than a few steps in front of him. In despair, he came upon an ox stable near a courtyard. He entered it and hid there. It was now midnight. The snow let up and it became lighter. Suddenly he saw a man in black with a sword and a spear in his hands sneak toward the stable. Holding his breath, the monk peeped out from the dark. He saw the man in black look around as if he was waiting for something. After a long while things were thrown out from within the courtyard. These appeared to be clothes or the like. The man in black tied these into two bundles. Then a girl climbed over the wall from within the courtyard. In the light of the moon shining on the snow, the monk saw all this clearly. After the girl came down, the man lifted the two bundles to his shoulder on the spear, and without saying anything to her, walked away. The girl followed him. This is not a place for me to stay, thought the monk. The man and the girl must be eloping. When they find her missing tomorrow, the people in the yard will trace the girl by the footprints in the snow. If they see a monk, they will surely put the responsibility for seduction on me. I will have to leave at once. But since he did not know the way and was in a hurry, he rambled aimlessly in a trance.

After he walked about ten *li* or so, he slipped and fell into a pit that was an abandoned well. Fortunately it had no water in it, but it was deep and wide. In the moonlight coming from above, he saw a corpse whose head and body had been severed, but the body was still warm. Obviously it had been killed just a moment before. The monk was more terrified, but he could not climb out of the well. He was at a loss as to what to do.

At daybreak he looked more closely at the body and found it to be the girl who had climbed over the wall the previous night. How could this have happened, he wondered. Then, in confusion, he heard many people's voices above. When they looked down into the well, they cried, "Here is the gangster!" A man was let down into the well holding a rope. Scared and frozen in freight, the monk was too weak to struggle. So he was easily tied up. The man struck him on his bald head and he saw stars. Unable to make an explanation for being there, the monk felt he was at the brink of Hell. After the man tied the monk up, he was pulled out of the well as was the body. At the sight of the body an old man among the group of onlookers howled. "You bald ass!" he berated the monk, "why did you kidnap my daughter and kill her in the well?"

"I am a monk from the eastern veranda on Gongshan Mountain," said the monk. "And for the last twenty years I have never left the monastery. Yesterday evening a monster entered my yard and devoured my fellow monk. As I ran for my life I arrived here. When I took shelter from the snow in an ox stable I saw a man in black come, and then a girl jumped over the wall and followed him away. Fearing I might get involved, I tried to flee. Unexpectedly I dropped into this well and saw the murdered body there. How could I know the reason for this? I have not left my mountain for years. How could I have made the acquaintance of a woman and have kidnapped her? And for what reason would I have killed her? I hope every one of you has an insightful judgment." When he finished, some of the people who had visited his monastery said they recognized him. They knew he was a monk with attainment in self cultivation. But since there was no explanation for the dead girl in the well, they could not defend him. So he was escorted to the county court.

Seeing a crowd come with a tied up monk and a body, the county magistrate asked them what this was about. The old man replied, "My family name is Ma and I am a native of this county. The dead one is my daughter, eighteen years old. She had not even been engaged yet. Only in recent days did a couple of match-makers come to propose marriage. This morning when I got up I found my daughter missing. As I looked for her, I saw footprints in the snow of the back yard. I realized she must have gone over the wall and run away. I traced the footprints to a well where they disappeared, but there was blood on the ground. As I looked down into the well I saw my slain daughter and this monk. Who can the murderer be if not the monk?" When the magistrate asked the monk how he would explain this, the monk said, "I am an ascetic monk from Gongshan Mountain and for the last twenty years I have never left there. Last night a monster entered the yard and ate my fellow monk. I had no choice but to break my vows and run down the mountain for my life. Unexpectedly I was haunted by a sin in my former life and was thus entangled in the meshes." Then he related what he had seen in the ox stable and how, as he had tried to avoid further trouble, he had fallen into the well and seen the body. "Just send a man to Gongshan, my lord," he added, "and let him see if the monk of the western veranda is still there and how he was devoured, and you will know that what I am saying is true." Following this proposal, the magistrate sent a man to the mountain to find out the facts and report back immediately.

When the man arrived at the yard of the monastery, he saw the other monk, safe and sound, sitting on the western veranda reading a sutra. Seeing the man, the monk stood up and greeted him. The man told him what the monk of the eastern veranda had done and added, "Since he said that he fled from the mountain because he saw a monster enter the yard and eat a man, the magistrate told me to come to check out the monk's statement. Since you are here, can you tell me what monster came last night?" "There was no monster," replied the monk of the western veranda. "But at the second watch when we two were reciting sutras each on his own veranda, my friend of the eastern veranda opened the gate and went out. Long ago we two swore never to go out of the gate and during the past twenty years we have both kept that oath. Seeing him leave by himself, I was surprised. I ran after him and shouted at him, but he simply didn't hear me. Because I must abide by my pledge never to step out, I dared not chase him further. What happened to him at the bottom of the mountain is quite beyond me."

When the man reported this to the magistrate, the magistrate said, "The bald wretch is treacherous!" He had the monk brought up and interrogated him again. The monk, however, insisted on what he had said before. "The monk to the western veranda is safe and sound. What monster entered the yard? You left the mountain on the same night the girl was killed and you were found in the same well. Can there be such a coincidence in the world? Evidently you are the murderer. Yet you are trying to deny it!" The magistrate put the monk to torture, shouting: "Tell the truth!" "Since an unsettled debt in my former life pesters me," said the monk, "death is my only outcome. But I have nothing to confess." Enraged, the magistrate inflicted all sorts of cruel torture on him. "You needn't torture me any more," said the monk, "let me admit to the murder." Seeing the monk so cruelly tortured and yet giving no details, the plaintiff thought to himself, my family never had any contact with this monk, how can he have seduced my daughter? Even if he could have seduced her, why wouldn't he run away with her but kill her instead? If he killed her, why didn't he escape? Why should he be in the same well with the body? He may have been wronged. He came forward and told the magistrate what he thought. "You may be right," the magistrate said, "but he cannot be a good person since he fell into a well at night. Besides, he told an absurd story. He must be engaged in some shady activity. But since the lethal weapon has not been found and no spoils were discovered on him, the case cannot be settled. I will imprison him. You may go out and conduct your own investigation. There must be some questionable signs relating to your daughter. She must have made secret contacts with somebody and there must be some objects missing from your house. Have a careful search for these and you may get a clear idea regarding the murder." All concerned parties took these directions and left the court. The monk went into prison to suffer more.

Let's leave them aside now and turn to Ma. A magnate of Yizhou, he was addressed by the locals as Squire. He had a daughter who was extremely beautiful. She had fallen in love with Mr Du, her cousin, since childhood. They swore secretly to became man and wife. But Du was poor. Despite the fact that he had sent match-makers to Ma several times, the Squire turned down all his offers because the Squire disliked his poverty. Ma did not know that his daughter was set on marrying Du. It was her wet nurse, the woman who had breast-fed her, that delivered letters and messages between her and her lover. Being an evil woman, the nurse purposefully stirred the girl's passions and, by offering services undercover, she intended to defraud the girl of her money and belongings. Knowing what the girl wished, the nurse served as a go-between and aroused even more the desires of the girl and her lover — just short of bringing them together.

After the girl had grown up, some other families sent match-makers. The Squire settled on one of the suitors and the betrothal contract was about to be signed. In desperation the girl turned to the wet nurse for help. "I only love my cousin Du," she said, "but they want to marry me to someone else. What can I do?" Thereupon the nurse hit upon a sinister plot. "Du made suit several times, but the Squire did not consent," she cajoled the girl. "You certainly cannot marry him openly. The only way for you is to carry on a secret affair with him after you have married another man." "How can I do that when I am married to someone else?" asked the girl. "Since I have made up my mind to go with Du, I won't marry at all." "Can you decide the matter?" asked the nurse. "I have an idea; you may have it done before you get married." "How shall I 'have it done'?" asked the girl. "Let me set a date," replied the nurse, "and you can go with Du to a strange prefecture, taking a lot of money for the journey, and spend a happy time there. By the time your family has found you, the two of you will have been united for a long time. A daughter of a family with a good reputation cannot divorce and remarry. Besides, nobody else will take you then. This is the only way out." "A marvelous arrangement!" said the girl.

"But you must fix a precise date for him." "Just leave it to me," the nurse assured her.

Let me tell you the situation in the household. Ma, the Squire, was extremely wealthy. The nurse had long set her eyes on the gold, silver, gems and jewelry, and boxes full of clothing in the girl's chamber. Since she coveted these treasures, how could she let them fall into another's hand? She had a son called Blacky Niu, who was a dishonest man. He often associated with gamblers and wrestlers and made friends with scoundrels. Sometimes he even pilfered. When the treacherous nurse promised to fix a date with Du, she went instead to her son, instructing him to take Du's place, carry the girl away somewhere and sell her to make a fortune. After the nurse and her son had worked out the plan, she went to the girl saying, "The date is fixed for this night. Move your things to the ox stable outside of the walls in the moonlight, climb over the wall and you will see him." When the girl asked the nurse to go with her, the nurse said, "That won't do. If you go alone, they will not find out your whereabouts for the time being. If I go with you, they will know that I am involved, and will turn to my family. Won't I be in trouble then?" Not having made the appointment face to face with Du, the girl believed the nurse's words. Perhaps misfortune was her lot. She believed that she would unite with her lover, Du, and fulfill her long-cherished wish. As a result:

While she was to give her heart to the bright moon,
The bright moon shed its light upon a dark ditch.

That night the girl and the nurse wrapped up her things and threw them over the wall. Then the girl climbed over the wall the moment the monk was peeping out from the dark. Seeing a man in black going ahead, the girl believed it was Du who had dressed himself in black to escape notice. So she followed him with little fear. As she arrived at the well, she saw in the bright moonlight that the robust, dark-faced man was not Du. Not realizing the consequences, the girl uttered a cry of alarm. Blacky Niu warned her to be quiet, but he could not stop her. I have so many belongings of hers in my bundles, he thought to himself, if I take this legged matter along, her protests may lay the truth bare. Then I will lose both her and her belongings. It's better to finish her off. Drawing out his sword, he slit her neck. A supple girl like she could not stand such a cut and in a short while the beautiful girl withered in the wilderness. It was her impure idea that led her to this end. When she died, Blacky Niu threw her body into the well and ran away with her belongings. Who could have foretold that an ill-starred monk would be his scapegoat and suffer in prison.

Story teller, you may say, if things go like this, the world is totally devoid of justice! Well, gentle readers, "The net of Heaven's law has large meshes but it lets nothing through." Justice has long arms and by and by each will receive his requital.

When the Squire found his daughter missing, he led a crowd to search for her and came upon the monk. After a time of entanglement, the monk was sent to prison. But Ma had never checked the things in his house. When he returned home, Squire Ma thought the matter over again and suspected that the monk might have had nothing to do with the murder. As he entered his daughter's room and saw all the boxes empty, he realized that she must have gone away with somebody by a prior agreement, but he could discover nothing suspicious about her daily activities. If she had eloped with an adulterer, why should she have been killed? This remained an enigma. As he could not think of any reason, he posted a list of the lost items and offered a prize for information about them. Hearing that the girl had been killed, the nurse as the only one who knew the truth was on edge. I let him take her away, she thought in resentment against her son, why did he do this? She contacted her son in secret, blamed him and enjoined him, "Be careful! Taking a life is a matter of grave consequences!"

After some time, however, Blacky Niu relaxed his vigilance and went to a gambling house with some money. Unfortunately the coins always fell with the head upward* and after awhile all his money was gone. But he was too fervent about winning to have the patience to leave. Standing there and looking on at the game, he could not hold himself back. Reaching his hand into his pocket, he took out a pair of gold-embedded hair clasps. Getting a loan on them, he joined the game again, hoping to win back his money. But beyond his expectation his money changed hands again. He had to leave the casino in reluctance. The pawned hair clasps, not retrievable, fell into the hands of banker Fatty Huang.

When Fatty Huang brought these hair clasps home, his wife saw them. "Where did you get these?" she asked. "Don't take anything of unknown origin, or you may get into trouble." "Of course I know where they came from," replied Fatty Huang. "They are Blacky Niu's mortgage." "There it is," said his wife. "Blacky Niu hasn't a wife. Where did a single man get these things?" "You are right," Fatty Huang replied, and then he had an idea. "The girl of Squire Ma was killed and the items on the list of missing objects are mostly hair ornaments. Blacky Niu is the nurse's son. Could these hair clasps be stolen from that girl?" "You can go to the Squire's house to take out a loan on the clasps," said Huang's wife. "He'll surely say something. If he recognizes them, we can get a prize. Isn't that a good idea?" So they agreed on the matter.

The next day Fatty Huang, taking the hair clasps, went to the Squire's storehouse. There he ran into Squire Ma as he was just walking out. "I have brought something for you," said Fatty Huang. "If you recognize them, give me a prize. If not, let me use them to obtain a loan." He handed the hair clasps to the Squire. Ma recognized them to be his daughter's. "Where did you get these?" he asked. Fatty Huang

---

*In olden times six coins were tossed in gambling. Those who had six heads lost the game.

related how Blacky Niu had borrowed money on them for gambling. "Needless to say," the Squire nodded, saying to himself, "the mother and son collaborated." Treating Huang with hospitality, the Squire had him write this statement: "This pair of gold-embedded hair clasps was pawned by Blacky Niu. This is the truth." The Squire told Huang, "Don't let anybody know about this." Giving Fatty Huang half of the offered prize, he promised to give the remainder to him when the case was settled. Fatty Huang, having hit upon a fortune, left quite pleased.

Entering the house with the two hair clasps in hand, Squire Ma asked the nurse, "Tell me how my daughter ran away." "It's funny," said the nurse, "you were here and I was too. Nobody knows how she left. How would I know? Why do you ask me?" Showing her the hair clasps, Squire Ma asked, "How did these come from your house if you don't know?" The guilty-conscienced nurse then understood that her son had betrayed himself. Her face turned pale, her heart thumped in fright. "Maybe they were dropped by the roadside," she said, hemming and hawing, "and were then picked up by somebody." Seeing her face turn now red now pale, the Squire decided she must be hiding something, but he did not let on. Instead, he had Blacky Niu brought in, tied up and hauled to the county court. "For what am I guilty," Blacky Niu shouted jumping. "Why have you tied me up?" "No roaring, please," said the Squire. "Someone has accused you of murder. Explain the matter to the authorities the best you can."

The county magistrate immediately convened court. Squire Ma submitted Fatty Huang's statement and the hair clasps, saying, "Here are the stolen goods and testimony. I entreat my lord to investigate the matter." "Who is Blacky Niu?" asked the magistrate. "Does he have any relation to your family?" "He is the son of my daughter's nurse," replied the Squire. The magistrate nodded, saying, "So he must be implicated in the case." Calling Blacky Niu in, the magistrate asked him, "Where did you get these hair clasps?" Unable to find a proper excuse, Blacky Niu had to acknowledge that they came from his mother. Thereupon the magistrate summoned the nurse and said to her, "You alone are accountable for the seduction and murder. I will find out the truth from you." He commanded to torture her. Unable to stand the torment, she confessed in vague terms, "The girl had close contacts with Du. She made an appointment with Du for elopement at night. All I know is that she jumped over the wall. But I don't know anything about what had happened afterwards." Then the magistrate turned to Squire Ma, "Do you know this Du?" he asked. "Du is a nephew of mine," replied Ma. "Several times he proposed marriage to my daughter. I turned him down because of his poverty. I never knew what he did in secret."

Accordingly the magistrate summoned Du. Du had often engaged in secret meetings with the girl and they were deeply in love. He regretted the girl's death during the alleged elopement, but he didn't know what had actually happened. The magistrate asked him, "Why did you elope with Ma's daughter and kill her on the way?" "We are cousins," replied Du, "and it's true we often exchanged intimate letters in secret. But when did we agree to elope? Who delivered the message? Who can be a witness?" The magistrate then called in the nurse and confronted her with Du. The nurse could only talk about the usual secret contacts between Du and the girl, but as to the appointment for an elopement, she could not hold on to her allegations. Having learned about the many missing things, Du defended himself. "Find where the stolen goods are, my lord," he said, "and you will know I am innocent." After careful consideration, the magistrate thought to himself, it seems to me Du is too weak to commit a murder and Niu is too rude to be a philanderer. There must be someone who assumed Du's name. He then had Blacky Niu and the nurse severely tortured. The nurse had to confess that she had let her son assume Du's name and meet with the girl, but she did not know what had happened later. Blacky Niu, however, was stubborn. Trying to put the responsibility on Du, he shouted: "If the girl invited him, it had nothing to do with me." Then an idea dawned on the magistrate: "The monk said the other day that he saw a man in black bring the girl away at night. If I let him come to recognize who that man is, everything will be clear." So he ordered the monk to be brought from prison.

When the monk came into the courtroom, the magistrate said to him, "You said that night when you were in an ox stable you saw a man in black take things and the girl away. Could you recognize the man if he were here?" "Though it was during the night," said the monk, "with the moonlight and reflection from the snow it was almost as bright as day. I have practiced meditation for a long time and have a keen sense of sight. If I see the man, I certainly can identify him." Calling in Du, the magistrate asked the monk, "Is this the man?" "No," said the monk, "the man was of sturdy build, nothing like this frail scholar." Then the magistrate summoned Blacky Niu and again asked the monk, "Is this that man?" "Yes," affirmed the monk. The magistrate sneered at Blacky Niu, "So your mother's word is proved. If you are not the murderer, who else is? Besides, the stolen goods are here. How can you defend yourself? The pity is that the monk suffered in prison for a time in your stead." "It is my debt from a previous life that makes me suffer," said the monk, "so I blame nobody. Fortunately the Buddha's Heaven is near and my lord has made a wise judgment to right the wrong." Again the magistrate had Blacky Niu cramped, saying to him, "You might have gone away with the girl, but why did you kill her?" "At first she took me to be Du," Blacky Niu confessed. "When we arrived at the well, she found that I was not and started shouting. So I killed her in a hurry." "Where did you get the knife at night?" asked the magistrate. "Because I consort with wrestlers, I carry sharp tools on me. Furthermore, having to act at night, I have to guard myself against surprise attacks. So I had a knife with me." "I knew it was not Du who committed the murder," said the magistrate. Having their full statements recorded, he then had the nurse flogged to death and announced that the rapist and murderer, Blacky Niu, would be executed when the stolen goods were fully recovered. Du and the monk were released. All concerned parties were dismissed. Of this we'll say no more.

The monk of the eastern veranda returned after having been scourged in court and having stayed in prison for a time. Upon returning to his mountain and seeing the monk of the western veranda, he told him all that he had experienced. "We were meditating together," said his partner. "Nothing happened that night. Why did you alone have a vision and undergo such tribulations?" "I don't know," responded the monk of the eastern veranda. As he went back to his room, he believed the hardship he had experienced must have stemmed from inadequacy in his self-cultivation attainment. He confessed his sin to the Buddha and prayed that the Buddha would show him visions of his previous life. Sitting on the rush hassock he meditated for three days and three nights. When his mind sank into absolute tranquillity, he suddenly apprehended that Squire Ma's daughter had been his concubine in a former life, a person whom he had scourged and locked up on a groundless suspicion. This was his unpaid debt. Because he had become a monk in this life and practiced austerity, the debt could have been annulled. But that night when he heard the weeping, he felt sad and, as soon as he relaxed his concentration, a specter appeared, which led him to nightmares until he was compelled to confront his former enemy and repay his debt by undergoing flogging and imprisonment. Having acquired a thorough understanding of the cause and result, he strengthened his religious devotion . After that he and his fellow monk of the western veranda never left the mountain again. Later he passed away in a sitting posture with his palms held together in front of his breast.* Thus the moral of this poem is proved:

---

*It was a popular belief that a Buddhist monk with the utmost attainment dies in a sitting posture.

The life's a debt in former incarnation;
The world, a constant lifeless being.
If you are not aroused by carnal feeling,
You are absolved from any obligation.

Tale 18

To Seize Possessions a Vicious Son-in-law Plots Against
  His Nephew;
To Continue the Lineage a Filial Daughter Hides Her
  Brother

It is related that during the Yuan Dynasty there was a rich man surnamed Liu and named Congshan who lived in Dongping Prefecture. He was addressed as Squire. He was sixty and his wife, Li, was fifty years old, and he had an enormous family fortune. He had no son, but he did have a daughter whose pet name was Yinjie. He had married his daughter to a certain Zhang Lang, who was thirty years old while Yinjie was twenty seven. Zhang Lang was a mean, greedy and crafty man. He had sent the match-maker to the Lius to offer his proposal only because he saw that Liu was wealthy and had no son. Now that he was Liu's son-in-law, he believed the riches would eventually be his, and he gloated over the matter. Liu, however, kept a tight hold of the family wealth and gave no sign of delivering it to his son-in-law.

Liu had two considerations: The first was that his brother, Liu Congdao, and his brother's wife, Ning, had both died and left behind an orphan whose pet name was Yinsun. By this time he was a twenty-five-year-old knowledgeable student. Since he had lost his parents in childhood, his bequest was now gone and he had to live on the generosity of his uncle. Liu gave the child special treatment considering he was a blood kin, but his wife was partial to her daughter and son-in-law. To make things worse, his wife had been on bad terms with the boy's mother when the latter was alive, so she shifted her resentment onto the child, regarding him as a thorn in her flesh. Fortunately Liu always tried to shield the child. Still, because of his wife and son-in-law, he could not look after him with the kind of tenderness he wished. Because of this, he always felt uneasy. The second consideration was a maid servant named Xiao Mei. Seeing her to be diligent, Liu's wife had her wait on him. Thereupon Liu took her as his concubine. She had become pregnant and Liu hoped that the child to be born would be a boy. Because of these considerations, Liu had not handed the household wealth over to his son-in-law. Zhang Lang, however, was too cunning and stubborn to give up. He purposefully disseminated discord between his mother-in-law and Yinsun. Yinsun could not stand the humiliation. Liu Congshan, on his part, wanted to save the family from further trouble, so he secretly gave Yinsun some money and let him find a new dwelling and start a trade. Yinsun rented a house, but being a student, he did not know how to do business. So he had to rely on donations from his uncle.

Seeing that Yinsun had been driven out, Zhang Lang hatched a sinister scheme. He was quite uneasy about the baby that would soon be born to Xiao Mei. If the baby was a girl, half of the fortune would go to her; if, however, the baby was a boy, the whole fortune would belong to the baby. He would have no share at all! In order to prepare his plot against Xiao Mei, he discussed the matter of the family fortune with his wife, Yinjie.

Yinjie, however, was a filial daughter and, after all, she was a woman and had no more than a woman's outlook. If her cousin Yinsun got a share of the family property, she would oppose it on the ground that she was the flesh-and-blood daughter of the family; if her father had a son, she would be happy, because a male child was her father's ardent desire. She was sincere in her wish to make the old man happy. Realizing that Zhang Lang harbored no good intentions and that her unwise mother sided with Zhang, she was afraid Xiao Mei could not deliver the baby in safety. At that juncture Zhang, pleased with his success in getting Yinsun expelled, hatched a plot to harm Xiao Mei. If we two or three collaborate, thought Yinjie, it will not be difficult to humiliate her. But his jealousy may rob my father of a successor to the family line! No, that won't do. If I don't use my wits to safeguard Xiao Mei's labor, I will be committing a crime against my father and will be condemned by posterity. But if my husband sees that I am not cooperating with him, he may do something in secret. So I'd better protect Xiao Mei by making use of his scheme.

Do you, readers, know what plan she worked out? Read on.

Yinjie had an aunt, her father's cousin, living in Eastern Village. The aunt was close to Yinjie. Yinjie planned to have Xiao Mei deliver the baby in her aunt's home, thinking it was as good as entrusting the fatherless baby to her. Thereupon she went to Xiao Mei and said, "Since Master Yinsun has been driven out from this house, Zhang Lang has set out to monopolize the family property. Seeing you pregnant, he has become very jealous. And my mother is on his side. You should take good care of yourself, Aunt.*" "Since you are good enough to tell me this," said Xiao Mei, "I know your boundless kindness comes from your consideration for the Squire. But how can I guard myself against the scheme? I beg you to look after me in this matter." "Am I unwilling to help you?" replied Yinjie. "But this is a

---

*In olden times a child called a father's concubine "aunt."

matter of property and something so secret that even a husband and wife don't talk about it with each other. If he eventually arranges a trap, how will I know?" "What can I do then?" Xiao Mei said tearfully. "Wouldn't it be better to tell the Squire everything and ask for his opinion?" "The Squire," said Yinjie, "is old and has limited resources to protect you. Besides, if we make this public, everyone's feelings will be hurt and they will become your enemies. It will be harder for you to stand. I have a plan to talk over with you." "What plan do you have?" asked Xiao Mei. "I have an aunt in Eastern Village and she is close to me," said Yinjie. "I mean to entrust you to her. You can give birth to the baby at her home. I will ask her to look after you and feed the child when it is born. I will take care of your food, clothing and other expenses. I will tell my mother and husband that you left because you are dissatisfied with life here. They are only too eager to see you go, so they will not investigate the matter. I will wait until they become less narrow-minded towards you. When my mother changes her mind and your baby has grown up, I will find an opportunity to tell the Squire and let him take you back. Then they can do nothing against you. I see no safer way to handle the matter than this." "Your kindness is so great that I cannot repay you even with my own life!" responded Xiao Mei. "I am driven to this," said Yinjie, "because I don't want to see the Squire deprived of an heir. Fearing that you may be victimized, I have no other choice but to make this plan behind my mother and husband's back. If you have a son and gain favor in the future, don't forget me." "Your kindness will be branded in my memory as if imprinted on a printing block," said Xiao Mei. "How can I ever forget it?" So settled, they waited for the right opportunity.

One day the Squire was about to go to his farm to look over the harvest. Remembering that Xiao Mei was pregnant, he feared his son-in-law might be jealous of Xiao Mei and his daughter might be unfaithful. In the hope of avoiding trouble he entrusted the management of the house holdings to them. Still he dreaded that his wife might cause trouble for Xiao Mei. He called her in and asked: "Do you know how to brew wine in a borrowed urn?" "No," she replied, "how is it done?" "We borrow an urn from others and brew wine in our house. When the wine is done, we return the urn to its owner. This means that we use his urn only temporarily. Now Xiao Mei is pregnant. If she gives birth to a son or daughter, I will regard the child as yours. Then you may decide to keep Xiao Mei in the house or sell her away. I simply borrowed her belly to get the baby. Isn't that the same as brewing wine in a borrowed urn?" Hearing this, his wife said, "You are right. I will look after her. You can rest assured and go in peace to the farm."

Then, asking Zhang Lang to bring out all the deeds signed by debtors in recent years, the Squire bade Xiao Mei light a lamp and he burned them all. As Zhang Lang reached out his hands to snatch some from the fire, his fingers were burned and he groaned in pain. The Squire smiled. "Can money come so lightly?" he asked. "The money we've lent to other people is what we have accumulated throughout our lives," said his wife. "Why have you burned the deeds?" "Without these sinful coins," replied the Squire, "perhaps I can have a son. Even if I have slim hope for a son now, without the money I will be carefree and nobody will covet my belongings. What is the good of money, and why should I cudgel my brains to exploit others? It's better to accumulate merits to my credit in the nether world. I have burned these deeds, yet I still have enough property to support my family. Maybe Heaven will sympathize with me and grant me a son. Who can tell?" With this, he left for the farm.

Hearing his father-in-law's words, Zhang Lang realized they were directed at him, and he became even more resentful. It is obvious he suspects that I've got it in for Xiao Mei, he thought to himself, so it is meaningless for me to play a good guy. Why not fulfill my plan while he is away on the farm? This will save me trouble in future. As he talked about it with his wife, Yinjie realized the situation was desperate. A few days earlier she had told her aunt about her plan. Now she directed Xiao Mei to go and hide herself there. She lied to her husband, "Xiao Mei, the servant, knows we have no good intentions. This morning I told her to go out to buy wool yarn. She hasn't returned yet. Perhaps she has taken this opportunity to flee. What should we do?" "It's not uncommon for a maid servant to flee from her master's house. If she's gone, it will save us trouble." "But father might be annoyed if he finds out," said Yinjie. "We didn't beat or berate or offend her," said Zhang Lang. "It is she, herself, who left our house. Father cannot blame us. Let's tell mother and ask her for her opinion."

Then the couple went to tell the mother about Xiao Mei's disappearance. The mother said, "You are talking lightly! The Squire at his advanced age is overjoyed to see that there is some hope for a son, and he is waiting at the farm for the good news. How can this have happened? Have the two of you schemed to get rid of her?" "She left the house very early this morning," said Yinjie, "and we had nothing to do with it." Although the mother was suspicious, she was partial to her daughter and son-in-law and hoped that what they said was true. Since she, too, thought that there would be peace if the maid servant left, she did not probe into the matter further. Fearing that the Squire might be vexed or suspicious, the three of them immediately went to the farm to inform him.

The Squire felt his heart thumping when he saw them all arrive, thinking that they were heralding the birth of a male baby. Then, as he heard their report, he was benumbed. She's left because things were too hard for her at my house, he thought to himself, it is alright for her to go. The only pity is that she left with the baby. Then he heaved a sigh. Judging from the attitude of the family, I'm afraid that even if Xiao Mei gives birth to a son, the child might not be safe. Let Xiao Mei go and find herself a good place to live. Why should I detain her and put the lives of her and her baby in danger? His eyes brimming with tears, he held up his anger and blamed his ill fate. On second thought, he said to himself: All their designs are aimed at my property. Why should I be a miser and hoard money to their advantage? My family line cannot be continued anyway, so why shouldn't I give alms away while I am alive? With resentment in his heart, he posted announcements everywhere that he would be distributing alms to the poor at Kaiyuan Temple the next day. Zhang Lang hated to see the money given away, but seeing that his father-in-law was in a bad mood, he dared not protest.

The next day the family went to Kaiyuan Temple with money to give away. When they arrived, they saw throngs of poor people. The Squire ordered that an adult beggar be given one thousand coins and a child beggar, five hundred. Among the beggars there was a certain Liu the Ninth, who had a child. He worked out a plan and discussed it with an elder beggar. "If I take alms with the child," Liu the Ninth said, "we will be considered one household and will get only one thousand. So I will let the child go up by himself and say he is all by himself. In this way I can get five hundred coins more. You may be a witness and speak for the child. When we get the money we can divide the five hundred between us and use it for drinks." Thus Liu the Ninth and the child announced themselves separately. "Does this child belong to another family?" asked Zhang Lang. "Yes," said the elder beggar. So the child got five hundred coins, which Liu the Ninth took away. As the elder beggar came to get his share, Liu the Ninth said, "The child is mine. How can you take my money? Why don't you imitate me and have a son of your own?" "We agreed to divide the money," said the other beggar, "why should you take all of it? Are you unreasonable simply because you have a son?" So they began to fight. Liu asked what this was all about and told Zhang Lang to reconcile them. Liu the Ninth, however, was insensible. Pointing at the elder beggar, he called him names relating to the fact that his was an heirless household nonstop. "I have a son," he shouted, "so I have got the alms. It's none

of the business of your heirless household!" Zhang blushed, but he
failed to make the man shut his mouth. All this was not lost on Liu,
who broke into a wail, saying, "We who have no sons are so miserably
treated!" As his grief knew no end, his wife and daughter felt the pain
and joined him in crying. Zhang Lang did not know what to do.

As they were giving out the money, a man came up and saluted Liu
and his wife. The man was none other than Liu Yinsun. "Why are you
here?" Liu asked him. "Uncle and Aunt," he said, "the money you
gave me has been used up. Having heard that you were distributing
money here today, I have come to borrow some." Seeing that his wife
at his side said nothing, Liu put on airs. "Why didn't you do business
with the money I gave you?" Liu asked. "Your nephew can only read,"
said Yinsun, "but he doesn't know how to follow a trade. The money
has been drained away on food and daily necessities, so it is gone."
"You good-for-nothing!" Liu said. "How can I have so much for you
to squander?" He was about to strike the nephew when his wife made a
show of reconciling them. Yinjie and Zhang Lang said to Yinsun,
"Father is angry. You should go." Yinsun, however, would not go, but
kept on importuning. Brandishing his walking stick, Liu drove him out.
The other people believed he was really angry and so they did not step
forward to dissuade him. As Yinsun ran away, Liu ran after him until
they had gone about half a *li*. Yinsun didn't know why his uncle was
acting like this. Why does my uncle behave so oddly today? he
wondered. Seeing nobody else around, the Squire called, "Yinsun," at
which Yinsun stopped and knelt down. Stroking him, Liu said with
tears in his eyes, "Oh my child, your uncle has suffered a lot for the
lack of a son. You are the only flesh-and-blood heir of mine. Your
aunt lacks sense, but she is kind-hearted. She is blinded by prejudice
and doesn't understand that another's flesh cannot become warm in
her breast. Zhang Lang is by nature a bad man. One day he may be
disobedient. I will find one way or another to persuade your aunt. You
should visit our ancestral graves on festival days. In a couple of years I

will make you extremely wealthy. Now I have two silver ingots in my boots. I have put on a show of driving you out in order to give you the money behind their backs. You may take it to cover your daily expenses. But you mustn't forget what I have just said." Saying yes to all this, Yinsun left. Liu turned around, collected his things and went home.

Realizing that his father-in-law had given away a great deal of money, Zhang Lang, though his heart ached, believed that the remaining family holdings were enough for him, since there would be no reason to waste any more. So thinking, he was complacent and began to make decisions for himself. He was trying to arrange the family affairs in his own way so as to show he, a Zhang, was the master of the household. By and by he neglected his parents-in-law as if the family belonged only to the Zhangs and not to the Lius. Liu, of course, was discontent. Even his wife, who had been partial to Zhang Lang, was unwilling to accept such an outcome. Fortunately Yinjie did her best to intercede between them, but Zhang Lang was a strong-willed man reckless of consequences. Besides, Yinjie, as a woman, by and by got used to her husband's ways and in the end took sides with him. While she was hardly aware of the situation, intelligent people could not stand the way the household was managed.

One Pure Brightness Day* everybody visited their ancestral tombs. Since Zhang Lang now had the Lius' property in his hands, he had to take up the duty of arranging the visit. Having prepared two boxes of sacrificial food, Zhang went with his wife to the tombs. In previous years he would always visit the Lius' ancestral tombs first and then the Zhangs'. This year he made a decision to visit his own ancestral tombs first. "Why don't you visit my family's ancestral tombs first, as we used to," Yinjie asked him, "and wait there until my father and mother

---

*Pure Brightness Day falls around April 5th. It is a traditional festival when Chinese people visit their ancestral tombs.

arrive?" "You are married to me," said Zhang Lang, "and, after death, will be buried in the graveyard of the Zhangs. It is only right to go to the Zhang ancestral tombs first." As Yinjie could not dissuade him, she had to comply. Of this we will say no more.

Liu and his wife left the house after Zhang Lang had gone. As they neared the tombs, Liu said to his wife, "I think they have probably been in the graveyard for a long while." "Zhang Lang has set the sacrificial food in an orderly way and he and our daughter are waiting for us," replied his wife. But as they arrived at the graveyard, they found it to be quiet and there was not a soul there. When they looked closely at the tombs, they saw they were covered with some fresh soil and there were ashes of burned paper coins and the earth was wet with a libation. Clearly realizing that it was Yinsun who had been there, Liu said deliberately, "Who has been here first?" Then he turned to his wife and said, "It's strange! Since our daughter and son-in-law haven't been here, who can have done this? Could it be a man with another family name?" After waiting for awhile, they still did not see Zhang and their daughter come. Liu became impatient. "Let us make obeisance to our ancestors first," he said. "Who knows when they will come!"

Then he asked his wife, "Where shall we be buried after we die?" Pointing at a high mound, his wife said, "The trees there look like tall umbrellas. I think that is a good place." Liu sighed. "You and I are not that blessed," he said. Then, pointing to a low marshy spot — such spots were called spots for extinct families — he told her, "You and I will have to be buried there." "We have a lot of money," said his wife, "so we can pick any place we like! Why should we be buried in that spot for extinct families?" "The high mound emitting dragon's breath," said Liu, "is a burial spot for people who have offspring, so that their descendants will be prosperous. You and I have no son. Who will cede such a good burial spot to us? The only place for our bones is the low marshy ground. We have no descendants, after all, and so we will not need a good spot." "Who says I have no descendants?" retorted his wife. "I have a daughter and son-in-law!" "Oh, I've forgotten that," said Liu. "Since they have not come yet, let's have a chat. Tell me what is my family name?" "Who doesn't know it is Liu!" she replied. "Is it necessary to ask such a question?" "Oh, I see," he continued, "my family name is Liu. And what is your family name?" "Li," she replied. "Why do you live in the house of us Lius if you belong to the Li family?" asked Liu. "Don't be funny," his wife replied. "I came because I was married to you, the Lius." "Do neighbors call you Madam Liu or Madam Li?" the Squire asked. "As the old saying goes, 'follow the man you marry, be he a fowl or cur.' My bones and flesh belong to the Lius, how can I be called Madam Li?" "Now I see your bones belong to the Lius. What is the family name of our daughter, then?" "Her family name is Liu, too." "And that of the son-in-law?" "Zhang," replied his wife. "Will our daughter be buried in the Lius' tombs or the Zhangs' after her death?" "She will be buried in the Zhangs'." At this Mrs Liu suddenly felt like weeping. Seeing the truth dawning on her, Liu said, "Now tell me, how can we say they are Liu's descendants? Isn't our family going to be extinct?" At this his wife cried loudly. "How come you are thinking of this?" she asked. "We are really miserable because of the absence of a male heir!" "Now you've got the idea," Liu said to her. "If we have no son, any male child from the Lius is an offspring of the line. He will pay visits to the Lius' ancestral tombs while he is alive and, when he dies, he will be buried in the same graveyard. What does our daughter, once married to another's house, have to do with us?" Hearing Liu's analysis, the woman suddenly saw the light. Moreover, thinking of the airs her son-in-law had assumed and seeing that he had not come with her daughter to the graveyard, she began to be angry with him.

As they were talking, Yinsun came to pick up his spade. Seeing his uncle and aunt, he prostrated himself in salutation. Liu's wife, having changed her attitude, found Yinsun somewhat dearer. "What are you doing here?" she asked. "Your nephew has come to add some soil to the tombs." replied Yinsun. "A blood relative is a blood relative, after all," she said to Liu. "Yinsun has come and has added earth to the tomb, but our daughter and son-in-law haven't come yet." Liu intentionally provoked Yinsun. "Why haven't you brought boxes of sacrificial food," he asked, "and set the offerings in an orderly way in front of the tombs, but have conducted such a perfunctory ceremony?" "Your nephew has no money," Yinsun replied. "He begged three cups of wine and a piece of paper from others. With these he expresses his respect for his ancestors." "Did you hear, Mother?" Liu asked his wife, "Those who have boxes of sacrificial food have not come because they are not the descendants of the Lius." Liu's wife was moved too. Then Liu asked Yinsun, "See the high manor house over there that even crows can't surpass and the tombs with stone sheep and tigers in front of them? Why didn't you go there, but instead here?" "Do you know whose tombs those are?" the mother chipped in. "Why shouldn't he visit Liu's tombs since he is one of the Liu's descendants?" "There you are, Mother," said Liu, "Yinsun is an offspring of the Lius. Didn't you say that your daughter and son-in-law are the Lius' descendants?" "I was wrong," she said, "From now on Yinsun will live in our house. You are one of my family members. Please forgive me for my faults." "Your nephew dares not bear grudges," said Yinsun. "I will look after your food and clothing," said Liu's wife. Liu bade Yinsun thank her with courtesy. Yinsun prostrated himself before her, saying, "I look to my aunt to take care of me, a descendant of the Lius." When she heard this, tears trickled down her cheeks.

While she was so moved, Zhang Lang and Yinjie arrived. Liu and his wife asked them why they had come so late, Zhang Lang said, "I went to my ancestral tombs before I came, so I am late." "Why didn't you come here first?" Liu's wife asked. "You kept us two waiting for half a day!" "I am the Zhangs' offspring," replied Zhang Lang. "According to propriety I should tend to the Zhangs' affairs first."

"And your wife?" she asked again. "She is the wife of a Zhang." Hearing that Zhang's words tallied with what Liu had said, the mother was enraged. She glowered, saying, "If you are an offspring and wife of the Zhangs, why should you have the Lius' property in your hands?" Snatching the case of keys from her daughter, she said, "From today on, you Zhangs are Zhangs and we Lius are Lius." Then, handing the keys to Yinsun, she added, "We Lius will manage our household!" Even Liu himself had not anticipated that she might be so determined. Still less did Zhang Lang and Yinjie, who had been shielded by her, know why this had happened. Why does Mother change her ways, they wondered in astonishment. They did not know that the mother had been convinced by Liu. As Zhang Lang set up the sacrificial offerings, Liu and wife roared in anger, "Liu's ancestors do not eat the Zhangs' leftovers! The sacrificial ceremony will be held later." Thus they parted, each in a gloomy mood.

When Zhang Lang and Yinjie returned home, Zhang grumbled, "I didn't expect that because I visited my own ancestors' tombs first I would incur such trouble. Even the family riches have now been robbed by Yinsun. How can I endure this? What is most odd is the fact that this was Mother's decision!" "Father and Mother believe that Yinsun is the only blood kindred of the Lius," said Yinjie. "That's why they did this. In the past you planned to do harm to Xiao Mei; she was aware of it and left. If she were still here and had given birth to a brother of mine, Yinsun would not have the opportunity to lord it over us. If my own brother had a share of the property, I would not object; but I really can't bear the situation of the whole household falling into Yinsun's hands!" "We have been his enemy," said Zhang Lang, "now that he is entrusted with the management of the household, we will have to be humble before him. We'd better plead with Mother for help." "Can we count on Mother for help if she herself made the decision?" responded his wife. "But I have a plan to prevent Yinsun from being the master of the house." "What plan?" asked Zhang Lang.

Yinjie, however, did not tell him. "You'll see," she said. "Don't ask about the details."

The next day Liu spread a dinner and invited his neighbors. In front of them he declared the family property would go to Yinsun. The mother was willing. Hearing this, Yinjie sent Zhang Lang away because she knew he would otherwise be embarrassed. She then sent a message to her aunt in Eastern Village to send Xiao Mei home. Xiao Mei had given birth to a son in Eastern Village. The son was now three years old. Yinjie had secretly sent food and clothing to the mother and son without letting her family know, lest Zhang Lang might develop another sinister plot. She had planned to tell her parents about the child when he was a little older. Now, unwilling to accept the arrangement that Yinsun was to be the owner of the household, she had to bring the mother and son to her home at once.

The following day she said to Liu, "You may refuse to recognize your son-in-law as your heir, Father, but do you refuse to recognize your daughter as well?" "Who says I don't recognize you?" said Liu, "but you are not as dear to me as Yinsun." "I am your own daughter," said Yinjie, "why am I less dear than he?" "You belong to the Zhangs, while he belongs to the Lius." "Even so," said Yinjie, "is it necessary that he be the owner of the family fortune?" "If there was another child as dear as he," replied her father, "the child would have a share of the property. But where is such a child?" "Likely there is one," Yinjie said, smiling. Liu and wife did not pay much attention to her words since they believed she had said them out of anger. Then Yinjie called Xiao Mei into the parlor with her son. "Isn't this a child as dear as Yinsun?" Yinjie asked her parents. Seeing Xiao Mei, Liu and wife were very surprised. "Where have you been?" they asked. "Didn't you run away?" "Who ran away?" retorted Xiao Mei, "I needed to look after the child." "Which child?" asked Liu. "Here he is," said Xiao Mei pointing to her son. Bewildered with joy, Liu said, "Is this the child you have given birth to? Am I dreaming?" "Ask your daughter and she will explain everything," replied Xiao Mei. Liu and his wife urged Yinjie to tell them everything immediately.

"Listen, father," Yinjie said, "and I will tell you the story from beginning to end. When Xiao Mei had been pregnant for half a year, Zhang Lang, jealous, might have plotted against her. If Xiao Mei had trouble, I realized, father at such an advanced age would be dispossessed of a successor to the family line. So I talked with Xiao Mei and entrusted her to my aunt in Eastern Village. There she delivered this child. During the past three years she was looked after by my aunt, and her food and clothing were attended to by me. I had planned to tell you the truth when the child was a little older. But now, seeing that father has taken Yinsun as his only blood kindred, I have invited her here. The child is not like a daughter. Isn't he dearer than Yinsun?" "Thanks to your daughter," said Xiao Mei, "and her thoughtful arrangements, the child has been kept safe."

Hearing this, Liu awoke as if from a dream or drunkenness. He was most grateful to his daughter. Xiao Mei let the child call him "Dad," at which Liu was almost stunned with joy. "Our own child is, after all, partial to us," he said to his wife. "Our daughter bears the family name of Liu and she shields the Lius. She did not follow Zhang and ruin her brother. Now with this child, our family line will not be broken and our tombs will not have to be in a marshy spot. All this is because of my filial daughter. I won't be ungrateful. Now I have an idea. I will divide the property into three parts, giving one each to my daughter, nephew and son. You'll each keep your own part and live in harmony." Thereupon he sent for Zhang Lang and presented him, Yinsun and the child to the neighbors. Inviting the neighbors to a feast, Liu divided the family fortune thereupon. Then they were dismissed, everyone satisfied.

After that even Liu's wife loved the child dearly, let alone Liu and Xiao Mei. With the boy under Yinjie and Yinsun' protection, Zhang Lang, though jealous, could do nothing against him. In the end the boy